In Pursuit
of Peace

In Pursuit of Peace

21 Ways to Conquer Anxiety, Fear, and Discontentment

JOYCE MEYER

WARNER
Faith

New York   Boston   Nashville

Warner Faith
Time Warner Book Group
1271 Avenue of the Americas, New York, NY 10020

Visit our Web site at www.twbookmark.com

The Warner Faith name and logo are registered trademarks of
Warner Books.

Printed in the United States of America
First Warner Books Printing: September 2004
10 9 8 7 6 5 4 3 2

Library of Congress Cataloging-in-Publication Data

Meyer, Joyce
    In pursuit of peace : 21 ways to conquer anxiety, fear and
discontentment / Joyce Meyer.—1st Warner Faith ed.
        p. cm.
    ISBN 0-446-53195-2
    1. Peace—Religious aspects—Christianity   I. Title.
    BT736.4.M47   2004
    248.4—dc22   2004009488

Contents

❧

v

Contents

Part 3
BE AT PEACE WITH OTHERS

Introduction

The first forty years of my life, I lived without the blessing and benefit of peace; therefore, I can say from experience, life without peace is *miserable*. One cannot enjoy life without first having peace. Without it, we live in turmoil—always worried, anxious, and upset about something.

I came to a point in my life of being so hungry for peace that I was willing to make whatever changes were necessary in order to have it. As a result of that decision and the investment I made during the following years, I now enjoy a life of peace that often passes understanding. In other words, I enjoy peace *during* the storms of life, not just when the storms don't exist. I am not saying that I have arrived at a state of perfection in my pursuit of peace, but I have made a lot of progress. As the apostle Paul said in Philippians 3:12, I have not arrived but I press on.

There were times in my life when I could be peaceful if everything was going my way, but since that seldom occurred, I rarely had peace. Now I have learned to change what I can change, accept what I cannot change, and regularly seek wisdom to know the difference. What I can do, I do with God's help; what I cannot do I turn over to Him so He can work. This leaves me free to enjoy my life.

A life of frustration and struggle, a life without peace, is the result of trying to do something about something you cannot do anything about. The apostle Paul said, "Be anxious for nothing, but in everything by prayer and supplication, with thanksgiving, let your requests be made known to God; and the peace of God, which surpasses all understanding will guard your hearts and minds through Christ Jesus" (Philippians 4:6–7 NKJV).

Once we realize we are struggling with something and feel upset, we need to start praying and immediately turn the situation over to God. You and I are not called to a life of frustration and struggle. Jesus came so we could have righteousness, peace, and joy (see Romans 14:17). He said, "The thief comes only in order to steal and kill and destroy. I came that they may have and enjoy life, and have it in abundance (to the full, till it overflows)" (John 10:10). The Word teaches us to "search for peace (harmony; undisturbedness from fears, agitating passions, and moral conflicts) and seek it eagerly. [Do not merely *desire* peaceful relations with God, with your fellowmen, and with yourself, *but pursue, go after them!*]" (1 Peter 3:11, italics mine).

Simply desiring peaceful relations is not enough. We're to pursue peace with God, peace with ourselves, and peace with our fellow man. In this book, I will share with you many things within these three areas of relationships that needed to change in order for me to enjoy peace.

If you sincerely want a life of peace, you will need to be willing to change too. Peace does not just come; we have to pursue, crave, and go after it. Walking in peace must be a priority, or we will not make the effort needed to see it happen. I spent years praying for God to *give* me peace and finally realized He had already provided peace, but I had to *appropriate* it.

Jesus said in John 14:27, "Peace I leave with you; My [own] peace I now give and bequeath to you. Not as the world gives do I give to you. Do not let your hearts be troubled, neither let them be afraid. [Stop allowing yourselves to be agitated and disturbed; and do not permit yourselves to be fearful and intimidated and cowardly and unsettled.]" We will refer often to this verse throughout this study.

We can see that Jesus has already provided peace, so now we must take action and stop responding to unpleasant things by being upset. Being upset certainly does not change anything, but it does make us—as well as the people around us—miserable.

Jesus made the statement recorded in John 14:27 after His death and resurrection and prior to His ascension into heaven. There were many things He could have taught His disciples, but He chose to talk about peace. This fact alone reminds me of how important peace is. What a tragedy it would be if we spent our lives without peace when it was available all the time.

Some people don't have peace with God because they are not born again and need to trust Jesus Christ to be their Savior. But some, even Christians, still lack peace because they have not responded to the leading of the Holy Spirit simply to do what is right. They don't have peace because they are living in disobedience or they have built up a bad habit of worrying over the years. And some people don't have peace because they are mad at God. Perhaps they prayed for something and it didn't happen. Perhaps somebody else got what they wanted. Perhaps somebody they loved died, and they don't understand why, or they were praying for a healing and didn't get it.

There are many, many reasons why people don't trust God, but in order to enjoy peace, we must learn to trust Him in all things. We must trust that God is totally and completely just, which means He always makes wrong things right if we continue to lean on Him. The Bible says we know "in part." I believe God has an individual plan for everyone. God is perfect; He never does anything wrong. We don't know everything, and we're not ever going to know everything. Sometimes we make ourselves unhappy because we don't *trust* enough.

We always want God to change our circumstance, but He's more interested in changing *us* than He is our situation. A lot of people have faith to ask God for deliverance *from* something, but they don't have enough faith to take them *through* anything.

Job said, "Even though He slay me, yet will I trust Him" (see Job 13:15). If we're asking God for something and don't get it, then we have to believe God knows more than we do. We need to trust God beyond what we see and beyond what we know. We cannot have peace without that trust in God.

We tend to think that the persons with the greatest faith are the ones who get the miracles. I'm not really sure about that, myself. We make so much out of miracles when they happen. We think, *Oh, what great faith they have! They got a miracle.* But I think the ones with the greater faith are the ones who *keep their peace* even when they don't get the miracles they wanted. I think the greater faith is in those who have to walk it out and decide to love God anyway. The people who don't get everything they're asking for, and who might not understand why, but yet continue to love and praise God, are truly trusting God. They stay in church, give their tithes and offerings, and stay full of peace. That is remarkable faith, in my opinion.

Thomas wanted proof that Jesus really had risen from the dead. He said he would not believe unless he could see in Jesus' hands the marks made by the nails and actually put his fingers into the nail prints and put his hand into Jesus' side. Jesus allowed Thomas to do so but told him that those who believed without having to see were blessed and happy and to be envied (see John 20:24–29).

We all would enjoy a miracle breakthrough every time we had a need, but we should have enough faith to stay the course if God chooses to take us on the long, hard route.

If you are ready to do whatever you need to do to enjoy a life of peace, this book is for you. I cannot promise that all your unpleasant circumstances will change, but I sincerely believe you can have and enjoy peace no matter what your circumstances are if you are willing to learn how to respond to people and situations the way Jesus did.

I pray that the Holy Spirit will enlighten you and grant you revelation as you press toward a life of peace. The book includes twenty-one ways you can do this. Even after you have completed the book, I suggest you read it often to remind yourself of the principles of peace. If you find you are slipping back into old ways (something we all do at times), go back over the principles and see where you have begun to backslide. I pray this will be one of those books you can use the rest of your life to help you maintain peace, which I believe is one of the most important benefits and blessings that God has given us.

ᔓ Part 1 ᔒ

Be at Peace
with God

*Therefore, since we are justified (acquitted, declared righteous, and given
a right standing with God) through faith, let us [grasp the fact that we]
have [the peace of reconciliation to hold and to enjoy] peace with God
through our Lord Jesus Christ (the Messiah, the Anointed One).*

—THE APOSTLE PAUL, *Romans 5:1*

PEACEKEEPER #1

Trust the Lord of Peace

❧⦿❧

God wants us to enjoy life and see good days. In fact, God's Word tells us to *search* for peace, and seek it eagerly (see 1 Peter 3:11). We are not to merely *desire* peaceful relations with God, with our fellow men, and with ourselves, but we are to pursue and go after peaceful relationships!

The first way to find peace is in learning to trust God through a relationship with Jesus Christ. Jesus is the Prince of Peace. We cannot have peace with God, others, or ourselves without His lordship in our lives. The Bible says that Jesus is our wisdom from God (see 1 Corinthians 1:30). His Word teaches us how to live properly. He doesn't just give us wisdom—He *is* our wisdom. Through trusting the Prince of Peace and having a personal relationship with Him, we actually have indwelling wisdom from the Lord's presence in us.

If we would get still long enough to let that wisdom rise and minister to our minds, we wouldn't do so many foolish things. Too many times, we react through our emotions and we don't pay any attention to the wisdom in our hearts. We tend to make decisions according to our thoughts rather than living by discernment and according to what the Holy Spirit is placing in our hearts. Consequently, we get ourselves in trouble.

I believe that Jesus is everything we need in any situation. He is sufficient to meet the need for every circumstance that we will ever face. So, we certainly must learn how to go to Jesus for much more

3

than just salvation or a ticket into heaven. We need to take Him as our everything in life, including as our Prince of Peace.

Jesus Governs Our Lives

Isaiah 9:6–7 says, "For to us a Child is born, to us a Son is given; and the government shall be upon His shoulder, and His name shall be called Wonderful Counselor, Mighty God, Everlasting Father [of Eternity], Prince of Peace. Of the *increase of His government and of peace there shall be no end*" (italics mine).

The government that is upon the shoulders of Jesus is not a political government; the verse is referring to the governing of our lives. We are not supposed to be running our own lives. In fact, we are not capable or qualified to run our own lives. Not one of us is intelligent enough to know what is best. That is why we should be thankful for God's interference.

I like the promise that there will be no end to the increase of His government and peace. The more His government increases in my life (the more He governs my life, my thoughts, my conversations, my decisions, and my actions), the more peace I am going to have.

Peace doesn't come from success and money and promotions and feeling good about everything in life. We find peace in the kingdom of God, which is righteousness, peace, and joy within us. Being right with God, knowing we are right with God, and doing the right thing out of knowing who we are in Christ is a process, but it leads us to peace, and peace leads us to joy.

And if we don't have righteousness, peace, and joy, then we are not enjoying the kingdom of God as we should. Sometimes we may need to take a vacation from all the other things we look for and instead seek the kingdom. Matthew 6:33 says, "Seek (aim at and strive after) first of all His kingdom and His righteousness (His way of doing and being right), and then *all these things* taken together will be given you besides" (italics mine).

We work and struggle and strive at "all these things," such as food and clothing and position in society. But what we should be doing is searching out God's kingdom; we should seek Jesus and His government in our lives. Colossians 1:10 says, "That you may walk (live and conduct yourselves) in a manner worthy of the Lord, fully pleasing to Him and desiring to please Him in all things."

BE A DISCIPLE OF JESUS

Jesus said, "If anyone would come after me, he must deny himself and take up his cross and follow me" (Mark 8:34 NIV). If we want to have peace, we have to stop following other voices; we must be God pleasers, not man pleasers, and we must choose to follow Jesus on a daily basis.

For many years, I was in a church that gave me a great foundation about salvation, but I never learned much past that. I had many problems in my life, but I wasn't getting any victory over any of them. I certainly didn't know how to pursue or go after peace. Satan distracted me by getting me involved with many activities that did not produce good fruit in my life.

I was not taught to study God's Word myself, and because I didn't know the Word of God, I wasn't aware of the many deceptions that can grossly mislead people. For example, before I was in ministry I worked at an office where a coworker studied astrology. At the time, the things she talked about seemed to make sense (because I had no knowledge of God's Word on this subject). She believed the position of the planets and stars directed her life. She said there were even optimum times to get a haircut to have the best results.

Today, advice is easy to obtain from psychics, tarot card readers, sorcerers, and people skilled in divination who would like to run people's lives. They may give information that seems to make sense, but it will not produce lasting peace in a person's life. As I look back at those early years of being a believer, I am sad to say that nobody in my church told me not to follow these voices of deception. No one warned me that the Bible clearly says those who practice these types of things will not enter the kingdom of heaven (see Revelation 21:8). We are to follow God, not psychics, astrology, mediums, tarot card readers, or any such thing. God's Word actually says that these things are an abomination to Him. To enjoy peace, we must be led by the Lord of Peace.

To be a disciple of Jesus means to study His teaching, imitate His life, and correctly analyze the Word of Truth (see 2 Timothy 2:15). We will have God's power to live our lives well if we devote our attention to God's Word and allow Jesus to transform us by following the peace that He alone can give.

Peace is our inheritance from Jesus, but we have to choose to follow Him daily. Colossians 3:15 teaches us that peace is to be the "umpire" in our lives, settling every issue that needs a decision. To gain and maintain peace in our hearts, we may have to learn to say no to a few things.

For example, if we don't feel peace about something, we should never go ahead and do it. And if we don't have peace *while* we are doing something, then we shouldn't expect to have peace *after* we have done it. Many people marry others they didn't have peace about marrying, and then they wonder why they don't have peace in their marriages. Many people buy expensive items they didn't have peace about buying, then continue to lose their peace every month when they have to make payments on them.

I want to repeat the text I used previously because it is vital to living life well. Colossians 3:15 says to let the peace from Christ "rule (act as umpire continually)" in our hearts. The presence of peace helps us decide and settle with finality all questions that arise in our minds. If you let the Word have its home in your heart and mind, it will give you insight *and* intelligence *and* wisdom (see v. 16). You won't have to wonder, *Should I or shouldn't I? I don't know if it's right. I don't know what to do.* If you are a disciple of Christ, He has called you to follow peace.

Dave, my husband, and I were trying to make a decision on a large purchase we needed to make. We called some of our board members from the ministry and presented the need to them, asking, "What do you think?"

They all gave their opinions, but as I listened to them I knew suddenly that I didn't have peace about going forward with the plan. We have learned by experience to wait if we don't have peace for something. Everyone agreed to wait on God to give us all peace before we proceeded.

I was out shopping recently and went into a children's clothing store. It was one I had not been in for perhaps a year or more. I saw some items that I thought would be perfect for two of my granddaughters. They were little pink shirts with rhinestone hearts on them. It was Valentine's Day and I wanted to give them something, so I called my daughter to check on their clothing sizes before making my purchase.

She said, "I cannot believe this! I was in that shop last night, looking at those exact shirts, but I didn't have peace about spending any money. I really wanted to buy them for the girls but felt I needed to honor God by not doing something I did not have peace about." Then she said, "Mom, I believe God is blessing me because I obeyed Him." She was very excited.

Letting her girls receive the shirts as a gift was much more fun than purchasing them. Had she disobeyed what she felt in her heart and done what she did not have peace about, she probably would have been uncomfortable in her spirit, perhaps even miserable. We both got to be part of a miracle because she chose to follow peace!

Following the Lord of peace may mean that you have to make some adjustments in your life. You may not be able to do everything your friends do. You may not be able to buy everything you want.

You may not be able to have something just because a friend, or a sister or a brother, has one. You may have to wait. But I believe that peace is the most important, the most valuable thing we can have. If we follow peace, we will end up living holy lives and thoroughly enjoying them.

Many people cannot hear from God because they have too much turmoil in their lives. Their insides are like a freeway during rush-hour traffic. They literally don't know how to be peaceful; it is as if they are addicted to turmoil. They keep things agitated and stirred up, seemingly on purpose. In fact, they get comfortable living in a state of chaos. It has become their normal state, even though in God's economy it is not normal at all.

It sounds strange, but when I started learning to be peaceful, I was *bored* at first! I was so accustomed to having something major going on in my life all the time that I wondered, *What am I supposed to do with myself?* Romans 3:17 says, "And they have no experience of the way of peace [they know nothing about peace, for a peaceful way they do not even recognize]."

That describes how my life used to be. I had no experience at all in enjoying a peaceful life; I did not even know how to begin. I had grown up in an atmosphere of strife, and it was all I ever knew. I had to learn an entirely new way of living.

But now I'm addicted to peace. As soon as my peace disappears, I ask myself how I lost it and start looking for ways to get it back. I am believing that as you read this book you will become so hungry for peace with God, peace with yourself, and peace with others that you will be willing to make whatever adjustments you need to make in order to have it. I am also believing that you will begin to follow peace at all times, because peace will lead you into the perfect will of God.

Jesus said that if we follow Him, He will give us peace (free of charge). In fact, He said He will bequeath His own peace to us (see John 14:27).

THE GOSPEL OF JESUS BRINGS PEACE

I want to see people love God's Word and put it first place in their lives. I believe there is an anointing on the Word; it has inherent power that makes positive changes in us. The Word of God is truth, and John 8:32 says, "And you will know the Truth, and the Truth will set you free." Truth sets us free from turmoil and leads us into a life of peace when we follow it.

The gospel of salvation through Jesus makes peace available to us *in all areas* of our lives. First Corinthians 1:21 says that when people failed to find God through earthly wisdom or by means of their own philosophy, God saved people through the preaching of salvation "procured by Christ." *Strong's Exhaustive Concordance of the Bible* says the Greek word translated as "save" in that verse is *sozo,* which means God "delivers, protects, heals, preserves, saves and makes whole" those who believe, trust in, and rely on Him.

We will experience peace in our personal lives when we stop trying to do so many things ourselves and just rely on God to deliver, protect, heal, and save us, as He wants to do.

And God will also lead us to peace in our relationships. Ephesians 2:14 is an awesome Scripture that says, "For He is [Himself] our peace (our bond of unity and harmony). He has made us both [Jew and Gentile] one [body], and has broken down (destroyed, abolished) the hostile dividing wall between us." Where there is no unity, no harmony, God Himself will break down and abolish the walls that divide people. He has broken down walls between so-called classes of people. He makes equal those who have higher education and those without any education at all. Somebody with a lot of money is no better to Him than somebody without money. The preacher is no better than the person who cleans the toilets.

The Lord loves each of us unconditionally. The hand of God uniquely created and personally designed each of us. That doesn't mean that we don't need some sandpaper to smooth our rough edges or polishing to make us shine. We all need to change and grow, but we can still be at peace about who we are without comparing ourselves with somebody else. We can stop thinking we are flawed because we are not like anyone else we know. We must have peace with ourselves before we can have peace with others.

I believe God wants you to have peace about where you are in your spiritual growth and to realize that you won't always stay the way you are. Anyone seeking God regularly is always changing, but we can enjoy where we are on the way to where we are going.

In the next chapter, I will share more about how we can surrender our will to God's leading. He doesn't want us to wait to have peace until we have all the things that we may want and desire or think are necessary to our lives. He doesn't want us to be jealous or envious of those who have the things we want and don't have, or those who can do what we can't do. He wants to prove to us that *He is* our peace.

God has an individualized, customized plan for your life. As you trust Him, He will bring it to pass in His timing, not yours. Waiting on God's plan and timing is wise because His ways are always best. He is the Lord of peace, and as you surrender your heart and life to Him, you will experience the peace that passes understanding.

PEACEKEEPER #2

Make Peace Through a Surrendered Will

తా౨ ౬ా

The apostle Peter challenged believers to find "every kind of peace and blessing, especially peace with God, and freedom from fears, agitating passions, and moral conflicts" (1 Peter 5:14). Surrendering our wills in order to maintain agreement with God is the foundation for all peace in our lives. God has a good plan for each of us, but when we go against His will by pursuing our own wills, we experience turmoil rather than peace. God is the source of all peace, and it stands to reason that He will not release peace to us unless we are following His ways and not our own. God desires for us to live free from fears and agitating passions, and He does not want us to be in bondage to immorality of any kind.

The Bible teaches that God will lead us by the presence of peace. Again, peace is the umpire in our lives that lets us know if we are in God's will or out of it. Ask yourself the following question, and be honest with your answer: Are you walking in God's known will to the best of your ability, or are there areas in your life in which you know you are not obeying God?

You will not experience peace if God is pulling in one direction and you are pulling in another; you will feel as if you are being torn apart. God will not force us to do what is right. He shows us what to do but leaves the choice to us. If we make right choices, we will reap good results that we can be happy with; if we make wrong choices, all we have is regret. Many individuals want their lives to change, but they don't want to do what God is showing them to do. If we are really serious about having change, we must follow God, no matter how difficult it is.

Carnality and God do not mix well together. We are called to walk in the Spirit, to be guided and willingly controlled by the Holy Spirit, who will lead us to make choices that make and maintain perfect peace.

We read in the book of Jonah how God told him to go to Nineveh and preach repentance to the people there. But Jonah did not want to, so he went to Tarshish, which, according to geography, is the exact opposite direction from Nineveh. Running from God does not help us to be at peace with Him.

What happens when we go in the opposite direction from where God has directed us? What happened to Jonah? When he boarded a ship and headed in his own direction, a storm arose. Many of the storms we face in life are the results of our own stubbornness, and nothing else. We may try to blame them on other things and people, but the truth is that in many instances, we have been disobedient to the voice and leadership of God.

The violent storm that came upon Jonah frightened the men on the ship, and they knew if something did not change, they would all die. They cast lots to see who was causing the trouble, and the lot fell on Jonah. They asked Jonah what he had done that made God so angry. He knew he had disobeyed God, so he told the men to throw him overboard in order to deliver them from danger. They did as he requested; the storm stopped, and a great fish swallowed Jonah. From the fish's belly (not a pleasant place), he cried out to God for deliverance and repented of his stubborn ways.

The fish vomited Jonah upon the dry land and in chapter 3, verse 1, we see that the word of the Lord came to Jonah a second time, and it was no different from the first time: God told him to go to Nineveh and preach to the people there.

No matter how long we avoid God's instruction, it is still there for us to deal with when we stop running. God's will makes us uncomfortable only as long as we are not pursuing it. In other words, we always know when something is just not right in our lives. Eventually we see that being *in* God's will, not *out* of His will, is what brings peace and joy to us. We have to surrender our own wills, because walking in our self-centered ways is what keeps us unhappy.

Running from difficult things never works long term. I know a woman who ran from everything in life that was difficult. She ignored things she needed to deal with, including abuse in her home. She lived in fear and actually had a very miserable life. She ultimately carried so much turmoil she had a complete mental and emotional breakdown, and she has never totally recovered. Pretending that her problems did not exist did not make them go away. They were there, pressuring her, all the time. God was trying to lead her to deal with her conflicts, but she would not trust Him enough to do so.

God never leads us anywhere that He cannot keep us. If God is leading you to deal with some unpleasant situation in your life, don't run from it. He promises to be with you at all times and never to leave you, or forsake you.

Surrender can be frightening when we first begin to practice it because we don't know what the outcome will be if we yield ourselves to God's will. However, once we have surrendered, and we begin to experience the peace that passes understanding, we learn quickly that God's way is better than any plan we could ever devise.

Not knowing exactly what will happen in the future, but trusting God to take care of us and enjoying peace, is far, far better than erroneously thinking we have life all figured out while continuing to live in fear and anxiety. To enjoy peace with God, we must become comfortable with not knowing what the future holds. There is no such thing as trust without unanswered questions. If God is leading you to do something difficult, just begin to take baby steps of faith, and after each one He will show you what to do next. We don't have to have an entire blueprint for the future; we don't need to have all the answers. All we need is to know the One who knows, and that is Jesus Himself.

We must realize that we are not nearly as smart as we think we are. God's Word advises us not to be conceited in our own wisdom and not to think more highly of ourselves than we ought. God has the answers; we don't. We need to seek Him, and He will lead us.

Proverbs 3:5–7 are some of my favorite Scriptures, and ones I have to return to frequently. They say, "Lean on, trust in, and be confident in the Lord with all your heart and mind and do not rely on your own insight or understanding. In all your ways know, recognize, and acknowledge Him, and He will direct and make straight and plain your paths. Be not wise in your own eyes." Notice we are told to "be not wise in [our] own eyes." To me that simply means we should not even think that we are smart enough to run our own lives. We need an attitude of humility that helps us lean on God for everything. An independent, I'll-do-it-myself attitude and dependence on God can't coexist.

Reasoning, struggling, and trying to figure out everything in life will steal our peace. God says to trust Him with all of our hearts and minds. I used to say I trusted God, yet I worried; therefore I did not truly trust Him. As I learned to keep my "ways" before God for alteration according to His will, He started guiding the events of my life, and the quality of it improved greatly.

God Leads Us by Peace

One of the major ways we hear from God is through peace. As I mentioned before, peace is our umpire in life. "And let the peace (soul harmony which comes) from Christ rule (act as umpire continually) in your hearts [deciding and settling with finality all questions that arise in your minds, in that peaceful state] to which as [members of Christ's] one body you were also called [to live]" (Colossians 3:15).

We are to follow peace. If our decisions and actions produce peace, we know God approves and we are safe in going ahead. If we don't have peace, we need to stop or at least wait. What we are doing or considering may be wrong, or the timing may be wrong.

People do so many things they don't have peace about, and then they wonder why they have big messes in their lives. If we follow His Word, God has promised us that we will enjoy blessed and peaceful lives. He also warns us that we will be miserable and live in turmoil if we follow our own will and walk in our own ways (see Deuteronomy 28:15-33).

I hear people say things like this all the time:

- "I know I shouldn't do this, but—"
- "I know I shouldn't buy this, but—"
- "I probably shouldn't say this, but—"

What they are saying is, "I know this is wrong, but I am going to do it anyway." They have a check in their spirits, a little bit of an uncomfortable feeling deep inside, a "knowing" that the action they are taking is not right or good for them, but they won't surrender their wills to God's leading.

We have to learn to release our plans when we don't have peace and wait to find God's good plan for our lives. When we sense we are losing our peace, we should know that it means danger to press on the way we are going. We really need to have a healthy fear of not following peace. We should respect what God says in His Word about peace being the umpire in our lives, and let peace make final decisions for us.

Over the years, I have learned many things, but one of the most significant is the importance of walking in peace and staying in the rest of God. It is God's will for us to live free of upset and frustration. He wants us to enjoy our lives, and we cannot do that if we don't have peace.

Do you enjoy a peaceful atmosphere most of the time? Do you keep your peace during the storms of life? Are you at peace with God? These are important questions. We need to take a "peace inventory," checking every area of our lives to see if we need to make adjustments anywhere. Jesus said, "My peace I've given unto you." If He gave us His peace, He wants us to walk in it and enjoy it.

We must resist the devil at his onset. The minute we sense that we are losing our peace, we need to make a decision to calm down. Even allowing ourselves to become upset places us out of God's will. To establish it in our hearts, let's look again at what Jesus said:

> Peace I leave with you; My [own] peace I now give and bequeath to you. Not as the world gives do I give to you. Do not let your hearts be troubled, neither let them be afraid. [*Stop allowing yourselves to be agitated and disturbed;* and *do not permit yourselves to be fearful and intimidated and cowardly and unsettled.*] (John 14:27, italics mine)

We can see plainly from this Scripture that Jesus has provided the peace, but we must appropriate it, not letting our hearts be troubled or afraid. We cannot just passively wait to feel peaceful. We are to pursue peace and refuse to live without it. As Jesus said, "Stop allowing yourselves to be upset."

In 1 Peter 3:10–11, the Bible teaches us that if we want to enjoy life and see good days, we should keep our tongues free from evil, we should do right and search for peace and harmony with God, with ourselves, and with our fellow man. These Scriptures have had a major impact on my own life, and I pray they will impact yours. They are core principles to enjoying peace in our lives.

What is life worth if we are at war in our relationship with God, people, and ourselves? Not much of anything, as far as I am concerned. As I mentioned, peace with God is the foundation for all peace in our lives. How can we be at peace with ourselves if we are not at peace with God, and how can we enjoy peace with other people if we don't have peace with ourselves?

There may be personal issues you need to settle with God before you can enjoy peace. There may be things that God has been dealing with you about for a long, long time that you have been ignoring. Remember, ignoring God's will does not change it. You can go around the same mountains again and again, pass through storms, or find yourself in uncomfortable places the way Jonah did, but when all is said and done, God's will is still the same.

Do you sense a tug-of-war inside yourself about some issues in your life? If so, I encourage you not to spend one more day in turmoil. Face the issue, and give God the right of way. In other words, lay your ways down and adopt His ways. Make a decision to stop running and deal with any issues God may be placing before you. Are you doing something that is bothering your conscience? If so, that is God letting you know He is not pleased with that action or decision. Your conscience is actually intended to be your friend; it is a great blessing in life. It will keep you out of trouble if you learn to respect and listen to it.

When God has His will for our lives and we have other wills, life gets hard and uncomfortable. But we can have and enjoy peace by surrendering our wills to God's. God will not surrender to us; He is waiting for our surrender.

TRUTH LEADS US TO PEACE

We gain peace with God through facing the truth about the changes He is asking us to make. God never asks us to do something without giving us the ability to do it. Truth is not easy to face, but it is the avenue to peace. When we hide from, avoid, and evade God, we are usually running from His will for us.

A man once told me he had run from God's truth for so long he had finally run past himself. He meant that he had totally lost himself and any understanding of what God wanted for him. He was confused and miserable. He felt like a total failure, as if he had completely wasted his life. He was depressed, discouraged, and without vision for his future.

I don't think I have ever seen anyone who was more unhappy and pitiful than he was. Why? Because he had spent his life doing what he wanted to do, what he felt like doing, rather than walking in God's plan for him. He was reaping what he had sown, just as we all ultimately do.

I thank God for the ability to turn around and go in the right direction. That is actually what true repentance is. It is not just a feeling of being sorry, but also a decision to go in the right direction from now on. We get into trouble through making a series of wrong decisions, and we will get our lives straightened out by a series of right decisions. It took more than a day to get into trouble, and it will take more than a day to get out. Anyone who is ready and willing to make a real investment of time and right choices can see his or her life turn around for the better. God's mercy is new every day. He is waiting to give you mercy, grace, favor, and help; all you have to do is say yes to whatever God is requiring.

The miserable man I referred to did what was right for about two years, and his life really began to change. He had every opportunity to have a great life, but he did not "keep on keeping on." He eventually went back to his old ways.

Recently I talked with a Christian sister who was very depressed and felt as if she was on the edge of a nervous breakdown. As we talked, I discovered she had spent years not making right decisions and then found herself overwhelmed with the outcome of her own poor choices. She had not raised her children in church, and she said they were out of control and impossible for her to manage. She had been very difficult to get along with, and the result had been the loss of several friendships and family relationships. She certainly had serious problems, and I did not have an easy answer for her.

She wanted me to tell her what to do, so I seriously pondered before the Lord what I should suggest. All I could tell her was that she needed to start making right decisions, and eventually they would overtake the crop she was now reaping from her previous bad decisions. People usually want to overcome a lifetime of bad choices in a short period of time without much effort on their parts, or they want other people to deliver them from the messes into which they have gotten themselves.

I sincerely felt compassion for her, yet I also realized she had been a Christian for over twenty-five years and had spent much time (at least in the early years of her walk with God) studying God's Word and ways. I felt she knew better than to behave the way she had. When we lack knowledge, we often experience a "special grace" in our lives from God. However, once we have knowledge of God's Word, we become responsible to apply it to our lives, and I personally believe we reap what we sow much quicker as knowledgeable persons than as ignorant ones.

God wanted to work with this sister and help her. He would give her mercy and grace and another chance, but there really was no easy answer like the one she appeared to be seeking. We cannot do right a few times—we must continue on. Jesus said, "If ye *continue* in my word, then are ye my disciples indeed; and ye shall know the truth, and the truth will make you free" (see John 8:31–32 KJV).

Both the brother and the sister I have mentioned gained help in their lives through applying God's principles, but they did not maintain. They did not *continue* in the truth they had learned. Galatians 5:1 teaches us to stand fast in the liberties we have; that means to gain and maintain. It has helped me to realize that I will need to stand fast for the rest of my life.

We cannot get lazy and start letting things slip. Each time God convicts us of wrong behavior, we need to listen to Him. Anytime we lose our peace even slightly, we need to stop and find out what is wrong. That loss of peace is God letting us know something is not going the way He wants it to go.

19

We gain a right relationship with God through complete surrender to Him, and through repentance of all of our sins. We maintain it through *continued* right living: making right choices, honoring our consciences, and following peace. Being a successful Christian is a full-time job; we must be on guard all the time against the deceptions of Satan.

Just going to church for one hour on Sunday morning is not enough to maintain peace. We need megadoses of God's Word, prayer, and regular fellowship with God and other godly people in order to stand fast in God's will.

Peace with God is available to every person, but we cannot have it on our own terms. Surrender seems so frightening because we are not sure what God may require. Will we suffer? Will God ask us to do things we don't want to do or don't even know how to do? Will we ever get to have any of the things we want? We all have these questions.

We may not get things our way, but we can trust that God's way is better. God is a good God, and He said that He has good things planned for His children: "For I know the thoughts and plans that I have for you, says the Lord, thoughts and plans for welfare and peace and not for evil, to give you hope in your final outcome" (Jeremiah 29:11).

We should not be afraid of harm, because God is not an ogre, He is not mean. He is good. Everything good in life comes from God. He wants us to trust Him, and when we take a step of faith to do so, we will see the goodness of God manifested in our lives. The more we surrender, the better life becomes.

The Holy Spirit Fills Us with Peace

In Acts 2:4, we see that believers were *all* "filled with the Holy Spirit," and later in Ephesians 5:18, we find the instruction to "be filled with the Spirit." One Scripture tells us what happened on the day of Pentecost, and the other is a command.

What does it mean to be filled with the Spirit? It does not imply a state of high excitement, or being perfect in all of our ways, nor is it a state in which we have no need for growth. It is having our entire personalities yielded to the Holy Spirit and being filled through and through with His awesome power *daily*. It is daily surrender; it is yielding to God's ways and plans for our everyday lives.

The following Scriptures are absolutely wonderful; I encourage you to meditate on them often.

May He grant you out of the rich treasury of His glory to be strengthened and reinforced with mighty power in the inner man by the [Holy] Spirit [Himself indwelling your innermost being and personality] . . . [That you may really come] to know [practically, through experience for yourselves] the love of Christ, which far surpasses mere knowledge [without experience]; that you may be *filled [through all your being] unto all the fullness of God [may have the richest measure of the divine Presence, and become a body wholly filled and flooded with God Himself]!* (Ephesians 3:16, 19, italics mine)

Just imagine having your personality filled with the Holy Spirit of the living God and being a body wholly filled with God Himself! The apostle Paul was a man filled with the Holy Spirit; he was also a man who had forsaken all to follow Jesus. Any area of our lives that we hold back from God is an area where we cannot be filled with His Spirit. I encourage you to open and surrender every room in your heart to God. Your time is His, your money is His, as are your gifts and talents, your family, your career, attitudes, and desires. He wants to be involved in every area of your life: how you dress, whom you choose for friends, what you do for entertainment, what you eat, and so on.

After conversion, Jesus is our Savior, but is He our Lord? Any area we claim as our own is one we have not surrendered to the lordship of Jesus Christ.

I lived a defeated life for many years simply because I was not fully surrendered. I had accepted Jesus as Savior; I had enough of Jesus to stay out of hell, but I had not accepted Him as my Lord, I had not accepted enough of Him to walk in victory. There is a difference. I lacked peace because I was still trying to manage my own life.

The blessedness of being filled with the Spirit is clearly visible in the change in the people's lives after Pentecost. Peter, for example, who had displayed great fear in not being willing to even admit that he knew Jesus, became a bold apostle who stood in the streets of Jerusalem and preached the gospel so fervently that three thousand souls were added to the church in one day. Complete surrender brings good change into our lives. Surrender to God actually opens the door to the things we desire, and yet we waste our own energy trying to obtain access to them our own way.

Realize that every act of obedience brings with it a corresponding blessing. Consecration, commitment, yielding, surrendering, obeying: all these words may sound frightening, but remember that fear is not from God. Fear is from Satan; he uses it to prevent us from entering God's plan for our lives. He uses fear to prevent progress. Each time we feel fear, we should recognize it as opposition from the enemy of our souls.

I share more about living a Spirit-filled life in my book *Knowing God Intimately*. I encourage you to read that book if you feel you need to surrender to the Lord in a deeper way. Being filled with the Spirit is like finding the "pearl of great price" that the following verses speak of:

> The kingdom of heaven is like something precious buried in a field, which a man found and hid again; then in his joy he goes and sells all he has and buys that field. Again the kingdom of heaven is like a man who is a dealer in search of fine and precious pearls, who, on finding a single pearl of great price, went and sold all he had and bought it. (Matthew 13:44–46)

The kingdom of heaven, as God intended us to enjoy it, includes being wholly filled with the Holy Spirit. These Scriptures teach us that we must "sell all" to buy the pearl of great price. That simply means we surrender everything we now have in order to gain the one thing we truly need to enjoy kingdom living. The kingdom of God is righteousness, peace, and joy in the Holy Spirit (see Romans 14:17).

Perhaps as you read this book today, you realize you have something against someone. Perhaps God has dealt with you to give up some bitter attitude, but you have stubbornly held on to it, feeling justified in your anger. I tell you that if you will surrender that attitude, God will give you peace in the place of it.

You may spend many days feeling sorry for yourself or being jealous of what someone else has. God has asked you to lay aside those bad attitudes and be content. If you will do so, His peace and joy will fill your life.

People may have more possessions than you do, but they can never have more peace and joy than you do if you follow the leading of the Holy Spirit. It is not what we own that makes us happy and peaceful; He is our joy and our peace.

A Consecrated, Dedicated Life Results in Peace

God's Word instructs us to be vessels fit (consecrated) for the Master's use. To be consecrated is to be set apart for a special use, as these verses explain:

> But in a great house there are not only vessels of gold and silver, but also [utensils] of wood and earthenware, and some for honorable and noble [use] and some for menial and ignoble [use]. So whoever cleanses himself [from what is ignoble and unclean, who separates himself from contact with contaminating and corrupting influences] will [then himself] be a vessel set apart and useful for honorable and noble pur-

poses, consecrated and profitable to the Master, fit and ready for any good work. (2 Timothy 2:20–21)

To God, we are precious treasures. According to His great plan, we are vessels He has set aside for a special purpose. God wants to show His glory through us. He wants to use us to bring others to Himself. We are His representatives, His ambassadors here on earth. God is making His appeal to the world through His children (see 2 Corinthians 5:20).

To dedicate is to give, to offer to another, or to set aside for a purpose. If I were to say a room in my house is dedicated to prayer, that would mean I wanted that particular room used primarily for that purpose and not for other things.

I own some dresses that I use only for fancy parties. I have set them aside in a certain place in my closet and keep them inside garment bags for protection. This makes them special; they are not used for ordinary purposes but are set apart for special purposes. That is the way God views us; we are not to be used for the world's purposes, but for God's. We are in the world, yet Jesus tells us we are not "of" the world. Don't be worldly, adopting its ways and methods. Even after we have dedicated ourselves to God, we should rededicate ourselves to our real purpose, as the following verse encourages: "I APPEAL to you therefore, brethren, and beg of you in view of [all] the mercies of God, to make a decisive dedication of your bodies [presenting all your members and faculties] as a living sacrifice, holy (devoted, consecrated) and well pleasing to God, which is your reasonable (rational, intelligent) service and spiritual worship" (Romans 12:1).

It is not too much for God to ask us to dedicate every facet of our being. It is actually our worship and spiritual service. Under old covenant law, God required animal sacrifices to atone for sin. He no longer wants dead sacrifices; He wants us offering ourselves as "living sacrifices" unto Him for His purpose and use.

There is nothing we can offer to God that He has not first given us, so we are only offering what already belongs to Him anyway. In reality, we are stewards, not owners. Andrew Murray taught in his book *Consecrated to God* that if God gives us everything and we receive everything, then what comes next is very clear: We must give everything back to God again. God gives us a free will so we can freely and willingly give ourselves back to Him. He does not want robots, who have no choice, serving Him. He wants us to *choose* Him! What a privilege, what an honor to give ourselves willingly to Him.

Offer Him your mouth to speak through, your hands to touch through, your feet to walk through, your mind to think through. Dedicate every area of your life to Him, remembering that anything we give to the Lord He gives us back many times over, and we get it back in much better condition than when we gave it.

When I gave my life to the Lord, it was an absolute wreck. He has now given me a life that is wonderful and beyond imagination. Ephesians 3:20 states that He is able to do much more than we could ever imagine if we will give Him the opportunity.

God wants you to enjoy a life of peace, the peace that passes understanding, and it begins by being at peace with Him. This requires regular surrender, consecration, dedication, and a willingness to let God be in the driver's seat of your life at all times. But beware; you have an enemy who plans to make it difficult to surrender your life to God. Next, we will look at what God's Word says about that enemy.

PEACEKEEPER #3

Know Your Enemy

༄ ⁓❧

If finding peace is a struggle for you, it is a sign that your enemy is working hard to keep you from receiving what is rightfully yours. Are you confused about who your real enemy is? According to God's Word, your enemy is not a person, or even circumstances—it is Satan himself. Knowing your enemy, and the weapons that God has given you to defeat him, is the third way to keep in perfect peace with God.

"For we are not wrestling with flesh and blood [contending only with physical opponents], but against the despotisms, against the powers, against [the master spirits who are] the world rulers of this present darkness, against the spirit forces of wickedness in the heavenly (supernatural) sphere" (Ephesians 6:12). We can never win our battles if we are fighting against the wrong source in a wrong way. The source of our troubles is Satan and his demons. We cannot fight him with carnal (natural) weapons, but only with supernatural ones that God gives us for the destruction of Satan's strongholds (see 2 Corinthians 10:4).

What exactly are these weapons? I believe the weapons God gives include His Word used in preaching, teaching, singing, confession, or meditation. Our weapons are righteousness, peace, and joy in the Holy Ghost, and we can and should use these against Satan, our enemy. Yes, peace is a weapon! The Bible talks about putting on the shoes of peace. Righteousness is a weapon! "By [speaking] the word of truth, in the power of God, with the weapons of righteousness for the right hand [to attack] and for the left hand [to defend]" (2 Corinthians 6:7).

Through faith in Christ we are placed in right standing with God. And by faith, we are covered with His robe of righteousness (see Isaiah 61:10 AMP). In other words, because we are trusting in Jesus Christ's righteousness to cover us, God views us as right instead of wrong. His righteousness becomes a shield that protects us from Satan. He absolutely hates it when a child of God really knows who he or she is "in Christ."

In and of ourselves, we are less than nothing; our righteousness is like filthy rags, for all have sinned and come short of the glory of God (see Isaiah 64:6; Romans 3:23). But we are justified and given a right relationship with God through faith.

"Therefore, since we are justified (acquitted, declared righteous, and given a right standing with God) through faith, let us [grasp the fact that we] have [the peace of reconciliation to hold and to enjoy] peace with God through our Lord Jesus Christ (the Messiah, the Anointed One)" (Romans 5:1). This Scripture teaches us that righteousness brings peace and joy. When we feel all wrong about ourselves, we do not have peace. Satan seeks to condemn us in order to steal our peace. Remember that Satan is your enemy, and you need to know that it is he who tries to make you feel bad about yourself. He works to steal your peace.

Satan uses people and circumstances, but they are not our real enemy; he is. He finds things and people through whom he can work and delights in watching us fight and war without ever realizing he is the source.

When Satan used Peter to try and divert Jesus from going to Jerusalem to complete the task God had sent Him to do, "Jesus *turned away* from Peter and said to him, Get behind Me, Satan! You are in My way [an offense and a hindrance and a snare to Me]" (Matthew 16:23, italics mine). Satan used Peter, but Jesus knew that Peter was not His real problem. He *turned away* from Peter and addressed the source of His temptation. We need to look beyond what we see or initially feel and seek to know the source of our problems too.

Usually we blame people and become angry with them, which only complicates and compounds the problem. When we behave in this manner, we are actually playing right into Satan's hands and helping his plans succeed. We also blame circumstances and sometimes even God, which also delights Satan.

Yes, we need to know our enemy—not only who he is but what his character is like. The Bible encourages us to know the character of God so we can place faith in Him and what He says. Likewise, we should know Satan's character so we do not listen to or believe his lies.

SATAN IS A LIAR

First and foremost, Satan is a liar, and Jesus called him "the father of lies" (John 8:44 NIV). All lies originate with him. He lies to us in order to deceive us. When a person is deceived, he believes lies. This is a terrible condition to be in, for one does not know that he believes lies. The lies are his reality because he believes them.

For example, I believed the lie from Satan that I would never overcome my abusive past. I believed I would always be tainted, second best, and soiled merchandise because of the things that had happened to me in my childhood. As long as I believed these things, I was trapped in my past. I could not really go forward and enjoy the future God had always planned for me (see Ephesians 2:10). I could not receive it because I was not aware of it. I believed what Satan said because I did not know what God had said.

I was miserable, hopeless, bitter, and in turmoil all because Satan was lying to me, and I believed his lies. When I began to study God's Word and His truth started renewing my mind, I knew Satan for what he is: a liar!

People who have had long-standing financial pressure are often convinced by Satan's lies that things will always be the way they are. The enemy tells them they will never have anything, never own a decent car or have a nice house. They believe they will never have enough, and so it becomes reality for them. We receive what we believe, whether what we believe is positive or negative.

God's Word says that He wants us to prosper (see Deuteronomy 29:9). It states we can and will be blessed in every way when we walk in God's statutes. Satan seeks to keep people hopeless. Hopelessness steals our God-given peace and joy.

Refuse to be hopeless. Be like Abraham, of whom it is said that although he had no reason to hope, he hoped on in faith that God's promises would come to pass in his life. As he waited he gave praise and glory to God, and Satan was not able to defeat him with doubt and unbelief (see Romans 4:18–20).

SATAN IS A THIEF

I often repeat John 10:10, which states that "the thief comes only in order to steal and kill and destroy." The passage is referring to Satan and his system. Just as God has a system that He encourages us to live by, and He promises blessings if we do, Satan has a system and his hope is that we will live by it so he can steal our blessings. Remember, he wants to prevent us from having righteousness, peace, and joy.

He steals through lying, and all of his tactics are connected in some way. They are all perverse in nature and the opposite of anything God would have for us. Satan steals from us through fear. Actually we receive from Satan through fear, just as we receive from God through faith. One might say that *fear is faith in what Satan says*. Fear threatens us with thoughts of harm or disappointment. Satan shows us a circumstance and then makes us afraid it will never change. God wants us to believe His Word is true even while we are still in the midst of the circumstances. Romans 8:37 says, "Yet amid all these things we are more than conquerors and gain a surpassing victory through Him Who loved us."

In God's economy, we must believe before we will see change or the good things we desire. Satan seeks to steal our vision and hope for the future. He tries to steal our sense of right standing with God through guilty feelings and condemnation, through self-rejection and even self-hatred. He steals our joy because the joy of the Lord is our strength, and he wants us to be weak.

Satan is a thief. He tries to steal every good thing that Jesus died to give us. Jesus gave us peace as our inheritance, but Satan does everything he can to rob us of it.

Recognize your enemy, know him, and stand aggressively against him.

SATAN IS A LEGALIST

You may already have deep furrows in your brow, trying to figure out what I could possibly mean by the statement that Satan is a legalist. This is what I mean: He pressures us to be perfect, to live without making mistakes, to never, never break any of the religious rules. When we do make mistakes—which everyone does—he then tries to make us feel condemned by our guilt because we have not followed all the rules and regulations.

What rules and regulations am I talking about? The ones some so-called religious organizations and systems impose. These include things like praying for certain amounts of time, doing good works, reading a certain amount of the Bible each day, observing religious holidays, and using various formulas that will supposedly give us God's approval.

When Jesus stated in Matthew 11:28, "Come unto me, all ye that labour and are heavy laden" (KJV), He was talking to people who were struggling while trying to live under the law, but who were always failing. There is nothing wrong with any of the rituals I have listed, and they are in fact good Christian disciplines. But if we view them as something we *have to* do to gain God's approval, rather than something we *want to* do because we love Him, they

30

minister death to us instead of life. They become a burden rather than a joy. The Word teaches us that the law kills, but the Spirit makes alive (2 Corinthians 3:6).

Jesus had much to say about religion, and none of it was good. Why? Because religion in His day was, and often still is, man's idea of what God expects. Religion is man trying to reach God through his own good works. The Christian faith teaches that God has reached down to man through Jesus Christ. By placing our faith in Jesus Christ, we receive the benefits from the work He has done for us. His work, not our own works of religion, not following rules and regulations man prescribes, justifies us and makes us right with God, as these Scriptures confirm:

- For no person will be justified (made righteous, acquitted, and judged acceptable) in His sight by observing the works prescribed by the Law. (Romans 3:20)
- [All] are justified *and* made upright and in right standing with God, freely and gratuitously by His grace (His un-merited favor and mercy), through the redemption which is [provided] in Christ Jesus. (Romans 3:24)

Many might describe a Christian as "someone who goes to church." This, of course, is not a Christian. A Christian may go to church, but one does not *become* a Christian through church atten-dance alone. I can sit in my garage all day, and that won't make me become a car. A Christian is someone who has had his heart changed by faith in Jesus Christ. He has had a change in his moral nature (see 2 Corinthians 5:17). He is not just someone who has agreed to follow certain rules and regulations and observe certain days as holy.

Religion is filled with rules and regulations one must follow to be part of a certain religious group. Christianity, however, is agree-ing to follow the leadership of the Holy Spirit entirely. We must remember that God has invited us into personal relationship and intimacy with Him through the death and resurrection of Jesus Christ. His invitation is not to be in a religious organization, where we strive to follow rules in order to gain acceptance and right standing with Him.

Religious rules and regulations steal peace and joy. They rob us of what Jesus died to give us. Through religion we become works oriented, rather than faith oriented. We pray because we are *supposed* to, rather than because we *want* to. We study the Bible because we are obligated; we have made it a rule. We have been taught that we *should,* so we do because we are *afraid not to.* We may do good works, but our motive is wrong if we do them to gain acceptance from God, rather than to reach out to someone in love because of what Christ has done for us. Religion causes us to live under the tyranny of the "shoulds" and "oughts."

Religion is the topic of discussion in John 9. The religious leaders were upset because Jesus had healed a blind man on the Sabbath. You see, with religious people, everything must be on the right day and done in the right way—their way. The results don't really matter as long as you follow their rules. If you don't follow the rules, they will not validate you.

The Pharisees interrogated the blind man over and over to learn exactly how Jesus did this work that gave him sight. They felt that Jesus must be a common sinner because He worked on a holy day.

Finally the man said, "I don't know all the answers to your questions. All I know is I was blind, and now I see." Then he asked the religious leaders if they wanted to be Jesus' disciples, at which point they became enraged and stormed at him (see John 9:27–28).

The Bible says the religious leaders sneered and jeered at the man's question. Isn't it a shame they could not rejoice with him? But then again, rejoicing with others is not what those types of people do. Enjoyment is foreign to them, and they want to make sure nobody else enjoys himself or herself either. Righteousness, peace, and joy are not part of their religious system. The man whom Jesus had healed had a very simple answer: "I was blind, and now I see." God intends Christianity to be simple, but religion and its systems can become very complicated and confusing.

I know many people who have struggled a lifetime to follow all the rules, and they still feel like failures. This is not God's will for His children. Again, Jesus said that He came that we might have *and enjoy* our lives (see John 10:10).

You might ask, "Doesn't God want us to be holy? Doesn't He want us to do good things?" The answer is yes, a thousand times yes. But we don't *accomplish* holiness through our good works. Christ Himself imputes holiness to us as a gift from God. We receive holiness by faith, not by good works. First Thessalonians 5:23 states, "And may the God of peace Himself sanctify you through and through." It is God Himself who will do it, we don't do it, and it is impossible for man to sanctify or make himself holy.

Jesus seriously chastised the religious leaders—the scribes and Pharisees—of His day. In Matthew 23, He called them "pretenders" and hypocrites because they demanded that others do things they were not doing themselves. He said they were play actors. They did good works, but their hearts were filled with wicked things. They paid their tithes and followed other rules, such as fasting, but they did not treat people justly and fairly. Jesus said they tied up heavy loads for others to carry but would not help bear the burden.

Like many others trying their best to serve God, I have experienced judgment and criticism from various people. Most of those people have been "religious" folks who actually don't know me at all. They assume and presume and accuse, but they never come to me in a loving manner to give me an opportunity to share anything about my life with them. They don't like anyone who does not do things "their way."

They are faultfinders who magnify every flaw they can find but never bother to examine or even mention any of the good fruit that has come from my ministry over the years. In Matthew 7:17–20, Jesus explained that we will know people by their fruit. He did not say, "Examine people, and if you find any fault at all, broadcast it to

33

everyone you know, hoping to ruin their reputations." Faultfinders are angry with anyone who has prospered or succeeded. Their "ministry" becomes criticizing the ministry of others. This is a sad state of affairs. Jesus has called us to love Him and to love one another, not to be faultfinders in the body of Christ.

People like this have deeply hurt me in the past, as they have many others, but I must remember that even Jesus Himself was attacked by the religious people of His day. Satan attacks, hoping to get people to quit and give up. He wants to drain us and wear us out, but God gives us endurance and makes strong in Him.

Satan is the author of this legalistic system that sucks the life out of people. The Holy Spirit ministers life to people. The Holy Spirit adds to us, Satan steals from us. In John 10, Jesus was making reference to the scene regarding the man who had been born blind when He said, "The thief comes only in order to steal and kill and destroy. I came that they may have and enjoy life, and have it in abundance (to the full, till it overflows)" (v. 10). Remember that Satan is a liar, a thief, and a legalist. Don't be deceived by him any longer—know your enemy!

SATAN IS A TROUBLEMAKER

The word *trouble* in *Webster's II New College Dictionary* is defined in part as: "distress, affliction, danger or need; malfunction, to stir up or agitate; to inconvenience or bother." Needless to say, we all experience these things on a rotating basis.

When people accept Jesus Christ as Lord and Savior and begin to study His Word, when they make progress in any way, Satan launches an all-out attack against them. He wants to entangle people in trouble so they will focus on the wrong things. He wants us to focus on things we cannot do anything about, rather than growing in God.

Mark 4 illustrates what is called the parable of the sower. It tells us of four types of ground onto which someone sows seed. In this parable the seed is the Word of God, and the ground is the heart conditions of mankind. Verse 15 says, "The ones along the path are those who have the Word sown [in their hearts], but when they hear, Satan comes at once and [by force] takes away the message which is sown in them."

Verse 17 says that some have the Word sown in their hearts, but "they have no real root in themselves, and so they endure for a little while; then when trouble or persecution arises on account of the Word, they immediately are offended (become displeased, indignant, resentful) and they stumble and fall away."

Verse 19 says, "Then the cares and anxieties of the world and distractions of the age, and the pleasure and delight and false glamour and deceitfulness of riches, and the craving and passionate desire for other things creep in and choke and suffocate the Word, and it becomes fruitless."

We can see from these verses that Satan works diligently to cause trouble and bring distractions.

The Word teaches that Satan will attack us for a season, and if we pass all of our tests, if we endure the testing and remain firm in our faith, he goes away for a while and waits for another time to attack. Luke 4:13 confirms his tactics: "And when the devil had ended every [the complete cycle of] temptation, he [temporarily] left Him [that is, stood off from Him] until another more opportune and favorable time."

This verse refers to Jesus' temptation in the wilderness. Even Jesus Himself was not immune to Satan's being a troublemaker. The Bible never promises us a trouble-free life, but we do need to know who the source of our trouble is. It is Satan!

Hold your peace. Satan may be a troublemaker, but Jesus is your Trouble Solver. He is your Deliverer, your Hiding Place. These times of testing, too, shall pass.

Satan tries to cause trouble in virtually every area of our lives. He does not attack every area at one time, but eventually he gets to everything. He will bring inconvenience of every kind, and it seems the wrong thing never happens at the right time. Problems never come when we are ready to deal with them.

He may attack people in their finances, relationships, physical health, mind, emotions, job, neighborhood, or projects. The apostle Paul said there were times when he was abased and times when he abounded (see Philippians 4:12). In other words, he experienced good times and hard times, as we all do.

We recently invited four different men from four different parts of the country to be guests on our television show. These men were all involved in the restoration of morality in America. They were all praying for revival. Dave and I are also very interested in this, and we wanted to impact the nation with some special programming along these lines.

Two of the four men had major delays with their flights. One had a flight entirely cancelled and was very late, and another sat on the runway for two and a half hours without any real explanation except that it was raining. What was Satan trying to do? He didn't want them to come at all, but if they were going to come, he wanted them to be upset when they arrived.

Two out of four of our guests having this type of trouble is more than coincidence. Satan sets us up to get us upset! He wants to steal our peace because our power is connected to it. I have learned that my ministry does not have much effect if I am not ministering from a heart of peace, so I strive to stay in peace at all times. Satan tries to steal my peace, and with God's help, I try to keep it.

We can trust God not to allow more to come on us than what we can bear (see 1 Corinthians 10:13). Paul also said that during all those times, he had learned to be content (satisfied to the point where he was not disquieted or disturbed.) It sounds to me as if he always kept his peace, no matter what was going on in his life.

This is an example we should seek to follow. Paul actually told the believers to follow him as he followed Christ. He believed he was doing what Christ would do. Jesus is "the Way." When we follow Him, we always end up enjoying a great victory.

Nobody likes trouble, yet we all have it. Everybody gets upset about it, and it never does any good. It is time for change! Don't go around and around the same mountains all of your life—learn a different approach.

I spent years getting upset every time trouble came, and Satan prized my response. I was following his lead, not the leading of the Holy Spirit. My response gave Satan power over me. The outer storms of life have no real power over us unless we let them rage on the inside of us. We cannot always do something about how life turns out, but we can do something about our inner responses.

I know you have probably heard the statement, "Attitude determines altitude," and it is very true. A good attitude will take you farther in life than most other things. I had a bad beginning in life; Satan had brought trouble for me as long as I could remember, and I had a bad attitude. I was filled with self-pity, bitterness, and resentment. I was jealous of those who had experienced an easier life than I had.

Jesus taught me to have a good attitude. He said I could not be pitiful and powerful at the same time, and He let me know that I had to choose which path I would take. By the grace of God and the help of the Holy Spirit, I made the right choice, and although it has been a long journey, it has been worth it.

Remember that peace must be aggressively pursued. I am encouraging you to adopt a new attitude toward trouble. Remember that what the enemy means for harm, God intends for good, and all things work together for good to those who love God and are called according to His purpose (see Genesis 50:20; Romans 8:28).

The Wearing-Out Tactics of Satan

Daniel 7:25 says that Satan seeks to wear out the saints of the Most High God. How does this wearing out take place? Often his work is barely noticeable, because he slowly tries to wear us down—a little here and a little there. Satan sends people to irritate us just as he did with the apostle Paul (see Acts 16:17–18).

A woman followed Paul and Silas, crying out that they were servants of the Most High God. This she did for many days. It annoyed Paul, it grated on him that she *continually* shouted the same thing all throughout the day. Paul finally turned to the woman and cast an evil spirit of divination out of her. Satan hopes we will just be aggravated and never deal with the situation aggravating us. He does this to wear us out.

Felix used his authority to postpone Paul's trial and keep him in prison. He wanted money from Paul, so he continued to send for him (see Acts 24:26). We know this went on for at least two years: Paul continued to argue about uprightness and purity of life, and Felix continued to prolong Paul's sentence without trial.

When people continue to be irritating, it has a different effect than someone who is irritating once or twice. In Judges 16:16, we see that Delilah pressed Samson *daily* until her deception worked, and he revealed the secret to his strength.

Likewise, Satan seeks to wear me out in various ways, but one of his favorite tactics is through trouble with employees—and not just one employee, but several in a row. For example, we might have to deal with several people who are initiating strife with other employees or remind people we have hired them to do specific jobs, not to run the ministry. Not too long ago, we had to deal with three issues concerning pornography in a ten-day period of time. That had never happened before, but suddenly we had three separate situations to confront.

You may be shocked to think that people working in a Christian ministry would have problems with something like pornography or commit such obviously disobedient acts, but they are tempted the same as everyone else, if not more so. Satan worked through their weaknesses and used them to drain me of much-needed energy.

I want you to pay particular attention to the fact that I said it had never happened before, and *suddenly* we had *three* issues with pornography at one time. That sounds like a wearing-out tactic of Satan to me. Satan not only attacked the people involved, but also the people who had to deal with the issue. He often works through other people to get to leaders of ministries. If Satan cannot get to you directly, he may try to work through the weakness of someone you know or love, hoping he can upset you through them.

Once we had a trusted employee steal from us. We had chosen him to help with a special financial project in which he had to count a lot of cash. We selected him because we "knew" we could trust him. Then five hundred dollars was missing, and at the same time, this man's wife was sharing how she had mysteriously found five hundred dollars in her mailbox at work. We questioned him, along with everyone else involved in the project, and of course, he denied any involvement. We had no proof and had to let the situation rest; however, we were convinced in our hearts he was the guilty party. A few months later, he and his wife quit working at the ministry and moved back to their hometown.

A few years went by, and one day we got a call from him, asking our forgiveness for stealing the money. I was glad for him because he could not have had peace with God until he told the truth and asked for forgiveness from God and us. This situation was most unfortunate for the man and his family, but Satan also used it to try to wear us out. It is draining when you trust people and find out they are dishonest.

These, of course, are isolated cases, and 99.9 percent of our employees at the ministry are quality people who walk in truth and integrity. But Satan does seek to find someone to work through to bring aggravation and trouble.

Another way he might seek to wear me out is through something I mentioned earlier: judgment from people in the world or the church who know absolutely nothing about the ministry, or the price we have paid to get from where we began to where we are today. People are jealous of the success of others, but they don't want to do what they did to get there.

I have to remind myself all the time that it is not my concern what people think of me; my concern is what God thinks of me. I will stand before Him, not anyone else, on Judgment Day. I want to have a good reputation because I know people cannot receive from me if their hearts are not open, but I cannot make myself responsible for what everyone thinks of me, and you cannot make yourself responsible for what everyone thinks of you.

It seems these situations also come in groups. A long time may go by without any occurrences at all, then suddenly it seems that the faultfinders and troublemakers come from every direction. Satan knows it takes more than one attack to wear us out, so he relentlessly comes again and again.

Satan seeks to wear out the saints by stealing our time, forcing us to deal with trouble that he starts. He actually would like us to spend our lives trying to put out the little fires he builds.

What is the answer? James 4:7 says we are to submit ourselves to God, resist the devil, and he will flee. We see that we have to *resist* the devil. When should we resist him, how long should we wait, how much should we put up with before coming against him? The Bible teaches us as Christians to be patient, but we are not to be patient with the devil. First Peter 5:9 shares a wonderful and most important principle; it says, "Withstand him; be firm in faith [against his onset—rooted, established, strong, immovable, and determined]." We are to resist the devil *at his onset*. I have benefited greatly over the years as a result of this Scripture.

When Satan attacks, we should immediately begin to praise God; in this way, we resist Satan. When he speaks lies, we should speak truth. The instant we sense an attack, we should draw near to God and pray. The Bible tells us to be alert for when we can practice prayer. Several times the Word of God instructs us to "watch and pray." This means to watch for things going wrong in our own lives or the lives of others and immediately pray—don't wait— *pray!*

Another way to resist Satan is to apply the blood of Jesus by faith to the situation. Just as the Israelites were delivered from death by putting the blood of a lamb on the lintels and door frames of their homes during Passover (see Exodus 12:1–13), so we can apply the blood of our Passover Lamb, Jesus, by faith and be protected.

Remind Satan of the cross on which Jesus totally defeated him; remind him that he is already a defeated foe and that you will not be deceived or deluded in any way. Let him know that you recognize that it is he who is coming against you and that you won't blame people, God, or life.

Satan wants us weak and worn-out; that way we have no power to resist him. He knows that if he gains a foothold, he can get a stronghold. As I said before, *resist the devil at his onset!* Be aggressive; don't wait to see what will happen. If you wait, you won't like it. Stir yourself up in the Holy Ghost, fan the embers of your inner fire, and don't let it go out during trouble. Remember that Jesus, the Victory, lives inside you—you have the Victory!

Matthew 11:12 teaches us that the kingdom of God has suffered violent assault, and violent men seize it by force. When we study the original Greek of this word *violent* (as defined by *Strong's Exhaustive Concordance of the Bible*), it reads more like this: "The kingdom of God has suffered violent attack, but the *energetic* take it by force." The *Amplified* version adds: They take it "[as a precious prize—a share in the heavenly kingdom is sought with most ardent zeal and intense exertion]."

Satan loves a lazy man or woman; he knows that our inactivity is victory for him. We are to resist Satan in the power of the Holy Spirit; if we do, we will trouble him instead of his troubling us. As one minister said, "Trouble your trouble."

You will trouble your enemy by keeping peace when he tries to bring you worry, fear, and dread. Read on to see how to overcome these common temptations.

PEACEKEEPER #4

Don't Worry About the Future

⚜

Worry, fear, and dread are classic Peace Stealers. Anxiety is a problem for many, if not most people, and it is a sure sign that they are not pursuing peace with God. These Peace Stealers are all things God tells us in His Word not to do, because all of them are a total waste of energy; they never produce any good results.

Worry can drain our energy, make us grouchy, and even make us sick. Worry has many negative side effects and none that are good. It is totally useless! We worry simply because we don't trust God. We worry because we think we can solve our own problems if we dwell on them long enough. We worry because we are afraid things in life won't turn out the way we hope.

The only solution to worry is total abandonment to God and His plan. Even when unpleasant things happen, which they do in everyone's life, God has the ability to make them work out for the good if we continue to pray and trust Him (see Romans 8:28).

TAKE LIFE AS IT COMES

Like most people, I resist things I don't like. One day the Lord said to me, "Joyce, learn to take life as it comes." That does not mean I am to lie down and become a doormat for the devil and people who would abuse me; it does mean there are many things that I can do nothing about, so it is pointless to fight them.

If we are traveling somewhere and suddenly find ourselves in heavy traffic due to an accident or bad weather, it doesn't do any good to resist it. Only time will change it. Worry will not change it, being upset will not change it, so why not relax and find some way to enjoy the time?

God has equipped us to handle life as it comes, but if we spend today worrying about tomorrow, we find ourselves tired and frustrated. God will not help us worry! Each day has enough for us to consider, we don't need to anticipate tomorrow's situations while we are still trying to live out today.

Jesus said, "So do not worry or be anxious about tomorrow, for tomorrow will have worries and anxieties of its own. Sufficient for each day is its own trouble" (Matthew 6:34). This is some of the best advice any of us will ever receive.

Ask yourself: What good does it do to worry?

Tell yourself: It does not do any good at all. It never solves the problem, it actually adds to it.

Most of the things we worry about are solved in time; sometimes they even solve themselves. Somehow an answer comes, and all the time we spent worrying was a total waste.

I have realized that when I worry, it is because I am really concerned about me. Worry is rooted in selfishness, just like so many other sins. Worry is a sin because it is not faith, and Romans 14:23 states that "whatever does not originate and proceed from faith is sin."

Usually when I worry, it is rooted in what I fear people will think of me, what people will say about me, what will happen to me, or what I am going to do. All of us worry about other people and what they will do or what may happen to them, but we can do less about them even than we can about ourselves. If we cannot even control our own destinies, how can we hope to control someone else's?

Worry definitely torments us. There is always, absolutely always, something to worry about unless we consciously choose not to.

Peace and worry do not cohabit together. If you intend to enjoy a life of peace, worry is one thing that you will have to give up.

The Lord wants us to be free from all anxiety and distressing care. He wants us to be free to serve Him without being "drawn in diverging directions" (1 Corinthians 7:34). He does not want our interests to be divided between Him and the things in this world we feel we need to worry about.

We should strive to keep our lives as simple as possible; it helps us to have fewer temptations toward worry. The more we are involved in, the more we face temptation to be concerned in new areas. I have discovered, for example, that the less I know, the less I worry. I was the type of person who wanted to be "in the know," but now I would much rather have peace.

Paul even went so far as to instruct people to consider remaining single in order not to have spouses they would have to please. He said "The unmarried man is anxious about the things of the Lord—how he may please the Lord. But the married man is anxious about worldly matters—how he may please his wife" (1 Corinthians 7:32–33).

It is certainly not wrong to get married, but Paul's point was that we should keep life as simple as possible so we are free to serve the Lord. Married or single, we should seek simplicity in our daily lives.

Let God Take Care of You

God wants to take care of His children, and He has promised to do so: "Casting the whole of your care [all your anxieties, all your worries, all your concerns, once and for all] on Him, for He cares for you affectionately and cares about you watchfully" (1 Peter 5:7).

We can either try to take care of ourselves, or we can trust God and He will do it for us. Psalm 55:22 says to cast our care on Him, and He will sustain us. The Holy Spirit is a gentleman, and He will not force His help on us. We must ask for it.

We can say that we trust the Lord, but He also wants to see the fruit of it. One of the ways we show our trust in God is by refusing to worry and be anxious.

Because of being abused in my childhood, I learned at an early age to take care of myself. Those I turned to for help had let me down; they disappointed me, so I vowed not to trust people. It took me a while to learn that God is definitely not like people; if He says He will do something, He never fails to do it.

I was thrilled to learn that God wanted to take care of me, but learning how to cast my care so He could do His job was a long lesson. It seemed so foreign to me not to worry about situations. I still need more growth in this area, but at least I'm not where I once was.

I admit that worry has been a problem in my life. I had many burdens at a young age and didn't know anything else to do except worry. I formed bad habits, and they have not been easily broken. It seemed I was literally addicted to worry and reasoning. I could not settle down and feel peaceful until I thought I had an answer to my situation. The main problem was that I always had some sort of situation; therefore, I rarely had the pleasure of being at peace.

If you are one of those people who seem to worry about everything, I want you to know that I know how you feel. I do believe the Lord can and will deliver you. There are biblical principles you can learn that will bring freedom from the bondage of worry. Retire from self-care! Make a decision to let God take care of you.

First Peter 5:6 says we are to humble ourselves under the mighty hand of God, so in due time He might exalt us. It says in verse 7, as we've seen, to cast all our care on Him, for He cares about us. These two verses together are saying that humility leads us into freedom from worry. We will worry as long as we think we can solve our problems, but humility says, "I need God, I need help."

Proud people are independent, but God requires us to be totally dependent upon Him. Habakkuk 2:4 teaches us that the soul of the proud person is not right within him. Part of the soul is the mind, and God does not consider our minds to be "right" when we are worrying. The just and righteous man lives by faith; he leans on God for everything.

First Peter 5:5 states that God resists the proud but gives grace (help) to the humble. Humble people know they are nothing without God, that they can do nothing of any real value without Him. I did not even begin to enjoy any measure of freedom from worry until I faced the fact that I was not able to solve my own problems.

If we know what to do, we should do it; if we don't, we should admit it.

MEDITATE ON THE WORD

If you know how to worry, you know how to meditate. It means to think of something over and over. Meditation on God's Word is one of the major ways you can find deliverance from worrying. Just as we once formed a habit of worrying (meditating on the problem), we can form a new habit of meditating on God's Word. Take portions of Scripture that comfort you, and roll them over and over in your mind. Do it on purpose!

As soon as you are facing a difficult situation that tempts you to worry, begin to confess and meditate on Scripture. In this way, you do warfare with the enemy of your soul (Satan).

When you begin to worry, go find something to do. Get busy being a blessing to someone; do something fruitful. Talking about your problem or sitting alone, thinking about it, does no good; it serves only to make you miserable. Above all else, remember that worrying is totally useless. Worrying will not solve your problem.

FEAR

Worry cannot exist without fear. We can fear things into existence. Fear looks into the future and imagines the worst that can happen. "Fear hath torment," according to 1 John 4:18 (KJV). Anyone who has experienced fear can say a loud *Amen* to that statement. Fear definitely torments!

Having revelation on God's love for us and placing our faith in that love is the only antidote for fear. We can relax and live free from worry and fear when we know that God is good and that He loves us. He loves us with a perfect, full, and complete love. He loves us unconditionally, which means there are never days—not even moments—when God does not love us. Knowing this helps us feel better about ourselves, and it also delivers us from tormenting negative emotions such as worry and fear.

God is on our side, and no matter what happens, He has promised never to leave us or forsake us. He said, "Fear not, for I am with you." Meditate on this Scripture until it becomes a reality in your life: "There is no fear in love [dread does not exist], but full-grown (complete, perfect) love turns fear out of doors and expels every trace of terror! For fear brings with it the thought of punishment, and [so] he who is afraid has not reached the full maturity of love [is not yet grown into love's complete perfection]" (1 John 4:18).

God loves you, and you can live without fear because He does. He has promised to take care of you, to meet your legitimate needs. I am not promising that God will give you everything you want. There are times when we want things that God knows would not be good for us. He promises in Luke 11 that if we ask for bread, He will not give us a stone; likewise, if we ask for a stone, He will not give us a stone when what we need is bread. God will always do what is best for us, and we need to trust that. That kind of faith leads us into lives of peace that passes understanding.

Know God's Character

God is faithful, and because faithfulness is embedded in His character, He cannot fail us or let us down. Experience with God gives us experience with His faithfulness. We have needs, and He meets them time and again. He may not always do what we would like, but He does do the right thing. He may not be early, but He is never too late.

I have seen God come through multitudes of times during the years I have been serving Him. I can truly say, *God is faithful.* He has given me needed strength, answers that came just in time, right friends in right places, open doors of opportunity, encouragement, needed finances, and much more. There is nothing we need that God cannot provide.

God is good. Goodness is one of His many wonderful character traits. When something is part of an individual's character, we can expect him to respond in that way every time. God is not good only sometimes, He is good all the time. He is good to people who don't deserve it. He helps us even when we have done dumb things, if we will just admit our mistakes and ask boldly for His help. We can always ask God for help: "If any of you is deficient in wisdom, let him ask of the giving God [Who gives] to everyone liberally and ungrudgingly, without reproaching or faultfinding, and it will be given him" (James 1:5).

What good news! God will give us wisdom when we have trials—He will show us the way out. All we need to do is ask, and He will give without finding fault with us. Amazing! We don't have to be afraid that God will not help us because we have been weak or made mistakes.

Another one of His character traits is mercy. Mercy chooses to be good to people who, in reality, deserve punishment. His mercy is new every morning. I have always said that God makes a new batch of mercy daily because we used up all of yesterday's supply.

Study the character of God (I have a tape series available on the subject); it will increase your faith and help you not to worry or be fearful. Remember that fear is a demon spirit Satan sends out from hell to hinder our progress. Fear stops us and even drives us backward. It causes us to shrink back. Hebrews 10:38 says, "Now the just shall live by faith: but if any man draw back, my soul shall have no pleasure in him" (KJV).

The *Amplified* translation of that verse says if we draw back and shrink in fear, God has "no delight or pleasure" in us. This simply means that God is not delighted when, through fear, we are cheated out of what Jesus died for us to have and enjoy. We must keep going forward in God's plan and never fall back. Satan hates progress, and more than anything, he uses fear to prevent it.

I believe fear is the master spirit Satan uses to control people. It seems that so many of our problems are rooted in fear. The only answer to fear is to face it with courage. Courage is not the absence of fear—it is going forward in the face of it. Courage overrides fear; it refuses to bow its knee to it. The only acceptable attitude toward fear is: *I will not fear!*

To fear is to take flight or to run away. We are truly afraid if we run from what God wants us to confront. When the Israelites were afraid of Pharaoh and his army, God told Moses to tell them to "fear not; stand still and see the salvation of the Lord" (see Exodus 14:13).

We will never see or experience God's delivering power if we run from things in fear. Stand still, and see what God will do for you. Trust Him; give Him a chance to prove His faithfulness and goodness to you.

When fear knocks on the door, send faith to answer. Don't speak your fears; speak faith. Say what God would say in your situation—say what His Word says, not what you think or feel. The book of Mark relates an account of a woman who had been bleeding for twelve long years. She heard of Jesus and believed that He could help her. "For she kept saying, If I only touch His garments, I shall be restored to health" (Mark 5:28).

The very next verse says, "And immediately her flow of blood was dried up . . . and [suddenly] she felt in her body that she was healed." This woman received her miracle because of faith, but notice that her faith said something.

Whatever is in our hearts will come out of our mouths. Are you speaking fear or faith? Both can produce results. Faith produces positive results, and fear produces negative ones. Did the woman sense any fear? I believe she did. The Bible records that the crowds were so heavy that people pressed Jesus from all sides. I am sure the woman looked at those people and thought, *How am I ever going to get to Jesus? What if I cannot press through to Him?* The devil offers fearful thoughts of that nature.

But the woman made a choice: In the presence of fear telling her she wouldn't make it, she pressed on! She did not shrink back in fear, she pressed on, and that is exactly what God wants all of us to do. She pushed forward and kept speaking her faith, and she got her miracle.

Jesus told the disciples that if they had "faith [that is living] like a grain of mustard seed," they would *say* to the mountain, "Move," and it would move. He further said that with faith, nothing would be impossible to them (see Matthew 17:20).

We see that once again Jesus told us that faith *says* something. I ask again, what are you saying in your situation? When trouble comes, are you able to keep a good confession?

In Matthew 21:21, we find Jesus saying basically the same thing to the same group of men. He was reminding them that if they had faith and did not doubt, even if they *said* to the mountain, "Be cast into the sea," it would be done. The mountains mentioned in these verses refer to obstacles in our way.

Imagine having that kind of power! God wants us to have power, but He also wants us to have spiritual maturity. He would not allow us to use His power for carnal, personal desires. We are His representatives on earth, and our goal should be to see His kingdom come and His will be done on earth as in heaven.

During our trials and tribulation, during the times of what Paul called "abasing," we should hold fast our confession of faith in Jesus, wait patiently, and know that He will never fail us.

What we talk about has a lot to do with our level of personal peace. Why? Because Proverbs 18:20 teaches us that we must be satisfied with the consequences of the words we speak. The next verse adds, "Death and life are in the power of the tongue, and they who indulge in it shall eat the fruit of it (for death or life)."

We can encourage ourselves with our own conversation, or we can discourage ourselves. We can decrease and even eliminate our peace or increase it. I encourage you to be accountable for your words—they are powerful!

DON'T BELIEVE YOUR FEELINGS

God wants us to enjoy lives of peace. Jesus provided it, and we must aggressively pursue it and hold on to it. Second Corinthians 5:7 says that we walk by faith and not by sight; that means we do not make decisions by what we see or feel. We have to search our hearts, where faith abides, and live from there. The kingdom of God is *within* us, and we are to follow those inner promptings that lead to righteousness, peace, and joy in the Holy Spirit.

Feelings can mislead us and steal our faith more than any other single influence. The problem with feelings is that they are ever changing. We can feel one thousand ways about the same thing in thirty days. One minute we may feel like doing a thing, and the next minute we don't.

Feelings provoke us to say things that are unwise; we talk a lot about how we feel. Do you believe the god of your feelings or the God of the Bible? This is a question we must all ask ourselves. More than anything, people who come to me for help and counsel tell me how they feel. We should be telling each other what the Word of God says, not just how we feel.

Our feelings do not convey truth to us; Satan can use them to deceive and lead us astray. Emotions are unreliable; don't believe them. Respond with your heart, where the Spirit of God abides, and see if you then have peace. Check with your heart, not your emotions, before making decisions.

For example, I may meet individuals with whom, in the natural,

I would like to form relationships. They may have gifts or talents that I think would benefit my ministry. But the more I am around them, the more uncomfortable I become in my spirit about them.

I can sense strongly if people are phony or their motives are impure. I may not have anything natural to base my knowledge on, but the inner sensing will not go away, and I do not have peace about making alliances with them. I have learned to trust those promptings of the Spirit but to distrust emotional feelings. I may want to do something in my flesh but know in my spirit it is the wrong thing to do.

I remember one woman we hired at the ministry. This woman seemed to have strong gifts of leadership, and some of our key leaders wanted to promote her. I had a sense that something was not right but could find no natural reason for my feelings. We desperately needed good leadership, so I finally relented, even against what I sensed within, and agreed to put the woman in a place of authority.

She seemed to function in that position well for a while, so I assumed I must have been wrong. But after a period of time went by, we began to have complaints of her mistreating other employees. She was always very respectful to me and other people in authority, but to those under her leadership she was a different person.

A phony is a person who pretends to be one thing to one group of people but is quite another at other times. I know she had the ability to be respectful because she treated me well, but she abused people when she thought she could get away with it. I absolutely despise that kind of attitude.

More than anything, Jesus despised the phonies of His day. He rebuked openly and often those who behaved well when someone was watching them but who, inside, were devouring wolves. People can pretend for a while, but under pressure the real person always shows up. I realized later that I should have listened to those inner promptings. God was giving me discernment about the woman that would have prevented a lot of heartache and wasted time and money had I listened.

There are intuitive (spiritual) feelings we should respect, but most of our emotional feelings will lead us into trouble if we obey or follow them. Emotions will tell us to bow down to fear, when actually that fear will destroy us if we don't resist it. They tell us to give up on things that God intends us to finish or to purchase things we cannot afford and don't even need. Satan uses our emotions to wreck our lives. Not only does Satan come against us through our emotions, but he also wars against our thoughts.

Examine your thoughts and feelings carefully. Don't follow them unless you are sure they are conveying God's will.

LET PEACE BE YOUR UMPIRE

Paul told believers to let peace decide with finality every question that came up. We are to follow peace. If we will remember that, we will have lives we can really enjoy, not ones we just endure. I hate to see people with lifeless attitudes, people who are just going through the motions and enduring each day. I was one of those people for a long, long time, and I know from experience that we must press into peace and joy if we intend to have them. Satan definitely tries to steal the best in life. He is not enjoying himself and does not want any of us to enjoy life either.

If we would obey the teaching from Colossians 3:15, which says peace is to be the umpire in our lives, we would save ourselves unbelievable misery. We open the door for many difficulties in our lives through doing what we think or feel rather than following peace.

I've mentioned that, out of fear of being lonely, some people marry people whom deep down inside they don't have peace about. I married out of fear when I was very young, and it ended in divorce a few years later. As I have mentioned in my teachings, I felt like used merchandise because of my father's abuse. I was afraid that nobody would ever want me, so I married the first boy who showed interest in me. I think I knew it would never really work, but the fear of being lonely caused me to ignore the lack of peace I felt inside.

My first husband had lots of problems himself, and I know God was warning me that I would only get hurt more, but I took a chance. I gambled that maybe I could make a wrong decision and get right results. This, of course, was very foolish, and because of my decision I added another five years of torment and mistreatment to the ones I had already experienced. By the time my first marriage ended, I was twenty-three years old and could never remember being truly happy or having any real peace in my life.

It was not until I learned, many years later in life, to follow peace that I broke these negative patterns in my life. Peace is a wonderful thing; it leads us into many other blessings. We should be completely unwilling to do without it. As Psalm 34:14 states, crave peace, inquire for it, require it, and go after it! Don't let worry or fear steal your peace.

Don't Live in Dread

Dread is closely related to fear. We might say it is the forerunner to fear. I believe a lot of people dread many things and yet don't realize what a problem it is. We dread everything from getting out of bed to going to work, doing dishes, driving in traffic, paying our bills, confronting issues, and just about any little thing we can think of.

Why do we dread something we have to do anyway? Through the power of the Holy Spirit, we can enjoy every aspect of life. An unbeliever may not be able to avoid dread, but a believer in Jesus Christ can. We have supernatural strength and ability available to us. Unbelievers have to depend on their feelings, but we can go beyond feeling and live by faith.

How we approach any situation makes all the difference as to whether we will enjoy it. We will, of course, be miserable if we approach driving to work in traffic with a negative, complaining attitude. It won't do any good, because we must drive to work anyway.

It is actually extremely foolish to dread things we must do and know we will do. The main thing dread does is steal the peace and joy of life. It also drains us of energy and strength we need for the day.

God commanded the Israelites to "dread not," nor fear their enemies (Deuteronomy 1:29). Can something like traffic be an enemy? Yes it can, if we perceive it that way. Anything that we don't want in life, that hinders or aggravates us, we can perceive as an enemy. We are not to dread or fear anything—we are to live courageously and boldly.

Dread drains, faith energizes. Being negative drains us while being positive energizes us. Millions of people in the world today are tired. They see doctors who cannot find any real reason for their condition, so they tell them it is stress. Often we take medication for conditions that would be totally solved if we would eliminate worry, fear, and dread from our lives. If we will make a decision to approach every aspect of life, no matter what it is, with a pleasant, thankful attitude, we will see major changes for the better, even in our health.

The future is coming, no matter how much we fear or dread it. God gives us what we need for each day, but He does not give us tomorrow's grace or wisdom today. If we use today trying to figure out tomorrow, we feel pressure because we are using what we have been allotted for today.

Probably one of the greatest ways we show our trust in God is by living life one day at a time. We prove our confidence in Him by enjoying today and not letting the concern of tomorrow interfere.

It made a big change in my life when I began to gain insight from the Holy Spirit on this problem of dreading things. This truth about living one day at a time greatly increased my peace and joy.

I learned that it really was not the event I was facing that was so bad—it was dreading it that made it bad. Our attitudes do make all the difference in the world. Learn to approach life with a "I can do whatever I need to do" attitude. Don't say that you hate things like driving to work in traffic, going to the grocery store, cleaning house, doing laundry, changing the oil in the car, or cutting the grass. These chores are all part of life. Don't let the events of life dictate your level of joy. It is the joy of the Lord that is your strength. Be joyful that you are going to heaven, that you have someone who always loves you, no matter what. Look at and concentrate on what you do have, not what you don't have.

Everyone has to attend to some unpleasant details in life. We would not know what God's peace was if we never had any difficulty to go through. It is in these difficulties that we learn how valuable His peace is to us.

Some things are certainly more naturally enjoyable and easier to do than others, but that does not mean we cannot purposely enjoy the other more difficult tasks. We can choose to have attitudes of joy and peace. Usually, if we don't feel like doing something, we automatically assume we cannot enjoy it or have peace during that time, but that is a deception. We grow spiritually when we do difficult things with a good attitude.

I don't always feel like being nice and pleasant, but I can choose to in order to honor God. We live for His glory, not our own pleasure. Dreading things does not glorify God. He wants us to live aggressively, to be alive and face each day with courage. How would any parents feel if their children got up each day and said they feared and dreaded the day the parents had prepared for them? They would, of course, feel terrible. God is a parent—He is our parent. The psalmist David said, "This is the day which the Lord has brought about; we will rejoice and be glad in it" (see Psalm 118:24). Notice he said, "We *will* rejoice," not "We *feel like* rejoicing."

What Does the Future Hold?

The future holds a mixture of things we will enjoy and things we would rather do without, but both will come. In Philippians 4:11–12, Paul experienced abasing and abounding, but he also stated that he was able to be content in both, and we also have this option (and ability) as a gift from God.

Jesus promised us that in the world we would have tribulation, but He told us to "cheer up" because He had overcome the world and deprived it of power to really harm us (see John 16:33). Dreading hard times will not prevent them from coming, but it will make them even more difficult than they would have been. Make life as easy as possible; don't dread it. Face it with courage and say, "I will not fear, because greater is He that is in me than he that is in the world" (see 1 John 4:4).

No mortal really knows what the future holds, only God knows, and He does not usually tell us what it is. Why doesn't He reveal more to us about the future? Because He wants us to trust Him that everything will work out for our ultimate good, that all things work together to help accomplish His will for each of us. We may not know what the future holds, but we can be satisfied to know Him, the one who does know.

I spent some time today thinking about the future, and I realized that everything out there won't be something I will welcome with open arms. I will face things that I would rather not have to deal with, but I cannot stop them, so I may as well embrace and go through them with a smile on my face.

I am convinced of one thing: I may go through difficulties, but God also has wonderful things planned for me. He always balances things so we don't become discouraged and defeated by too many difficult days without good ones in between. Remember, God never allows more to come on us than what we can bear, but with every temptation He also always provides the way out.

I have noticed in my life that when I have truly had all I can take, something happens to relieve the pressure for a while. I get built up, rested, and have times of joy, then perhaps go another round with the trouble. When I feel I have reached my limit, I pray for good news, because the Bible says that good news nourishes us, it encourages us and strengthens us. Another Scripture says that David prayed for God to show him evident signs of His goodwill and favor (see Psalm 86:17); I also pray for that, and God always gives me what I need when I need it.

Remember, James 4:2 says we have not because we ask not. Ask God for good news—ask Him to encourage you. Too often in life, we go to people for encouragement or even get angry at them when they are not giving it to us. We should go to God because He is the God of all comfort (see 2 Corinthians 1:3).

We would not need faith if everything in life went the way we wanted. We would need no patience if we never had to wait for anything. Faith and patience work together to bring our break-throughs. While we are waiting, let us do so with joy and peace. This shows that we are children of God.

The whole world lives in fear and dread, but God's children should not. We are to behave differently from the people in the world; we should let our light shine. Just being positive in a nega-tive circumstance is a way to do this. The world will notice when we are stable in every kind of situation.

Make up your mind right now that all of life does not need to make you feel good in order for you to face it with peace and joy. Make a decision that you will not dread anything you have to do. Do it all with a thankful attitude. There are people who are sick and diseased or perhaps in the hospital who would absolutely love to be able to move about enough to do what you may be dreading.

I never considered driving down the street to get a cup of coffee a huge privilege until after I had been hospitalized with breast cancer and had surgery. When I was released, I asked my husband to take me out for a coffee and a drive through a local park. It was amazing how much joy I felt.

I was doing a very simple thing that was previously available to me every day, yet I had never seen it as a privilege. When I had faced the possibility of death or long-term treatment for cancer and discovered I would not only live but was pronounced well, I suddenly loved life so much that very simple things brought extreme joy.

Our son went on an outreach with a team of people who go visit the homeless each Friday evening. After helping in this ministry, he called me and said, "If I ever complain again, please knock me down and then kick me for being so stupid!" He was appalled at himself for the things he had murmured about in the past once he saw by comparison how some people were living. We would all feel exactly the same way.

Those without a place to live would love to have a house to clean, while we dread cleaning ours. They would delight in having a car to drive, even an old one, while we complain about needing to wash ours or take it in for an oil change.

I am sure you are getting my point. We lose sight of how blessed we are most of the time, but we should work at keeping it in the front of our thinking. Be thankful you can do anything, and don't dread things you have to do.

Choose to bless God all the time, no matter what is going on, as David did: "I *WILL* bless the Lord at all times; His praise shall continually be in my mouth" (Psalm 34:1, italics mine).

PROSPERITY AND PROGRESS

God certainly wants all of His children to enjoy prosperity and progress, but once again I want to remind you that worry, fear, and dread can stop and hinder both of these. This verse says all that I am trying to say: "Then you will prosper if you are careful to keep and fulfill the statutes and ordinances with which the Lord charged Moses concerning Israel. Be strong and of good courage. Dread not and fear not; be not dismayed" (1 Chronicles 22:13).

The negative expectations of worry and dread hinder and prevent progress. Live courageously, live with faith, and keep a good confession.

Good things will not just fall on us; we must aggressively pursue them like the woman with the issue of blood pursued Jesus. She refused to take no for an answer, and she got her miracle breakthrough. We can have the same results if we press in and press on instead of drawing back in fear and dread. God will either give us a breakthrough, or at the very least He will give us grace to go through whatever we need to and enjoy our lives while we are doing it.

Recently a group of pastors asked me a question: Besides God Himself, what one thing had helped me get from where I started in ministry to the level of success I currently enjoy? I immediately said, "I refused to give up!" There were thousands of times when I felt like giving up, I thought about giving up, I was tempted to give up, but I always pressed on. I thank God for the determination He gives us.

Don't let life defeat you—face it with boldness and courage, and declare that you will enjoy every aspect of it. You can do that because you have the awesome power of God dwelling in you. God is never frustrated and unhappy. He always has peace and joy, and since He lives in us and we live in Him, surely we can attain the same thing.

Right now, as I am writing this portion of this book, I have a terrible backache. I did some new exercises yesterday and apparently strained some muscles, but I will not dwell on the pain and let it ruin my day. I have something to accomplish today, and by God's grace, I will do it. I will not worry that I might still have the same pain tomorrow or dread it if I do. Whatever we go through, God will always be with us. I choose to believe that Jesus is my Healer and that His healing power is working in my body right now!

When tempted to worry, Dave always says, "I am not impressed." He believes we should be more impressed by God's Word than our problems. He says if we don't get *impressed,* we won't get *depressed,* then *oppressed,* and ultimately perhaps even *possessed* by our difficulties. No matter what you are facing right now, God has a great life planned for you. It includes prosperity and progress in every area of life. It includes great peace, joy unspeakable, and every good thing you can imagine. Refuse to settle for anything less than God's best for you!

Don't Be Double-Minded

❧ ❦

Double-minded, indecisive people are always miserable; they certainly don't enjoy peace with God. Nothing is worse to me than being between two decisions and not making either one of them. I am usually a very decisive person. At times in life I have made decisions too fast and made mistakes. I have also found that I can slip into being double-minded and indecisive if I am not careful.

I believe this is something the devil tempts all of us with at various times. He does anything that steals our peace because he knows that without peace, we are without power. We often don't make decisions because we don't want to make mistakes. But making no decision is still a decision *and* a mistake. Decide to decide! It will produce peace in your life, as long as you don't second-guess yourself and fall back into being indecisive once again.

Stick with your decisions unless you are definitely shown that they are wrong. Sometimes we find out whether a decision is right or wrong only by making it and seeing what happens. Making a wrong decision is not the end of the world, in most cases, and it is usually better than making no decision.

Some people do nothing most of their lives because they are afraid to commit to action. I hope you are not one of those people, but if you are, I want to help you. Please realize you need to start somewhere. Begin with smaller things, and work your way up to major decisions.

Don't Be Afraid of What People Think

Most of us would not mind making a mistake if we thought we could make it privately. It is not the mistake, but people knowing about it that bothers us. We are afraid of what people think, and yet their opinions cannot really harm us. Our indecision can.

Many people have destroyed their lives by being overly concerned about what others think. Saul lost his kingdom and the opportunity to be king because he cared so much about what people thought that he disobeyed God on more than one occasion.

We have all experienced having to choose between God and people. It really should not even be a contest, but somehow it always is—at least until we are delivered from the fear of man.

Can someone's *thoughts* really harm us that much? I think I have finally realized that if someone wants to judge me, he will find some way to do it, no matter what I do; therefore, I may as well follow my heart and get about enjoying my life.

We will be judged, criticized, and misunderstood at various times in life, and we really can't do much about it. Fear of people's thoughts about our decisions only prevents us from making progress. We decide nothing and then nothing happens, with the exception that we remain frustrated while going back and forth and being confused about what we should do.

Satan always threatens us with, "What if . . . ?" He shows us the most terrible thing that *could* happen, and it always revolves around our making a mistake. When needing to make a decision, we must remember that there is as much of a chance that we will be right as wrong.

We will never fulfill our destinies if we have undue concern over what people think. Let them think what they want. If they think wrong thoughts, they will pay the price by being miserable. Wrong thoughts can do nothing except produce misery. Many people blame their unhappiness and lack of peace on their circumstances when it really is rooted in their own lousy thinking.

People who can break free from caring about what other people think will instantly upgrade their level of living. They will increase their joy and their peace one hundredfold.

BE CONFIDENT

God wants us to live with confidence and approach life boldly. Being indecisive is neither. Make a decision today to start being decisive. It will never happen if you don't. It may be a bold move for you if you have spent a lot of your life in fear and indecision, but it is necessary if you really want to enjoy a life of peace. Indecision is not a peaceful place.

Put your confidence in Christ and who you are in Him, not in what people think of you. We cannot base our worth on what others have said or how they have treated us. People who are hurting will hurt others. If you have come into contact with people who are hurting, they may hurt or reject you. They may have transposed their pain onto you, when in reality you were not the real problem at all.

Know yourself! Know your heart, and don't wait for other people to dictate to you the truth about your value. Don't assume you are wrong every time someone does not agree with you. Believe that God's wisdom dwells inside of you. Believe you can make decisions. There is no point at all in believing something negative about yourself when it is just as easy to believe something positive—and it's certainly a lot more beneficial.

People who are indecisive are usually more passive in nature or insecure. They are fear-based and should be faith-based individuals. Is fear, or faith, motivating most of your actions?

A believer without confidence is like a jumbo jet sitting on the runway with no fuel in it. It looks good but goes no place. People who are indecisive are the same way. They may have all the qualities needed to be successful, but if they refuse to make decisions, they go nowhere and accomplish nothing. Progress begins with a decision.

BE COURAGEOUS

Courage is a vitally necessary quality if we intend to do anything worthwhile with our time here on earth. Leaders are not always, or even usually, the most gifted people, but they are people with courage. They step out when others shrink back in fear. They take bold steps of faith, they do things that to other people might even seem foolish or unwise, but they are willing to take a chance. They may be wrong occasionally, but they are right enough of the time that it doesn't matter.

I would rather try to do a lot and accomplish a little than try to do nothing and accomplish all of it. If I try nothing, I will accomplish nothing. The worst thing that can happen is I will be wrong, and that really is not the end of the world. After all, nobody is right all the time. I would rather take a chance on being wrong and trying to accomplish something than definitely be wrong because I have done nothing.

God expects us to increase, to be fruitful and multiply (see Genesis 1:28). He admires courage; in fact, He demands it from those who will work alongside of Him. The Lord told Joshua that he was to take Moses' place and lead the Israelites into the promised land. There was one stipulation: He had to be strong and of good courage.

> Be strong (confident) and of good courage, for you shall cause this people to inherit the land which I swore to their fathers to give them. Only you be strong and very courageous, that you may do according to all the law which Moses My servant commanded you. Turn not from it to the right hand or to the left, that you may prosper wherever you

go. . . . Have not I commanded you? Be strong, vigorous, and very courageous. Be not afraid, neither be dismayed, for the Lord your God is with you wherever you go. (Joshua 1:6–7, 9)

It doesn't matter what qualities or provisions we do not have, as long as God is with us. He is all we need. He makes up for anything we are lacking. God told Joshua, "As I was with Moses, so I will be with you" (Joshua 1:5). Moses was great because God was with him and he took courageous steps to do what God told him to do. The same thing would hold true for Joshua—and will be true for any one of us who follows God's ways in these areas. His way is not one of shrinking back in fear, but of going forward courageously in faith.

God's way is one of being decisive. We are not to make decisions so quickly that we don't give them proper thought and prayer. We should seek wisdom and be sure we are following peace. But once we have done all we can do to assure we are making a right decision, as far as we know, there is nothing else to do except be courageous and do something, lest we do nothing.

DECIDE BY YOUR HEART, NOT YOUR HEAD

A person who needs to have everything all figured out will not be courageous. People who do courageous things follow their hearts. They may not always fully understand why they feel courage, but they are bold enough to follow it. I am not suggesting we follow our emotions, which would not be good since they are rather unstable. But we should follow our born-again spirits, our hearts.

People who do bold things step out in faith even though they have no real proof they will even work. They make decisions by discernment. *Discernment* means to be able to grasp and comprehend what is obscure. It is the ability to see what is not obvious based on circumstances. A person might say he makes decisions by his "gut." This simply means he does what he believes is *right* even if he feels uncomfortable. Jesus Himself did not make decisions based on natural knowledge.

> And shall make Him of quick understanding, and His delight shall be in the reverential and obedient fear of the Lord. And He shall not judge by the sight of His eyes, neither decide by the hearing of His ears; but with righteousness and justice shall He judge the poor and decide with fairness for the meek, the poor, and the downtrodden of the earth (Isaiah 11:3–4)

We see from this Scripture that He did not decide "by the sight of His eyes," or the "hearing of His ears," yet He was of "quick understanding." If we follow our hearts, we can understand quickly what we could not learn by natural means in a lifetime. It is sad, but most people are afraid to operate in the supernatural realm; they want to understand everything in their minds.

One year a man was helping me do my income tax. When he observed that we gave 10 percent of our income to the church each year, he promptly told me that we were giving too much, that it was not necessary, and we should stop.

He was looking at our giving in the natural and could find no reason why we would want to do such a thing. We were looking at it according to our knowledge of God's Word. We understood spiritually what we were doing and believed that if we gave, God would always take care of us. I tried to explain God's principles on sowing and reaping to him, but he insisted that even if we wanted to give, it did not need to be that much, especially since we didn't have an abundance left over after giving to the church and paying our bills.

This is an example of a natural man not understanding the spiritual man. First Corinthians 2:14 explains that the natural man cannot understand spiritual things because they must be spiritually discerned. This simply means that spiritual things take place in the born-again spirit of the inner man, not in the natural mind.

This is one of the reasons God's Word instructs us to let peace be the umpire in our lives, deciding with finality everything that is questionable. If we could go two ways, which way do we go? What do we decide? We decide to do what we have peace in our hearts about, what we are comfortable with inside of us. God speaks and communicates to the heart of man, not necessarily to his head. We know God in our hearts. He dwells in our hearts.

This is the reason people who depend on their intellects have a difficult time believing in God. They don't see Him, they don't feel Him, and many of His principles don't make sense to their natural minds.

Naturally speaking, what sense does it make to tell people that they will have increase if they give away some of their money? It makes no sense at all. The Bible says that the first will be last, and the last will be first. That makes no sense to my mind, but I know by spiritual understanding that it means when we try to push ourselves forward into first place, we will end up last. When we wait on God to promote us, even if we start out last, we will end up first.

I am very grateful for discernment and spiritual understanding. I appreciate the fact that you and I, as believers in Jesus Christ, filled with His Spirit, can make decisions courageously because we can trust what is in our hearts.

If you have been having difficulty making a decision, try this: Let your mind rest. Don't be *thinking* about what you should do. Then see what is in your heart—what do you *know* inside that you should do? Whatever you have peace about, do that.

A person might want to purchase a new car but not have real peace about it. Emotional excitement is not peace. If you are confused, you are not in God's will. He is the Author of peace, not confusion. Satan wants you confused. It is really very simple: If you don't have peace, don't buy the car. If you do purchase it without peace, I can guarantee that later on you will be sorry that you did. You will either have purchased something that will not meet your needs, it will require a lot of maintenance, or it will create financial pressure.

We don't have to know why God is not giving us peace to do a certain thing; we just need to follow His leading. He is not obligated to explain, but we are obligated to trust Him.

THE DOUBLE-MINDED MAN IS UNSTABLE AND UNRELIABLE

In James 1, we find that when we need wisdom we should ask God for it, and He will give it—but we must ask in faith. We are not to waver, hesitate, or doubt. The person who does these things will receive nothing he asks for from the Lord. Why? If the man cannot settle on something and make a decision about what he believes, how can God give him anything? "[For being as he is] a man of two minds (hesitating, dubious, irresolute), [he is] unstable and unreliable and uncertain about everything [he thinks, feels, decides]" (James 1:8).

The double-minded man is unreliable and unstable. This is not a reputation anyone wants to have. I want people and the Lord to be able to depend on me, to know that I mean what I say and won't change my mind without a very good reason.

Paul told the Corinthians that when he said yes to them, it meant yes. He promised that yes would not end up being no (see 2 Corinthians 1:17–18). In other words, Paul was promising not to be double-minded. He was telling the church members that they could count on him to be stable, and he would keep his word to them.

Integrity is extremely important for every person, and especially for those who lead others. How could Paul expect to be respected if he was unreliable? He couldn't, and neither can we.

I want to be in relationship with people I can depend on, people I know who are decisive, stable, and reliable. I want to be able to trust people. Good relationships are built on trust. I was recently involved in an event that required people to sign up ahead of time, indicating whether or not they would be attending. We had nine hundred people say they were coming, and only seven hundred showed up. Very few of them made any effort to cancel or even communicate that they were not coming. The problem was twofold: First, they did not keep their word, and second, we had purchased and cooked meat for nine hundred, and since seven hundred showed up, we obviously had lots of meat left over.

This was inconsiderate on their parts and harmful to them spiritually because they didn't honor their commitment. This is a widespread problem today in our society. Most people don't think anything at all about saying they will do a thing and then changing their minds without any good reason, except they did not feel like doing what they said they would do. Their excuse is "I changed my mind."

The very least we can do when we have made a commitment and cannot or will not keep it is to make a phone call and say so. Don't just leave people hanging, not having any idea what happened.

Those who didn't attend the event I mentioned thought it didn't really matter. But it always makes a difference if we don't do what we say we will.

Our word is a verbal contract. This verse shows that God considers it to be a vow: "When you vow a vow or make a pledge to God, do not put off paying it; for God has no pleasure in fools (those who witlessly mock Him). Pay what you vow. It is better that you should not vow than that you should vow and not pay" (Ecclesiastes 5:4–5).

We should take these Scriptures to heart and view them seriously. Don't make commitments rashly without giving thought to whether or not you are prepared to follow through. I am sure that some of the two hundred people who failed to show up had good reasons for not doing so, but I am equally sure that most of them just plain didn't see the need to keep their word.

When we keep our word, even if it is inconvenient for us to do so, it shows good character. We should be concerned about our example because the world is watching those of us who claim to be Christians. They want to see if we are all talk, or if we are living what we are saying we believe.

I have witnessed people signing up for things and not showing up numerous times during my years of involvement with people in the church. I started out being shocked because I assumed church people could be trusted, but I quickly learned that just because someone goes to church, he is not automatically honest and truthful.

The ones who don't keep their word always have an excuse of some kind, but I don't believe they have peace. We cannot be double minded, unreliable, and unstable and enjoy peace at the same time. We may try to override the feelings of conviction about not keeping our commitment, but its presence nibbles away at the peace God wants us to enjoy.

One of the ways to maintain peace with God, with yourself, and your fellow man is to do what you say you will do. Once you have made up your mind, don't change it unless you have no other choice.

DON'T BE DOUBLE-MINDED, EVEN IN SMALL MATTERS

Although I am usually very decisive, I have been known to be double-minded about little things, like what to wear or where to go and eat. God showed me that even being double-minded in these things places pressure on me and robs me of available peace. I like my meals, for example, to be perfect. I think of one restaurant that has the salad I like, but then another comes to mind that has wonderful coffee. Then I remember the pasta dish I love at another one, and before I realize what I am doing, I have spent a half hour or more going back and forth in my mind and in conversation with others about where I want to eat.

It's so bad that it has become a family joke. My son says to me early in the morning, "You better start thinking now about where you want to go eat, so you have a decision by tonight when it is time to go." Or when I tell him to make a reservation at a restaurant for all of us, he might say, "I will check with you in two hours and see if the decision is still the same, so I won't have to change the reservation three times between now and then."

I am doing better, but I still find myself falling into the trap of being double-minded in this area simply because I want to get a perfect meal—and there is probably no such thing.

I have a large classic-movie collection and I often get double-minded about which movie I want to watch. I may choose three or four and keep going back and forth. I read the back of the box and ask others in the family what they think. I make a decision, but then I might ask people who have seen the movies which one is the best and change my mind again. Sometimes I get so frustrated that I end up watching nothing. I turn the television on and flip from channel to channel for an hour and then go to bed. This is a ridiculous waste of time, and it is another habit I am in the process of breaking. As you can see, I am not perfect in this area either, so if you need to change too, we can change together.

My main point is that even being double-minded in small things, which would not seem to matter very much, can still steal your peace, and it is simply not worth it.

The only way to find out if I will enjoy a movie that I have not seen is to start viewing it. If it does not suit me, I can try another one, but at least I need to do something besides be double-minded.

According to Scripture, it is the little foxes that spoil the vine. In other words, it is not always big things that cause misery; often it is small, almost imperceptible things—things we would not think matter at all.

Some people who lack peace search in all the wrong places for the sources of their problem, but it may simply result from being indecisive, even in the small matters of everyday life. To overcome this, they must practice being decision makers in less-consequential situations, and it will help them gain confidence for larger issues.

CHOOSE WHOM YOU WILL SERVE

Joshua was obviously a man who had his mind made up about what he was going to do, and it didn't matter to him what others did. He said, "And if it seems evil to you to serve the Lord, choose for yourselves this day whom you will serve, whether the gods which your fathers served on the other side of the River, or the gods of the Amorites, in whose land you dwell; but as for me and my house, we will serve the Lord" (Joshua 24:15). We should not wait to see what other people will do before making our own decisions, especially when it comes to serving God.

James talked about believers who cannot make their minds up whether they want Jesus or the world when he wrote: "Come close to God and He will come close to you. [Recognize that you are] sinners, get your soiled hands clean; [realize that you have been disloyal] wavering individuals with divided interests, and purify your hearts [of your spiritual adultery]" (4:8). James referred to people with divided interests as "spiritual adulter[ers]": They choose the world as a friend, therefore making God their enemy.

We cannot serve God and the world. We are in the world, but the Bible instructs not to be like it. We can live in it, but we cannot love it. God must have first place at all times.

Keeping the Lord first requires consistent decisions and a refusal to be double-minded. Just about the time we make a decision to do the right thing, someone will come along and try to convince us to compromise. We have to stand firm on what we believe is right for us.

James referred to those who cannot decide whether they want God or the world as "sinners" and told them to purify their hearts of being double-minded. Satan tried to tempt Jesus with the world and all it had to offer, but Jesus quickly responded by quoting

Scriptures to him. Jesus knew what He wanted, He knew what was really important, and He stood firm on His original decision to do what God had sent Him to do (see Luke 4).

Temptation will come. It is a defining moment in our lives each time we face temptation yet remain firm on what we know is right. The devil's ultimate plan is to destroy us. He may make sin look inviting in the beginning, but in the end, we will be sorry if we fall into his trap.

I repeat, don't be double-minded. Make up your mind to serve the Lord, and don't bow down to the devil or anyone through whom he is trying to work. Be like Joshua: Have a firm attitude toward others who try to move you off of your righteous stand. No one else will stand before God and give an account of your life, only you will (see Romans 14:12), so make your own decisions.

Every decision is a seed you sow, and every seed produces a harvest. *Before* changing your mind and giving in to temptation, ask yourself if you want to reap the harvest of the seed you are being tempted to sow.

The Bible is literally filled with promises of good things to those who follow God's commands. Decide to follow Jesus, and don't ever change your mind.

In Luke 10, we see that Jesus visited two sisters named Mary and Martha. These women had quite different natures. One was very interested in *seeking* Jesus; the other was interested in *impressing* Him.

Martha was busy about much serving. She wanted everything to be clean and in the right place. She became angry with her sister, Mary, because she was sitting at the feet of Jesus, wanting to learn all she could and enjoy Him while He was present.

Martha even complained to Jesus and told Him to tell Mary to get up and help her. Jesus replied by saying, "Martha, Martha, you are anxious and troubled about many things; there is need of only one [thing]. . . . Mary has chosen the good portion [that which is to her advantage]" (Luke 10:41–42).

Mary made a firm choice, and even when Martha became angry with her, she did not change her mind. We must realize that people will often get angry with us if we don't make the choices they want us to make, but we should remain steadfast and follow our own hearts.

Learn to relax and be more like Mary. Martha believed that she had to take care of everything herself. She wanted everything to be perfect. Sometimes we can find ourselves like Martha, tense even when we don't have anything to be tense about. It isn't really our circumstances that make us tense; most of the time it is our own approach to life. In the next chapter we will examine ways to relax and enjoy trusting God's faithfulness to take care of us.

PEACEKEEPER #6

Stay Supernaturally Relaxed

❧

The longer we know the Lord, the more relaxed we should become when we face situations that try to steal our peace. Previous experience with God is valuable because we learn that somehow He always comes through. Each time we face a new crisis, we can remember that even though He may not have done exactly what we wanted Him to do, He always did something that worked out. Relaxing in the face of trials helps us to maintain our peace with God.

New believers who do not have personal examples on which to build their confidence in God must be more dependent on examples in the Bible of God's faithfulness. The testimonies of other believers can also greatly encourage them.

Remember, Jesus said that we are to come to Him when we have problems, and He will give us rest. The *Amplified Bible* translates His words as: "Come to Me, all you who labor and are heavy-laden and overburdened, and I will cause you to rest [I will ease and relieve and refresh your souls.]" (Matthew 11:28).

That sounds to me like Jesus wants us to live in a relaxed state, not tense, uptight, worried, or anxious about yesterday, today, or tomorrow. We can stop reasoning and trying to figure out what we need to do. And the Lord doesn't want us to be upset with other people who aren't doing what we want them to, either.

Jesus wants us to trust Him and relax. I call this being *supernaturally relaxed*, because in the natural we may have difficulty learning how or finding time to relax. But when God adds His *super* to our *natural,* we end up with *supernatural.* We can have supernatural relaxation!

Jesus was saying, "Come to Me about anything, because I always want to help you with everything." There's nothing too little and nothing too big to take to Him. You can't take too much. You can't have too many requests.

JESUS INTERCEDES FOR US

I believe that in order to stay relaxed, you must understand the present-day ministry of Jesus. Jesus keeps working on your behalf as long as you keep your trust in Him. Even as you are reading this book, you can pray: "Lord, I leave all my situations and circumstances in Your hands. I leave the past behind. I know I can trust You to work all my situations together for my good. Things are going to be different from now on, because I am going to relax and simply enjoy You."

Release your confidence in God through faith-filled words, and through short little prayers throughout your day. Every prayer doesn't have to be long and eloquent. Pray your way through the day.

One of the most blessed present-day ministries of Jesus is that He is interceding for us. The Word says of Jesus: "Therefore He is able also to save to the uttermost (completely, perfectly, finally, and for all time and eternity) those who come to God through Him, since He is always living to make petition to God and intercede with Him and intervene for them" (Hebrews 7:25).

All that Jesus asks of the Father, God answers. So whatever He is praying for me, whatever He is praying for you, we're going to get it! Jesus never stops praying for us. This means that we can relax, because the Word promises that Jesus sits at the right hand of the Father and intercedes for us (see Romans 8:34).

In order to stay supernaturally relaxed, it is important to understand the relationship between the Vine (Jesus) and the branches (us, the believers). John 15:4–5 teaches that Jesus is the Vine, and the Father is the Vinedresser. He cuts away any branch that doesn't bear fruit, but He cleanses and repeatedly prunes every branch that continues to bear fruit to make it even more productive.

I realized a long time ago that pruning is just a fact of life. We are pruned if we do bear fruit and pruned if we don't! According to *Webster's New College Dictionary,* the word *prune* means to cut off or remove living or dead parts, to shape or stimulate growth, to remove or cut out as unnecessary, to reduce, to remove the superfluous or undesirable. In other words, God is going to deal with us because we are as branches that should be bearing fruit, ultimately so the world can pick that fruit and be fed. God wants us to meet people's needs, be a blessing to them, and live for His glory.

The more strength of Jesus' life that we receive through Him, the Vine, the more fruit will grow on us, the branches. But branches don't have to struggle to bear fruit, just as we don't have to labor or be heavily burdened to produce good results in our lives. We don't reach our goals by trying, but by believing. We're supposed to abide in Jesus, and as we just "hang on" the Vine, Jesus will pour His life into us so that we bear fruit.

ABIDE IN CHRIST

All we need is more of Jesus! The more we relax and trust Him, the more we are abiding in Him. I have never seen a peach tree frustrated, upset, and all stressed-out trying to produce peaches. The tree rests in the ground, and the life from the vine flows into the branches and produces fruit. This is God's will for each of us: resting in Jesus and producing good fruit.

Whenever I return home from ministering in conferences, I renew and revitalize myself by abiding in Jesus. I pray, meditate on His Word, and spend time with Him. I say, "Thank You, Lord, for strengthening me. Thank You for refueling me. I need You, Jesus. I can't do anything without You."

I know I must abide in Him if I want to bear good fruit. Abiding replenishes the energy I use in my conferences. For many years I ministered in my conferences, returned home, and went right back to the office or out on another trip without spending the time I needed with the Lord. I always ended up worn-out, depressed, crying, and wanting to get out of ministry because of the pressure.

If we drive our automobiles without filling up the tanks, we ultimately run out of gasoline and break down somewhere on the road and have to be towed in. We can do the same thing as individuals. We will break down mentally, physically, emotionally, and spiritually if we don't stay full of Jesus by abiding in Him.

Most mornings, Dave and I spend from two to three hours with the Lord, praying, reading, meditating, pondering, writing, resting, trusting, and abiding in the Lord. By the time I face my family or work responsibilities, I'm full of good fruit in case anybody has a need. Sometimes people "pick on us," and when they do, we want them to be able to pick good fruit.

If I abide in Jesus, the Vine, I'll always have what I need to give to others. If I don't spend time with the Lord, I will become like the fig tree that was full of leaves but without fruit. The Bible said Jesus was hungry when He saw a fig tree in the distance, and He went to get something to eat from it, but there was no fruit on it. So He cursed it and He said, "Fruit will never grow on you again" (see Matthew 21:19). I remember thinking that it wasn't the fig tree's fault. Then I read that when the fig tree has leaves, it is also supposed to have fruit. I believe He cursed it because it was a phony—it had leaves but no fruit.

I think a lot of people are like fruitless fig trees. They have all the Christian paraphernalia (the leaves), but they don't have the fruit of real faith in their lives. They look like they have the lives of Christians: They have the bumper stickers, the fish on their cars, the big Bibles they carry to work, and they say, "Praise the Lord" on a regular basis. But when a coworker goes to them, hungering for kindness, patience, mercy, or love, they don't have what is needed—there's no fruit (good works or pleasant attitude) because they have not been hanging (abiding) on the Vine. They also live with the curse of not having the fruit of peace in their own lives.

I am afraid not to spend time with God because as a minister of God's Word, I don't do anything fancy when I teach. I know that if I don't have the anointing from abiding in Christ, I'm finished before I ever open my mouth.

Jesus said that if we dwell in Him, He will dwell in us. If we live in Him, He will live in us. He said that we cannot bear fruit without abiding in Him. But if we *live,* which implies daily abiding, in Him we will bear *abundant fruit* (again see John 15:4–5). Whether it is teaching or anything else I do in life, I have learned by experience that I need Him and cannot do anything of real value without Him. Unless the Lord builds the house, we labor in vain that build it (see Psalm 127:1).

To have peace, it is very important that we abide in Christ, and this means to spend time with Him on a consistent basis. In the world we live in today, a little bit of time with God is not enough. God has to be first in our thoughts, in our conversations, in our finances, and in our schedules. Don't try to work God into your schedule; work your schedule around Him. Put Him first, and everything will work properly.

If you put God first in everything, then you will find yourself getting things done supernaturally. He may even send someone to help you whom you were not expecting. I have had two people tell me recently that God moved on the hearts of people they knew to help them with housework or other duties; the helpers said they felt that God placed it on their hearts and wanted to do it without charging any fee.

This same thing happened to me many years ago, when I started my ministry. I had four young children, no money, and not much time to prepare for ministry. God sent a friend who offered to help me two days a week without pay.

I want to say again, if you put God first in everything, then you will find yourself getting things done supernaturally. Putting God first is not about having all the Christian paraphernalia I mentioned that we might refer to as "fig leaves." Don't forget that when Adam and Eve found themselves in trouble, they covered themselves up with fig leaves too. Fig leaves weren't adequate to meet their need to cover themselves, so God provided the sufficient covering for them (see Genesis 3:21).

We are not capable of making ourselves fruit-bearing Christians. Bearing fruit is the work of the Holy Spirit, and God gets the glory. God promises to graft us into Himself so that His life pours through us (see Romans 11:17).

The picture of being grafted in to the vine is an interesting concept because it requires taking a branch that is almost dead and wrapping it tightly to a living vine. This process brings life back into the almost-dead branch. This branch cannot do anything but receive life from the Vine. Like grafted branches, we are simply to relax in God's presence and let His abundant life flow through us.

TRUST YOURSELF TO GOD

There is nothing that we can give to God, except ourselves. We can show appreciation for all He has done for us and praise Him for His goodness.

Trust yourself to God; He wants you! He wants to take care of you and be your everything. Total surrender of your life will bring an awesome peace with God—the peace that passes understanding.

We will keep our peace if we surrender our guilt for past sins to God. God wants us to ask for and receive His free gift of forgiveness, which has always been available to us. I encourage you to form a habit: When you ask God to forgive your sins, follow up by saying, "I receive that forgiveness right now, and I let go of the guilt."

Learn how to receive; see yourself as a branch hanging onto the Vine. All you can do is receive life from that Vine. Confess, "I receive, Lord. I give myself to You, and I receive You as my everything in life: my Savior, Lord, Strength, Peace, Righteousness, Joy, Justification, Sanctification, and all other things."

All the branch does is receive what the Vine offers. To *receive* means to act like a receptacle and simply take in what is being offered. To stay supernaturally relaxed, become a receiver and live by grace, and not by works or fleshly effort.

Living by grace is trusting in God's energy, instead of our own work and effort, to do what needs to be done. And look what Christ can do: Hebrews 1:3 says that He upholds and maintains and guides and propels the universe by "His mighty word of power"!

God makes this earth and all of the planets and stars spin perfectly through space. We don't even know how big the universe is. If He can do that, shouldn't we relax, knowing He can take care of us too? If He can run the entire universe, surely He can manage each of us.

Hebrews 1:3 goes on to say that Jesus "accomplished our cleansing of sins and riddance of guilt" by offering Himself, then He *sat down* at the right hand of God. Sitting down is a picture of being relaxed because the work was done.

So, Jesus is relaxed. He's taking care of the universe, but it's not even an effort for Him. Why isn't He running around heaven, worried about our situations? Why isn't He wringing His hands, trying to figure out what to do? Surely there must be a lot of work involved in keeping this whole universe running. Yet He does it and remains perfectly calm. As we learn to live in Him, we, too, can enjoy this supernatural ease and relaxation.

RELAX IN THE KEEPING POWER OF GOD

A lady who works for me says that she doesn't have a "big" testimony. She just grew up in the church, loving God. She got married, was filled with the Holy Spirit, then came to work for us. Through our ministry, she was moved by the testimonies of drug addicts and people who have suffered abuse. One day she asked God, "Lord, why don't I have a testimony?"

He said, "You do have a testimony. Your testimony is that I kept you from all of it." God had kept her from the pain that results from being separated from Him. The keeping power of God is a great testimony!

Psalm 91 teaches that He will give His angels charge over us, and they will protect and defend us. This same woman was sitting in a boat one day, reading that very chapter. Her husband was fishing when the boat hit a wave and the lawn chair she was in fell over. She banged her head on the side of the boat at the same time she was reading about God's protection. She said, "Lord, I don't understand this! The Bible says that You'll protect me, and here I've hit my head."

God said to her, "You're not dead, are you?"

It's true that a few things happen in our lives that we don't like, but what has God kept us from that we never even knew Satan had planned against us? I marvel at the fact that we can drive in traffic and stay alive. We need to thank God for His keeping power. We can relax knowing that He is our Keeper. Daily, God protects us and keeps us from the power of the enemy. We are sealed in the Holy Spirit and preserved for the final day of redemption when Jesus will return.

I don't know how I've done what I've done over these past years. I look back at my calendars, and I see how hard I've worked. I read some of my prayer journals and remember some of the things I've gone through with people, and the hurt I've felt. I think, *How did I ever get through that?* But God held me together. He strengthened me. He kept me. And I can see now that I worried about a lot of things I didn't have to worry about because they worked out okay anyway. God has a plan, and He is working His plan. We can trust that and relax. Psalm 145:14 says, "The Lord upholds all those [of His own] who are falling and raises up all those who are bowed down."

This continual care of God is uninterrupted in our lives. There's never a moment when He's not taking care of us. The Bible says that God never sleeps nor slumbers. When you go to sleep at night, He stays up and watches over you. You can relax.

SIMPLY BELIEVE

The Bible tells us that we are to live sanctified lives, but then it turns right around and says God will do the work to sanctify us. We are to simply put our trust in Him, hang on to the Vine, and He does the work through us, as these verses promise: "And may the God of peace Himself sanctify you through and through [separate you from profane things, make you pure and wholly consecrated to God]; and may your spirit and soul and body be preserved sound and complete [and found] blameless at the coming of our Lord Jesus Christ (the Messiah). Faithful is He Who is calling you [to Himself] *and* utterly trustworthy, and He will also do it [fulfill His call by hallowing and keeping you]" (1 Thessalonians 5:23-24).

The disciples asked Jesus, "What must we do to be working the works of God? What must we do to please God?"

Jesus replied, "This is the work (service) that God asks of you: that you believe in the One Whom He has sent [that you cleave to, trust, rely on, and have faith in His Messenger]" (John 6:29).

Joy and peace are found in believing, according to Romans 15:13. Simple, childlike believing enables us to live with an ease that releases joy and peace. Hebrews 4 teaches us that those who have believed enter the rest of God.

As believers, we are supposed to *believe*. Otherwise we'd be called *achievers*. But we're *believers*, and to be believers we must first learn how to *be* instead of *do*.

Relax; all the good things that God has planned for you will come to you through Him, not through your works. Romans 11:36 confirms, "For from Him and through Him and to Him are all things. [For all things originate with Him and come from Him; all things live through Him, and all things center in and tend to consummate and to end in Him.] To Him be glory forever! Amen (so be it)."

To be at peace with God, we have to learn how to *maintain* peace. Maintaining requires watchfulness and daily attention. As we will continue studying in the next chapter, we must avoid strife with others in order to stay supernaturally relaxed.

Avoid Strife to Maintain Peace with God

❧

I've discovered over the years that peace is one of the greatest gifts God has given to us. But Satan works incessantly to steal our peace, so we must be aware of his tactics and be determined to live peaceful lives so we can live powerful lives. Once we have peace with God, we must learn to maintain it in order to enjoy it every day of our lives. Maintaining peace means that we must pursue peace, crave it, and go after it with all of our might.

Peace and power work together. Peace allows the anointing of God's presence to flow through our lives. That grace gives us the power to live the way God wants us to live, and to enjoy what God has provided for us.

I believe that the level of peace we walk in and the level of prosperity we have are directly connected. We can prosper from God's blessings, but if we lose our peace in the process, we may also lose our prosperity too.

The loss of peace opens a door for the devil to rob us. Ephesians 4:26–27 verifies this when it says if we become angry, we should not let the sun go down on our anger. It says we should not give the devil any such foothold in our lives.

There was a time when our ministry was growing so fast that it was actually creating problems. We couldn't hire enough people. We didn't have enough space, and we had difficulty keeping up with the growth. It was important to keep our peace, but I felt that we were running to keep up with God all the time. He was blessing us, but we had to learn how to handle the blessings and stay peaceful.

The loss of peace can come from anything that causes us to feel we are on overload. Problems may make us feel that way, and even success and growth can make us feel overwhelmed sometimes. At that time in our ministry, we suddenly found ourselves needing to deal with things we had never dealt with before, and we had to learn to trust God in an entirely new way.

We wanted to grow and prosper, but we strongly felt that God had instructed us to maintain our peace in order to do so. God works in an atmosphere of peace, not in turmoil and strife. I believe that God opens the door for many people to be blessed, but they quickly lose the blessing because they allow their emotions to rule when they should be diligent to walk in peace.

One of the ways we maintain peace with God is by maintaining peace with the people in our lives. Our new growth meant we had to make a lot of new decisions, and Dave and I had to work at staying out of strife because we did not always agree.

Avoiding strife with people is such an important aspect of peace that I have devoted an entire section of this book, which you will read later, to teach the various ways God has taught me to maintain peace with others as unto the Lord. But because the way we treat other people is important to God, I also want to make clear how maintaining peace in our relationships with others helps us to be at peace with God.

God does not like it if I mistreat someone. It grieves His Holy Spirit, and I feel a sudden loss of peace. I remember one night when I could not sleep. I tossed and turned until five o'clock, at which time I finally asked, "Lord, what is wrong with me? Why can't I sleep?"

He instantly showed me a situation from the previous day when I was quite impatient and rude to someone. I never apologized; I justified my actions and went on my way. I had grieved the Holy Spirit, and the loss of peace was keeping me awake. As soon as I repented of my sin, my peace returned and I went to sleep. And the next day, I also apologized to the person as soon as I could.

As servants of the Lord, we must not have strife, because where there is strife, there is neither power to enjoy life nor prosperity in any area, including our relationships. Peace and prosperity are two components of the abundant life that God wants us to have. We cannot represent Him properly if we are in strife.

The relationship between Abram (later Abraham) and Lot illustrates the importance of maintaining peace in our relationships with others. Genesis 12 records the covenant of peace that God made with Abraham and his heirs. Abraham became extremely rich and powerful because God blessed him. God chose him to be the man through whom He would bless all the nations on the face of the earth.

I find it interesting that in the very next chapter, Genesis 13, strife came between the herdsmen of Lot and Abraham's cattle (see v. 7). Strife is the exact opposite of peace. God gave Abraham peace, and Satan went immediately to stir up strife. God wanted to bless Abraham, and Satan wanted to steal his blessing.

Sometimes God's abundance can cause problems that lead to strife. He had blessed Abraham and Lot with so many possessions and cattle that the land could not nourish and support them. They had to regroup.

The Bible says that Abraham went to Lot and said, "Let there be no strife, I beg of you, between you and me, or between your herdsmen and my herdsmen" (Genesis 13:8). He told Lot that they were going to have to separate, so Lot should choose the land he wanted, and Abraham would take what was left.

Abraham took a humble position to avoid strife, knowing that if he did what was right, God would always bless him. But Lot, who would have had nothing if Abraham hadn't given it to him, chose the best part: the Jordan Valley. Abraham didn't say a thing; he just took the leftovers. He knew God would bless him if he stayed in peace. People who walk in peace in order to honor God cannot lose in life.

But then God took Abraham up on a hill and said, "Now, you look to the north, to the south, to the east, and the west—and everything you see, I'll give to you" (see vv. 14–15). What a great deal! Abraham gave up one valley, and God gave him everything he could see.

HUMILITY BRINGS PEACE

God honored Abraham's humility and blessed him abundantly with fruitful land. I believe that God's got a good plan for all of us, but prideful attitudes can prevent us from having all that God wants us to have. A bad attitude is one of the most important things on which we can work with God to overcome.

The Bible says that strife and contention come only by pride. You cannot have strife if you don't have pride. Pride was Lucifer's sin, and it is so deceptive that proud people don't know that they are proud. When people are deceived by pride, they blame others for everything that goes wrong and fail to see their own faults.

Romans 12:16–17 says,

Live in harmony with one another; do not be haughty (snobbish, high-minded, exclusive), but readily adjust yourself to [people, things] and give yourselves to humble tasks. Never overestimate yourself or be wise in your own conceits. Repay no one evil for evil, but take thought for what is honest and proper and noble [aiming to be above reproach] in the sight of everyone.

Some people are basically impossible to get along with, but I love Romans 12:18, which says, "*If possible, as far as it depends on you,* live at peace with everyone" (italics mine). We can't do their part, but we *must* do our part of maintaining peace with others.

I challenge you to be a maker and a maintainer of peace today and every day of your life. Go the extra mile to keep peace—even if it means apologizing to somebody when you really don't think you're wrong. I'm not suggesting that you let everybody take advantage of you. But I am suggesting that you live life with humility so you can enjoy peace and the blessings that result from it.

The Bible says there are times that we will look like sheep being led to the slaughter. But right in the midst of all these things, we are more than conquerors. If two people are arguing, the one who is proud, stubborn, and refuses to apologize is the loser, not the winner. The one who looks like a sheep on his way to disaster but humbles himself and says, "Look, I don't want any trouble. If I was wrong, I'm sorry. Please forgive me" is the winner. He took the position that Jesus would have taken if He were there, dealing with that same situation.

Humility is *hard* on our flesh. But the Bible tells us to walk in the Spirit, not in the flesh. We need to learn how to follow the leading of the Holy Spirit. We also need to recognize when we are not following the ways of the Lord.

People use the phrase, "Well, I got in the flesh," but we need to learn how to get out of it just as quickly as we got in. We mustn't get selfish and stay that way for long periods of time. The Bible says not to let the sun go down on our anger (see Ephesians 4:26). God knew there would be times when we would get angry, but as soon as we know we're angry, we can keep that emotion from controlling us. We can come back to a place of peace before the day is over. It requires some humility and a decision.

We can be Peacemakers and Peace Maintainers. To do so, we will have to treat people nicely who haven't been so nice to us. We can have abundant lives, but we will have to do what the Bible says in order to have it. God's promises of a good life are for "whosoever will"; not just whosoever will receive the promises, but whosoever will *obey* what He tells them to do. Then the promises will be enacted in their lives.

That's why it is so important to know what the Word of God says, and let God work it out in our lives through our obedience to Him. It is hard to say we are sorry, but we can do all things through Christ. He will give us the grace to be Peacemakers.

One morning, Dave corrected me about something when I wasn't feeling good. My first thought was, *Oh my, not this morning!* I was in Africa, preaching. I was already fighting jet lag, my back was hurting, my eyes were extremely dry, I was tired, and in general I did not feel good when my husband decided to correct me.

Why is it that when somebody corrects us, the first thing we do is get mad? That's what I did. Now, I had gained a little bit of control over my emotions, so I didn't *show* my anger. But inside, I was not happy.

Naturally, the first thing we want to do when people correct us is start telling them everything that's wrong with them. Dave was describing a certain situation where he felt I hadn't shown him respect. My response was, "Well, there are many times when you don't show *me* respect."

He said, "We aren't talking about me. We're talking about you." Talk about a flesh burner! Whoa! Lord, have mercy!

Now, I've learned a few things after twenty-five years in ministry. I was getting ready to preach that morning, and I knew better than to get into the pulpit with strife in my heart! Strife steals our peace and shuts down the anointing. So, I started praying for two things.

I said, "God, help me keep my mouth shut." That's the first thing to pray for if you don't want war. Never overestimate your own ability to keep quiet just because you want to. You have to *pray* for help in this area.

Then I said, "God, if he's right . . . give me the grace to receive it." I've learned that just because we don't *think* somebody's right, that doesn't mean they're not.

It is interesting how human beings have problems with being corrected. That same spirit of pride that causes us to mistreat people will also prevent us from receiving correction.

The Bible says, "Only a fool hates correction" (see Proverbs 15:5). If you correct a wise man, he becomes wiser. If you correct a fool, he gets angry and won't even consider receiving it.

Why is it so devastating when somebody tells us we're not doing something right or tells us, "I need you to change this"? I believe that our insecurity can cause our pride to rise in defense and say, "Nobody's going tell me anything. I'm right, and everybody else is wrong." If we don't learn to recognize this Peace Stealer, we will go around the same stupid mountain, again and again, dealing with the same problems.

Prayer Brings Peace

Well, it turned out that God showed me Dave was right. I made my first round of apologies, but I really wasn't sincere. I was still a little bit mad, because though I agreed with God that Dave was right, I still didn't like the way he told me. I didn't like his attitude or his timing. I was willing to say that I was wrong, but I wanted also to talk about what Dave had done wrong. He wouldn't talk about that.

I could *feel* my flesh just screaming. I had to pray, "God, give me grace. Give me the grace to forgive. Help me talk to Dave. I don't want to talk to him. God, help me talk to him." When we get mad, a wall goes up. We say silently, "You hurt me, and I am not letting you back into my life to do it again." I know this is exactly the way we all are. Then we just become polite. We talk only if we absolutely have to and use very few words. We answer questions with a simple yes or no, but we offer no further conversation. We avoid the person who hurt us as much as possible.

Dave knew I was hurting, but he also knew I was really trying to do what was right. Even when we are trying to do right, our flesh can still hurt. God's Word teaches us we are to die to self. That means we say yes to God and His will and no to our flesh that wants to rebel. Dave reached out and patted me on the arm or leg to show love and understanding while I was trying to get over the correction he gave me.

We were traveling with many people on the plane that day, but I didn't want to talk to anybody. They were all asking, "Why are you so quiet?"

I said, "I'm just having a quiet day." But the truth was I was hurting too bad to talk. My emotions were whacko, and I really wanted to just be left alone. The entire day was a struggle for me not to cry or scream. It was very difficult for me to be civil to people, but I knew that God was dealing with me and correcting me. I knew I needed to submit to His dealings if I was going to make progress and overcome in the area of being disrespectful.

Sometimes, even after we choose to do what is right, we may hurt for a while. It is the pain that is doing the good work in us. It is actually changing us and making us better.

I have learned that if we don't listen to God when He tries to correct us, then He will bring pressure from some other direction to get our attention. I am sure God had been dealing with me for a long time about my disrespectful attitude toward Dave and some of the wrong things I said to him, but I was not listening to God. So he led Dave to correct me.

I had a bad habit, and God knew that He needed to help me get free if I was going to do all He had for me to do in the ministry. The Lord wanted to bless my life, but my attitude was hindering Him.

I kept praying for God to give me grace to submit to His dealing and no longer be angry with Dave. I wanted to do right and knew that grace is the power of the Holy Spirit to help us do what we can't. After some time went by, I felt much better and knew God had done a work in me that would help me enjoy more peace in my life.

If you want to be a maker and maintainer of peace when somebody hurts you, you better not think that you can do it just by decision or self-will. Start praying, because emotions are strong, and they are a controlling force in our lives. Pride gets all tangled up in our emotions and causes strife and eventually lots of broken relationships.

Strife causes stress that can even lead to sickness and disease. God did not create us to live in the war zone all the time. We are supposed to have peace, and when something happens to disturb our peace, we have to work to get it back.

We've seen that the Word says to live in harmony with others, and be ready to adapt and adjust ourselves to people. We want them to adapt to us, but God puts the responsibility on *each one* of us to give ourselves to humble tasks.

When Dave corrected me, it didn't really take me all that long to get my attitude right again. Well, perhaps it was a couple of days (though it seemed like a month), but forty-eight hours was a big improvement over the way I used to stay offended for weeks. Isn't it amazing how time goes so slowly when we're upset about something?

Finally, I knew that I had the grace to give a sincere apology. So, I said to my husband, "Look, I'm really sorry. If I've ever spoken disrespectfully, please forgive me. I don't want to do that, but you know my mouth gets me into trouble sometimes." Everything was fine after that. Peace returned!

God has dealt with me since then about my mouth. Most of us say things that hurt and wound other people. I probably will have to endure correction in this area again, but I really do want to be all that God wants me to be. My desire to please God motivates me to go through whatever I need to in order to be in His perfect will.

PEACE RELEASES ANOINTING

I encourage you always to pursue peace. You won't have peace with God until you have peace with the people He has placed in your life. It is important to understand that in order to have peace with God, you must work through whatever issues are causing strife in your life and quickly bring closure to them. Don't pretend everything is okay when you are eaten up inside with strife.

God knows everything that goes on behind closed doors, including the doors to our hearts. If our relationships aren't right, our lives won't be right. And if our private lives are not right, our public lives are not right. Whatever we do in private affects our public lives and ministries.

Pride will absolutely ruin us. But the mighty God who dwells inside of us gives us the power to humble ourselves and say, "I'm sorry," even if we don't feel like it.

If you need to come to a new level of peace in your life, make a decision to become a maker and maintainer of peace. The Word says, "Blessed (enjoying enviable happiness, spiritually prosperous—with life-joy and satisfaction in God's favor . . . regardless of their outward conditions) are the makers and maintainers of peace, for they shall be called the sons of God!" (Matthew 5:9).

It's one thing to be a *child of God,* but to be called a *son* or a *daughter of God* implies a level of maturity: someone who can handle blessing, responsibility, and authority that children cannot manage.

The blessing of peace keeps the anointing and power of God flowing through our lives so that, like Abraham, we can bless other people on God's behalf. God gives gifts to people, and He wants to fill those gifts with His anointed presence to bring blessing. It might be a gift to preach and teach God's Word, to sing, to lead, to encourage, or to administrate.

There are certain character qualities that God will bless (anoint with power) and certain qualities that He won't. Exodus 29 gives a detailed description of where the priest was to put the anointing oil. It was to be on the utensils, the altar, the priest's garments, and the turban on his head, but he was not to put anointing oil upon the flesh. God will not anoint our fleshly actions or our fleshly behavior.

We have to learn to surrender our wills to God and let the Holy Spirit lead us if we want to maintain peace and carry its anointing power in our lives. But first and foremost, I encourage you to pursue peace through prayer today, and be determined to keep the strife out of your life. Without peace you won't have the power to enjoy life. Pursue peace with God, with yourself, and with your fellow man.

If you lack peace, pray something like this: "Father, I pray for peace with You. I don't understand everything that is going on in my life. It's not going the way I want it, but I am deciding to trust You. Help me to have peaceful relationships, and give me the power (the anointing of Your grace) to be a maker and a maintainer of peace with others, in the name of Jesus. Amen."

In the next part of this book, I will explain seven ways that I found to have peace with myself before I could focus on keeping peace with others. Through wisdom from God's Word, you can learn to have peace and enjoy your life every day, wherever you are. So next, let's look at how slowing down will help you to keep peace with yourself.

～Part 2～

Be at Peace
with Yourself

*Now the mind of the flesh [which is sense and reason without the Holy
Spirit] is death [death that comprises all the miseries arising from sin,
both here and hereafter]. But the mind of the [Holy] Spirit is
life and [soul] peace [both now and forever].*

—The apostle Paul, *Romans 8:6*

PEACEKEEPER #8

Stop Rushing

Much of the world is in a hurry, always rushing, yet very few people even know where they are going in life. If we want to be at peace with ourselves and enjoy life, we must stop rushing all the time.

People rush to get to yet another event that has no real meaning for them, or that they really don't even want to attend. *Hurry* is the pace of the twenty-first century; rushing has become a disease of epidemic proportions. We hurry so much, we finally come to the place where we cannot slow down.

I can remember the days when I worked so hard and hurried so much that even if I took a vacation, it was almost over by the time I geared down enough to rest. Hurry was definitely one of the Peace Stealers in my life and still can be, if I do not stay alert to its pressure.

Life is too precious to rush through it. I find at times that a day has gone by in a blur; at the conclusion of it I know I was very busy all day yet cannot really remember enjoying much, if any, of it. I have committed to learn to do things in God's rhythm, not the world's pace.

Jesus was never in a hurry when He was here on earth, and God is absolutely not in a hurry now. Ecclesiastes 3:1 states, "TO EVERYTHING there is a season, and a time for every matter or purpose under heaven." We should let each thing in our lives have its season and realize we can enjoy that season without rushing into the next one.

It is permissible to enjoy our morning coffee or tea without feeling we must hurry to get to the next thing. We can get dressed calmly without rushing. We can leave the house in a timely fashion, without frantically running out the door already behind schedule. Rushing is a bad habit, but we can break bad habits and form good ones to replace them.

The way we get a day started is important. Often how we start is how the entire day goes. I have found if I allow the "hurry-up" spirit to grab me early in the day, everything within me gets into high gear, and I never seem to slow down or really relax the rest of the day. Hurry creates pressure that in turn creates stress.

Stress is the root cause of many illnesses and is therefore something each one of us desperately needs to resolve. God did not create us to hurry, rush, live under pressure and stress day after day. Jesus said, "My peace I leave with you." He wants us to have peace.

Pace is very important in life. Our pace not only affects us but others around us. I don't like to be around people who are always in a rush; they are usually short-tempered and impatient. They certainly don't minister peace. They make me feel as if I also need to hurry, which I am desperately trying to avoid.

I have noticed in fine-dining restaurants that the hostess who seats people walks very slowly while leading customers to their tables. The waiters or waitresses don't rush the table for orders; they give you plenty of time to think. I am sure this is because they want the customers to enjoy their experience, and they know that will not be possible if they are rushed.

When following one of the hostesses who is exuding peace simply by the way she walks me to the table, often I am behind her thinking, *Get going, you're moving too slow.* Then I am reminded (I am sure by the Holy Spirit) that I don't need to be in a hurry to enjoy the nice meal I am about to pay for.

Our pace of living affects the quality of our lives. When we eat too fast, we don't properly digest our food; when we rush through life, we don't properly digest it either. God has given life to us as a gift, and what a pitiful shame to do nothing but rush through each day and never, as they say, "stop to smell the roses." Each thing we do in life has a sweet fragrance, and we should learn to take it into ourselves and enjoy the aroma.

RUSHING BEGINS IN THE MIND

Rushing begins in the mind, just as all actions do. *I have to hurry* is a thought pattern we should avoid. When other people say to us, "Hurry up!" we can learn to resist following their suggestion or demand. It unsettles us and makes us feel rushed when thoughts constantly fly through our minds, one following upon another (especially thoughts that go in many different directions).

Those of us who have a bad habit of rushing need to decide that we don't have to do this. We can do only one thing at a time! When we hurry, we make more mistakes and often forget things that end up costing us more time than we would have used had we maintained a godly pace.

Did you know that you can think things on purpose? You can choose what you think about, and by doing so you help assure what your actions will be. Yes, you can purposefully think thoughts such as *I don't have to hurry. I have time to do whatever I need to do.* Speaking such affirmations out loud is also helpful.

Positive statements help give direction for future actions. Get up in the morning, and as soon as you feel rushed, say, "I am glad I don't have to hurry. I have all the time I need. I will do things today at a pace that enables me to enjoy each task."

This may sound strange, but the Bible teaches us to speak of the nonexistent things that God has foretold and promised as if they already exist (see Romans 4:17). God created the world with words, our words also hold creative power; words affect our futures. Take a step of faith, and try saying what you want, not just what you have at the current time, and I believe you will enjoy positive results.

If we feel hurried, we usually say, "I am so sick and tired of hurrying all the time! That is all I ever do: hurry, hurry, hurry." Statements like those may be facts describing the way things are, but circumstances don't have to stay that way. I repeat, *say what you want, not what you have.*

Peace of mind must precede peace in our lives. This verse promises perfect peace to those who keep their minds on God: "You will guard him and keep him in perfect and constant peace whose mind [both its inclination and its character] is stayed on You, because he commits himself to You, leans on You, and hopes confidently in You" (Isaiah 26:3).

Thinking too much about everything we have to do sets the wheels in motion for rushing. We often feel overwhelmed when we think of all the future will require of us. This type of thinking is called *anxiety.* As we discussed earlier, when we spend today trying to figure out tomorrow, we struggle simply because God gives us grace, which is His strength and power, one day at a time. When we try to live tomorrow today, even if only in our minds, we feel pressured and begin to lose peace.

We will never enjoy the peaceful and fruitful lives that God intends for us unless we learn to think right. I repeat what I have said on many occasions: *Where the mind goes, the man follows.*

LEARN TO LIVE WITH MARGIN

Living without margin is one of the main reasons we feel we need to hurry. To live with margin means to leave room on either side of planned events or appointments to take care of unexpected things that come up. We seem to plan our days in an unrealistic way, as if everything will go exactly according to our plans and desires, which it never does. One unplanned phone call or traffic jam can change our entire timetable. One set of misplaced car keys can upset a whole day's scheduling.

I was feeling tremendously rushed every day at the office. I raced in and flew through my many appointments, and I am sure that I made all the people I met with feel as if I could hardly wait to get rid of them. I was always behind schedule and never got finished. At the end of every day, I was frustrated and went home feeling totally drained. It was so bad that I actually got to the point where I literally despised even going to the office.

Then I learned about the principle of adding margin to my life, and I feel like a new person. I told my secretary that I wanted her to find out how much time each person who needed to meet with me felt he would require, and then just add ten to fifteen minutes to each appointment. This margin would cover any unexpected things that came up during the meeting, and if we didn't use the margin, it would be an extra blessing.

Now, one of our managers might be scheduled to meet with me for one hour, but when we finish in forty minutes, it is glorious! I almost always get finished with my day's schedule and usually have some time to spare. Adding margin has been one of the biggest blessings in my life. I was always the type of person who never wanted to waste one moment, therefore, I planned everything to the second so I had no downtime.

If Dave and I needed to be on a flight leaving at ten o'clock, I wanted to arrive at 9:30 or 9:45, rush through the ticket counter, run down the hall, and hurry to get on the plane. Dave refused to do this because he is not a person who is willing to hurry. He has one pace—it is called *Peaceful*. He insisted we arrive at the airport no less than one hour early; this caused many arguments between us literally for years. I must say, though, that he was right, and I was wrong.

Having breathing room between planned events of the day is healthy, and it is actually mandatory if one is intending to enjoy his or her life.

One of the worst things a person can become is a busy man or woman. I have noticed upon meeting people and asking how they are that most respond, "Busy," and many say, "Tired." Surely life is meant to be more. If our testimony of life is "I'm busy and tired," that is very sad indeed.

Margin is another word for *wisdom*. It makes absolutely no sense to live without it, and nothing truly succeeds without it. We know from experience that we always encounter things we did not plan for, so why not plan for the unplanned, which is what margin is?

KNOW YOUR LIMITS

We are not all alike, nor do we all have the same tolerance level. Some people, by virtue of their temperaments or even natural stamina, can do more than others. Know yourself, and don't be ashamed to admit you have limits. Don't try to keep up with some other busy person you know—just be yourself.

I can accomplish a lot; I thrive on activity. Some of the people who work with me comment often that they don't know how I do all that I do. God has given me a lot of natural drive, and I am very passionate about what I am called to do; but I have had to face the fact that I have my limits, and so does everyone else.

I spent years pushing past my limits and eventually became ill and very discouraged, thinking, *If this is all life is, I would rather go to heaven.* After pushing myself beyond reason and becoming very ill three different times, I knew I needed to change.

I finally admitted I had limits and saw that it was not wrong to have them. I had to face the fact that I was not able to do everything I or other people wanted me to do. I had to make choices just like everyone else. I had to be willing to say no to people who wanted to hear yes, and even to things I really wanted to do.

High achievers often feel it is a personal failure to say, "I can't do any more than I am doing." That is, of course, wrong thinking, and Satan uses condemnation to destroy people. Many "driven" people are just insecure people who are getting their worth and value from their accomplishments in life.

I heard a story about a woman who worked in a shipyard, and her job was cleaning the ships. She believed that her job had value because she was doing it, not that her value was based on the job she did. This gave her wonderful freedom to enjoy herself, her job, and all of life. Many people would feel belittled by her job, but not her—she knew *she* had value. Our attitudes about ourselves really do affect all of our lives.

Learning that my worth and value are rooted in God through Christ has been life-changing. Quite often, people strive to have prestigious jobs so they feel important; this causes a lot of heartache in life. I know because I experienced it. I once was seeking promotion and success, but for all the wrong reasons. We could all learn a lesson from this woman's story. *You make what you do important;* you are not important because you do it.

I believe that some people don't have peace with themselves because they actually don't approve of themselves, and they over-commit while trying to find worth. They stay busy trying to accomplish something that will make them feel important and valuable. When we come to terms of peace with ourselves, we don't have to live to impress people; we are free to follow the Holy Spirit, who always leads us into peace and balanced living.

"I can do all things through Christ" (Philippians 4:13 KJV) doesn't mean what some people try to make it mean. We can do *what we are called to do,* but we cannot do everything *we would like to do,* nor everything everyone else would like us to do. We have limits! God Himself has placed these limits on us. Only He has no limits. He gives us the energy and grace to do what He wants us to do. Jesus said He came that we might have and enjoy life, and I don't believe that is possible as long as we are rushing.

God gives us all gifts and talents, but they are not all the same. The Giver of the gifts is the same, but the gifts differ. He hands them out according to His will and for His overall purpose in life. God makes sure that everything in life is taken care of.

Sometimes Dave and I notice people doing jobs like washing

windows on high-rise buildings or walking on construction beams high in the air, and we marvel that God calls someone to do every task that needs to be done. We would not want to do what these people seem to enjoy doing, but then they probably would not want to do what we do either. It has been helpful to me to realize that God gives us all talents and limits. We can do well and with peace only what God has assigned to us. Being overcommitted in order to feel good about ourselves is not wisdom and will never minister peace.

According to James Dobson, overcommitment is the number-one marriage killer. I have discovered that Satan wants us to be either uncommitted or overcommitted. His entire goal is to keep us out of balance, one way or the other. First Peter 5:8 says, "Be well balanced . . . for that enemy of yours, the devil, roams around like a lion roaring . . . seeking someone to . . . devour." Satan cannot devour just anyone; he has to find someone who is out of balance.

The world applauds our being overcommitted, but heaven doesn't. A busy person with too much to do is usually considered a success by the world's standards, but not by God's. How can we be successful if we fail at relationships (which are usually what suffer the most in the life of a busy person)? Most extremely busy people don't even take the time to really know themselves, let alone anyone else.

What is the point in parenting children if they are all going to be strangers to you? Why be married if you never have anything left of yourself to share with your marriage partner? I can remember coming home so tired each night that I could not even think, let alone have meaningful conversation. I thought I was doing my duty, being responsible—but now I realize I was being deceived, and the deception was aimed at destroying the life Jesus desired for me to have.

Don't give your family and friends the scraps you have left over while you give the world your best. The world will let you down in the end. It will take everything you have and disappear when you are in need. I don't mean to sound cynical, but even Scripture verifies my comment. Solomon wrote, "So I hated life, because what is done under the sun was grievous to me; for all is vanity and a striving after the wind and a feeding on it. And I hated all my labor in which I had toiled under the sun, seeing that I must leave it to the man who will succeed me" (Ecclesiastes 2:17–18).

The writer of Ecclesiastes was a "busy" man, one who tried everything that could be tried and did everything there was to do. Yet, at the end of his experience, he was unfulfilled and bitter.

How many people have given all of themselves to something that never gave anything back? A great example of this is what motivational teachers refer to as "climbing the ladder to success only to find that it was leaning against the wrong building." It's true, I've never heard of any person who has said on his or her deathbed, "Gee, I really wish I had spent more time at the office."

I recently talked with a woman in ministry whom I have known for many years. I saw her at one of my conferences and noticed right away that she seemed unhappy and totally worn-out. The joy, zeal, and enthusiasm she had previously were no longer there. I invited her to come early the next day and speak with me.

When I asked her if she was all right, she told me that she had a serious case of burnout. She said, "For the first time, I am not enjoying everyday life. I have worked so hard and given myself to meet everyone's needs without requiring anything for myself. Now I am bordering on being bitter and fighting the temptation to quit and give up."

This woman needed balance; she needed to review all of her commitments and see which ones were really producing the fruit she was called to produce. Not everything that seems good is actually God's will for an individual. In fact, *good* is often the enemy of the *best*. We can easily lose our focus and get sidetracked. We are busy all the time, we work hard, but we don't get the things accomplished that minister fulfillment to us as individuals.

I believe when we are in the will of God and giving ourselves to what He has called us to do, we will sense satisfaction and fulfillment. We will get tired, but it will be a tired we recover from, not one that never goes away. When we are flowing in God's will, our schedules always leave time for good relationships.

Great relationships are one of the most precious treasures in life, but we must feed them regularly by putting time into them. If you find you have no time to develop and maintain strong, intimate relationships with God, with yourself, and with your family and friends, then you are absolutely too busy.

We all need to take a serious inventory of what we are doing with our time, get out the pruning shears, and as the Spirit of God leads, cut things out of our lives until we no longer have to rush. *Then* we will be able to live with peace and joy.

Realizing that we have limits and cannot do everything, and then making choices to do what is most important, will definitely increase our level of peace. Peace equals power; without it, we live weak, frustrated lives. Remember, we should strive to let the peace of God rule in our lives as an umpire. If we have peace, we can keep doing what we are doing, but if we do not have peace, we know we need to make a change. If you hear yourself complaining all the time, it is an indication that you need to make some adjustments. If you are doing what God wants you to do, you should not be complaining about it.

TAKE CHARGE OF YOUR SCHEDULE

I remember murmuring about my schedule to the Lord, complaining how terribly busy I always was. He responded in my heart by saying, "You make your schedule. If you don't like it, change it. I never told you that you had to do all the things you are doing." He put the responsibility right back on me.

If we are honest, we really are the only ones who can do anything about the busyness of our lives. We complain frequently about being overworked and too involved, but we never do anything about it. We expect everyone to feel sorry for us because we are under pressure that we place on ourselves. We say we would love to have just one free evening at home with nothing to do. Yet when, by some miracle of God, we find ourselves alone for the evening, we are so tense from all our other hurrying that we cannot sit still and enjoy it.

One evening at about 5:15 PM, when I was home alone working on this book, our electricity suddenly went out. We were without power for three hours, and I was absolutely amazed at how I kept looking for something I could do. I eventually decided I would go to my aunt's house because she did have power, so I could find something to do there. I got in my car, started it, headed down the driveway, pushed the button to open our electric gate, and realized we had no electricity, therefore the gate would not open. There was a way to open it manually, but I didn't know how.

I finally thought, *Well, I guess God has trapped me in this house with absolutely nothing to do but look out the window, and He probably has a lesson in it for me.* Perhaps the lesson is found in Psalm 46:10: "Be still, and know that I am God" (KJV)!

Two days later we had a bad storm, actually one of the worst I can remember, and hundreds of thousands of homes—including ours—in St. Louis were without power for over twenty-four hours. I settled in more quickly the second time but found it amusing to watch how not only I, but also others in our neighborhood responded to having nothing to do. One of our sons, who had shared that day how tired he was from a recent trip and needed to rest that evening, got in his car and went to the office because the power was on there. I think it is safe to say that most of us are addicted to activity.

Make your own schedule. Don't allow circumstances and demands from other people to make it for you. Simplify life. Do what you really need to do, but don't be afraid to say no to things that take your time yet produce few positive results.

I recently spoke with a young woman who had a husband, small children, and a part-time job. She shared how she felt so pressured by all of life, and how she committed to things, then resented doing them. She was even beginning to resent the people who were asking her to do them. Her attitude was becoming bitter, and she was confused.

I strongly encouraged her to be realistic about what she could sanely accomplish and remain peaceful. I suggested that she simplify her life as much as possible. In other words, I encouraged her to be in charge of her own schedule.

BE HONEST WITH YOURSELF

What is stress? Stress is too much to do in too little time. A fight with someone you love. A boss who is never pleased. Car trouble. Too little money and too many bills. Another red light when you are already late. The Internet not working when you desperately need it.

Actually, situations themselves do not cause stress; it is our reaction to the situation that is the real problem. For example, we blame the red light for being there at the wrong time when, in reality, we should have left home sooner, leaving some margin in our schedule. Only the truth makes us free. As long as we are making excuses for the stress in our lives rather than taking responsibility, we will never experience change.

I spent years trying to get rid of everything that bothered me and found out it was impossible. I wanted all of the people around me to change so they would never upset me; I also discovered that is not going to happen. Out of desperation to enjoy peace in my life, I became willing to change my approach to life. One of the things I had to do was slow down!

In 2 Timothy 4:5, Paul gave Timothy instructions about his life and ministry, saying, "As for you, be calm and cool and steady, accept and suffer unflinchingly every hardship, do the work of an evangelist, fully perform all the duties of your ministry." Paul then said, "I am . . . about to be sacrificed [my life is about to be poured out as a drink offering]" (v. 6). Paul knew his time on earth was almost up, and he was giving Timothy instructions that he might not get another opportunity to give.

If we were dying and wanted to impart last words to those we were training, I believe we would choose things we felt were very important. Paul said, "Be calm"; in other words, "Don't let things upset you. Live your life at a pace that enables you to enjoy it. Even when difficulties arise, accept them, and keep doing what God has called you to do."

Calm is the picture I get of Jesus when I think of Him and His earthly ministry. (We will talk more about the fruit of living a calm life in a later chapter.) I don't ever picture Jesus rushing from one thing to the next, being impatient with people who were not moving as fast as He wanted them to. Jesus lived in a manner that allowed Him to be discerning about what was going on around Him. He knew of danger before it approached and was able to avoid things that Satan had planned for His destruction. We need this kind of spiritual sensitivity in our own lives. We will not have it if we don't slow down.

Carefully Choose
What You Need to Be Involved In

We cannot be involved in everything and remain calm, cool, and steady. My own definition of hurry is this: *Hurry is our flesh trying to do more than the Spirit is leading us to do.* If God is leading us to do something, surely we should be able to do it and remain peaceful. He is the Author and Finisher of our faith, according to Hebrews 12:2, but He is not obligated to finish anything He did not begin. Often we begin projects in the flesh, and when we feel overwhelmed, we start praying for God to do something. We should learn to pray *before* we make plans, not afterwards.

Don't engage in everything that is going on around you. Choose carefully what activities you need to participate in. I often refer to it as "choosing your battles carefully." There are many things I could get involved in at my office that I have learned to just stay out of and let some other qualified person handle. Previously, I wanted to be part of everything, especially things that pertained to some problem at the ministry. I learned the hard way that I simply cannot be involved in everything; too much is going on for me to do that. I pick my battles now, and it has greatly increased my level of peace.

Moses was trying to be involved in too much, and in a moment of intense frustration, he told God the burden was too heavy for him. The Lord told him to choose seventy other qualified men, whom He would anoint to give them authority, then let them help with the burden of trying to lead millions of people through the wilderness (see Numbers 11).

If we don't learn to delegate work and authority, we will always feel overwhelmed. Please notice I said, work *and* authority. Don't ever give someone responsibility without the authority that goes with it. I found myself at times trying to give someone else a job to do while still wanting to be in control of it. By doing this, I was not relieved of the burden I had. My actions said to the other person, "I don't really trust you," which destroyed that person's confidence and affected the outcome of his work.

In Exodus 18, we see another situation in which Moses was overworked, only this time Moses' father-in-law, Jethro, saw all that Moses was doing for the people and told him it was too much. There are times in our lives when someone else will recognize what we can't see. We should be open to hearing that it is time to delegate some of our workload to another qualified individual.

Jethro told Moses that if he did not make a change, he would wear out both himself and the Israelites. Even people get worn-out when we don't let them help us, if God has put them in our lives for that purpose. They will feel stifled, unfulfilled, and frustrated. I believe we frequently lose people because we will not permit them to do what God has assigned them. If you have the idea that you are the only one who can do what needs to be done, you need to seriously consider what I am saying. Don't let pride destroy you—ask for help!

Exodus 18 talks about leaders who could oversee thousands, hundreds, fifties, and tens of people. Not everyone is qualified to lead the same number. If you are anointed to lead thousands and won't let others lead the tens, fifties, and hundreds, you will burn out, lose your peace, and not enjoy your work or your life.

Moses was wise enough to heed what his father-in-law said. He began to judge only the hard cases among the people while allowing other qualified people to judge the easier ones. He actually preserved his ministry by asking for help. We often have the mistaken idea that if we let others help us, we will be losing something, when actually the exact opposite is true.

I firmly believe that God provides for whatever He assigns to us. He will make sure we have all the people we need to help us, but it is not their fault if we won't rely on them.

If you find yourself trying to do something and you don't have the help you need, you might need to ask yourself if you are doing the right thing. Why would God ask you to do something, then sit by and watch you be frustrated and miserable because the burden is too much? God meets all of our needs, including the people we need to work alongside us. This passage of Scripture gives an example of this act of wisdom.

So the Twelve [apostles] convened the multitude of the disciples and said, It is not seemly or desirable or right that we should have to give up or neglect [preaching] the Word of God in order to attend to serving at tables and superintending the distribution of food. Therefore select out from among yourselves, brethren, seven men of good and attested character and repute, full of the [Holy] Spirit and wisdom, whom we may assign to look after this business and duty. But we will continue to devote ourselves steadfastly to prayer and the ministry of the Word. (Acts 6:2–4)

Had the apostles not recognized their need for help, their priorities would have remained out of line and their true assignment unfulfilled. They would have ended up frustrated, just like the people they were trying to serve. They could have lost their peace, and therefore, their power. It is very possible that the loss of peace was what triggered their decision to ask for help. This is a very good example for us to follow.

A mother can delegate some of the household chores to her children. True, they may not do the job as perfectly as she would, but they will relieve some pressure and also learn, as time goes by, to do chores with more excellence. No matter what station we are in, we can always delegate some of our responsibilities to others at the right time, therefore making it possible to do what we are assigned to do in life with peace and enjoyment. When you start to feel frustrated and begin losing your peace, ask yourself what you are doing that you could delegate to someone else.

I heard a man say that his wife desperately needed more time, so she "bought" some by hiring household help to do some of the chores. I thought this was a good way to look at it. We all feel occasionally that we are out of time—that there is never enough. "Buy" some time by either hiring someone to help or assigning chores to available people.

Once again, I want to stress that whoever you assign to jobs probably won't do the job *exactly* the way you would. Look for a good outcome, and don't be so concerned about the methods they use. We may all get to the same place by taking a different route, but the important thing is that we arrive. One person may prefer dusting the house before vacuuming the floors, while another may want to vacuum first and dust later. I can't see that it makes any difference as long as both jobs get done. We should be humble enough to admit that *our way* of doing things is not the *only way*.

When we have to consistently hurry, we have not managed our lives well. We have shoved too many things into too little space, or we are trying to do more than our share and not allowing others to help us.

Once you learn to slow down, you will have time to evaluate your real priorities in life. The first place I suggest you begin is in self-acceptance. In the next chapter we will observe how deep peace begins when you learn to love who God made you to be.

PEACEKEEPER #9

Accept Yourself

❦

Many, perhaps even most people, are not at peace with themselves, and they may not even be aware of it. Our enemy, Satan, begins to work early in our lives, poisoning our thinking and attitudes toward ourselves. He knows we are not a threat or danger to him if we have no confidence.

Our goal is not to be self-confident but to have confidence in who we are in Christ. We should know the value of being children of God and the position it gives us. As children of God, we can pray boldly in faith, knowing that God hears and answers our prayers. We can look forward to the inheritance that is ours by virtue of our personal relationship with Jesus. We can enjoy righteousness, peace, joy, good health, prosperity, and success in all we lay our hands to do, intimacy with God through Jesus, and many other wonderful benefits.

We can develop godly character and be used mightily by God to lead others to Christ and help hurting people. Yes, our lives can be absolutely amazingly wonderful through Jesus; however, Satan is the deceiver, and as such, he seeks continually to steal what Jesus died to provide for us.

If you are not at peace with yourself, you won't enjoy your life. You are one person you never get away from, not even for one second. You are everywhere you go, therefore, if you don't like and accept yourself, you cannot possibly be anything other than miserable. Also, if we don't accept ourselves, we will find it hard, if not impossible, to accept others.

Our faults stand between us and self-acceptance. We think that if we could only behave better, we could like ourselves. We are proud of our strengths, natural gifts, and talents, but we despise and are embarrassed by our weaknesses. We rejoice in our successes and feel depressed about our failures. We struggle and strive for perfection, but somehow it always eludes us. Our pursuit is in vain.

Andrew Murray said in his book *Consecrated to God* that we are "not perfected, yet perfect."

Perfect in Christ

God's Word states that if we are willing to share His sufferings, we shall also share His glory (see Romans 8:17). We have a command (or perhaps it is a promise) in Matthew 5:48: "Be perfect, therefore, as your heavenly Father is perfect" (NIV).

In the past, I had always received that verse as a harsh command, yet it could be God's promise to us that because He is perfect and is working in us, we can also look forward to sharing in His perfection. I think the *Amplified Bible* makes the verse easier to understand: "You, therefore, must be perfect [growing into complete maturity of godliness in mind and character, having reached the proper height of virtue and integrity], as your heavenly Father is perfect."

The apostle Paul said that although he had not already been made perfect, he pressed on toward the goal. He then said that those of us who are imperfect should be thus minded, to let go of what was behind (mistakes) and press on. In essence, he was saying that in God's eyes, by faith in Jesus Christ, he was perfect, yet he was not totally perfected (see Philippians 3:12–15).

Was there ever a time when Jesus was not perfect? The answer must be no; we know that Jesus was and is always perfect, the spotless, sinless Lamb of God who was found worthy to take away our sins. Hebrews 7:28 confirms His perfection, saying, "For the Law sets up men in their weakness [frail, sinful, dying human beings] as high priests, but the word of [God's] oath, which [was spoken later] after the institution of the Law, [chooses and appoints as priest One Whose appointment is complete and permanent], a Son Who has been made perfect forever."

This Scripture tells us plainly that Jesus was made perfect forever, yet Hebrews 5:8–9 says that although He was a Son, He *learned* obedience through His sufferings and thereby *became* perfectly equipped to be the Author of our salvation. This makes it clear that He was perfect, yet was also being perfected. At each moment of His life, He was totally perfect, and yet He needed to be perfected through suffering in order to become our Savior.

Perfection is a state God's grace places us into through our faith in Jesus Christ, and He works in and through us in degrees of glory. I saw my babies and my grandchildren as perfect. I even said many times as I looked at them, "You are perfect." On the other hand, they had faults; they needed to mature, grow, and change.

We must learn to see ourselves in Christ, not in ourselves. Corrie ten Boom taught that if you look at the world, you will be oppressed, if you look at yourself, you will be depressed, but if you look at Jesus, you will be at rest. How true it is that if we look at ourselves—at what we are in our own abilities—we cannot be anything except depressed and totally discouraged. But when we look to Christ, "the author and perfecter of our faith," we can enter His rest and believe that He is continually working in us (Hebrews 12:2 NIV).

According to Andrew Murray, there are degrees of perfection: perfect, more perfect, and most perfect. There is perfect and waiting to be perfected. This is simply another way of saying that God has made us to be perfect, and we are growing into it. It is like a child saying, "My mother gave me her wedding dress to use when I get married, and I am growing into it year by year. It is still my dress, even though it does not fit me yet."

We always say, "Nobody is perfect." What we mean is that nobody manifests perfect behavior, and that is a correct statement. Our behavior, however, is quite different from our identities. The Bible says that faith in Jesus makes us righteous, but in our experience, we don't always do the right thing.

Well, if we are righteous, why don't we always do right? Simply because we are still growing into people who do what is right. We do less and less wrong, and more and more right, the longer we serve God. Consider this verse: "For our sake He made Christ [virtually] to be sin Who knew no sin, so that in and through Him we might become [endued with, viewed as being in, and examples of] the righteousness of God [what we ought to be, approved and acceptable and in right relationship with Him, by His goodness]" (2 Corinthians 5:21).

I have said for years, "My *who* is completely different than my *do*." In other words, who I am *in Christ* is one thing, and what I do *in myself* is a completely different thing altogether. We are to *become* examples of righteousness.

When we are born again, we receive new identities; God makes us His children, just as when my children were born, they became Meyers. They will never be more or less Meyers than they were on those days. In one moment of time, each became forever and completely a Meyer. Did they always act like a Meyer? Did they always act the way we would have liked our children who represent us to act? Of course not, but they were nonetheless Meyers.

Religion frequently teaches us to *do things right* (follow rules and regulations) to prove *we are right* with God. True Bible Christianity teaches the opposite: we cannot *do right* until God has *made us right* with Him, which He does at our new birth.

Second Corinthians 5:17 says, "Therefore, if anyone is in Christ, he is a new creation; the old has gone, the new has come!" (NIV). We suddenly become new creatures. I like to say we are new spiritual clay. We have in us the stuff we need in order to learn how to act the way God wants us to act.

It is vital for us to understand these things if we are to ever accept ourselves. We must believe that even though we are not where we need to be, neither are we where we used to be. We are, this very moment, perfect in God's eyes and on our way to perfection.

SELF-ACCEPTANCE IS A FOUNDATION FOR PEACE

We have no foundation of peace if we don't have peace with God and ourselves. Peace with God should take us to the foundational principle of having peace with ourselves. If God loves us unconditionally, then we can love ourselves unconditionally. If He accepts us, we should be able to accept ourselves. Peace within ourselves, which is self-acceptance, is based on God's *having made us* perfect and righteous in Christ; it is not based on our own works and behavior.

In His Word, God refers to us (His believers) as being "holy." Romans 12:1 says to offer our bodies a living sacrifice, "holy" and acceptable unto God. First Corinthians 3:17 explains that God's temple is "holy," and we (believers) are His temple. Ephesians 3:5 speaks of God's "holy apostles (consecrated messengers) and prophets." These Scriptures, and others like them, clearly show that God views us as holy, perfect, and righteous. We either accept it or we reject it, and the choice we make greatly affects how we view ourselves.

We are the house of God; we are His home. He has come to live in us; we are His new base of operation, so to speak. He works through us (His born-again children) to draw the world unto Himself.

He wants peace in His house! Have you ever screamed to your children, "I want some peace in this house"? I have, and chances are you have too. Hear God gently saying that to you right now, and come to terms of peace with who you are.

Accept yourself right where you are, and let God help you get to where you want to be. He loves and accepts you each step of the way. He is changing you from glory to glory (see 2 Corinthians

3:18). Get into agreement with God, and you will see new power in your life unlike anything you have experienced before.

Being at peace with yourself in light of who God is transforming you to become will give you a firm foundation upon which to build a good life. Remember, Satan wants you weak and powerless; God wants you to be strong and powerful, ready to enjoy life, so He can use you for His purposes on earth. But we cannot grow spiritually and become perfected for His use until we are at peace with ourselves.

ARE YOUR FAULTS DISTRACTING YOU?

To make spiritual progress, we need to keep our eyes on Jesus instead of ourselves. Hebrews 12:2 teaches us to look away from all that will distract us from Jesus, who leads us and is the Source of our incentive to have faith, and who will bring our faith to maturity and perfection.

When we keep our eyes (our thoughts) on everything that is wrong with us, it prevents us from paying attention to the Lord. We need to see everything that is right with Him and believe He is working to reproduce it in us rather than taking a continual inventory of all of our faults. We should not have our eyes on other people, comparing ourselves with them; we should have our eyes on Jesus. He, not other people, is our example to follow. We will eventually stand before God, not people, and give an account of our lives.

And get your eyes off yourself; don't meditate on everything you think you do right, or everything you think you do wrong. Focus on who God says you are.

The Holy Spirit will convict you in areas where you need it, and when He does, your response should not be to feel condemnation. It should be appreciation that God cares enough about you to send His Spirit daily to help you stay on the narrow path that leads to life.

When I learned to respond to God's correction (conviction) with appreciation instead of condemnation, it closed a door to Satan that I had allowed to remain open all of my life. We cannot grow without conviction of our sins, yet if we always respond with condemnation, that also prevents our growth. God intends that conviction of sin lift us up and out of wrong behavior, but condemnation presses us down and holds us prisoner to the sin. We can never get beyond something we stay condemned about.

VERBALIZE YOUR ACCEPTANCE OF YOURSELF

Many people have a bad habit of saying negative, downgrading things about themselves. This is dangerous and wrong. Words are containers of power; they carry either creative or destructive influence. Proverbs 18:21 states that the power of life and death are in the tongue, and those who indulge it will eat the fruit of it for life or death. In other words, I can speak death or life to others, my circumstances, and myself.

Previously in my life, I had a bad habit of saying ungodly, negative things about myself. What was in my heart came out of my mouth, just as Matthew 12:34 confirms, and I saw that truth operating in my life. I had a bad attitude about myself; I didn't like myself, so I said things that were proof of what was in my heart.

I frequently ask in conferences where I am teaching, "How many of you regularly say negative, downgrading things about your own self out of your own mouth?" Most in the audience raise their hands.

Negative self-talk is a big problem that we need to seriously address. If you don't understand the tremendous power of words, please obtain and read my book entitled *Me and My Big Mouth*.

As I gained revelation from God's Word, I began to see how devastating this bad habit of speaking against myself was, and I slowly began to replace those bad things I said with good things. It was initially a step of faith, because I felt foolish standing around by myself, saying good things about myself. I started doing it when alone because I certainly did not have the boldness to say anything complimentary about myself in front of anybody. Instead of saying, "I am so stupid" when I made mistakes, I changed my response to "I made a mistake, but God loves me unconditionally, and He is changing me." Instead of saying, "I never do anything right," I said, "I am the righteousness of God in Christ, and He is working in me."

I am not suggesting that we form a habit of telling people how wonderful we think we are—that would be prideful and unacceptable behavior. But we should say good things rather than bad things when the occasion arises.

For example, if someone asks you what your gifts, talents, and abilities are, don't say, "I don't have any. I'm really not very smart." Say, "God has gifted me to do many things," and then describe the things you are good at.

Perhaps you are good at encouraging people; that is a gift from God. Or you may love simply to help people, and that is one of the greatest gifts God gives. I don't know what I would do in life if I did not have people who just help with whatever needs to be done. You may not have gifts that are "showy," but that does not make them any less important.

Ask God to forgive you for all the times you have said negative things about yourself, your life, and your future. Make a decision to start speaking in positive terms to everything in your life, including yourself.

Say out loud several times a day, "I accept myself. God has created me with His very own hand, and I am not a mistake. I have a glorious future, and I intend to go forward and greet each day with peace and joy."

For years, I wished I were just a little thinner, that my voice were not so deep, that I didn't talk so much, that I were not so straightforward in my approach to people, and so on. I have since discovered that many of the things I didn't want were the very qualities I needed in order to do what God has called me to do.

How can we ever have peace within ourselves if we always want to be something we're not? How can we have peace if we are mad at ourselves because we are what we are, or under condemnation because we are not perfected in behavior?

I recently read a statement by Watchman Nee that blessed me; he said that "we shall forever be what we are." He did not mean that God isn't changing us in behavior as we grow in Him, but he did mean that God has given each of us a specific temperament, and we shall always be, at the root, those persons God made us to be.

God gave me my bold voice and personality. I can learn not to be harsh and rude, but I will always be bold and aggressive. I am a preacher and teacher of God's Word. I am a mouth in the body of Christ, so to speak. God uses my mouth. I will always talk a lot. I can learn not to enter into idle talk, which we will discuss later, or say things that hurt people; but I will never be a quiet, soft-spoken person.

You will always be you, so accept the basic you and let God be God in your life. Stop wrestling with yourself, focus on your strengths, and enter into peace.

Focus on Your Unique Strengths

Part of self-acceptance is realizing that you are unique in yourself and will never be exactly like someone else. God wants variation, not boring sameness. Actually, if we look around, we see that God is extremely creative. We enjoy different flowers, trees, birds, weather. It seems that a lot of what God has created has many varieties, even people.

Don't struggle to be a carbon copy of someone you admire. You are unique, and there is something you can do that nobody else in the entire world can do exactly the way you can. God had to teach me the all-important lesson of not comparing myself with others and competing with them or their abilities. He had to teach me to "be free to be me" before He could use me the way He had planned.

I taught home Bible studies for five years, and then for one year, God sort of sat me on a shelf and I did nothing. During that year I decided I needed to settle down and live a "normal" life. I decided I needed to be a "normal woman." I had always thought my hopes and ambitions were out of the ordinary, but Satan was tormenting me with thoughts that I was really weird and something was wrong with me.

I kept my house clean and neat but had no real interest in decorating to the degree that many of my friends did. They went to craft classes and had home-decorating parties on a regular basis. I could hardly sew a button on my husband's shirt, while one of my friends made clothes for her entire family. I felt destiny calling me while they were totally content doing things that really bored me. What they were doing was important also, it just was not what I was called to do.

I began to think that I just needed to straighten up and be what a woman "ought to be." I wasn't sure exactly what that was, so I tried to pattern myself after other women I knew. One friend was really sweet in nature, so I tried to speak softly and be sweet like her. Another had a garden and canned vegetables, so I tried that. I also took sewing lessons and attempted to make some clothes for my family. I was miserable, to say the least. I had forced myself into a mold that God had never designed for me.

All of these carnal ideas were birthed out of deep-rooted insecurities left over from my abusive past. I was insecure in who I was, I felt deeply flawed, and I had a shame-based nature, so I kept trying to reshape myself into what seemed acceptable to the world.

Woman preachers were not exactly at the top of the list of what the world applauded, especially in 1976 when I began, and even more so in the denomination we were part of. I am sure these fleshly efforts of mine grieved the Lord, yet He allowed me to go through the process of comparing, competing, and being miserable until I finally realized I was not *weird*, I was *unique*. Something unique has value because it is one of a kind, whereas something just like many others is not as valuable.

I was comparing myself to wonderful women who were operating in their natural, God-given abilities. They were happy because they were doing exactly what God had assigned to them. I was unhappy because I also was trying to do what God had assigned to them to do. God patiently forms each of us in our mother's wombs with His very own hand. When you consider your strengths, remember this verse:

> For you created my inmost being;
> you knit me together in my mother's womb.

126

I praise you because I am fearfully and wonderfully made;
   your works are wonderful, I know that full well.
My frame was not hidden from you
   when I was made in the secret place.
When I was woven together in the depths of the earth,
   your eyes saw my unformed body.
All the days ordained for me
   were written in your book
before one of them came to be. (Psalm 139:13–16 NIV)

We are not accidents, not something that just got thrown together with no forethought. Each of us is here on purpose, chosen to live in this particular time period on purpose. Fighting yourself is like fighting God, because you are His handiwork, predestined to good works (see Ephesians 2:10).

When Paul was converted, he certainly had heard about the great apostle Peter. I am sure Peter was someone everyone looked up to because of the great way in which God used him and the strong gifts he expressed. Peter was a leader among leaders. One would think that Paul would have sought out Peter for approval and friendship, yet we see just the opposite. Paul went away into Arabia and remained there for three years first, then he finally went to Jerusalem to become acquainted with Peter. Then, after a period of fourteen more years, during which he ministered where God led him, he went to Jerusalem again to meet with Peter and some of the other apostles (see Galatians 1:17–2:12).

Paul had confidence in his call and did not feel the need to compare himself with Peter or anyone else. We see evidence of this fact in other Scriptures: In Galatians 1:10, Paul stated that if he had been trying to be popular with people, he would not have become an apostle of the Lord. Why? Because following people rather than God can get us on the wrong paths for our lives. God does not want copies—He wants originals. Paul was an original, not a copy of Peter or the others, and that is how God wants it.

In the beginning of my ministry, I tried to get into several different groups of well-known preachers. I wanted their approval, and I wanted to compare what I was doing with what they were doing to see if I needed to change anything. Although I made improvement the year I spent "doing nothing" (except struggling to be what I thought was a regular woman), I still had insecurities and would have become a carbon copy of someone else if I had had the opportunity to do so.

I was quite frustrated when God would not allow me to have friends in ministry at that time, but I didn't understand that He was training me personally and did not want any interference in those early days of preparation for my calling.

Insecure people are not good at saying no! They are not good at being different; they usually bend in the direction everyone is going, rather than following their hearts wholly. When God was ready to promote our ministry to a more visible platform, one of the things I often heard was, "You are a breath of fresh air! You're unique, not like everyone else out there." That does not mean all the others were not wonderful and needed, it simply means we need variety.

Paul's message was the same as Peter's, yet with a different emphasis, and that is the way it should be in order for people to mature spiritually. We often fear being different; we are bored with sameness, yet somehow we feel safe with it.

Comparing ourselves with others and trying to be like them will definitely steal our peace; it is one of the most frustrating things we can go through. Beware of comparing any aspect of your natural or spiritual life with anyone else's—it will produce only turmoil.

Spiritual Comparisons

I remember hearing one preacher talk of how often he saw Jesus. I had never seen Jesus, so I wondered what was wrong with me. Another person I knew prayed four hours every morning. I could not find enough to pray about to keep praying for four hours and always ended up bored and sleepy, so I wondered what was wrong with me. I had no gift to remember large portions of Scripture like someone I knew, who memorized all the Psalms and Proverbs as well as other entire books of the Bible, so I wondered what was wrong with me. I finally realized that nothing was necessarily wrong with me because I could not do what they could. The fact was, I was preaching all over the world, and none of them were doing that.

Whatever we cannot do, there are many other things we can. Whatever someone else can do, there are also things they cannot. Don't play the devil's game any longer. Don't compare yourself with anyone in any way, especially not spiritually. We can see other people's good examples, but they must never become our standard. Even if we learn from them how to do something, we still will not do it exactly the same way.

Dave taught me how to play golf, and he taught me according to how he swung the golf club, but I don't swing mine the way he does and never will. We see this same example over and over. I hold the steering wheel of the car differently from the way he does, we apply the brakes differently, when I iron a shirt I start with the collar, my friend starts with the sleeve. What is the difference how we iron the shirt as long as it gets ironed properly?

I know people who say they have never felt the presence of God, and it really frustrated them when they heard others say things like "Did you feel God in this place tonight?" Some have great emotional experiences when they are born again or receive the baptism of the Holy Spirit, while others take it completely by faith and feel absolutely nothing, although they do see the fruit in their lives later.

At some time or another, I think we all fall into the trap of wondering why we are not like others we know or why we don't have the same experiences they do, but it *is a trap*—and a dangerous one. We are caught in a snare set by Satan when we enter into spiritual competition and comparison and become dissatisfied with what God is giving to us.

We should trust that God will do the best thing for each of us and let Him choose what that is. If we trust God in this way, we can lay aside our fears and insecurities about ourselves. How we respond to God in different areas can be the result of many different things, such as our natural temperaments, past teachings, and levels of natural boldness. For example, Thomas was a doubter and God loved Him, but He also corrected him for having little faith. Seeing and feeling are great, but Jesus said, "Blessed are those who believe and have not seen" (see John 20:29).

I am sure we would all like to see into the spiritual realm and have an abundance of supernatural experiences, but being frustrated if we don't only steals our peace and certainly does not produce visions of Jesus. I have had some "experiences" with the Lord, but I have also gone for many years without anything but faith.

I went through all the frustration, all the wondering what was wrong with me, wondering if I had committed some sin and God could not get through to me, wondering, reasoning, anxiety, unrest, no peace. . . . Then I found the answer: *Don't compare your spiritual life with that of anyone you know or anyone you read about.* Be yourself. You are unique, and God has a plan just for you.

COMPARING CIRCUMSTANCES

Comparing your circumstances with those of other people will steal your peace and cause confusion about God's unique plan for you. Remember, the devil wants to devour the blessings that God has set for you. The Word says to "withstand him; be firm in faith [against his onset—rooted, established, strong, immovable, and determined], knowing that the same (identical) sufferings are appointed to your brotherhood (the whole body of Christians) throughout the world" (1 Peter 5:9).

This Scripture shows us that we are to resist the devil quickly, stand firm against him at the onset of his attack, and know that everyone is going through difficulties in life. When we are in tough times, it seems Satan taunts us with thoughts that no one has it as bad as we do, but that is not true. There is someone in much worse circumstances than ours, no matter how difficult your or my situation may seem.

Realizing this builds gratitude and thankfulness, rather than self-pity, in our hearts. We should not be glad that others are suffering, but it does help us not to think we are the only ones waiting for a breakthrough from God. No matter how long we may have been waiting for God to do something we have prayed about, someone else has waited longer. No matter how sick, or poor, or lonely, or frightened any one of us may be, someone, somewhere is in worse condition.

God never promised us a life without trials; in fact, He promised us the opposite. He said there would be trials but that we should not fear them. "For He [God] Himself has said, I will not in any way fail you nor give you up nor leave you without support. [I will] not, [I will] not, [I will] not in any degree leave you helpless nor forsake nor let [you] down (relax My hold on you)! [Assuredly not!]" (Hebrews 13:5).

The presence of trials and tribulations does not mean that God has forgotten us or that He does not love us. We sometimes look at someone who seems to be having a wonderful life while we are suffering and ask, "God, why don't You love me the way You do that person?" We are tempted to think the same old question: *What is wrong with me?*

No matter what Satan uses, his purpose is the same: He wants us to think something is desperately wrong with us, and that we should have someone else's life or be like someone else. He wants to keep us from self-acceptance and the freedom to be who we are and *enjoy our lives.*

Don't despise your life and wish for another just because you are going through trials. If you had someone else's life, your trials might well be worse than the ones you have now. Besides, whatever you are going through right now, remember, *this too shall pass!*

Look beyond where you are, see with the eyes of faith, and believe God for even the impossible. The Bible says that Abraham had no reason at all to hope, but he hoped on in faith that God's promise to Him would be fulfilled (see Romans 4:18). A hopeful mind and attitude ministers peace and joy, while fear and discouragement steal both.

Don't concentrate on your problems; keep your mind on Jesus and His good plan for your life. As you read God's promises in the Word, adapt the Word as a personal letter to yourself. For example, paraphrasing Isaiah 26:3 as a personal letter to you, God is saying, "I will guard you and keep you in perfect and constant peace as you keep your mind on Me, because you commit yourself to Me, lean on Me, and hope confidently in Me."

Where the mind goes, the man follows. If we let our minds dwell on negative things (our problems instead of God's answers), our problems seem to multiply. The more we think about a problem, even a little one, the larger it seems to be.

I can honestly say now that I like myself. I admit it took a long time to get from where I was to where I am, but I really had nothing better to do than press on in God, and neither do you. For much of my life, I literally hated myself, and I know now that type of attitude is insulting to God, who carefully made us.

It costs nothing to be positive and believe that God can change you and your life. Jump-start your blessings by saying you love your life, and be thankful in all things, no matter what the circumstances may be, knowing this is God's will for you.

Each time you are tempted (which you will be) to compare yourself, or any aspect of your life, with anyone else, resist Satan at his onset. Don't even entertain thoughts of comparison to others. You are an individual, you are unique, and you have a right to enjoy your life, which must include enjoying your unique self.

Embrace your life. Wrap your arms around yourself right now as an act of faith and say out loud, "I accept myself, and I love myself in a balanced way. I'm not selfish, but I do affirm myself as a child of God, and I do believe He has created me and has a purpose for my life."

ACCEPTING YOUR UNIQUENESS
OPENS THE DOOR TO BLESSINGS

I mentioned earlier that God had put me "on a shelf" for a one-year interval during my ministry, at which time I decided I had a wild imagination and was not really called to ministry at all. I tried to be what I thought the world expected me to be as a woman, wife, and mother. I felt during that year that God was doing absolutely nothing in my life; I saw no progress in my ministry, so I concluded that it was over when actually it was only about to begin.

During that year of comparing, competing, and finally coming to the realization that even if I was less than perfect, I still had to be me, God was actually doing one of the greatest works in me He has ever done. He was setting me free to be me! This had to take place before God could promote me into the next level of my ministry. Right at the end of that year of trials, our family began going to a new church in town, and a short while later, I found myself teaching a weekly Bible study that was eventually attended by over four hundred people.

I became an associate pastor at that church, taught Bible college three times a week, and learned a great deal that prepared me for the next challenge of my ministry, which included the media ministry that I am currently enjoying. Our daily television program is available to 2.5 billion people, we are on 350 radio stations, and I've had the privilege of writing nearly 60 books, as well as other very fruitful outreaches.

Our television program is aired around the world in 21 different languages, and we are adding new ones all the time. We air in the nation of India in 11 languages and recently had the great privilege of doing a major conference in Hyderabad. In 4 days, we ministered to 850,000 people with 250,000 decisions for Jesus Christ. Wow! What a privilege to be part of something like that.

None of this would be happening today if I had not stopped comparing myself with others and competing with them. It is vital for your future that you take this seriously and ask God to reveal any areas of comparison in your life.

If God has a plan for you and me, He certainly won't bring it to pass as long as we are trying to be other people. God will never give us grace to be people other than ourselves. Without grace, life is filled with struggle, it is not a life we enjoy; but with His grace (power of the Holy Spirit), we can enter the rest (peace) of the Lord and experience joy unspeakable and full of glory.

When I was trapped in self-rejection, comparing and competing with many of the people God had placed in my life, He led me to an article that was life-changing for me. I want to share excerpts from it with you, and I pray it blesses you as it did me.

The following article about "the consciousness of sin, and longing for holiness" was a letter Hudson Taylor, missionary to China in the 1800s, wrote to his sister and was later reprinted; it is entitled "The Exchanged Life." Hudson Taylor wrote:

Every day, almost every hour, the consciousness of sin oppressed me. I knew that if only I could abide in Christ all would be well, but I could not. I began the day with prayer, determined not to take my mind off of Him for a moment; but pressure of duties, sometimes very trying, constant interruptions apt to be so wearing, often caused me to forget Him. . . . Each day brought its register of sin and failure, of lack of power. To will was indeed present with me, but how to perform I found not. . . .

The last month or more has been, perhaps, the happiest period of my life; and I long to tell you a little of what the

Lord has done for my soul. I do not know how far I may be able to make myself intelligible about it, for there is nothing new or strange or wonderful—and yet, all is new! In a word: "Whereas I was blind, now I see. . . ."

I felt the ingratitude, the danger, the sin of not living nearer to God. I prayed, agonized, fasted, strove, made resolutions, read the Word more diligently, sought for more time for retirement and meditation to be alone with God—but all was without avail. Every day, almost every hour, the consciousness of sin oppressed me. . . . I hated myself; I hated my sin; and yet I gained no strength against it.

I felt I was a child of God: His Spirit in my heart would cry, in spite of all, "Abba, Father," but to rise to my privileges as a child [of God], I was utterly powerless.

I thought that holiness was to be gradually attained by diligent use of the means of grace. I felt that there was nothing I so much desired in this world, nothing I so much needed. But the more I pursued and strove after holiness, the more it eluded my grasp, till hope itself almost died out. . . . I knew I was powerless. I told the Lord so and asked Him to give me help and strength. . . .

When my agony of soul was at its height, a sentence in a letter from dear [John] McCarthy [in Hangchow, China] was used to remove the scales from my eyes, and the Spirit of God revealed the truth of our oneness with Jesus as I had never seen it before. McCarthy, who had been much exercised by the same sense of failure, but saw the light before I did, wrote (I quote from memory) "But how to get faith strengthened? Not by striving after faith, but by resting on the Faithful One."

As I read I saw it all! "If we believe not, He [remains] abideth faithful." I looked unto Jesus and saw (and when I saw, oh, how joy flowed) that He had said, "I will never leave you."

"Ah, *there* is rest!" I thought. "I have striven in vain to rest

135

in Him. I'll strive no more. For has He not promised to abide with *me*—never to leave me, never to fail me?" And . . . He never will!

Joy will flow in our lives when we get our eyes off of ourselves and onto Jesus—off of what is wrong with us, and onto what is right with Him. Finally, when we realize that we are one with Him, we can live the "exchanged life" rather than a frustrating one.

Jesus took our old lives and has given us new ones. His life is in us, and He has given us His peace (see John 14:27). His joy is ours. He was made poor so that we might be made rich; He took our sin and gave us His righteousness; He took our sicknesses and diseases and the pain of our punishment and gave us His strength. Yes, He took everything bad and has given us lives to enjoy along with the peace that passes understanding.

Remember, Jesus said, "I came that [you] may have and enjoy life, and have it in abundance (to the full, till it overflows)." So enjoy the strengths that God has given to you, and focus on the life He wants you to enjoy. In the next chapter I will share with you how to avoid the paralysis of self-analysis and find peace by keeping your priorities in focus.

PEACEKEEPER #11

Keep Your Priorities in Order

❧◦❧

I believe that one of the reasons people lose their peace and fail to have the things they want is because they get their priorities out of line. There are so many choices to which people can give their time and attention. Without clear priorities, people can become paralyzed with indecision; I call this *paralysis of analysis.*

Some of the choices we have are bad options and are easy to recognize as something to avoid, but many of our options are good. Yet even good things can get our priorities all messed up. What is a top priority for somebody else could be a problem for us. So we have to be careful that we don't just do what everybody else is doing. We need to do what God is leading us individually to do.

When setting our priorities, it's important to understand that Jesus is the holding power of all that is good in our lives. Colossians 1:17 says, "And He Himself existed before all things, and in Him all things consist (cohere, are held together)." That is why He should always be our first priority. Jesus holds everything together.

A couple can't have a good marriage if Jesus isn't holding it together. In fact, people won't have good personal relationships with *anybody* if Jesus is not leading and influencing individuals to love each other. Finances are a mess without Jesus. Our thoughts are clouded and confused without Jesus. Our emotions are out of control without Him.

Colossians 1:18 continues: "He also is the Head of [His] body, the church; seeing He is the Beginning, the Firstborn from among the dead, *so that He alone in everything and in every respect might occupy the chief place [stand first and be preeminent]*" (italics mine). Jesus is the head of the church body; therefore, He alone, in every respect, should occupy the chief place, stand first and be preeminent, in each of our lives.

That means if Jesus is not first place in our lives, then we need to rearrange our priorities. Matthew 6:33 says that if we seek the kingdom of God and His righteousness, that all other things will be added to our lives. The *Amplified Bible* translation of this verse says we are to "seek His way of doing and being right."

Seeking the kingdom means finding out how God wants things done. Finding out how He wants us to treat people. Finding out how He wants us to act in situations and circumstances. Finding out what He wants us to do with our money. Finding out what kind of an attitude we should have. Even finding out what kind of entertainment Jesus approves of for us.

Our lives will not be blessed if we keep God in a little Sunday-morning box and let Him have our priority attention for only forty-five minutes, once a week during a church service. As long as we are here in this world, we will have to resist becoming like the world—and it is a daily battle. *The church is full of worldly, carnal, fleshly believers, and that is why we are not affecting the world the way we should be.*

If Christians were putting Jesus first in everything, then the world would be in a better condition. There are, of course, sincere, God-fearing, dedicated believers in every church and in society, but not nearly as many as there should be. Each of us should remember the importance of walking in the Spirit, not in the flesh. The world is watching us, we are Christ's representatives; God is making His appeal to the world through us (see 2 Corinthians 5:20).

ESTABLISH GRACE AS YOUR PRIORITY

Our first priority of life should not be to earn a living or get an education. In fact, First Corinthians 8:1 says that "knowledge causes people to be puffed up," but love "edifies." This tells us that focusing on our love-walk is a more important priority than learning a career skill. (I am not saying that God is against higher education, but wouldn't it be an awesome world if everyone were required to spend four concentrated years of education to learn how to walk in love?)

Often we don't think about what our priorities are, but we still have them. Our priorities are whatever is first in our thoughts and in how we plan our time. Having real peace in our lives requires making God first above all other things that demand our attention.

If you put God first in your finances, first in your time, first in your conversation, first in your thoughts, first in your decisions, your life will be a success. I am living evidence of this truth. Before I learned to put God first, I was living in the worst messes that anybody could have. I had a bad attitude and couldn't think two positive thoughts in a row. I didn't like anybody, and nobody liked me. The abuse in my childhood had left me full of bitterness, resentment, and unforgiveness.

Even when I became a believer, I still thought I could achieve approval only through good works. I didn't understand the simple fact that Jesus loved me, and God's grace just didn't make any sense to me. But eventually I learned that God's grace is better than our works.

Works breed reasoning and anxiety that will eventually strangle our peace. Grace and works are two totally different entities, which cannot partnership together. If grace has anything to do with works, then it's no longer grace, and if works have anything to do with grace, then they're no longer works. Romans 11:6 explains, "But if it is by grace (His unmerited favor and graciousness), it is no longer conditioned on works or anything men have done. Otherwise, grace would no longer be grace [it would be meaningless]." Even after putting God first, I had to learn to let grace (God's power) bring about the fruit of my ministry.

I had no peace when I tried to accomplish through works what was in my heart to do. As you will read shortly, I couldn't even enjoy a relaxing bubble bath as long as I thought works would help me find my answers. It was several years ago that God brought this vivid lesson to my attention.

I had already seen tremendous growth in our ministry through national radio and TV. My secretary at that time, who was also our office manager, and her husband, who was our bookkeeper, lived in an apartment in the lower level of our home. They had been with us for several years and took care of our house and teenage son whenever we traveled.

Consequently, we talked a lot about business in our house. God had been trying to teach me that I needed to delegate work and stay out of some things if I wanted to have peace in my life. He had been showing me I should let Dave handle some of the things that frustrated me, and that I didn't even have to know about them. I could just go on about my business.

But one night, I knew Dave was going to discuss some business matters with that couple, and I wanted to hear them too. Even though God had instructed me to let Dave handle many of the things that were stealing my peace, I still wanted to get in on *everything*. So this particular night, I put aside some things I really needed to do in order to sit in on their meeting. They just kept talking about other things, and it seemed to me that they weren't going to discuss business issues after all, so I finally said something about getting started.

Dave said, "Well, we're just not ready yet. Why don't you go ahead and take your bath?" So, reluctantly, I went upstairs and ran the bathwater and got into the tub, but as soon as I did, I heard everyone talking downstairs and realized they were starting their business meeting. There I was, a grown woman, nearly fifty years old at the time, and I wanted to hear what they were saying so badly that I got out of the bathtub and tried to listen to their conversation through the grate in the floor!

When that didn't work, I went to open the bathroom door so I could listen from the stairway, when suddenly the Holy Spirit made me realize how stupid I looked. I remember His saying to me, "Why don't you just get in the bathtub, Joyce, and mind your own business?"

I tell all this to help you realize that I know firsthand how difficult it is to let go of works and to trust God's grace to carry us where we want to go. I know how difficult it is to delegate jobs to other people and then trust that those jobs will be done properly without any involvement from us.

If we cannot let the grace of God work for us in small areas, we will never learn to let it work for us in the big ones. I was so nosey, I could not even stay in the bathtub when I thought Dave was discussing business and I wasn't going to know what was going on. That being the case, how could I ever advance to trusting God to take care of larger matters?

God wants you to understand that you have two choices: You can enjoy your life while He takes care of what needs to be done for you, or you can labor and struggle in vain through your own works. He is willing to build your life or allow you to do it, but His grace and your works are not both going to bring results that you want. If you choose His grace, you will have to lay aside the works of your flesh you are planning to do.

God wants us always to be in a position of trusting Him. Worry is the work of our flesh and is unscriptural. Worry, reasoning, and frustration are internal types of work that do not please God. To worry is to torment yourself with disturbing thoughts, and is a clear indicator that God is not first in your life.

GOD'S GRACE IS SUFFICIENT FOR TODAY

God will give you all the grace you need for today, and He will also give you grace for tomorrow, but as I've said, tomorrow's grace won't show up until tomorrow. The grace of God is just like manna was to the Israelites; every morning the manna came down out of the sky and was enough for that day. Whenever someone tried to store up provision for the next day, it rotted. It's the same way with grace. We are to learn to live our lives one day at a time.

When we have to stand in faith and believe God for a breakthrough in an area, we want to know immediately when the answer will come. God's answer is that it will come—one day at a time. And worrying or trying to make it happen will not help it come any faster.

The Lord's Prayer will help you stay in peace while you are waiting for a breakthrough. In Matthew 6:11, Jesus taught us to pray, saying, "Give us this day our daily bread." God wants us to pray *every day* for whatever provision we need for that day. Jesus also said to "stop being perpetually uneasy (anxious and worried)" about our lives (v. 25).

I realized I was frustrated as soon as I got up in the mornings. I was always in such a hurry, no matter what I was doing, I had my mind on the next thing I needed to do. As I was brushing my teeth one morning, I discovered I was hurrying because I was thinking about making the bed, and God told me, "Slow down. Brush your teeth."

God continued to show me how misplaced priorities were robbing me of the peace and enjoyment in my life. I'd rush to make my bed, but because I never kept my mind on what I was doing, I was already anxious about the next thing I needed to do. As I started making the bed, I thought, *I better lay out some meat to thaw for dinner.* So I'd leave the bed half made and rush downstairs to get meat out of the freezer, but on the way there I'd see a pile of dirty clothes and think, *I better put those clothes in the washer and get the laundry started.* Just as I put soap in the washer, the phone would ring, so I ran back upstairs to the kitchen to answer the phone.

While I talked on the phone, I realized that I needed to load the dishwasher, so I put a few dishes in the dishwasher as I talked. But then whoever was on the phone said, "Would you like to go to town with me?" and I'd think, *Well, I do need to get some stamps to mail some letters,* so I'd hurry to get dressed to go to town.

I'd carry on like that all day, never finishing what I started. By the time Dave came home, everything was in shambles and he asked casually, "So, what did you do all day?"

That offended me and I threw a fit, saying, "What do you mean, what did I *do* all day? I've been running around here like a maniac trying to work!"

Now, that is not the way to enjoy your life. That is anxiety! And anxiety is work that never accomplishes anything.

Peace begins with our keeping priorities straight moment by moment. It is a challenge to thoroughly enjoy every moment that God gives us. But when we learn to do this, we will enjoy our days. When we learn to enjoy our days, we will find that we are enjoying our lives.

We can learn to *enjoy* making the bed, doing laundry, and washing the dishes. We can enjoy getting meals for our families, going to the grocery store, and taking time to talk with friends. If we don't enjoy every phase of our day, we will miss the life that God intended for us to enjoy.

Life cannot just be filled with things that are fun to do. But we can enjoy the more mundane things that we *need* to accomplish by staying filled with the Holy Spirit. Ephesians 5:18 says, "Ever be filled and stimulated with the [Holy] Spirit." We can do this by singing spiritual songs while we work, and by keeping an attitude of praise in our hearts and talking to the Lord as we work. We stay filled with the Holy Spirit by giving thanks to God as we go about our daily tasks (see vv. 19–20).

If you have never hummed a little tune as you worked, you will be surprised at how quickly this simple act lifts your spirit. The Lord designed us, so He alone knows what it takes for us to enjoy our lives and be free from anxiety. Keeping a melody in our hearts and an attitude of praise toward God will keep Him in first place on our list of priorities.

I challenge you to examine your life and ask yourself: How much of my life am I wasting on anxiety? You won't have peace if you waste too much of it. Time is something that we can never get back. Learn to enjoy all of your day. Have fun even while doing strenuous chores. And don't waste time worrying or being frustrated about circumstances that you can't change.

GIVE GOD THE BEST PART OF YOUR DAY

I've trained myself now to start each day by giving God the first-fruits of my time. I've realized that I'm not going to get through the day peacefully if I don't spend time with God.

So, each morning, I get coffee, and usually while still in my pajamas, I just spend as much time with God as I need to in order to feel I can behave properly and walk in the fruit of the Spirit throughout the day.

When I first started doing this, I used the time to murmur to God about all my trials in life, so one morning the Holy Spirit spoke to me and said, "Now, Joyce, are you going to fellowship with Me this morning, or with your problem?"

I learned to use the best part of my day to give God the best part of my heart. Giving God the first moments of the morning helps keep my priorities straight for the rest of the day. In fact, I've written a little book that will help you get in the habit of beginning your day with God, called *Starting Your Day Right*. Each short devotion encourages you to meditate on God's Word during this time and reminds you to ask Him to help you rely on His grace your whole day.

Don't use this gift of time with God to meditate on your problems. Don't spend that time worrying about all the things that you want God to do for you that He's not done yet, or trying to figure out ways you can get Him to do them. During this time with God, set your heart as the psalmist did, who wrote, "But I trusted in, relied on, and was confident in You, O Lord; I said, You are my God. *My times are in Your hands*" (Psalm 31:14–15, italics mine).

The Bible says to "lean on, trust in, and be confident in the Lord with all your heart and mind and do not rely on your own insight or understanding. In all your ways know, recognize, and acknowledge Him, and He will direct and make straight and plain your paths. Be not wise in your own eyes" (Proverbs 3:5–7).

What's the sense in our saying that we trust God, then spending our day trying to figure out how and when our problems will be solved? God wants to hear us say, "Lord, I don't know how You're going to do this. I don't care how You do it. However You do it, I know it's going to be right. I can't do it anyway, so I'm not going to frustrate myself trying to figure out how I can do it, God. I trust all my circumstances to You. *My times are in Your hands.* Trusting You is my first priority in life."

STAY IN PERFECT PEACE

God wants us to enjoy perfect peace, and we cannot do that unless we give Him our worries. "Therefore humble yourselves [demote, lower yourselves in your own estimation] under the mighty hand of God, *that in due time* He may exalt you, casting the whole of your care [all your anxieties, all your worries, all your concerns, once and for all] on Him, for He cares for you affectionately and cares about you watchfully" (1 Peter 5:6–7).

The way you humble yourself under the mighty hand of God is to refuse to try to figure everything out. Reasoning and worry are works of our flesh. Remember, as I said at the beginning of this chapter, peace will come by grace, but not by works.

Ezekiel 20:40 says that we should bring the Lord our firstfruits, the choicest selections of all our offerings. To stay in perfect peace, we should give God the best of our time and our goods. We must be honest with ourselves about what our priorities really are and start making changes to keep God in first place.

Being too busy is not an acceptable excuse for not keeping focused on what is truly important. Everyone sets his or her own schedule. We need to establish boundaries, and we need to learn to say no when people ask us to do something that leads us away from peace (I will talk more about saying no in the next chapter).

Be honest with yourself as you examine how you spend your time. Don't give God your leftovers; don't give Him the part of your day when you're worn-out and you can't think straight or hardly keep your eyes open. Give God the firstfruits of your attention. Give Him the best part of your day. That's where your real priorities will be found.

God needs to be your priority in *everything* you do. From getting dressed to setting your schedule, you can ask God for wisdom to make choices that will glorify Him. You can intermingle your time with God into everything you do to such a degree that you can pray without ceasing (as I suggested earlier, pray your way through the day). As you become aware of His presence, it will not be possible to compartmentalize God or separate secular activities from sacred ones. Even ordinary events will become sacred because He is involved in them.

You can just talk to God as you go about your day, asking Him to direct you in the choices you are making and to empower you for the jobs you need to get done. As you acknowledge that God is always with you, you will keep Him first in everything you set out to do, and He will show you a direct path that will lead you to peace. You will experience pleasure, knowing you are partnering with God in all you do.

Following the moment-by-moment leading of the Holy Spirit will cause you to enjoy every day of your life. The Spirit of God is creative; His mercies are new every morning, so if you follow the leadership of the Holy Spirit, He will keep your priorities straight. He will make sure your time with Him is right, and that your family time is right, and that you are fulfilling the work He has for you to do.

God will also energize you by grace to do whatever He leads you to do. If your priorities get out of order, you will labor in vain and tire quickly. In the next chapter we will look at how making healthy choices will help avoid stress, exhaustion, and upset so you can learn to enjoy your quiet times with God.

PEACEKEEPER #12

Protect Your Health

ॐ

No matter what people own in life or what their positions are, if their health is not good, they will not enjoy anything. Good health is one of the greatest treasures we have; it is a gift from God. The psalmist wrote, "Bless (affectionately, gratefully praise) the Lord, O my soul, and forget not [one of] all His benefits—Who forgives [every one of] all your iniquities, Who heals [each one of] all your diseases" (Psalm 103:2–3).

The apostle John wrote, "Beloved, I would that you prosper and be in health, even as I know your soul prospers" (see 3 John 1:2). We should do all we possibly can to protect our health, both physically and emotionally. It is sad to see people in our society regularly abuse their bodies and then wonder why they get sick.

I have discovered that it is much harder for me to remain peaceful under any kind of opposition if I also have the added stress of not feeling well. If I am really tired, it is more difficult for me to get along with people or display the fruit of the Spirit.

I have had long periods of time in my life of not feeling well, and I have heard the doctors say over and over, "You are under stress." Their diagnosis always frustrated me because I did not know how to live any way other than under stress. I thought I had no choice except to do all the things I was doing, even though I often admitted, "I can't do all this. It is too much."

Stress-related illnesses are rampant. I asked Dr. Don Colbert, a nutrition expert whom I greatly respect, to share how stress affects our health and nerves. He wrote, "Approximately 75–90% of all visits to primary-care physicians are for stress-related disorders. Chronic stress has actually been linked to most of the leading causes of death, including heart disease, cancer, lung ailments, accidents, cirrhosis, and suicide."

Dr. Colbert agrees that individuals must learn to protect themselves against stress, saying,

> Few people realize that the fast-paced lives they are living, the increasing demands on their schedules, and the way that they cope or react to stress or stressful situations are all in their control. Yes, we all have a choice to continue this hectic schedule; we can choose to react by becoming more and more frustrated, or we can learn to limit the demands on our everyday lives and react in love rather than frustration.

The following excerpt from Dr. Colbert is a report he shared with me of how the Canadian physician Hans Selye accidentally discovered the effects of stress on the physical body.

> Selye's vision was not to discover the effects of stress but to discover the next new female sex hormone. He had made an extract from ovaries and injected the extract solution into rats. However, Selye was not very skillful with his injection techniques. He always dropped the rats and spent much of the morning chasing the rodents around the room, using a broom to get them out from behind a desk or a sink. At the end of a few months, Selye discovered that the rats had developed enlarged adrenal glands, shrunken immune tissues, and peptic ulcers.
>
> Selye, however, thought this was due to the ovarian extract that he was injecting into the rats. So, he tested another group, and he injected them with only saline solution. Due to his poor coordination, however, he also dropped these rats, chased them around his lab, and also got the broom after

them. At the end of the experiment, the control rats had also developed the enlarged adrenal glands, the shrunken immune tissues, and the peptic ulcers. Selye then figured out that the cause *was not what he was injecting,* but *the tremendous stress he was putting the rats under* while trying to inject them. He had literally stressed the little creatures out. Dr. Selye determined that when stress is maintained long enough, the body undergoes three distinct stages: (1) the alarm stage, (2) the resistance stage, and (3) the exhaustion stage.

The alarm stage is the fight-or-flight emergency system that God created in our bodies for survival. The brain sends a signal to the pituitary gland to release a hormone that activates the adrenal glands. Adrenaline then sends the body into high alert. The brain becomes focused, the eyesight sharpens, and muscles clench as the body prepares for fighting or fleeing. This amazing alarm system has enabled multitudes of people to survive vicious attacks from animals, auto accidents, and other traumas. The body's hormonal system returns to normal when the perceived attack is over.

However, this alarm reaction is being activated hundreds of times a day in many Christians due to deadlines at work, financial pressures, arguments with a spouse or children, traffic jams, as well as all the common stresses of modern life. In other words, frustration, anger, guilt, grief, anxiety, fear, as well as most other emotions, will also set off this alarm system, which can then lead to a heart attack or stroke.

Dr. Selye's second stage of stress is called the resistance stage. When someone is undergoing a chronic stress such as having a child on drugs or alcohol or in jail, long-standing marital problems, a chronic illness, long-term unemployment, or some other situation over which he feels he has lost control over an extended period of time, [this] generally leads to the resistance stage of stress. This is another emergency system that God has placed within us so that we may survive periods of famine, disease, and pestilence. During this stage, our cortisol and adrenaline levels become elevated. Cortisol is very similar to the medication *cortisone,* which doctors give to treat asthma, arthritis, chronic obstructive pulmonary disease, as well as numerous other illnesses. However, release of cortisol can lead to elevation of blood sugar, which can eventually lead to diabetes and weight gain, especially in the abdominal area. Over time, it can result in bone loss, which can lead to osteopenia and osteoporosis. Elevated cortisol also leads to hypertension, memory loss, sleep deprivation, and a compromised immune system.

The resistance stage is similar to having the accelerator of your car stuck to the floorboard. Your system is all geared up and is unable to gear down, even at night. Individuals in this resistance stage generally have insomnia, or they wake up at two or three in the morning and find it very difficult to fall back to sleep. After patients have been living in the resistance stage for months or years, they will eventually enter into stage 3 of stress, which is the exhaustion stage.

People have entered the exhaustion stage when they feel burned-out. Examples of this stage are individuals with chronic fatigue, fibromyalgia, most autoimmune diseases including lupus, rheumatoid arthritis, MS, and usually cancer. In other words, these people have had the accelerator pressed to the floor for so long that eventually they run out of gas, and the powerful, robust bodies that God has given them, which He designed for health, begin to degenerate and die. The body is more prone to bacterial and viral infections, allergies, candida, environmental illness, inflammation of joints, and severe fatigue.*

It is obvious from this report that stress destroys the body's immune defense system. Once the immune system breaks down, it can be a difficult and lengthy process to restore it back to full health.

*Reprinted with permission. For more of Dr. Colbert's advice on better health, please visit his website at www.drcolbert.com.

To restore the immune system, people have to do what they should have done to begin with: Get lots of good rest; eat good-quality food, not junk food with no nutritional value; maintain peaceful lifestyles; and live balanced lives, which include worship, work, rest, and play. And people need to exercise as their systems permit them.

But we shouldn't wait until we are forced into doing the right thing. Let's act voluntarily and keep our health. The symptoms of stress are real, and though we can take medicine to mask or alleviate them, the root cause of many illnesses that we have is simply a stressful lifestyle. Unless we deal with the lifestyle, we will always have a new symptom pop up in some new way. The world will not change, so we must.

Dr. Colbert instructs people who are suffering from stress to avoid overcommitment and learn to be satisfied in order to circumvent overspending. He writes,

> The majority of our stress comes from the demands everyday life places on us and our choosing to walk the frustration-walk instead of the love-walk: by trying to enforce unenforceable rules. By simply walking the love-walk instead of the frustration-walk, one will be able to pull the roots of stress out of his or her life.

Stress depletes our bodies, our immune systems become weak, and sickness and depression can set in. Some stress is actually good for us; you might say it exercises various organs in the body. God designed our bodies to handle a certain amount of stress; it is only when we continually push ourselves beyond reasonable limits that we break down under the strain. It is when we get out of balance that we open a door for sickness in our lives. Excessive stress over a long period of time eventually causes our organs to just plain wear out.

Each time we say, "I am exhausted," we should realize that we are exhausting something in our bodies also. We recover from normal stress through proper rest; however, we can cause irreversible damage when we don't get needed rest.

We live in stressful times, but by following Jesus' advice and casting our cares on Him, we can live stress-free in a stressful world. If we will exalt Jesus, lift Him up, and put Him first by following the leadership of His Spirit, we will not end up exhausted.

Is Jesus exalted, or are you exhausted? To exalt someone is to put him above other things, to make him first. To be exhausted is to be completely worn-out, having no energy and being susceptible to sickness.

There is a popular worship song entitled "He Is Exalted." I was trying to sing this song once during a time when I was extremely tired, and I got my words mixed up and sang to the Lord, "You are exhausted."

He stopped me and said, "No, Joyce, I am exalted. You are the one who is exhausted."

Remember, God will always energize us to do *what He leads us* to do. It is only when we go beyond His will to follow our own will or other people's that we are likely to get exhausted. Second Corinthians 2:14 says that God always "leads us in triumph." It is not His will for us to live defeated, weak lives; He wants us to be more than conquerors. His will for us is strength, not weakness and sickness.

ARE YOU SUFFERING FROM EXHAUSTION?

Are you excessively tired all the time, and even after sleeping, do you wake up feeling tired all over again? Do you go to doctors, but they cannot find anything wrong with you? You may be experiencing some of the symptoms of exhaustion, or what I call burnout. Long periods of overexertion and stress can cause constant fatigue, headaches, sleeplessness, gastrointestinal problems, tenseness, a feeling of being tied in knots, and an inability to relax.

Some other signals of burnout are crying, being easily angered, negativity, irritability, depression, cynicism (scornful, mocking of the virtues of others), and bitterness toward others' blessings and even their good health.

Burnout causes us to be out of control, and when this happens, we are no longer producing good fruit in our daily lives. Burnout steals our joy, making peace impossible to find. When our bodies are not at peace, everything seems to be in turmoil.

God established the law of resting on the Sabbath to prevent burnout in our lives (see Mark 2:27). The law of the Sabbath simply says we can work six days, but by the seventh, we need to rest and spend time worshiping God. Even God rested after six days of work. He, of course, never gets tired but gave us this example so we would follow the pattern. In Exodus 23:10–12, we find that even the land had to rest after six years, and the Israelites were not to sow in it the seventh year. During this rest, everything recovered and prepared for future production.

Everything rested on the Sabbath: people, servants, and domestic animals. These were days of complete relaxation for the mind, emotions, and body. In Leviticus 26, we see that much turmoil and trouble come due to ignoring God's ordinances.

Today in America, almost every business is open seven days a week. Some of them are even open twenty-four hours a day, seven days a week. I have heard that after the pilgrims landed on Plymouth Rock and began to establish America, a drummer walked through the streets, signaling everyone to go to church on the Sabbath. After church, they rested the entire day. Sabbath-breakers were actually arrested!

People say we are free from the law of the Old Testament and that keeping the Sabbath was part of that old system. That's good, because people who broke the Sabbath then were stoned. Thankfully, we are not to be legalistic about it, but we do need to honor the spirit of the Sabbath principle. Jesus said the Sabbath was designed for man, which simply implies that we must rest at least one out of seven days. When we make ourselves available 24/7, we are in danger of burnout.

People today are quick to argue that they cannot afford to take a day off, but I say that they cannot afford not to do it. We often hear, "I am too busy to do that. I would never get everything done if I did that." My answer is, "Then you are too busy, and something needs to change in your life."

When we are too busy to obey God's ordinances, we will pay the price. Remember, the Bible says we reap only what we sow. If we sow continual stress with no rest to offset it, we will reap the results in our bodies, emotions, and minds.

If someone says, "Well, my boss insists that I work seven days a week," then I would say to get a new job. I learned from the story of Epaphroditus, who was working with Paul in the ministry and became so sick from overwork that he almost died, that even if I am overworking "for Jesus" (in my way of thinking), I will still pay the price for abusing my body.

Regular time set apart for God is one of the quickest ways to restore a tired mind and body. Jesus invited us to rest when He called for those "who labor and are heavy-laden and overburdened." He promised to ease and relieve and refresh our souls. He even offered "recreation and blessed quiet" for our souls (Matthew 11:28–30). Just lay your burdens on Jesus, spend time with Him, rest in His presence, and you will experience a glorious restoration. God delights in restoring all things.

Don't Wait Until It Is Too Late

The question is not *Do you have stress?* Everyone has stress. The question is *Are you managing your stress?* Use wisdom, which is really sanctified common sense. Realize you cannot spend something you don't have. Spending what one does not have is what causes financial stress and ultimately financial collapse. Spending energy we don't have has the exact same effect except it's on our physical health, rather than the financial realm.

Our bodies warn us when they are running low on energy. We should respect them. I can remember conferences in which I conducted five sessions consisting of three hours each, and instead of going home to rest like I needed to, I went to the shopping mall.

Of course, I felt extremely tired, but I would not go home. My head hurt, my feet hurt, I was grouchy and often felt discouraged, but I would not rest. I was not respecting my body; I was not listening to the warning signals it was giving me. I have since learned better. If I am out doing anything and I start to feel I am running out of energy, I don't wait until I am completely depleted. I go home while I still have some strength. I have learned the dangers of total exhaustion and have a reverential fear of abusing my body.

I ignored warnings in the past and paid the price. I am encouraging you not to wait until it is too late, and you have lost your health. Begin right now to respect your body, and treasure the health God has given you. I am grateful to be able to say that God has restored me, and I feel good most of the time. I also must say that I will probably have to be extra careful for the rest of my life. Once we push our bodies past where God intended them to go, we have weaknesses that will show up quickly with the slightest provocation.

Faith and prayer work. God will restore. He is the God of restoration, but we must also realize that we cannot continually ignore warnings. God is merciful, but He is also just. He put natural safety alarms in our bodies to indicate when we need rest, and He teaches us what to do when those alarms sound. He means what He says: We are the dwelling places of the Holy Spirit, and we should not do anything to hurt God's temple (see 1 Corinthians 3:17, 6:19).

Frequent Upset Damages Your Health

I spent many years getting upset frequently. There were probably very few days when I did not get aggravated about something, and often I did so several times each day. As I studied God's Word and gained wisdom, I began to realize that this required a lot of energy. I was tired most of the time and didn't have any energy to spare, so I knew I had to calm down. Jesus told His disciples, as recorded in John 14:27, that they were to stop allowing themselves to be "agitated and disturbed." He told them, in essence, to relax.

I don't know how much energy is required to get really upset and then to try to calm down, but I am sure it is a lot. It takes energy to resist getting frustrated, but not nearly as much as going through the entire cycle.

Eventually I learned to resist becoming upset as soon as I felt distressed. I learned to talk to myself and actually calm myself down by doing so. I asked God for help each time I started to feel that I was losing my peace. I was learning to "hold" my peace, just as Moses told the Israelites to do. He reassured them, "The LORD shall fight for you, and ye shall hold your peace" (Exodus 14:14 KJV). Frequently losing our tempers or having fits is damaging to our health.

What we often do to our bodies reminds me of a rubber band: When you stretch it too far, it breaks, and you have to tie it into a knot for continued use. Let this occur several times, and eventually all you have is knots. Like a rubber band, we can be stretched only so far, and then we ultimately break under the strain.

All the upset stretches us beyond our limits, and ultimately we break, so we tie a knot and keep going, then another and another until we go to the doctor and say, "I feel as if I am tied in knots and cannot relax." We don't know how accurate the statement really is.

Psalm 39:4–6 says, in essence, it is useless to be in turmoil, and how true that statement is. It does no good at all. The only one fulfilled when we get upset is the devil. He sets us up to get us frustrated anyway, so of course, he is delighted. He is the thief who only comes to kill, steal, and destroy. He wants to kill us, steal our health, and destroy our bodies and minds. We should do as Jesus did and say, "Get thee behind me, Satan. You are an offense, and you are in my way."

We might look at our bodies and energy levels as a bank account. We have enough for our lifetime. But if we spend it all early, we will feel depleted in our later years. I hate to see young people abusing their bodies through eating junk food excessively, never resting, and even perhaps using damaging chemical substances. I have tried to speak to a few, but I always get the same response. "Oh man, I feel great, got all kinds of energy." They don't understand that if they overspend today, they will do without later on in life.

LEARN TO SAY NO

One of the reasons I previously found myself stressed-out, burned-out, and sick was from not knowing how to say no. We all want to please people, but we might kill ourselves trying to do so.

I wanted to take every ministry opportunity that came my way, but it just was not possible. We must all learn to let God's Spirit, and not other people's desires, lead us. Frequently people tell me that God has showed them that I am supposed to come to their churches or conferences and be their speaker. There was a time when that would pressure me because I thought, *If I say no, then I am, in reality, saying they didn't hear from God.*

Other people cannot hear from God for us. We are individuals and have the right to hear from God ourselves. I started realizing that no matter what they thought they had heard, I could not do the engagement with peace and confidence if I had not heard it myself. Remember, God has no obligation to help me finish something He did not tell me to do.

Dr. Colbert teaches that many people are unable to say no

because they have passive personalities. He explains that most people fall into one of three personality categories: passive, aggressive, or assertive. He wrote the following scenario to show a typical situation for a passive person:

If you are passive, you usually have problems expressing your thoughts and feelings and find it difficult to stand up for yourself. Other people, especially the aggressive type, tend to walk all over you; they are able to manipulate and even make decisions for you. Passive individuals usually feel guilty and like they have to apologize. They usually have poor self-esteem and maintain poor eye contact or look away and down to the floor when you talk with them.

I have found so many Christians who are passive, and much of the stress that they are under is directly related to their passivity. You see, when someone is passive, other people's problems become his problems.

For example, a passive person will not be able to say no when people ask him to do something. An aggressive person at work may ask a passive fellow employee to stay later to help him finish his work because he has an important appointment. The passive individual is unable to say no, so he stays overtime, doing the other person's work. This may create problems with his spouse, since he comes home late from work, and this trend continues because the aggressive person will continue to put more and more on the back of the passive person, and the passive person allows it. Many times this is because the passive person has a good heart and good motives, and he lets the fear of rejection control his life. Instead he should assert his feelings and ideas and risk not being accepted.*

Are you saying yes with your mouth while your heart is screaming no? If so, you will eventually be stressed-out, burned-out, and

*Reprinted with permission.

possibly sick. We just cannot go on like that forever without ultimately breaking down under the strain. Be true to your own heart.

Don't be afraid to say no. Don't fear the rejection of others. No matter how many people you please, there will always be someone who will not be pleased. Face it now, and get it over with.

Learn that you can enjoy your life even if everyone does not think you are wonderful. Don't be addicted to approval from people; if God approves, that is all that really matters.

Don't try so hard to keep other people happy that it costs you your joy, peace, and health. None of the people who put pressure on you will stand before God and give an account of your life; only you will do that. Be prepared to be able to say to Him, "I followed my heart to the best of my ability."

Being committed is very good, but being overcommitted is very dangerous. As I said earlier, know your limits and don't hesitate to say no if you know that you need to. Tell people when you don't have peace about being involved in a certain activity or project. They should respect your rights and want you to have peace in your life. If they don't, then it is clear they are not thinking of what is good for you.

Remember that people can be very selfish. It is good to be a blessing, to do things for others and serve them, but not to the point that we get sick trying to keep everyone we know happy. I am not saying that we should never do anything we don't want to do. There are always times when we will serve others sacrificially, but we must not let their desires control us and push us into exhaustion and high levels of stress.

God has assigned a life span to each of us, and although we don't know exactly how long we have on earth, we should certainly desire to live out the fullness of our years. We want to burn on, not burn out. We should live with passion and zeal, not with exhaustion; we should be good examples to others.

Learn to say no when you need to—it will help you stay healthy!

BEND BEFORE YOU BREAK

People with aggressive personalities have their own sets of stress inducers that can work havoc in their health. Dr. Colbert writes:

> People with aggressive behavior generally dominate, intimidate, and bully others, and they are very confrontational. They tend to view their own needs as priority, and they stop at nothing to get what they want. Most of us have encountered aggressive drivers who cut us off in traffic or shake their fists at us.
>
> God desires for Christians to be neither passive nor aggressive, but *assertive*. Assertiveness allows people to communicate confidently, boldly, and clearly their thoughts, feelings, and desires. But unless they were raised in loving, stable home environments where they received encouragement, freedom to express themselves, and discipline with love, support, and acceptance, most Christians never learn assertiveness.
>
> Many Christians grew up in dysfunctional families. Instead of being programmed for success, they were programmed for failure. They heard they were no good, that they would never amount to anything, that they were losers. Some children responded passively to this environment; some became angry and aggressive.*

While we can see the danger of being too passive, we can also see that being inflexible and aggressive will not lead to healthy situations. Learning to be adaptable, considering the welfare of those around us, is one way we can keep peace.

Don't expect the world to adapt to you; be ready to bend before you break. When you start to feel stressed because things aren't going your way, and you sense peace ebbing away, quickly see what you can change to relieve the pressure. Most often you will need to

---

*Reprinted with permission.

simplify, simplify, simplify. The more simple your life, the more peace you will enjoy.

Keep in mind that being assertive is the healthy goal you are working toward. Assertiveness is like leather: It is tough to tear apart and will show only a small indention under the impact of a hammer, while aggressiveness is like brittle sandstone that easily crumbles if it is struck with a hard blow. Likewise an aggressive person's temper easily breaks or snaps under pressure, but an assertive person is able to stay flexible and in one piece.

We can see from pondering this comparison why Satan's plans can thrive in the life of an aggressive person. He intends to break us by applying force and pressure. However, he will not succeed if in the process we are willing to bend and remain flexible. His plans cause the stiff-necked or stubborn individuals to crumble easily, so they fall apart.

I used to be one of those aggressive people, but I realized long ago that it was not worth it. A little humility can preserve a lot of health. The Word warns us: "Be not like the horse or the mule, which lack understanding, which must have their mouths held firm with bit and bridle, or else they will not come with you" (Psalm 32:9).

The Word tells us to resist the devil, but if we resist the wrong things in life, we sacrifice precious energy. Stop trying to change things you cannot change. Let God be God! Adapt when you need to, and the reward will be worth it.

Flexibility will cause you to look young when others appear older than they actually are, you will have energy while others are tired, and you will still be bearing fruit in old age, long after others have retired.

People break when they try to do something about something they cannot do anything about. They burn out when they are trying to get something that only God can give or trying to make something go away that only God can remove. Resisting everything in life that we don't want creates a pressure inside of us that does a lot of damage to our health.

We all have things happen that we didn't plan for. We may get dressed in the morning, and we find a spot on our clothing. We didn't plan for that and don't have time for it. We can be frustrated and upset while we change clothes, we can go out with the spot on the clothes, or we can choose peacefully to change clothes since we have a situation we cannot do anything about. Think about it. What is the point in getting upset about something that will not change as a result of our being upset?

I remember a time, while conducting a conference, when we sent some luggage home early in one of our ministry trucks, thinking we no longer needed it. When we arrived at the airport, we discovered we did not have our tickets. To our dismay, we remembered they were in the luggage we sent home. We shared our story with the ticket agent, who said he could do nothing about it; the only possible solution was for us to repurchase tickets.

I felt upset building within me, then remembered my own messages and simply had a little talk with myself. I said, "Joyce, this is something you cannot do anything about; getting upset won't change it. So buy the tickets, and go home."

These types of situations occur regularly in all of our lives. Preserve your health by no longer trying to do something about something you cannot do anything about! Learning to stay calm in potentially upsetting situations is a great victory. Stability in all kinds of circumstances indicates great spiritual maturity.

PEACE BRINGS RESTORATION

One of the stress inducers we face daily in our society is noise. We live in a noisy society. In order to enjoy a peaceful atmosphere, we must create one. Outer peace develops inner peace. Find a place where you can go that is quiet, a place where you will not be interrupted, and learn to enjoy simply being quiet for periods of time. I have a certain chair in my living room where I sit and recover.

The chair is a white recliner that faces a window to our yard, which is filled with trees. In the spring and summer, I can watch the birds, rabbits, and squirrels. There was a time when I would have considered that boring, but not any longer—now I love it.

When I return from a conference now, I go home, take a hot bath, and then sit in that chair. Sometimes I sit there for several hours. I may read a little, pray, or just look out the patio door window, but the point is I am *sitting still and enjoying the quiet*. I have discovered that quiet helps me recover.

Being still has a soothing effect on us. Peace produces more peace. If we find peaceful places and remain in them for a while, we will begin to feel calmness engulf our souls. We cannot live noisy lives continually and expect to feel peaceful.

Some people have to have some noise in their atmospheres all the time. They always have music, or the television or radio, playing. They want someone with them all the time so they can talk. Each of these things done in balance is good, but we also need complete quiet and what I call *alone time*.

Jesus made sure He had seasons of peace and alone time. He ministered to the people, but He slipped away regularly from the crowds to be alone and pray. "But so much the more the news spread abroad concerning Him, and great crowds kept coming together to hear [Him] and to be healed by Him of their infirmities. But He Himself withdrew [in retirement] to the wilderness (desert) and prayed" (Luke 5:15–16). Surely if Jesus needed this type of lifestyle, we do also.

In Luke 9, we read of one occasion when Jesus took Peter, James, and John with Him to a mountain to pray, and they saw His face transfigured (changed). Verse 29 says, "And as He was praying, the appearance of His countenance became altered (different), and His raiment became dazzling white [flashing with the brilliance of lightning]."

When we get alone and take time for prayer, we will also be changed: Our weaknesses will turn into strengths. Our countenances will reflect the peace of being in God's presence. Isaiah 40:31 confirms, "But those who wait for the Lord [who expect, look for, and hope in Him] shall change and renew their strength and power; they shall lift their wings and mount up [close to God] as eagles [mount up to the sun]; they shall run and not be weary, they shall walk and not faint or become tired."

Waiting on God quietly does more to restore our bodies, minds, and emotions than anything else. We need it regularly. Insist on having it; don't let anyone take it from you. Work your schedule around God; don't try to work Him into your schedule.

You may have tried everything to feel better, but I encourage you to take my suggestion and try regular doses of quiet. I believe you will see restoration and increased peace. Remember, outer peace helps develop inner peace. Rest in God's presence, and you will take His peace with you when you go back to normal activity.

If you have peace, you can minister peace to others. Jesus was able to speak peace to the storm only because He had peace within Him. I believe He had peace within because He regularly found time to rest simply in quiet and spend time with His heavenly Father.

I hope that you can see how important it is to relieve yourself of emotional stress in order to hold your peace. In the next chapter we will look at how balancing your spending habits is both a practical and powerful way to maintain the peace you have found so far.

PEACEKEEPER #13

Avoid Financial Pressure

❧⟡❧

According to a survey our ministry conducted, the number-one problem most people face is financial pressure. Being in debt and not having enough money creates terrible stress on people, and it definitely steals our peace. Financial pressure is also one of the major causes of problems in marriages and is the culprit behind many divorces and even suicides.

We realize that people can find themselves in unfortunate circumstances that they could not control, but usually people create financial pressure through a lack of wisdom. When you have more money going out than coming in, it will eventually cause major problems.

The first step in people's receiving help is to face truth about how they reached their current condition. Most people who are pressured by debt feel sorry for themselves, believing they are not at fault, thinking that they are not responsible for the debts they have.

If we are feeling financial pressure, we must ask, "Were my circumstances really beyond my control, or could things have been different if I had made better choices?"

Of course, we cannot blame our debts on someone else, and repentance is the first step to recovery. Spending more money than we have is a sin, just like any other excess in our lives, and it requires God's forgiveness.

Only truth sets us free. You may have heard the statement "The truth hurts," which is true, but staying in bondage hurts even worse. If we have managed our finances poorly, made unwise choices, or acted out of emotion, we should simply admit it to ourselves and to God, ask His forgiveness, and begin immediately reversing the situation through the power of right choices.

If your finances are causing you to lose peace, ask God for a plan, get professional help if you need it, and be willing to wait on obtaining things you desire. Making bad choices is what gets us in trouble, and making right choices is what will get us out of trouble. However, making one right choice will not undo the negative result that years of bad choices have caused.

Prepare to remain steadfast. Patience will be vital to work yourself out of financial stress, but it will be worth it in the end. Anyone can be financially blessed and stable if he or she really wants to be.

Every person can prosper. Every person can have financial security, but that man or woman must follow God's guidelines. To simplify it, we can say that His guidelines are to tithe and give offerings and use wisdom in spending. God will always provide what we need if we are givers. He may not always provide everything we would like to have.

God definitely wants to bless, radically and outrageously, all of His children. The Word says that the Lord takes pleasure in the prosperity of His servant (see Psalm 35:27).

God wants us to prosper, but not out of proportion to our spiritual growth. If people are immature or carnal, which means they live according to fleshly desires, they don't really need an abundance of money and things because they will probably use them only in selfish ways. Possessions can actually take us away from God rather than bring us closer to Him, unless we understand they are tools to use as a blessing in a hurting world. God will release more and more to us as we grow spiritually. Ask God for what you want and desire, but also ask Him not to give you any more than He knows you can handle.

CREDIT CARDS

Almost everyone uses credit cards. We use them for convenience. We pay with credit cards and then weekly write checks out of our account to cover the charges. We put the checks in an envelope until the bill comes. It is easy to charge things, but it is also easy to lose track of the total being charged.

I highly recommend that you either follow our example or keep a running total of items charged so you know at all times the state of your finances. Losing track of what is going on is probably one of the major causes for financial pressure.

Using credit cards responsibly is not a problem, but when people charge things they don't have the money to pay for, it is a problem. Many people don't know how to delay gratification. We are accustomed to instant everything: We want what we want *now!*

Are you spending tomorrow's prosperity today? You are if you are charging merchandise that you don't currently have the money to pay for. If you spend tomorrow's paycheck today, what will you do when tomorrow comes? You will have to use credit cards again, and the cycle will never end.

The amount of credit-card debt in the world is unbelievable. The pressure that the media put on people to acquire new products is amazing. We are merchandise-crazy in our society; the quest to have the newest items is out of control. People will work two jobs and ignore their families, sometimes losing them in the process, just to have bigger houses or newer model cars.

Are things really that important? Do you have drawers and closets full of things you went in debt to have that you really don't even enjoy now? Are you making payments on things that have already worn out or that you have lost track of? The world says, "Buy now, pay later," but that is not what wisdom says. Wisdom says, "Do now what you will be satisfied with later." We cannot be satisfied paying for something for months and even years after we no longer are using it. The desire for instant gratification is stealing many people's financial peace.

We know from Scripture that God wants His children to be abundantly blessed, and He provides the following plan for it to happen:

Will a man rob or defraud God? Yet you rob and defraud Me. But you say, In what way do we rob or defraud You? [You have withheld your] tithes and offerings. You are cursed with the curse, for you are robbing Me, even this whole nation. . . . Bring all the tithes (the whole tenth of your income) into the storehouse, that there may be food in My house, and prove Me now by it, says the Lord of hosts, if I will not open the windows of heaven for you and pour you out a blessing, that there shall not be room enough to receive it. (Malachi 3:8–10)

If we do what God tells us to do, He will never fail to do what He promises to do. His way works. Millions will testify to miraculous breakthroughs in their finances as a result of tithing (giving 10 percent).

As I mentioned at the beginning of this chapter, being willing to tithe and give other offerings as God leads is the first step to overcoming the pressure of debt. Many say, "I cannot afford to do that. After all, I am in debt!" I say, "You cannot afford not to do it. If you don't, you will stay in debt."

One way to remember the simple principle of financial gain is that tithing brings increase, while credit cards bring decrease to your financial peace. Most of us, at some time or other in our lives, experience firsthand the pressure of credit-card debt. Some people are wearing their tithe right now, or they are driving it, or they have used it up on a vacation they did not even enjoy or on other equally unwise things. Give to God what belongs to God, and He will always make sure you have your other needs met.

Early in our marriage, I begged Dave for a credit card. We didn't have much money, and I wanted to buy things. He really did not want to get one but finally relented.

We began with caution, but like most people, we ended up using the card for things we really did not need but simply wanted. Soon we had a huge balance and were making minimum payments, which never reduced the principal amount we owed. We were paying interest on things we had already used up and certainly could have done without.

Again, wisdom is to do now what will bring satisfaction and contentment later, while impulse is to do now what will later bring regret and even despair. Instant gratification—getting something we really want immediately—feels good, but later on, when we are paying and paying, we usually are not satisfied.

Dave was wise enough to refuse to live like that, so we cut up the card and kept making payments until we paid off the balance. We did without credit cards for years because we had proven we were not able to handle them. We did eventually get them again, but only after we had developed enough self-control to use them only for convenience in paying for things while in the store. Then we went right home and deducted the money from our checking account.

One of our managers has shared openly that he and his wife did the same thing as Dave and I, and millions of others, had done. When they decided to get out of debt, they paid for eight years on credit cards, while not using them, in order to pay them totally off.

When people are making payments on houses, one or two cars, school loans, furniture, perhaps other loans, and two or three credit cards, how could they possibly be anything other than stressed to the maximum degree? Very few individuals make enough to handle that kind of payment pressure.

No matter how much money someone makes, that is not the proper way to manage it. We have known of people who became bitter at their employers, thinking they were not paid enough to do their jobs, when in reality they were simply living beyond their means. Don't blame the results of a bad decision on someone else—only the truth will make you free.

Be very careful about making any kind of purchase on time payments, and when you do, be sure you look seriously at how long you will be making the payment and how much interest you will pay over the months or years involved. Ask yourself if you believe it will be worth it to you later on, as well as right now. Remember that emotions subside. We can all do things in excitement and be very sorry later on in life.

Through the convenience of the financial aids on the Internet, you can find a site that will give you an amortization schedule that will calculate how long it will take you to pay off a current debt. For example, if you have $20,000 of credit-card debt, which you are paying at $300 per month with an interest rate of 12.99 percent, it will take you 10 years to pay it off! And you will pay over $15,000 in interest charges! If you pay $500 per month, it will take you nearly 5 years to pay off the loan, but you will still pay over $6,000 in interest.

Obviously, the gratification that you may feel when purchasing items on credit will not be so tempting if you calculate the amount of interest and the amount of time it will take you to pay off your debt.

Filing Bankruptcy

If debt has overwhelmed you, you may have filed bankruptcy—or perhaps you are thinking about making that decision now. I don't mean any of what I am about to say to condemn anyone, but I do wish to make it plain how filing bankruptcy affects your credit rating later in life and sometimes follows you all of your life.

First, let me say there may be legitimate reasons to file bankruptcy. When I was eighteen years old, I was married to a man who would not work, committed adultery, stole things, wrote bad checks, and eventually ended up in prison. When we were divorced, I suddenly found that I was responsible legally to pay all of his debts. At that time I felt I had no choice, it seemed impossible and unfair for me to pay for his debt, so I decided to file bankruptcy. Had I known God as I do now and been aware of His Word and delivering power, I might have made a different choice.

It took a few years to overcome my bad credit rating. Bankruptcy should never be our first choice; we should do everything we possibly can to pay our debts. First Timothy 3 teaches us that Christians should have a good reputation with the world so no one has a reason to judge them. Not paying our bills does not help our reputation.

Today, filing bankruptcy is far too easy and becomes an answer for far too many people. It certainly should not be the solution for poor financial management. When people live excessively, they will eventually need to suffer to bring things back into balance. Bankruptcy may relieve current pressure, but it creates another type of pressure for years to come.

We find many people in financial trouble today; actually, the number is quite astounding. It is usually a result of poor management and choices. Some people have since learned wisdom and are making better choices, but they still find they are paying the price for past mistakes. God forgives us, but creditors are not quite as forgiving as God is. They want their money!

Even though God is forgiving, He expects us to pay for what we have taken from others. The Word says, "The wicked borrow and pay not again [for they may be unable], but the [uncompromisingly] righteous deal kindly and give [for they are able]. For such as are blessed of God shall [in the end] inherit the earth" (Psalm 37:21–22).

I believe God wants people to pay their debts, and He helps people, quite often through miracles, when they begin doing what is right. It is encouraging to hear of testimonies about how God has miraculously gotten someone completely out of debt. It is good to believe for a miracle, but at the same time, we need to do what we can.

As a matter of fact, I believe people don't receive miracles if they have not been sowing seeds of obedience to God. I tell people all the time, "If you do what you can do, God will do what you cannot do." Don't be the type of person who believes God for a miracle in his finances but who is not willing to do what he can do to help the process.

If you have poor credit and a lot of debt, you might have to work extra hard for a few years and show diligence in paying off your bills. Most companies will work with people having financial difficulty if the people are willing to do something. Even if you can pay only ten dollars per month on a loan balance, do what you can. Remember that God blesses diligence, but He does not bless laziness and excuses.

Don't take the easy way out (bankruptcy) just because you might be able to legally. Do all you possibly can in order not to have a bad financial reputation.

If you have already ruined your credit rating, I do believe you can overcome it, but you will need to be patient and persistent. If you are making financial decisions right now and still can avoid making bad choices, I pray this book will help you really think about what you are doing and the long-term effects of your choices.

Remember, what we sow today, we reap tomorrow, and tomorrow always comes. Too often people want instant gratification, and they don't think about tomorrow, but I repeat: *Tomorrow always comes.*

RESOURCES FOR FINANCIAL PROSPERITY

God gives resources to all of us. He is not a respecter of persons; He does not play favorites. God gives all of us time, energy, gifts, talents, and finances. If we make right choices with what we have, it will always multiply. If we make wrong choices, we deplete our resources and end up with nothing.

Let's take energy as an example. Most young people feel good, they have lots of energy and can go and go like the Energizer bunny. As I mentioned in the previous chapter, often they don't take care of themselves; they actually abuse their bodies and later on in life find themselves sick and facing serious health issues.

Time is another good example. We all have the exact same amount, yet some people accomplish a lot while others do nothing. Some people constantly say they have no time, yet they have as much as anyone else. Very often in my life, I have used my day to work on a book or teaching for an upcoming conference, while other people I knew played all day. A concert pianist spent a lot of time practicing while other children were playing. A person who wins a gold medal at the Olympics in figure skating practiced while others played.

Those who accomplished their objectives made a choice that brought an unusual reward. They were not just "lucky" or blessed more than others; they worked hard, and they used their time to accomplish their goals in life.

I am certainly not saying that we don't need to play at times, and I realize there have been times in my life when I was a workaholic, but God did say to work six days and rest one. Our world is way out of balance when people want to play more than work, and they too often seek entertainment.

People often ask me how I accomplish what I do, and the answer is *I work*. I don't feel that I am out of balance; I make sure I have fun and get rest, but I am also a hard worker. I am using my time to leave a legacy for the world in books, tapes, television, and radio programs. I want my being here to matter. I don't want just to pass through the world and take up space for eighty or ninety years, then die and have nobody remember I was here. I want people to be reading my books several hundred years from now, unless Jesus returns.

Time is a resource, and most people waste a lot of theirs. I heard myself say one day that I felt I "spent" a lot of my time getting dressed, putting on makeup, fixing my hair, getting my nails done, and so forth. God spoke to my heart and said, "That is right, you 'spend' time, so make sure it is worth it."

Any area of our lives can get out of balance. I strongly believe we should look as nice as possible, and to do so we must spend some time on personal grooming. Some people don't put in any time on their appearances, and others spend too much. All we really need in any area is balance.

Another resource is gifts and talents. Everyone can do things; they have abilities and should be using them. If we don't use something, we often lose it; or if it lies dormant, it doesn't do us or anyone else any good.

What am I doing with what God has given me? This should be one of the questions we regularly ask ourselves. If we are not satisfied with the answer, we need to make changes.

There are many things I cannot do; for example, I cannot sing well enough to do anything other than make a joyful noise, but I can talk. I have a gift of communication, and God is using it since I offered all my abilities and myself to Him. Everyone should stop moaning about what he or she cannot do, and start doing what he or she can do. If you use your resources, God will be pleased, and He will multiply what you have.

Matthew 25:15–29 teaches us about resources a master gave his servants. The Bible refers to these resources as "talents." In this passage of Scripture, the talents were money that the servants were to use properly until the master's return, at which time he would require an accounting. As you read the story, you will find that one took what he had been given and increased it five times. Another servant took his and increased it two times. Another did nothing with his, except hide it in fear that the master would be upset if he lost it.

When the master returned, he was very pleased with the two who had multiplied what he had given them, but he rebuked the one who did nothing. The master called him "wicked and lazy and idle" (v. 26) and took from him what he had and gave it to the one who had multiplied most.

This is God's way. He gives to all people what they can handle and waits to see what they do with it. Those who do nothing always become losers in life, and those who work hard, investing their resources and multiplying, always become winners. The master told the two who invested and had a good return he would put them in charge of more and allow them to share in their master's joy.

I believe people are happier and experience more joy and peace in life when they are using their resources. We all have a built-in knowledge that it is right to make progress and wrong to sit idle and watch life pass us by.

Usually people who do nothing are jealous of those who prosper. Don't be jealous of what someone has if you are not willing to do what he or she did to get it.

God expects us to manage what He gives us and to use it wisely so it will increase. We are not blessed in any way when we waste our resources, and we always pay the price for waste. One of our resources is the ability to work. In fact, the Bible instructs us to work!

For while we were yet with you, we gave you this rule and charge: If anyone will not work, neither let him eat. Indeed, we hear that some among you are disorderly [that they are passing their lives in idleness, neglectful of duty], being busy with other people's affairs instead of their own and doing no work. Now we charge and exhort such persons [as ministers in Him exhorting those] in the Lord Jesus Christ (the Messiah) that they work in quietness and earn their own food and other necessities. (2 Thessalonians 3:10–12)

This, of course, does not apply to those who are too old or ill to work. God provides for them in other ways, but those of us who can work, He expects to do so. God worked and then rested from His labors, and we should follow His example. Deuteronomy 28:11–12 declares that God will bless the work of our hands; He doesn't bless our laziness.

DISCIPLINE AND SELF-CONTROL

Relieving financial pressure will require discipline and self-control. The Bible teaches in many places the importance of discipline. If we don't discipline ourselves, our circumstances will eventually do it for us. God's Word tells us to be temperate, which means to be marked by moderation, to hold ourselves within limits (to compromise between two extremes or find the middle ground).

Clearly, we are to maintain balance. It is wrong to overspend, but it is also wrong to underspend. You may be at a point where you need to stop spending for a while, or perhaps you need to take some of your money and go do something with it. God gives us money not to hoard, but to enjoy. Wisdom saves some, spends some, and gives some.

My husband is a very good financial manager, and that is his motto: "Save some, spend some, and give some within your borders, and you will always be blessed!"

Don't let emotions rule you—discipline them. Don't let them take charge or lead your decisions. As I stated previously, emotions rise, but they also subside. Emotions can rally you to begin a thing, but they won't be there for the finish. You may experience excitement about making a purchase but feel depression when it is time to make the payment. Emotions are fickle—they change regularly. To depend on them is a foolish choice.

Part of discipline is always to know the state of your finances. Balance your checkbook regularly; if you do not, you may think you have more money than you do and write checks that will be returned, marked "insufficient funds." When that happens, the bank usually charges at least a ten- or fifteen-dollar fee for handling. This costs you more money and only adds to the problem.

It is amazing to me how many people write checks they don't have the money to cover. In our ministry, people have sometimes given offerings and purchased products with bad checks or credit cards that have already reached their approved limits.

This should not occur with anybody, but definitely not among Christians. We are the light of the world; we are supposedly setting an example for others to follow. We are to be excellent and show forth integrity. Obviously, writing bad checks does not help accomplish any of our biblical goals.

I realize we can all make mistakes. I have had a check returned a couple of times in my life. But it was because I just added wrong or forgot to deduct a check, not that I wasn't paying any attention to my finances.

Too many people spend money without knowing how much they have. I dealt with one person who seemed to have no ability to look ahead. If she had three hundred dollars in her account, she thought she could spend it. She forgot that she still had not paid her electric bill that month.

Look ahead at what bills are going to be due, and consider when your next paycheck will be, before spending money just because it is in your bank account. Never run your account to zero, because there will always be something that you did not expect. Put aside money for emergencies, and you will enjoy a lot more peace.

COMMON SENSE

Managing our finances is not really that difficult if we learn to follow some commonsense principles.

1. Tithe and give offerings regularly.
2. Don't spend more money than you have coming in.

3. Always know the state of your finances.
4. Always plan for emergencies.
5. Don't waste money.
6. Don't spend tomorrow's prosperity today.
7. Let emotions subside before you decide to make a purchase.
8. Use tremendous wisdom with credit cards.
9. Practice delayed gratification; resist impulse purchases.
10. Always follow the guideline of "Save some, spend some, and give some within your means."

SAVE SOME

Always save a portion of whatever income you earn, no matter how small it may be—make a commitment and stick to it. One gentleman shared that his father had taught him always to give 10 percent of everything he earned and to save 10 percent. He had been practicing his father's advice all of his life, and at the age of thirty-seven he already had a sizeable amount of money and no debt. His house and car were both paid for, and at a very early age he was able to work out of his home as a consultant, making his own hours, with no financial pressure at all.

Even saving 1 percent would be better than nothing. It would be a place to begin, and you could increase from there. Do something, lest you do nothing! Without some cash saved, you will never be able to buy things without paying interest. Save for things you eventually want to buy, save for retirement, save for emergencies. *Save—save—save.* Have several accounts at one time that you are putting some money into for future needs. Save all year for Christmas, for example, and when that time comes, you will be prepared.

When Dave was a young boy, he hid money in his socks. He paid cash for his first car, which was preowned, but he later paid cash for a new car when he was about twenty-two. That is amazing, but anyone can do it if he is willing to start saving and be diligent at it. Although Dave no longer hides money in his socks, he calls his various accounts his "stash" or his "socks." Everyone in our family has learned a lot about finances just by watching Dave. He is a very patient man and can wait on things he wants. He saves and does things at the right time.

As a result of his administrative gifts, we have been able to pay cash for everything at the ministry. We have been in ministry since 1976 and in our own ministry since 1985. Since incorporating, we have made payments on only one piece of equipment (a five-hundred-dollar copy machine). We even paid cash for the building we now occupy. That sounds almost impossible in today's economy, but it can be done.

Dave simply won't buy things for which he cannot pay. He had to do without some things in the beginning while saving, but once he gained momentum and had money saved, it put him, instead of the debt collector, in charge.

We could have borrowed money and built our ministry headquarters in one year, but we took five years to build it because we wanted to move in debt-free. Patience is always worth it in the end! I am certainly not judging anyone who cannot pay cash for everything he or she does, but I am sharing that it is possible through saving regularly.

SPEND SOME

I already mentioned the fact that some people actually need to spend some of their money. Maybe it's time you did something special for yourself; it ministers to your weary emotions to do so, and that is not wrong at all. I realize this may excite you, but make sure you are one who actually *needs* to spend. And I am referring to spending out of what you have saved. Don't spend what you need for other things, and whatever you do, don't go spend what you don't have.

The ones who actually *need* to spend are people who have a tendency to be excessive in saving. They hoard things, save everything for the future, and spend nothing for now. Most of the time, people hoard out of fear or greed. I noticed that when I began saving money, I accumulated a certain amount and thought it was awesome, and the more I saved, the more I wanted to save and became unwilling to spend any of it. I wanted a big balance in my account. I then noticed that when I refused to spend any, God stopped supplying. He wants us to enjoy what He gives as well as save for the future.

If I spent some as He directed, He then replenished it and gave more besides. It is like the principle of pruning bushes. Without pruning (cutting back), they can keep getting bigger and bigger, but they also become a problem. If we prune them, they grow right back, but in better shape and condition than before.

Some people won't spend anything on themselves because they don't feel they are worthy of anything. Some are martyrs; they want to be able to say that they never do anything for themselves, hoping it will invoke pity. Some people are just plain stingy, and they hoard everything because it makes them feel secure and powerful to own things. Whatever the reason, it is wrong to be out of balance. A balanced person saves some, spends some, and gives some.

If you are working your way out of debt, and as a result you are never able to spend anything on yourself, I believe God will do special things for you through other people. When you are doing your part, God always does His part. Ask Him to bless you supernaturally, but refuse to go deeper in debt.

GIVE SOME

Giving is actually one of the wisest choices anyone ever makes. The Bible says to give and it shall be given to you, and "good measure, pressed down, shaken together, and running over" will men give back to you (Luke 6:38). Giving is wisdom, because it actually causes increase. Learning to give is one of the greatest things that ever happened to me, and many others will testify to the same thing. I heard one woman, who has a very wonderful life, recently say, "My life is a result of giving." That is a statement we should ponder.

Are you a giver? If not, you should start today. God requires the first 10 percent of all of our increase (as we saw in Malachi 3). We are to give it to the "storehouse," the place or places where we are spiritually fed (see Exodus 34:26). In addition to that, He leads us to give other offerings at various times and on special occasions.

When you give, do it with a great attitude. Don't ever give as an obligation, but realize it is a privilege. Second Corinthians 9 gives us a lot of wonderful insight about the principles of giving. It says we should not give "reluctantly or sorrowfully or under compulsion, for God loves . . . a cheerful . . . giver, [whose heart is in his giving]" (v.7). The attitude with which we give is very important to God. We are to give to bless. God blesses us so we can be a blessing.

Many people find it difficult to give, especially when they are not accustomed to doing it. The basic nature of the flesh is to be selfish; we want to own things, not give them away. But when people receive Jesus Christ as Savior, their nature changes; they receive the nature of God. This nature comes as a seed on the inside of their spirits, and they are to water that seed with God's Word. As they do so, they begin to want to do what God would do. God is a giver; those who serve Him must be givers also.

Dave grew up in a church whose minister taught the blessing of tithing; therefore, we have been tithing since we got married. We have always seen God meet our needs. In thirty-six years of marriage, Dave has been without a job only about two days, if my memory serves me correctly. We had some tight years, but we always paid bills on time and never did without the necessities of life.

In 1976, when God touched my life and called us into ministry, we began giving more than ever. We wanted to go beyond our tithe. We endured times of testing, but we have never been sorry concerning the decision we made. We have continued to increase our giving over the years and have seen God be faithful to increase us as well.

I believe givers receive a harvest back in any area where they have need. Thank God He provides financially, but that is not the only area of provision. He gives us grace. "And God is able to make all grace abound to you, so that in all things at all times, having all that you need, you will abound in every good work" (2 Corinthians 9:8 NIV). We see from this Scripture that God gives grace in abundance so we have *all* our needs met.

FROM POVERTY TO PROSPERITY

If you have been making right choices and are enjoying prosperity, keep doing what you are doing. Don't ever backslide in the principles of wisdom you have learned.

If you find yourself in debt or in need, get started now doing what is right. If you don't, you will still be in the same situation next year, and the year after, and so on. Pay the price to have financial freedom and security. No matter how big of a mess you are in—*if you consistently do what you can do, God will do what you cannot do*. Remember the simple formula: save some, spend some, and give some within your means, and you will soon find your situation changing. Not having to worry about money will greatly increase your peace.

Keep Your Thoughts Above Life's Storms

Although people cannot see our thoughts, they can see the results of them. What is in our minds and hearts is what comes out through the words of our mouths. If we have troubled minds, we will not live peaceful, serene lives. We will not minister peace to others, because we cannot give to others what we do not have within ourselves.

Jesus said we are to be makers and maintainers of peace. Paul said to work for what makes for peace, unity, harmony, and agreement with others. It is very important to make peace a priority, but it begins inside of us.

As I said earlier, Jesus was able to quiet the storm outside because He maintained peace within Himself. Jesus did not have His mind on the storm even though it was raging against Him. While the disciples were frantic and fearful, Jesus slept. He had peace in the midst of the calamity and was able to actually calm it. He had peace; therefore He could speak peace to the circumstances.

Isaiah said if we keep our minds on the Lord, He will *give* us perfect and constant peace (see Isaiah 26:3). God's Word has a great deal to say about our minds and how we think. Proverbs 23:7 teaches us that as a man thinks, so will he become. I say it another way: Where the mind goes, the man follows. Thoughts precede actions!

CAN WE CONTROL OUR THOUGHTS?

We cannot control the thoughts that come to us, but we can control what we continue to think about. For many years of my life, I simply did what most people do: I thought about whatever came into my mind. I did not know I had a choice. The Bible teaches us that the mind is the area Satan tries to control. He offers thoughts for us to entertain on a regular basis; we can either keep them or cast them down and replace them with God's thoughts.

God's written Word is a record of His thoughts toward us and about the way we are to live. The Bible literally covers every area of life. If we order our thoughts and conversation according to God's Word, we will be amazed at how enjoyable and prosperous life will be. But first we must believe that we can choose our own thoughts and that we don't have to meditate on whatever happens to fall into our minds.

Second Corinthians 10:4–5 are important Scriptures for Christians to understand: "The weapons we fight with are not the weapons of the world. On the contrary, they have divine power to demolish strongholds. We demolish arguments and every pretension that sets itself up against the knowledge of God, and we take captive every thought to make it obedient to Christ" (NIV).

This passage of the Word explains that we have spiritual weapons with which we can demolish any argument that "sets itself up against the knowledge of God," and that we have been given divine power to "demolish strongholds" and "take captive every thought and make it obedient" to the knowledge of Christ. These verses teach us that Satan tries to build strongholds in our minds so he can dominate areas of our lives through wrong thinking.

Satan is a liar, and if we believe his lies, he has successfully deceived us in one or more areas. For example, Satan told me for years that I would never have a good life because I had been abused in my childhood. I did not know any different, so I believed what I thought. As I became a student of God's Word, I learned that even though my past had been unpleasant, God had a great future planned for me. I learned it was not too late for me, as Satan had been telling me for years.

God's Word renews our minds; it teaches us a new way of thinking. We can begin to think the way God thinks instead of the way the devil would like us to think. Instead of looking at a nice home and thinking, *I could never own a home like that,* we can think (and say), *God will bless me with a lovely home. He meets all my needs.*

Instead of thinking we will get cancer because three relatives in our family died of it, we can think, *The blood of Jesus protects me, His name is a hiding place for me, God's healing power is working in my body right now, making right anything that is wrong.*

Instead of thinking we absolutely cannot forgive someone who has hurt us, we can think like this: *I am hurting, and what has been done to me is wrong, but I trust God to vindicate me. I can forgive through the power of the Holy Spirit. I will pray for the one who hurt me, I will bless him, and God will give me double blessings for my former trouble.*

Think about what you think about. If you start to feel depressed, discouraged, or angry, stop and examine your thoughts. You will find that you have been thinking thoughts that are producing the negative emotions you are experiencing. We can make ourselves miserable or happy by what we choose to think about.

When writing about the effect stress has on our health, Dr. Colbert included the following review on the importance of keeping our thoughts in line with God's Word:

Perhaps the greatest stresses that one encounters are the [unexpected] storms of life. It may be a personal injury or illness of a family member, friend, or oneself, a marital separation or divorce, the death of a relative or close friend, being fired at work, a lawsuit, finding out your daughter is pregnant out of wedlock or has had an abortion, or that your child is on drugs. These are the storms of life that seem to occur at the most inopportune times. Most of us want these problems to go away, and when they don't, they leave us even more frustrated and stressed than before, and our minds constantly seem to dwell on the problem, with no answer in sight.

When confronted with a problem like this, the first thing we need to do is realize that in this world we will have tribulation—we have been promised that. Jesus said, "I have overcome the world" (John 16:33). And "many are the afflictions of the righteous, but the LORD delivereth him out of them all" (Psalm 34:19 KJV).

So, in other words, we should be able to accept problems as an inevitable part of our lives and see them as potential teachers rather than analyzing, meditating on, and struggling over them.

I once heard a preacher use the term "renting too much space in our minds out to problems." The preacher talked about a man who had bought an apartment complex and rented out 90 percent of the apartments to drug addicts, prostitutes, and gang members, and 10 percent of the complex to law-abiding citizens who actually paid their rent. Well, after a few months, the 90 percent had run off the other 10 percent. Then the drug addicts, prostitutes, and gang members took up the whole complex, and no one was paying rent.

A similar thing happens in our minds when we start pondering, mulling over, and worrying about problems over which we have no control. We end up renting too much space in our minds to these problems, and they eventually take over most of our thoughts. In other words, we dwell on the problem, not the answer. We forget the second part of the Scripture in Psalm 34:19: "Many are the afflictions of the righteous: *but the LORD delivereth him out of them all*" (KJV, italics mine).

Instead of renting so much space to our problems, we have got to learn how to turn the channel of our minds from the worry channel to the praise-and-worship channel, the joy channel, the appreciation channel, the love channel, or the laughter channel, and start focusing on the things that are good in our lives. When we focus too much on a problem, it only makes the problem stronger. Then fretting actually becomes a habit, and the habit becomes very difficult to break.

The average person has about fifty thousand thoughts a day, and for many, these thoughts are mainly pessimistic and negative. When you are confronted with a negative thought, you have the option of either ignoring it or inviting it in and analyzing it, meditating on it, and allowing it to rent more space in your mind.

When you do the latter, you begin to speak out the problem with your mouth, and it becomes a word. You ponder it more, and it becomes an action. You then analyze and meditate on it more, and it becomes a habit, and unfortunately for the majority of Christians, most of their problems are simply negative thoughts that have become habits.

When confronted with a problem that you have no control over, ask God what He wants you to learn from it. Try to find out what He is trying to teach you by permitting the situation to remain longer than you would like.

Do you need to be more patient, more forgiving, more loving? When you allow your problems to be your teacher rather than your punishment, you will begin to learn from them and develop godly character.

Therefore, when one of the storms of life comes on you, how will you react? Will you learn to ignore little, insignificant problems and not rent space in your mind to them? Will you instead change to the appreciation, joy, love, peace, and praise-and-worship channels? When a massive storm, like a hurricane, enters your life, will you allow your thoughts to actually bring you closer to the Lord? Can you practice love, forgiveness, patience, and all the fruits of the Spirit?

Many times, the storms of life actually show us what is really inside our hearts, and unfortunately most Christians fail the test; they react in the flesh, with anger, self-pity, hostility, unforgiveness, fear, or bitterness. I tell patients to practice the love walk during the little trials of life: Practice patience and kindness, instead of being envious or rude. Through intense practice we will be ready for the storms of life; and when they do hit, we will be able to turn the channel in our minds to the love, peace, joy, forgiveness—to all the fruits of the Spirit channel. And thus, we will weather the storm of life and see the storm as a teacher that makes us even wiser.*

We know the fruit of the Spirit dwells in us, but as Dr. Colbert's article illustrates, we never really know how developed it is until it is squeezed. Trials squeeze our fruit and reveal our level of spiritual maturity. We learn more about ourselves during trials than at any other time in life.

We must remember that God is not the author of our problems, but He will use them to help us once we have them. God is good, and He gets good out of everything if we trust Him to do so. Romans 8:28 teaches us that all things work together for good to those who love God and are called according to His purpose. All things may not *feel* good, seem good, or even be good, but God can cause them to work out for good! What the enemy intends for our harm, God means for good (see Genesis 50:20).

FIGHT THE GOOD FIGHT OF FAITH

Keeping our thoughts pure and in the will of God will be a lifetime battle. We must "fight the good fight of the faith," according to First Timothy 6:12. The mind is the battlefield on which we fight. Satan wages war in the realm of our thoughts because he knows that if he can control our thoughts, he can control us and our destinies.

Study again the following verses in the *Amplified Bible*, and ask God to help you really understand the depth of their meaning: "For the weapons of our warfare are not physical [weapons of flesh

---

*Reprinted with permission.

and blood], but they are mighty before God for the overthrow and destruction of strongholds, [inasmuch as we] refute arguments *and* theories *and* reasonings and every proud and lofty thing that sets itself up against the [true] knowledge of God; and we lead every thought and purpose away captive into the obedience of Christ (the Messiah, the Anointed One)" (2 Corinthians 10:4–5).

Paul said we are to lead every thought captive unto the obedience of Jesus Christ. That means we take authority over wrong thoughts and bring them in subjection to God's will. His will is His Word, so we must think according to His Word to be in obedience to Him. The devil likes to argue with us, tempt us to live in the mental realm of what reasoning dictates to us. He injects proud and lofty thoughts in our minds. He suggests that we are better than other people, saying they are wrong and we are right. He puts judgmental thoughts in our minds. We must cast down these demonically induced thoughts and replace them with humble thoughts of love and concern for others.

Since we are thinking most of the time, we will find the renewing of the mind quite a battle, especially in the beginning of our journey with God. When I initially started learning these principles, I felt all I did all day was cast down thoughts and watch them come right back.

I finally cried out to God, telling Him that I didn't know how to just *not think* about something. He replied that the answer was very simple; I was to form the habit of filling my mind with good things so bad things could find no room.

I was once an extremely negative person, but God has taught me and brought me about-face so that now I am very positive and really have an aversion to being around negative people. Negative thinkers are not the type of people with whom I want to work or fellowship. Romans 12:21 shares one of the most powerful principles in God's Word; it says that we overcome evil with good! It works in every situation.

Being good to people who have treated you badly is the way to win them and break the power of Satan. It is the open door to the radical blessings of God in our lives. Thinking good thoughts is the way to overcome the habit of thinking bad ones. Yes, good always overcomes evil.

God is stronger than the enemy: "You, dear children, are from God and have overcome them, because the one who is in you is greater than the one who is in the world" (1 John 4:4 NIV). This makes reference to the fact that God and everything He represents is greater than the devil and anything he represents. God is good, the devil is evil; therefore, good always overcomes evil.

If we walk in the Spirit, we will not fulfill the lusts of the flesh (see Galatians 5:16). We don't have to spend our lives fighting with sin, temptation, wrong thoughts, lusts of the flesh. We can choose the right thing, and the wrong thing will find no place to exist in us.

There will be times of fighting the good fight of faith, but as in any other war, if we win enough battles, we will eventually win the entire war.

LITTLE BY LITTLE

We overcome the devastations of our past ways of life little by little. We make a big mistake if we look at everything that is wrong in our lives due to many years of bad choices and expect to eradicate the results overnight.

God delivers us from our enemies little by little (see Deuteronomy 7:22). Expecting anything else only sets us up for discouragement. If you discover, as a result of reading this book, that you really have some problems with your thinking processes and need some big changes in your life, don't even think it will all happen overnight or even quickly.

Having your mind totally renewed is a process that can take years. Be thrilled about your progress, and don't be discouraged about what still needs to be done. Be excited about how far you have come, not depressed about how far you still have to go. Even realizing you have a problem is progress.

We have thoughts in literally thousands of different areas, and God deals with them one at a time. The Holy Spirit worked with me for a long time, helping me learn to think better thoughts about myself. Then we worked together on how I viewed other people, my past, my future, the world, my work, and so on. In the beginning of my journey with God, I felt defeated most of the time because I kept thinking about how far I had to go. No matter how much progress I made, I was overwhelmed by what still needed to be done.

Satan wanted to make sure I did not feel at all victorious, but eventually I realized I needed to be careful how I thought about my thoughts. I could think, *I will never change. I'll never be positive enough to overcome all the junk in my mind.* Or I could think, *I may still have problems in many areas of my thinking, but I have made progress, and I will continue making progress. Even if it takes the rest of my life, I will keep pressing forward and will enjoy new victories daily.*

At first, thinking in this new way was awkward, it was work, it required effort. Eventually, being positive was natural, and being negative felt all wrong. Thinking wrong thoughts actually makes me uncomfortable now; I feel a burden on my spirit when I do. Just think how someone would feel who was perhaps twenty-five years old and had never worn shoes in her entire life—when suddenly someone put shoes on her. She would definitely be uncomfortable. When God places this halter on our minds, it is uncomfortable at first; but it is the discipline that leads us into the good plan He has for us. He wants to transform our thinking, as this verse shows:

Do not be conformed to this world (this age), [fashioned after and adapted to its external, superficial customs], but be transformed (changed) by the [entire] renewal of your mind [by its new ideals and its new attitude], so that you may prove [for yourselves] what is the good and acceptable and perfect will of God, even the thing which is good and acceptable and perfect [in His sight for you]. (Romans 12:2)

When our minds are completely renewed, we will prove for ourselves what is the good and perfect will of God. We must think in agreement with God in order to manifest His glory.

Don't be in a hurry! I know from experience that it does not do any good. It only serves to make us feel defeated all the time. Our own wrong expectation sets us up for feelings of failure. I was a very impatient individual most of my life and finally realized that God would move in His timing, no matter how big of a hurry I was in.

I saw the problem in me once I began studying God's Word. I wanted immediate change, and when I didn't get it, I felt discouraged, frustrated, and defeated. But 1 Peter 5:10 states, "After you have suffered a little while, the God of all grace . . . will Himself complete and make you what you ought to be."

Why does He allow us to suffer? I believe the suffering begins when we realize we have a problem and that we cannot change ourselves—only God can. As we wait on Him, trusting Him for deliverance, we will see victory. The waiting tests our faith to see if it is genuine. Everyone goes through the same process, so we may as well settle down and enjoy the journey. If you struggle with keeping your thoughts above life's storms, I encourage you to read my book titled *Battlefield of the Mind*. It will help you learn to renew your mind and stand firmly on God's promises for your life.

We can be transformed from people who worry all the time to people who enjoy peace of mind on a regular basis, but we will have to fight the good fight of faith and not give up if everything does not change as quickly as we would like.

FORGET YOUR PAST

Thinking about the past, especially the bad, does not do any good. We can learn from mistakes we have made, but beyond that, the best thing we can do is repent of our mistakes and forget them.

God is greater than any mistake you or I have made in the past, and we have all made plenty of them. Everyone has some skeletons in his closet that he would rather not expose. God Himself encourages us to forget the past and move on: "Do not [earnestly] remember the former things; neither consider the things of old. Behold, I am doing a new thing! Now it springs forth; do you not perceive and know it and will you not give heed to it? I will even make a way in the wilderness and rivers in the desert" (Isaiah 43:18–19).

God is always doing something new. When we mentally stay in the past, we miss our right now, and our future. We must make an effort not to spend time on things that are useless. We talked about worry and how it does no good, so why engage in it? Dwelling on the past is another excellent example of spending time doing something that does no good. We can apologize to people if we have hurt them, we can ask God to forgive us, but we cannot undo what has been done, so moving on is the only real solution. As I said, we can learn from our mistakes, which is actually very valuable.

Through not using wisdom, you may have ruined a relationship, lost a job, made bad financial choices, or gotten involved in something that did not succeed. Whatever the case might be, take the lesson you learned with you and move on—there is nothing else to do. We learn from the Word of God and from life's experiences (see Proverbs 3:13).

God is merciful and does not hold our sins against us. Hebrews 4:15 states that He is a High Priest who understands our weaknesses and infirmities. That knowledge always comforts me, as I am sure it does you. God is not angry with you if you messed up.

The apostle Paul stated in Philippians 3:12–13 that one thing he definitely attempted to do was let go of what was behind and press on to the things that lay ahead. If he had to do this, perhaps we should not feel so bad when the same thing happens to us. Paul was a great apostle—he received about two-thirds of the New Testament by direct revelation from God—and yet he made mistakes and had to move past them. I am sure he did not permit himself to dwell on the past. We cannot get beyond anything we refuse to let go of mentally.

The Word confirms that not pressing on will rob us of the futures God has planned for us. Hebrews 11 talks of those who pressed on by faith, and verse 15 says, "If they had been thinking with [homesick] remembrance of that country from which they were emigrants, they would have found constant opportunity to return to it." Peter is a great example of a man who made a terrible mistake and had to let it go. God had called and anointed Peter to do something great. He had been one of Jesus' twelve disciples and was actually one of the three with whom Jesus frequently spent special time. Yet, at Jesus' crucifixion (His greatest agony, the hour of His need), Peter disappointed Him by denying that he knew Him. Peter was afraid; it was just that simple.

On resurrection morning, when Mary found the tomb empty, the angel she saw told her to go tell the disciples *and Peter* that Jesus had risen from the dead (see Mark 16:7). It has always really blessed me that the angel mentioned Peter by name. The others were lumped into a group called "disciples," but Peter was singled out. Why? Peter probably felt as if he no longer even had the right to be part of the group; surely his grief was intense.

I am sure Peter felt he had destroyed his chance to serve God, that he had made a fool of himself and failed miserably. Peter had gone out and wept bitterly after he realized what he had done, and that was his time of repentance. Since he had repented, Jesus had already forgiven him, but then He let Peter know that he did not have to live in his mistake. Jesus included Peter in His plans for the future.

If you have made mistakes and find yourself still stuck in the past, I strongly urge you to make a decision to let go. Stop thinking about the past, stop talking about it, and press on.

I also encourage you not to dwell excessively on past victories. Don't turn your past miracles and mighty feats into memorials that you admire; it may prevent you from doing even greater things in the future.

Matthew 6:3 teaches us not to let our right hand know what our left hand is doing concerning good works. I believe this statement partially means not to dwell on the good things we have done. Give God the glory, thank Him for letting you be involved, and then move to the next thing He has for you.

I led a women's ministry in St. Louis for about seven years. We built a weekly congregation with four hundred to five hundred women in attendance. We had wonderful times, learned and grew together, saw mighty works in women's lives, but the time came when it needed to be over. God had directed Dave and me to take our ministry to a larger part of the world. In order to do so, we had to let go of what was behind. It was hard to do and even harder for many of those in attendance. After all, I was moving on to something new, but some felt as if I was abandoning them. For years after we disbanded those weekly meetings, people kept talking to me about "the good ole days" when we had the women's ministry.

I was excited about the future, but they were hanging on to the past. Eventually many of those women were no longer involved in my life and ministry. When God moves, we must move with Him, or we will get left behind.

One of the women actually apologized to me on her deathbed, saying she had been angry with me for over ten years because she felt I had abandoned the women who depended on me. Of course, she realized she was wrong, but she had needlessly suffered emotionally for many years because she was hanging on to the "good ole past."

Had I allowed the emotions of my friends to dictate my decision, I would not be seeing the good fruit I see today worldwide. Life is always flowing and going somewhere; we must be able to go with the flow. Don't stagnate and make memorials out of what God might be finished with.

We will not find peace while living in the past. God's power is available for us to live today; yesterday is gone, and we must let it go mentally and emotionally.

FILL YOUR THOUGHTS WITH FAITH

Although we have already discussed worry, I want to say a few more things regarding excessive thinking about the future. We would all love to know what the future holds, but nobody knows except God and those to whom He reveals coming events. He may, from time to time, give us supernatural insight into what the future holds, but generally speaking, we must live by faith daily.

Having faith means that we don't see or have any natural proof of what tomorrow may hold. We believe for good things, we expect good things, and we wait on God. We may be disappointed occasionally, but in Christ we can always get quickly reappointed. We can shake off the disappointment or discouragement and move on with what God is doing.

I was pondering just this morning the future of our ministry. We have been in ministry since 1976, and many things have changed during those years. I realize that things will not be the same ten years from now, but I don't know exactly what they will be. Dave and I are getting a bit older, and we realize that we will not always be able to maintain the heavy travel schedule that we have now.

When I try to look into the future with my thoughts, I must admit I don't really see anything definite. I intend to keep doing what I am doing and prayerfully helping more and more people. I just believe whatever God does, it will all be good. I believe it is important for many of our readers to realize that even ministers and authors don't always have exact direction from the Lord; we walk by faith just like everyone else. I trust that God will always take care of us, that He will always do the right thing. God does not make mistakes—people do. Often we make ours from excessive personal planning that becomes so important to us we miss what God wants to do.

Making plans for the future is part of our thinking process. If we go overboard, we can cause ourselves a lot of misery. We expect things to go the way we have planned, then when they don't, we are unhappy and lose our peace.

God's plan is always better than ours, so we should be careful about making too many of our own. I always say, make a plan and follow your plan, but be ready to let it go quickly if God shows you something else. God should always have the right of way and the right to interfere with our plans at any time.

We cannot live without making plans; if we tried to live without a plan, most of us would do nothing. But there are people who are obsessive about making plans, and I have noticed they seem upset a good part of the time. Why? Simply because they are not in control, but God is. Make plans in areas that you need to, but don't plan your future so precisely that you create problems for yourself. One of the best pieces of advice we can receive is to live one day at a time.

These verses of Scripture teach us that God will get His way in the end, so be careful about excessive planning:

- The plans of the mind and orderly thinking belong to man, but from the Lord comes the [wise] answer of the tongue. Proverbs 16:1
- A man's mind plans his way, but the Lord directs his steps and makes them sure. Proverbs 16:9

Our minds can come up with what seem to be great ideas, but in reality they will not work because they are our plans, not God's. The Bible says that there is a way that seems right to man, but the end of it is death (see Proverbs 16:25). That does not mean we will literally die because of our plans, but it does mean they won't add to our lives, they will subtract from them. They will cause trouble and not minister peace and joy; they won't work.

We should thank God that our plans don't always work, once again remembering that God is smarter than we are, and His plans are better. I want His will in my life more than I want my own, and I am sure you feel the same way.

How much mental time do you spend planning what you will do tomorrow, or even the rest of your life? If it is too much, then I suggest you spend more time telling the Lord that you want His will, asking Him to make His plans come to pass for you.

The Word says that if we will roll our works on the Lord, He will cause our thoughts to become agreeable to His, and our plans will succeed because they will actually be His plans (see Proverbs 16:3).

What does it mean to *roll our works on the Lord?* I believe it means that we genuinely want His will, not our own, and that we avoid getting into works of the flesh by trying to make things take place according to our design.

I am grateful that I can usually discern when *I* am trying to make something happen and when God is behind it, making it happen. When God is involved, things flow, there is a certain holy ease about the project. He gives favor and opens doors; He provides. When it is all me, I struggle, there is not enough of anything, and I certainly have no peace or enjoyment.

No matter how strongly I want a thing to happen, I have learned it does no good to keep pushing a project in which God is not involved. Our works of the flesh produce no good fruit. Therefore, we should roll our works on the Lord and trust Him to put right thoughts into our minds, thoughts that will be in agreement with His will so they produce good things.

TRUST IS BETTER THAN KNOWLEDGE

We usually think we would like to know the future, yet in many cases if we did know all the future holds, we would be miserable and even afraid to go forward. Trusting God enables us to handle life one day at a time. God gives us what we need. We do not have everything we need right now for our future because it is not here yet, so if we did know the future, we would all feel overwhelmed.

I have discovered that I lose a lot of peace by what I know. Knowing is not all it is cracked up to be. Some things are better left alone. For example, I don't want to know if someone doesn't like me and has been talking unkindly about me; all it does is make me unhappy. Sometimes we are quite peaceful and then we receive some information, and suddenly we lose our peace over what we just learned.

I would love to know all the wonderful, exciting things that are going to happen in my future, but I don't want to know the difficult or disappointing ones. However, I realize both will be in my future. Just like everyone else, I will have good and bad times. I really believe I can handle whatever comes if I take it one day at a time, but knowing it all now would be too much. This is why God withholds information from us and tells us simply to trust Him.

Trust really is better than knowledge. Trust ministers peace, and that is very important. I suppose we can ask ourselves this question: Do I want peace or knowledge? I choose peace. How about you?

SET YOUR MIND ON THINGS ABOVE

The Word admonishes us to think about things above, not things on the earth. This does not mean to sit and think about heaven all day, but it does mean to think about what God would think about.

He thinks of high things, not low things; good things, not bad things. We can think about anything we choose to, but we must remember that we reap what we sow. Thoughts are definitely seeds that will always produce a harvest in our lives.

The Word says we are to "aim at and seek the [rich, eternal treasures] that are above, where Christ is, seated at the right hand of God" (Colossians 3:1). When we do this, we will indeed be raised with Christ to a new way of living. Verse 2 says to "set your minds and keep them set on what is above (the higher things), not on the things that are on the earth." This clearly means that we seek whatever we think about. Whatever we fill our minds with is what we are looking for, desiring, and will more than likely end up with. Remember, where the mind goes, the man follows.

Set your mind on eternal treasures where Christ is. The mind has a tendency to wander. Our powers of concentration are not too strong. This is partially due to the age in which we live. We have literally thousands of messages coming at us on a regular basis. Just driving down the highway is like driving through an encyclopedia. We might view hundreds of various types of advertisements on billboards and posters in a short drive.

We live in the age of information. As many as five or six things can be advertised during one commercial break on a television program, and this occurs numerous times in one hour. Most of the time, commercials are so overwhelming and even frustrating to me that I will not watch regular television programs. I either watch noncommercial stations or videos that I own. I want peace of mind, not so much information coming at me at one time that I cannot possibly take it in.

The Bible says to set our minds and keep them set. That basically means, think on right things and keep thinking on them—don't give up quickly. For example, if you think about starting an exercise program, you will need to keep your mind set to do it, otherwise you will quit when you get tired or sore.

Satan steals from us by getting us to change our minds about doing right things. He shows us what is difficult about everything we try to do. We have to remember that the Holy Spirit empowers us to do difficult things and to tell the devil so. Believe that you can do whatever you need to do for as long as you need to do it.

We can live the good life, but not if we don't set our minds and keep them set on good things. Be careful when choosing what to think about, for your thoughts help determine your future. God has a plan for you, but so does the devil! With whom will you agree?

Any thought that does not minister peace is one we should cast down and reject. God is the God of peace, not confusion and turmoil. Jesus is the Prince of Peace; He left His peace for us to enjoy.

If we begin to feel upset in any way, we should examine what we are thinking about. Sometimes thoughts are so vague that we are almost unaware that we are thinking them. We might, for example, have an underlying bitter thought about someone who has hurt us. Several times a day, this little vague thought comes to us and we don't think about it long, but it keeps coming back, and by the end of the day we have actually spent quite a bit of time dwelling on something we should not have on our minds.

Recently an individual aggravated me by seeming to be always in disagreement with me. No matter what I liked, this person never liked it, making simple decisions much more difficult. I just wanted to decide something and go on, but this individual always had to make a big deal out of things that were minor issues to me.

Although each time this occurred, I consciously made a decision to forgive the offensiveness and let it go, I found myself feeling irritated several times a day when I thought of this person. My mind reviewed events where we had disagreed, and I even began to anticipate the same behavior in the future meetings. I needed to show this individual another project and found myself dreading it because I "thought" I would face the same opposition as in previous encounters.

I finally got rather violent with the devil. Realizing that he was responsible for injecting these negative thoughts in my mind, I began saying out loud, "I get along quite well with _____, and we are able to make quick decisions together. We like a lot of the same things and enjoy harmony with one another."

Although I have never experienced agreement and harmony with the individual I am talking about, I desire to do so in the future, so I am calling those things that are not into existence as if they already existed. As I've mentioned, Romans 4:17 teaches us that God does this same thing: He "gives life to the dead and speaks of the nonexistent things that [He has foretold and promised] as if they [already] existed." We, too, can declare in faith what we believe is God's will for our situations because He created us in His image and encourages us to practice doing what He does.

It certainly is not going to help me in any way to keep thinking and saying what I have experienced in the past; it will only create more of something I don't want.

What if, even after making this good confession, my experience does not change with the person in question? I will continue to war against negative thoughts about this individual, because those thoughts make me feel bad inside, they steal my peace, and it is not God's will that I think bitter thoughts. I will continue to fight the good fight of faith, knowing that my reward will come from God.

THE MIND IS AMAZING

No matter what upsetting circumstances are going on in life, if we can get them off of our minds, they no longer upset us—it is as if they do not exist for us. When we recall them, they once again become part of our reality. No wonder Satan continually brings up things that steal our peace. He even uses other people to remind us of things we want to forget.

If we want to enjoy peace, we need to be willing to tell people that we don't want to talk about certain things. Recently I made a phone call to another minister I know, and he began telling me about a minister we both know, sharing details of a messy divorce situation, lies, and immorality. He explained the situation but then obviously wanted to go on and on, talking more about it. I started losing my peace and was feeling irritated, so I simply said, "Well, you have told me what I need to know, so let's go on to something else."

Was I rude? I don't think so. Once I would have listened as long as he wanted to talk and participated myself. But those were also days when I did not enjoy a peaceful life and didn't seem to know why. I have found that being a garbage dump for other people does not promote peace for me, and I want peace more than I want to know what is going on in everyone else's life.

Don't let Satan use other people to steal your peace through giving you upsetting information you don't really need, and make sure that the enemy doesn't use you to upset other people in the same way.

The mind is an absolutely amazing organ. Thoughts affect our emotions, our health, our futures, our attitudes, our relationships, and much more. Certainly we should be careful concerning them.

What we think about literally becomes our reality. We can think of something that is not even true, but our thoughts will make it real for us. I can imagine that someone is ignoring me and feel hurt when in reality he didn't even see me. The pain is the same to me although my mind manufactured it all.

Make sure your thoughts are not deceiving you. Find out what the truth is, knowing that the truth will set you free. Paul said,

For the rest, brethren, whatever is true, whatever is worthy of reverence and is honorable and seemly, whatever is just, whatever is pure, whatever is lovely and lovable, whatever is kind and winsome and gracious, if there is any virtue and excellence, if there is anything worthy of praise, think on and weigh and take account of these things [fix your minds on them]. Practice what you have learned and received and heard and seen in me, and model your way of living on it, and the

God of peace (of untroubled, undisturbed well-being) will be with you. (Philippians 4:8–9)

If we follow this advice, we will please God and enjoy much more peace. Having peace with God and with yourself is the foundation of having peace in life. But there is still more—you must have peace with the people around you. Only then will you enjoy the full, abundant life that God's Word directs us to enjoy.

Peaceful relationships are the real evidence of living a Spirit-led life. In the next section of this book, I will share with you seven ways to keep peace with others.

~ *Part 3* ~

Be at Peace
with Others

*So then, whatever you desire that others would do to and for you, even so
do also to and for them, for this is (sums up) the Law and the Prophets.*

—JESUS, *Matthew 7:12*

PEACEKEEPER #15

Esteem Others as Higher than Yourself

❧

The only way we can ever hope to have peace in our relationships is if we are willing to humble ourselves and esteem others the way Jesus does. This means that we are not to think we are too good, or too important, to be the ones who initiate the act of making and maintaining peace with someone else.

I realize that the things I will be suggesting in these next few chapters will sound easier to do than they actually are. Your heart may say *Amen,* but your flesh may cry out, "I cannot do this" when the time comes to act. However, humility inspires harmony in relationships.

Humility has an enemy called *pride.* Pride is the enemy of us all. While we reviewed in previous chapters that it is important to love ourselves and to be at peace with who we are, we must never consider ourselves as more important than anyone else. In fact, the real test of humility is to regard others as a prize, *better than ourselves.* These verses hold important keys to our keeping peace with people we encounter:

Do nothing from factional motives [through contentiousness, strife, selfishness, or for unworthy ends] or prompted by conceit and empty arrogance. Instead, in the true spirit of humility (lowliness of mind) let each regard the others as better

209

than and superior to himself [thinking more highly of one another than you do of yourselves]. Let each of you esteem and look upon and be concerned for not [merely] his own interests, but also each for the interests of others. Let this same attitude and purpose and [humble] mind be in you which was in Christ Jesus: [Let Him be your example in humility]. (Philippians 2:3–5)

Inspired by the Holy Spirit, the apostle Paul was telling us how to avoid strife through the true spirit of humility by regarding each other as better than *and* superior to ourselves. That is a difficult challenge because our flesh wants to shout, "But what about me?"

Yet, this Word clearly exhorts us to be of the same humble mind that Jesus displayed: to think of others as better than ourselves, to be more concerned for their interests and welfare than for our own, and to do nothing from conceit or empty arrogance. If we are obedient to this instruction, if we humble ourselves to tend to the needs of others, we will live in harmony and therefore be pleasing the Lord. Jesus taught us to respect all men and treat them with kindness.

Sometimes a person who does everything fast will look down on a slower person, even showing irritation. This kind of arrogance often shows up in people who are waiting in a line to be served at a fast-food restaurant. And a person who learns quickly may become impatient with someone who has to hear more than once how to do something. Truly humble people demonstrate patience, and even an *eagerness* to help the person who is weak where they are strong.

But we all have real faults, and this Scripture tells us very plainly how to handle the faults of others:

Brethren, if any person is overtaken in misconduct or sin of any sort, you who are spiritual [who are responsive to and controlled by the Spirit] should set him right and restore and reinstate him, without any sense of superiority and with all gentleness, keeping an attentive eye on yourself, lest you should be tempted also. Bear (endure, carry) one another's burdens and troublesome moral faults, and in this way fulfill and observe perfectly the law of Christ (the Messiah) and complete what is lacking [in your obedience to it]. For if any person thinks himself to be somebody [too important to condescend to shoulder another's load] when he is nobody [of superiority except in his own estimation], he deceives and deludes and cheats himself. (Galatians 6:1–3)

I have personally read and meditated on these Scriptures hundreds of times. I have a natural temperament that avoids humility, so I need all the scriptural help I can get. I do want to please God, and I am willing to do things His way, no matter how difficult it is. Reading these Scriptures reminds me that while misconduct should be confronted in a loving way, I will also have times of needing simply to bear and endure the troublesome faults that others have. Humility allows us to be patient with the mistakes of others. As we walk in love and pray for people, God will intervene and deal with their faults. We reap what we sow: If we sow mercy, we will reap mercy when we need it.

Even though we find it difficult at times to bear with the weaknesses of others, the Word of God actually strengthens and enables us to do God's will. When you are being tempted to be prideful, study and meditate on the Word, asking the Holy Spirit to do through you what you certainly cannot do by sheer willpower. Remember, pride is a sin, and it is the culprit behind all broken relationships.

The signs of pride include an unwillingness to admit fault, to take responsibility for one's actions, and to initiate making peace. Pride wants to do all the talking, and none of the listening. Pride is stubborn; it does not want to be instructed, it wants to instruct others.

Pride was Lucifer's sin; he said he would lift himself and his throne above God's! Therefore, we see that pride manifests in one's esteeming himself above the value of another, but God says we are all equal in His eyes. Lucifer, of course, was not equal with God, but as far as human relationships are concerned, no one is better than another.

AVOID UNREALISTIC EXPECTATIONS

We all have personal standards that we expect other people to meet, and we are disappointed when people fail to act the way we hoped. But is it really what they do that hurts us, or is it our own unrealistic expectations that set us up for the pain we feel when they don't perform to our standards?

God's Word tells us to expect things from God, but not from man. But how can we have relationships and not expect anything from people? In reality, there are some things we have a right to expect, but there are also expectations that we place on people that are not rightfully their responsibilities to fulfill. For example, my joy is not my husband's responsibility—although I thought it was for many years. If he was not doing what made me happy, I became angry. *I* thought he should be more concerned about my happiness and do things differently. It was *what I thought* that caused the problem, not what he did.

Dave and I have very few arguments now that I know my personal joy is my own responsibility, and not his. Dave should do things for me that make me happy, just as I should try to please him, but there were many years in my life when it would have been practically impossible for anyone to keep me happy. My problems were in me; they were the result of abusive treatment in my childhood. I was filled with bitterness, resentment, rage, anger, and self-pity.

There was no way I could ever be truly happy until I dealt with those things. Dave could not deal with them; I had to. I was placing responsibility on Dave to make up for pain he had not caused. I was literally trying to punish him for the unfair abuse that someone else had perpetrated.

Over time, I noticed that no matter had badly I acted, Dave remained happy. It irritated me but also served as an example. I eventually became very hungry for the peace and joy I saw in his life, which were not dependent on any of his circumstances. In other words, he never made me responsible for his joy. If he had been dependent on me to make him happy, he would have never enjoyed life, because I gave him no reason to rejoice.

Are you perhaps trying to make someone else responsible for things that only you can do anything about? Are you blaming people for your problems when Satan is actually your true enemy? Let us take responsibility and stop expecting people to do for us what we should, in reality, be doing for ourselves or trusting God to do.

If I give someone some of my time by doing a favor for him or her and then expect to receive the same thing in return, I am setting myself up for disappointment. He or she may not know of my expectation. When people don't know what we are expecting from them, it is unfair to become angry when they don't meet our requirements.

The Bible says when we give a gift, we are to expect nothing in return from people. It is God who returns to us what He wants us to have according to our investment and heart attitude (see Matthew 6:1–4).

We often think people should be able to read our minds when we should be willing to clearly communicate what we expect from them. If I have a certain expectation for return of a favor I am willing to grant, I should say in the beginning, "I will be glad to do this-or-that for you, and then would you be willing to do thus-and-so for me?"

I can say to Dave, "Well, I expected you to stay home tonight." But if I did not communicate my desire to him ahead of time, it is not fair later to blame him for something he did not even know I wanted. I agree that some people should frequently be more thoughtful than they are, but we should also be willing to ask for what we want and humble ourselves by being quick to forgive those who do not fulfill our wishes.

If you truly want to have peaceful relationships, examine yourself and ask God to show you if you have expectations for people that you should not have.

We all have times when perhaps we have worked really hard or endured a difficult trial and need some special blessing to balance things out. I have learned over the years to ask God to give me encouragement when I need it. True, He frequently uses a person to do so, but I put my expectations in Him as my source, and not on people.

I ask God to provide encouragement when I feel that I have reached a place in life where I need something special to happen. I spent many years getting angry with people when I had times like this because I looked to them to make me feel better. It never produced anything but strife and offense. People are not our source, God is.

Go to God, and if He wants to use people to bless you, He will; if not, trust that whatever He chooses is what is best for you at the present time. Even if God should choose not to give the encouragement immediately, you can trust that His timing is perfect in your life.

ACCEPT WHAT OTHERS HAVE TO OFFER

We expect people to give us what we would give them. We also expect people to love us the way we would love them, but this produces disappointment—and quite often, even more serious problems. We need to appreciate what other people are willing to do for us and receive their offerings with thankfulness.

One of the ways I show love is through communication. I say

uplifting things to people or spend time talking with them. My husband, on the other hand, is not a big talker. I have often wanted him to sit and talk for long periods of time, but he says what he wants to say and then prefers to be quiet. I will often go over and over the same thing, talking about it in different ways; Dave hates to do that. I have expected Dave to talk to me in the way I want him to, but he is not able to comply. It would be unnatural for him. Dave and I do talk and have good conversations, but I like to analyze things and people while he absolutely loathes doing that.

Another way I show love is to buy people things, so naturally I would like it if Dave bought me more gifts. He will let me buy whatever I want that we can afford, and he will buy me anything I ask him for, but he is not the type to go out shopping and bring surprises home to me on a regular basis. He is more logical, and his logic says, "Why should I spend all day shopping for a gift for you when you will probably take it back and exchange it anyway? Why not just let you go get what you want to start with?" I, of course, like most women, would like him to spend the day shopping for me just to know he did it.

One of the major ways Dave does show love for me is by protecting me. That is very important to him. He feels he is my covering and should make sure I am safe. For years, some of the things he did while trying to protect me irritated me immensely.

For example, Dave might tell me to make sure I bend my knees when I pick something up off the floor. He does that so I don't injure my back as I have in the past. I, however, don't want to be told how to bend over, so it has irritated me. When I get out of the car, he reminds me to watch for traffic. He is making sure I don't get hurt, but I have felt as though he thought I was dumb and couldn't cross the street without his advice. (I am sure you can see that my main problem was that I just plain did not want to be told what to do.)

After several years of his protectiveness becoming a bone of contention between us, I read an article explaining that not everyone shows love in the same way, and it set me free. I now realize that

Dave is showing me love in his way, and I received it wrong because it was not my way.

One of our daughters had a similar experience with her husband. She is very affectionate, like most women, and would like lots of pretty words, hugs, kisses, flowers, and candy. Her husband is not like that at all, so for years she felt that he was not showing her love. She even shared publicly in one of our conferences that she was very unhappy for a long time because of how she viewed her situation. She read the same article I did and realized that he did indeed love her very much. He showed his love by being a good provider, by taking care of things around the house, making sure the walk was shoveled during snow or ice so she didn't get hurt, and other things like that.

This does not mean that women have to settle for having no affection, but it does mean that women are different from men, they approach life differently, and we cannot expect our spouses to give us what we would give them.

Men are providers and protectors; God has designed them that way, and it only causes trouble when wives constantly try to make their husbands be something they are not. Should men show affection? Absolutely! But most of them will never demonstrate their affection as women do. Of course, there are men who are very affectionate and some women who are not, but I am making my statements based on what most women experience.

I am sure my husband would like it if I enjoyed sports with him, simply because it is something that really gives him pleasure. But I don't like playing or watching sports very much, and he has accepted that. I don't think he feels that I don't show him love because I don't watch football or play golf every week. I do play golf occasionally, and I do listen when he shares about sports he enjoys, but my enthusiasm level is certainly not what his is. He knows I love him, and he accepts me the way I am.

Being accepted by those we love is very important because we all want to receive acceptance. But are we giving it to others?

Remember, according to God's Word, we should esteem others as a prize—just the way they are—especially if we want to enjoy peace in our relationships with them.

I believe a humble attitude and a willingness to accept what demonstrations of love others offer to us may really help a lot of people, as it did me. Realize how your family and friends show love for you, and stop concentrating on how they don't. Be positive and not negative.

DON'T GRIEVE THE HOLY SPIRIT

We've already studied in previous chapters how stress causes a great deal of diseases. We know that the symptoms are real, but how many bottles of medicine are sold to combat emotional disorders when the root cause is actually a lack of peace in an individual's life?

I wonder how many cases of stress and depression are the result of strife between relationships in the home or on the job. We treat the symptoms of stress, but we often ignore the sin of pride as the underlying cause of our lost peace. Our general health is much better when we live in peace. Humility, always esteeming others as higher than ourselves, will keep us full of peace and free from grieving the Holy Spirit.

Ephesians 4 teaches us that we grieve the Spirit of God ("offend or vex or sadden Him") when we are not getting along with each other—when we lack harmony and unity. Paul exhorted us to let go of all bitterness, wrath, passion, rage, bad temper, anger, animosity, quarreling, clamor, contention, slander, evil speaking, abusive or blasphemous language, malice, spite, ill will or "baseness of any kind" (see vv. 30–31). If we are living in those conditions, no wonder the Holy Spirit is grieved! Yet many homes are filled with these demonstrations of strife every day.

But it is quite plain; in essence, the Word says we are to stay in peace at all times. The power of peace binds us together. The presence of the Holy Spirit produces peace, and Paul encouraged us to "be eager and strive earnestly to guard and keep" it (Ephesians 4:3).

The thought of grieving the Holy Spirit makes me very sad. I am willing to humble myself and resist strife when I remember that what I do affects the Holy Spirit. When He is grieved, we also feel that way because He lives in us.

AVOID BLINDNESS TO YOUR OWN FAULTS

One of the ways to maintain godly humility and promote peace in our relationships is to take a good, long, honest look at our own faults. Self-deception is one of our biggest problems as human beings. We easily and quickly see what is wrong with others but rarely, if ever, see what is wrong with us. We judge others, and the Lord tells us there is no justification for this: "Therefore you have no excuse or defense or justification, O man, whoever you are who judges and condemns another. For in posing as judge and passing sentence on another, you condemn yourself, because you who judge are habitually practicing the very same things [that you censure and denounce]" (Romans 2:1).

Why would we judge someone else for the same thing we are doing? Because we look at others through a magnifying glass but see ourselves through rose-colored glasses, a tinted glass that makes everything look lovely whether it is or not.

In our thinking, there is absolutely no justification for the wrong behavior of others, but for us there always is. We always seem to have some valid reason why we have behaved badly that excuses us from being responsible. For example, someone might be short-tempered with us, and we feel it was inexcusable for him or her to treat us that way. We might have treated someone the same way on another day, but we had done so because we felt ill or had a bad day at work.

In reality, we should practice being harder on ourselves than others simply because the Word tells us we will not be asked to give an account of their lives, but of our own: "Why do you criticize and pass judgment on your brother? Or you, why do you look down upon or despise your brother? For we shall all stand before the judgment seat of God" (Romans 14:10).

I read this Scripture often because it reminds me how God views my critical judgment of other people. Second Corinthians 13:5 says we are to examine ourselves, but we are usually examining others, which produces nothing but judgmental attitudes and eventually trouble.

Paul said to examine ourselves before God, not unto condemnation, but in order to recognize areas of need in our own lives, and to ask God for His help. But nothing will change if we are blind to the truth of our own shortcomings. Psalm 51:6 says, "Behold, you desire truth in the inner being; make me therefore to know wisdom in my inmost heart."

Jesus has paid for our freedom to see the truth, yet it does us no good until we are truthful with ourselves, about ourselves. We fear looking at ourselves; our pride keeps us from wanting to see our own selfish tendencies. The way we evade facing this needed truth about ourselves is by finding fault with other people instead.

But when we judge others, we are setting ourselves up as gods in their lives. We have no right to judge others; they are God's servants. James 4:12 says it very plainly: "[But you] who are you that [you presume to] pass judgment on your neighbor?"

Can you remember a time, or times, in your life when God has strongly convicted you of some fault? Perhaps some situation exposed it. Times like this tend to humble us, at least for a while.

I had always been short-tempered with people who gossiped about me, not admitting that there were times when I also gossiped about others. Then I got caught, and a friend who heard what I had said confronted me. I had no way out and was terribly humbled. For a while after that, I was very patient with other people who said things about me, but eventually my pride crept back in, and I had to be humbled all over again.

God tells us to humble ourselves, but if we don't, He will do it for us. He either corrects us privately, or if we persist, He will do it publicly. We either fall on Jesus (the Rock) to be broken, or the Rock falls on us to break us—the choice is ours.

If God begins to deal with us about some wrong behavior, there is no point at all in trying to avoid Him. When God admonishes me for my behavior in a relationship, it is particularly difficult for me if I feel the other person does the same thing that God is asking me to change. I have told God more than once, "This is not fair. What about the other person?" He always reminds me that *how* and *when* He corrects another is His business. All I need to do is receive my chastisement from Him without complaint or comparison.

I remember one particular time when God was strongly dealing with me about not being rude to my husband. However, I felt Dave was also being rude to me, and I told God so. I was so frustrated about God confronting me and not Dave also, that I went to Dave and asked him if God was correcting him about anything.

He pondered for a moment, and then with an innocent look on his face, he said, "No, I don't believe He is." I look back now and those events amuse me, but they sure were not funny at the time.

Being willing to be first to do whatever is right is commendable behavior. Being willing to do what is right, even if no one else ever does what is right, is something that God may call upon us to do. We also may have to do what is right *for a long time* before we will get right results, and we may have to treat people in our lives right (humbly love them) a long time before we begin reaping the good seeds we have sown.

CORRECT WITH SINCERE LOVE

Remember, we have a right to pray for people but not to judge them. Should we ever try to correct another brother or sister in the Lord, or someone in our families? Yes, as we read in the beginning of this chapter, there may be times when God will use us to confront someone for misconduct, but once again it must be with humility, not having an exaggerated opinion of our importance or spirituality.

Paul was an apostle, and therefore God used him to bring correction to the churches quite frequently. But he said, "By the grace of God given unto me, I warn you not to estimate and think of yourself more highly than you ought to" (see Romans 12:3). I have always been struck by the fact that Paul said he corrected people because of God's grace in him to do so, not just because he had an opinion and wanted to express it.

When we do anything by God's grace, it has God's power on it and therefore produces good results. When we try to correct people, but God has not given us the assignment to do so, we only cause trouble.

I quickly learned in the early years of my marriage that I am not my husband's teacher, nor have I been assigned the job of correcting him. There have been rare occasions when God has used me in that way with Dave, and each of those times he has received the correction. The times I just decided I was going to tell him a thing or two only initiated a small war between us.

When we do correct people, it should be because we truly love and care about them, not just because we want to tell them what is wrong with them and act superior. I do have an assignment from God that requires frequent correction of people, both in my teaching and among my staff. I try to maintain a truthful attitude about myself also, lest I become bossy with them.

I can be the boss and not be bossy. I always share with people what they are doing right as well as wrong, and I also try to admit my own faults with them as well because I find this puts people at ease.

BE WILLING TO BE WRONG

Most of us have an out-of-balance craving to be right about everything. My personal belief is that the need to be right rises from insecurity, which is also a manifestation of pride. If we have peace with God and are secure in ourselves, why do we need to be right all the time? Why can't we be wrong about something without feeling wrong about ourselves?

It is amazing, the fleshly feelings we have when we try to sit quietly and let someone else think he is right when we are convinced we're the one who's right. Dave and I both have rather strong personalities in many ways and neither of us enjoys saying, "I was wrong." We both do it at times, but we are still in the process of learning to enjoy it.

First Corinthians 13 says love doesn't demand its own way. That means there are times when we will have to give up what we think is our right to be right. It is amazing how many arguments we can avoid if someone is willing to say, "I think I'm right, but I may be wrong." Even if one party has the humility to say he could even *possibly* be wrong, it seems to dissipate the argument.

Sometimes we argue over things that don't even make sense—things so unimportant that they should be left entirely alone. Dave and I used to argue over directions on how to get to a place we were going; he wanted to go one way, and I thought another way was a little bit shorter. It would have been better to take a little longer to get there, if that ended up being the case, rather than argue about it. Most of the time there is more than one right answer, and peace is much more important than having your own way.

The Word says that a servant of the Lord must "have nothing to do with trifling (ill-informed, unedifying, stupid) controversies over ignorant questionings, for you know that they foster strife and breed quarrels" (2 Timothy 2:23). Staying out of strife is not a suggestion; it is a command from the Lord.

We lose our power when we lose our peace. We hinder the flow of our anointing, which is one of the most precious treasures we have, and we also hinder our blessings from flowing in abundance. Remember the example I gave in the beginning of the book about

Abraham and Lot? Abraham was so determined to stay out of strife that he allowed Lot to choose the best part of the land for himself, while he (Abraham) took what was left. God blessed Abraham and rewarded him for his right choice by telling him he could have all he could see as he looked north, south, east and west.

We can be prideful or peaceful. Pride says, "I am right" and has no willingness to even consider it might be wrong. Humility says, "I may be wrong, and it is not that important whether I am right or not."

I believe you can see why humility is the basis for any successful relationship. Even if only one person in the relationship will treat the other with loving humility, the relationship will flourish, because God promises to lift up the one that is humble (see Psalm 147:6). The Word also says that the one "who is of a humble spirit will obtain honor." In this light, we should never fear the consequences of adapting ourselves to the needs of someone else. In the next chapter, we will look at the rewards of being Peacemakers by remaining flexible and encouraging others.

PEACEKEEPER #16

Adapt Yourself to the Needs of Others

❧❧❧

The Word says, "If possible, as far as it depends on you, live at peace with everyone" (Romans 12:18). First Peter 3:11 makes this very clear: "Let him turn away from wickedness and shun it, and let him do right. Let him search for peace (harmony; undisturbedness from fears, agitating passions, and moral conflicts) and seek it eagerly. [Do not merely desire peaceful relations with God, with your fellowmen, and with yourself, but pursue, go after them!]"

Peaceful relationships seem to be fading away in our society. The divorce rate is still climbing, and the percentage of failed marriages is said to be even higher among Christians than other people in the world. What is wrong? Is it the stressful society in which we live, or is selfishness still on a rampage?

The Word says that in the last days will come "times of great stress and trouble [hard to deal with and hard to bear]. For people will be lovers of self and [utterly] self-centered" (2 Timothy 3:1–2). They will love money, be greedy, hard-hearted, disobedient, immoral, lacking self-control, and they will have no desire to make peace.

We are living in those times. These are days of great moral darkness, and we, as believers in Jesus Christ, must let our light shine out in the darkness. In practicality, that means we must let our behavior emulate that of Jesus and not be sucked into the world and its system. If people treat us badly, we cannot return evil for evil, but rather forgiveness and love so that others will see God's love in the way we treat people.

Unity among people is pleasant. It releases blessings from God and the anointing power of His presence (see Psalm 133:1–3). Unity, harmony, and peace in relationships won't just come to us; we must go after them with all of our might. We must not wait for someone else to make the first move; we must be Peacemakers; we must make and maintain peace.

One usually must be spiritually mature before he will choose aggressively to be the peacemaker. Jesus said the Peacemakers will be called "the sons of God" (Matthew 5:9). As I have mentioned before, He said "sons," not children, indicating maturity. We are called to lay aside childish behavior and make and maintain peace as responsible sons and daughters of God.

Not all people are as easy to get along with as others. It seems we all have some people assigned to us in life who are like sandpaper. They always seem to grate on us and make a habit of being difficult. They are never happy, no matter what we give or do for them. They regularly find fault and rarely, if ever, encourage us in any way. They are takers and not givers.

Then there are the people who have irritating habits. We love them; we may even be married to them, yet they have one or more idiosyncrasies that continue to rub us the wrong way. An example is those who feel they must give their opinion on everything, whether anyone asks for it or not. Then there are the people who dominate all conversations, to whom we rarely, if ever, get to express ourselves. Even when we try, they interrupt us. They may not even realize they are making conversation difficult; they may be doing something as simple as slurping their soup or popping their chewing gum, but the distraction throws off our concentration and frustrates us.

My point is that we all get opportunities to hold our peace and to be Peacemakers. I dare say that every person in this world has some challenging people in his or her life. Of course, we must remember that we are also challenges to others. Someone struggles with us, with our personalities and habits, just as we struggle with others.

Are You Reaping What You Have Sown?

We like the law of sowing and reaping if we are reaping good seeds we have sown, but we will also reap from the bad seeds we cast along our paths. I remember a time when I felt Dave was being particularly crude and rough in the way he was speaking to me. I immediately felt offended and began to complain to the Lord. He quickly reminded me that I had talked to Dave the same way for years and was only reaping on seeds I had sown in the past.

Actually Dave rarely talked to me in that brisk way, whereas I had probably spent many years being grumpy with him. I had improved and had forgotten about all the years I had spoken that way to him. We want other people to be patient with our faults, but we are not always willing to give others the same mercy and grace we want to receive.

Facing truth is one of the most beneficial things we ever do in life, but it must be truth about ourselves that we face. Truth sets us free; self-deception keeps us in bondage.

Why is it so painful to see ourselves as we really are? Simply because of pride. When we see ourselves in reality, the way others see us, our pride is hurt and we are embarrassed.

When someone talks unkindly about me, is he sowing seeds to reap unkindness, or am I reaping on what I have sown in the past? When we have an appointment and the other person is late, is he sowing seeds that will cause others to be inconsiderate, or are we perhaps reaping on times when we have been late for other appointments? These are questions we must ask ourselves.

We must be honest with ourselves and not go through life blaming others for everything that goes wrong in our relationships.

Pride causes us to be blind to our own faults, but God's Word encourages us to be careful when we think we stand, lest we fall. In other words, we shouldn't think more highly of ourselves than we ought to because this type of pride will also cause our own downfall (see Proverbs 16:18).

DON'T FORCE YOUR CONVICTIONS ON OTHER PEOPLE

It is arrogant of us to try to make other people agree with our convictions. For example, I try to eat reasonably healthy meals, and I have studied nutrition and its effects on the body. Consequently, I have strong opinions about how we should take care of ourselves. I do eat sweets, but only small amounts, and I am usually concerned when I see anyone regularly consuming large amounts of sweets and other foods that I know to be unhealthy.

I have tried to tell people that they are eating poorly, and they have not received my advice well, to say the least. I even had one person say, "If we are going to spend time together, I don't want you telling me what to eat all the time and making me feel guilty when I eat something you don't approve of."

The person went on to say, "I know I don't eat right, but I am just not at the place yet in my life where I am ready to do anything about it. I have lots of things wrong with me that I feel are more urgent than my appetite. So I am concentrating on what I feel God is dealing with me about, and I have no time to pay attention also to what you are dealing with me about."

The person sounded pretty harsh and actually did not display a good attitude toward me, but I got the point, and I have been less likely ever since to tell anyone how he or she should eat. We all tend to put our convictions on others; we think if they are priorities for us, they must be priorities for everyone.

The fact is that people have a right to make their own choices, even wrong ones. God will actually protect people's right to go to hell if that is what they choose to do. In other words, even as much as God wants them to spend eternity with Him, He won't force them, and we cannot force people to do things we want them to do either.

Romans 14 shares examples of how people were in a quandary about whether or not they should eat meat that had been offered to idols. Some thought it would be a sin, and others said the idols were nothing anyway and therefore could not harm the meat. Some could not eat because of their weak faith, and others ate because of their strong faith. Paul told them to let them each be convinced in their own hearts and not try to force their personal convictions on others. God seems to meet each of us where we are at in our faith. He begins with us at that point and helps us grow gradually and continually.

GIVE PEOPLE FREEDOM TO BE THEMSELVES

One of the most devastating things one can do to a relationship is try to make the other be what he or she can never be. We must accept people and not reject them when they don't change to suit us. We all seem to look at the way we do things as the standard for everyone, which is, of course, another manifestation of pride. Instead, we should see that God created us all differently but equally. We are not alike, and we all have the right to be who we are.

I am not speaking at this point about faults that God will deal with in time; I am speaking of our inherent, God-given traits that vary from person to person.

I talk a lot; Dave is quiet. I make decisions really fast, and he wants to think about things for a while. As I've mentioned, Dave loves all kinds of sports, and I don't really like any of them—at least not enough to put much time into them. Dave wants each item in a room to stand out, and I want everything to blend. I am sure you could tell similar stories about personal differences you have in your relationships with others.

I am a serious person (sometimes too serious), but I know people who seem to be serious about nothing. There are people I can say almost anything to and they are not easily offended, and then I know others who are very sensitive and I have to be more careful around them. I am blunt and straightforward, so sometimes I struggle with those who have tender personalities.

Why does God make us all different and then put us together and tell us to get along? I am convinced that it is in the struggle of life that we grow spiritually. God purposely does not make everything easy for us. He wants us to exercise our "faith muscles" and release the fruit of the Spirit, including love, patience, peace, and self-control.

If everyone pleased us all the time, if our faith was never stretched and our fruit never squeezed, we would not grow spiritually. We would remain the same, which is a frightful thought. There are two kinds of pain in life: the pain of change, and the pain of remaining the way we are. I am more fearful of remaining the same than I am of changing.

Dave and I argued and lacked peace in our relationship until we agreed to accept each other the way God had created us. I cannot say things were perfect after that, but they certainly improved. People cannot change people; only God can. We discovered it would be wiser to accept and enjoy each other while God was making whatever adjustments He wanted to make in His timing.

I learned that all people have God-given variations in their temperaments and therefore realized I was expecting people to be something they couldn't. I was asking for a response from them that they did not know how to give.

Some people are gifted with thoughtfulness, and others rarely think about doing things for other people. They are willing to do thoughtful acts if someone suggests it, but they don't take initiative on their own. The person gifted with thoughtfulness might also be impatient, while the person who is not very thoughtful (he will always forget your birthday) is extremely patient in every situation. We all have good qualities, but none of us is gifted in them all.

Accept people where they are, and trust God to change what needs to be changed in His timing, His way. Rejection is one of the greatest emotional pains we endure in life. I don't want to be the source of that kind of pain in anyone's life ever again. I finally realized I have more than enough faults of my own; I don't need to magnify anyone else's.

Tell people the good qualities you recognize in them; don't point out what you think they need to improve. Compliment, don't find fault. Accept, don't reject. Be positive, not negative. Be encouraging, not discouraging. You and I will never lack for friends if we will practice giving people the freedom to be themselves.

I honestly believe acceptance is something that all people crave. We cannot endure a person who constantly wants to turn us into something we don't know how to be. To be around such a person for too long is like living in prison.

We can easily fall into the trap of trying to change our children, as well as spouses, friends, and coworkers. We should merely encourage others to become all God has intended them to be. We must not expect to live our unfulfilled dreams through the lives of our family or friends. Everyone has a right to his or her own life.

Be Adaptable

One of the major ways to avoid strife and stay in peace is to be adaptable. We always want others to adapt to us, but they want us to adapt to them. Until someone decides to be adaptable as unto the Lord, strife and contention will rule, or in reality, the devil will rule because he is the one who instigates the turmoil to begin with.

The Word says, "Readily adjust yourself to [people, things] and give yourselves to humble tasks. Never overestimate yourself or be wise in your own conceits" (Romans 12:16). This Scripture has been very helpful to me. It is amazing how peace increases when we make the simple act of adapting or adjusting to someone else. This principle was once foreign to me. I wanted everyone else to do the adapting, and it never occurred to me to try adapting to other people's preferences.

When I tried, my flesh screamed out against it, because we are inherently selfish and our flesh always wants what it wants when it wants it. However, God calls us to follow the leading of the Spirit, not our flesh. The flesh was legally nailed to the cross with Jesus, and we have been resurrected to a brand-new life. We are called upon daily to put off the old man and put on the new man. This literally means to ignore the pleadings of the flesh and follow the Spirit of God.

Paul talked about buffeting his flesh, keeping it under discipline and self-control. This is all part of pursuing peace. For example, Dave and I planned to watch a movie tonight. We agreed to take our showers and prepare for the evening so we could begin the movie. I got ready, and Dave was sitting on the couch, reading a travel brochure about hotels around the world. I kept asking him to get ready because it was getting later and later. He kept saying "Uh-huh, okay" but was not moving. I could feel my flesh getting irritated, so I made a conscious decision to say nothing more and remain in peace no matter what happened.

Once I would have simply followed my feelings, and the entire evening would have been ruined. I would have nagged him until he either got up or got mad. I finally realized, somewhere along the way, that getting my way is highly overrated.

In other words, relieving the pressure the flesh feels when it does get its own way is not worth the pressure we endure from arguing and losing our peace to get it. When the flesh rules, everyone loses, except Satan.

An adapter is a device used to bring compatibility between two totally different parts. We use electrical outlet adapters when we travel to foreign countries. The outlets in the walls are different from the plugs on our electrical appliances, so we always take our adapters. One side plugs into our appliance and the other into the wall outlet, thus bringing the two into compatibility.

When we enter any type of relationship, we need to become willing to adapt simply because no two are ever exactly the same. Dave and I have recently become friends with a married couple. We like a lot of the same things, and it appears it will be a great relationship; however, we do have differences and will therefore need to adapt to one another. I am also certain from my experience with other relationships that the longer we know one another, the more things we may need to adapt to in each other.

What happens when one person in a relationship is willing to adapt, and it seems the other person never does? This, of course, makes it more challenging, but it has been a great help to me personally to remember that I am responsible to God only for my part, not what the other person does or does not do. We are not liberated to do wrong simply because someone else chooses to do wrong.

BE HAPPY FOR PEOPLE WHEN THEY ARE BLESSED

I love to be around people who are really happy for me when I am blessed or have something wonderful happen in my life. Not everyone is like that. We should pay heed to the Scripture that says to rejoice with those who rejoice and weep with those who weep (see Romans 12:15).

I received a very special gift a while back, and it was interesting to see how different people responded. Some said, "Joyce, I am so happy for you. It really blesses me to see you blessed." I knew they were sincere, and it increased my joy. It also made me want to pray that God would do something awesome for them too.

Another friend said, "I wish someone would do something like that for me." Actually this particular person almost always responds in a similar fashion when I receive nice things. Even when my husband does lovely things for me, the individual will say, "My husband just doesn't seem to know how to do things like that." These responses indicate a spirit of jealousy or some deep-seated feeling that she is not getting what she deserves in life.

At one time I was like that: I pretended happiness for people when God blessed them in some special way, but inside I didn't really feel it. At that time in my life, I compared myself to others and always competed with them because the only way I could feel good about myself was if I was ahead of or at least equal to others in possessions, talents, opportunities, and literally anything else you could think of.

I am grateful that God has worked in my life, and I can be genuinely happy for others when He blesses them. I must be honest, though, and say I still sometimes have a little problem if the blessing comes to someone I might consider an "enemy." You know the type—someone who has hurt you in some way. I am not responding perfectly yet, but at least I have made progress.

I love the friend I just mentioned, and in many ways she meets my needs. I know this friend loves me and this is just a small character weakness, so I let it go. But I also know it prevents me from wanting to share what God is doing in my life because I know she cannot be truly happy for me. I also believe it prevents her from being blessed. Dave and I both feel strongly that we will not receive blessings until we can be truly happy for the blessings of others.

All of these areas are ways in which we can adapt to the needs of others. When we can adapt ourselves to both their needs and their celebrations, we will enjoy lasting peace with them. If we are struggling in our ability to adapt to the needs of others, we must be careful to avoid foolish, unproductive comments that will quickly tear apart even close relationships. Next, we'll talk about how idle words can steal our peace.

PEACEKEEPER #17

Beware of Idle Talk

❦

The Bible teaches us to beware of idle talk—vain, useless words that do not minister life to either the speaker or the hearer. Believers are to speak words that are full of God's truth, that build up and encourage, but idle words cause life to drain out of relationships with one another. The Word says, "He who guards his mouth keeps his life, but he who opens wide his lips comes to ruin" (Proverbs 13:3).

Some people really seem to know the Word of God; they appear to have good relationships with God, yet when we are with them, we sense death instead of life through the words they speak. There is something about them that just doesn't seem right. Many of these people leak life and have nothing left but death because of their idle talk. They have received life from God, but they drain it away through unguarded, careless comments.

I believe that idle words can affect our health and even the length of our lives, but it is our spiritual lives that are quickly emptied when we indulge in vain, useless, idle talk. Other than obvious sin, idle words cause the most damage to our lives.

The Word says, "But I tell you, on the day of judgment men will have to give account for every idle (inoperative, nonworking) word they speak. For by your words you will be justified and acquitted, and by your words you will be condemned and sentenced" (Matthew 12:36–37). Imagine having God judge every idle word that we speak. This Scripture is not talking about unclean words, evil words, negative words, or even slanderous words. It speaks of ineffective, unnecessary words; idle words are those that have no value and are the faithless things we simply did not need to say.

What does the phrase mean, "They shall give account thereof" (Matthew 12:36 KJV)? I believe it means that we pay for them. They actually bring a curse with them, and in some ways, we endure the effect of it. Idle words steal our lives. The Word says clearly, "Death and life are in the power of the tongue, and they who indulge in it shall eat the fruit of it [for death or life]" (Proverbs 18:21).

You have probably heard the phrase, "You will have to eat your words before it's over," and this Scripture backs up the statement. We do eat our words! What we say not only ministers life or death to the hearer but also to us who speak them.

We can literally increase our own peace and joy by the things we say or the ones we don't permit ourselves to say. God's Word encourages us to think about what words we will use before we speak:

- The mind of the wise instructs his mouth, and adds learning and persuasiveness to his lips. (Proverbs 16:23)
- Be not rash with your mouth, and let not your heart be hasty to utter a word before God. For God is in heaven, and you are on earth; therefore let your words be few. (Ecclesiastes 5:2)
- Let every man be quick to hear [a ready listener], slow to speak, slow to take offense and to get angry. (James 1:19)

Words are containers for power, positive or negative. Words actually are a tremendous responsibility, and we should be more careful how we use them. Proverbs 6:1–2 says, "If you have given your pledge for a stranger or another, you are snared with the words of your lips, you are caught by the speech of your mouth."

Many relationships are destroyed because people speak foolish words that they don't even mean. People blurt out hurtful words that are very damaging. Wrong words cause a lot of problems because they are not easily retracted or erased from our memories.

As individuals, we are often uncomfortable if we are with people and nobody is talking. We seem to feel someone should be saying something all the time. During these times when we simply try to fill up the air space with words, we may speak idle words that cause problems. We can chatter on and on about things that don't even deserve discussion. Idle people with lots of idle time usually say lots of idle things.

Paul gave instructions about widows whom the church leaders were to support. He said younger widows should not be put on this list because they might become idlers and spend their time talking about things they should not mention. I believe Paul was assuming that younger women would have enough energy to work and be active. If they had nothing to do because the church was supporting them, it would lead to trouble. He wrote:

> But refuse [to enroll on this list the] younger widows, for when they become restive and their natural desires grow strong, they withdraw themselves against Christ [and] wish to marry [again]. And so they incur condemnation for having set aside and slighted their previous pledge. Moreover, as they go about from house to house, they learn to be idlers, and not only idlers, but gossips and busybodies, saying what they should not say and talking of things they should not mention. (1 Timothy 5:11–13)

I have been practicing thinking before I speak, and it is amazing to me how many times I realize that what I am about to say simply does not need to be said. It won't do any good; it does not build up or add to anyone. In many instances, what I was about to say could have been downright harmful, or at least useless. I believe forming this habit is adding peace to my life and the lives of those around me.

Idle words are one of the easiest ways to break unity and sabotage the power of peace. Apologies don't quickly repair the bad impression that heated, foolish words can leave. We can confess our sins, but how can we ever make amends for idle words spoken against other people? How can we repair someone's reputation that we have destroyed with foolish accusations? We may go to the person and ask forgiveness, but we cannot take the words back. Their message has already entered people's ears, and we have no way to eliminate them. You can pay someone back for something you steal, but you cannot repay the damage done by idle, careless words.

People who talk a lot (like me) are more apt to make mistakes with their mouths than quiet people are. Those of us who talk a lot will need to exercise even more caution than others. With much speaking, the tongue becomes heated, and in being overheated, it loses gentleness. Proverbs 15:4 says, "A gentle tongue [with its healing power] is a tree of life, but willful contrariness in it breaks down the spirit." We should strive to keep a gentle, wise tongue, for idle words are the opening through which our power for life leaks away.

GUARD YOUR HEART

Out of the heart the mouth speaks. If we permit wrong thoughts to dwell in our hearts, we will ultimately speak them. Whatever is hidden in our hearts, our mouths will sooner or later express openly. Satan may make an evil suggestion to us, he may try to plant a wrong thought; however, we need to be diligent to guard our hearts.

There is too much at stake not to use diligence in keeping our hearts full of God's truth. Our outer lives are only visible representations of our inner lives. If a tree is rotten, it will bring forth diseased and rotten fruit, and if it is good, it will produce good fruit.

We've seen that we must cast down wrong thoughts and bring them into subjection to God's Word (see 2 Corinthians 10:5). If we are thinking things that are contrary to God's Word, we must renew our minds with proper thoughts. We should think on good things, excellent, and noble things (see Philippians 4:8).

If the attitudes of our hearts are not in line with the heart of God, neither will the words of our mouths reflect His Word. Although you may sometimes say things in the heat of emotion, don't excuse yourself by saying that you did not mean what you said. Take responsibility before God, and ask for His grace to change if you are speaking idle words that are not full of faith or edifying to others.

Another example of idle words is those we speak to ourselves that upset us and get us in a bad humor. For example, we may have been dealing with a particular upsetting issue, which we have prayed about and have even cast our care on God. By doing so we have enjoyed peace even though we have an unpleasant situation. But then someone asks us about it, and in talking about it, we give gruesome details and discuss how unfair and painful the entire thing is. Soon we find ourselves upset once again.

We can actually upset ourselves by how we choose to talk about our situations. When we are filled with life, we are filled with peace; when we leak life, we experience a loss of peace.

SAY THINGS THAT EDIFY

Speaking idle words can become a bad habit. Thankfully, we can break bad habits and form good ones. Let us strive to form a habit of speaking words that edify people. Words of edification minister life, not death. Make a commitment to spread good news, and let all bad news stop with you. When someone tells you some kind of an unclean, unkind, or negative story, don't spread it to anyone else.

If you have an opportunity to stop people before destructive words escape their mouths, do so. To have these leaks in us completely stopped, we must get rid of our curiosity.

Most people are full of curiosity; even Christians are nosey. People tend to enjoy knowing all that is going on in other people's lives. Being delivered from this morbid curiosity, we will sin less. We will have less opportunity to speak idle words if we know less.

I must admit I have always been a curious person; I've said already that once I liked to be "in the know." But I discovered that I could be very peaceful and thoroughly enjoying my life and then find something out that immediately stole my peace. I then wish I had never asked a question or listened to what I just heard, but it was too late.

I have often paid for my curiosity with a loss of peace. I may have heard a negative or judgmental comment about me or someone else I love, and then suddenly I lost my peace. If only I had not heard it, if only someone had been wise enough not to speak it— but it is too late. The words have done their damage and cannot be retracted. We can help one another stay strong and enjoy the peace of God by not speaking idle words.

Our challenge is to "make every effort to do what leads to peace and to mutual edification" (Romans 14:19 NIV). The *Amplified* translation says we are to "eagerly pursue what makes for harmony and for mutual upbuilding (edification and development) of one another." I have made a point to repeat, throughout this study, that we must pursue peace. It seems that we must pursue all good things. The flesh has a natural negative bent; without restraint it will always go in the wrong direction, just as water will always flow to the lowest point unless a dam is built to prevent it from doing so.

Edifying others not only increases their peace and joy, it also increases our own. We feel better when we are saying kind things, things that minister life. We are to help develop one another, not destroy one another.

There are times when we think good things about other people we are with or know, yet plain laziness prevents us from opening our mouths to say the good things that are in our hearts. Be aggressive in saying good things and passive concerning saying evil things.

I am not naturally an exhorter, but I have developed a habit of looking for good and expressing it. Some people have this gift; they are called to be encouragers. It is, of course, easy and natural for these people to do what God has gifted them to do, just as it is easy for me to teach and preach the gospel.

For a long time, I simply made an excuse for not being exhortative by thinking, *I'm just not that way. I just don't think about it.* It even seemed uncomfortable for me to try to do, but God corrected me and told me to start doing it on purpose. There are many things we can choose to do on purpose that will help to increase our peace immensely. Saying good things to people is only one of them.

Establish a boundary in your own heart, and determine that you will not cross the line and speak careless, destructive words to or about others. As you will see in our next chapter, boundaries are important to protect peace in all of our relationships.

PEACEKEEPER #18

Establish Boundaries with People

꧁ ꧂

To enjoy peaceful lives, we should learn how to establish and maintain boundaries. Without boundaries, we have no ownership of our lives. We need to learn that even though people may be good at heart, without boundaries most will go farther than we would like them to, and they may even try to control us. Boundaries protect us.

Having an unlisted telephone number is a boundary. If I didn't have one, many people would call me all the time, asking me to meet their needs, and my own life would fall apart. We cannot be available to people all the time and enjoy peace in our lives. Saying no when we need to is not wrong or unchristian.

We are not offended to see the boundaries of fences on someone's property. They communicate "You can come this far, but no farther." Signs that say "Keep Out" are boundaries telling us "This is private property, and you are not welcome here." We accept boundaries in other areas of life yet often fail to establish them in our own lives.

Home owners who have boundaries on their properties are usually strict about maintaining them. People who put up fences might become angry with neighbors who violate their boundaries. People don't want their neighbor's dogs to do their business in their yards. People usually don't want the neighborhood children playing in their yards. People don't want their neighbors' daily newspapers collecting in front of their houses. When people purchase property, they pay for surveys to make sure their boundary lines are what they think they are, so they get all they are paying for.

We want to know our property boundaries—so why do we care more for a piece of property than we do our own personal lives?

Like many people, I was guilty of not establishing and maintaining boundaries in relationships for many years, but after seeing how this adversely affected my health and peace, I made some drastic changes. People don't always like boundaries, but we are definitely wise to establish them.

ESTABLISH BOUNDARIES TO PROTECT YOUR PRIVACY

We live very close to all of our children and our eight grandchildren. We wanted to live close because most of us in the family travel, and living near each other allows us the opportunity for quick visits. I can go to a son or daughter's house with my coffee cup in hand and chat for thirty minutes and return home. This helps keep our relationships strong and healthy.

When we first made this decision, I was a bit concerned about how I would handle the grandchildren wanting to go to Grandma and Grandpa's house all the time. This is certainly a normal desire for a grandchild. I knew I would not be happy if they just started showing up whenever they wanted to, so I talked with my children, and we agreed they would not let their children come over without asking or calling first. To some people that might seem strange, but it was vitally necessary for me because of my busy schedule.

Dave and I and our children talked about our boundaries, and as long as everyone respects them, we get along great. It is not wrong to have personal boundaries; it protects the privacy to which we are entitled.

What should you do when people don't understand the boundary you have set? Most of the time, when this is the case it is simply because it is not a boundary they need in their lives, so they don't understand why you do. People have different needs because of the differences in their personalities, as well as lifestyles.

We should respect each other's needs, not judge and criticize them. Some people are just plain selfish, they want to do whatever they want to do, whenever they want to do it, with no regard or consideration for anyone else. This, of course, is a wrong attitude, and being forced to respect other people's boundaries is actually good for these types of people. Selfish people can certainly steal our peace if we allow them to do so.

As I stated, everyone has different needs and boundaries. This is true even of our four grown children. One of our daughters wants people in the family to call her before stopping by, and the other says, "Come by anytime, the door is always open." We improve our relationships with others by respecting their boundaries. Respect is vital for good relationships.

Everyone in life has a right to privacy. There may be things we don't want people to know or see. No matter how close we are to someone, we all have a right to and a need for privacy. Even in a marriage, we need a certain amount of privacy. For example, I don't like for anyone to get into my purse without my permission, not even my husband. It is not because I am hiding anything—there is nothing in my purse that would be a problem for anyone to see—but it is my private space to keep my personal things, and I want others to respect my right to have that space.

I never get into Dave's wallet unless he asks me to. If I had an emergency and needed money, I would do it, but I don't go through his private things. I don't go through his briefcase, because that is another area where people keep things that are special to them. Once again, it is not because people are hiding something, it is simply to respect their privacy. By doing so, we are respecting their rights as persons.

I had a relative once who came to my house, and without asking, ate things out of the refrigerator. Often the person ate the last of something, not caring whether or not we had any plans to use it ourselves. This is rude and unacceptable behavior. I had to talk to this person about it, though this individual really should not have even put me in the position to need to say something.

Sometimes we pressure others and cause them work because we don't respect their privacy properly. Some people ask questions they should not ask, some are nosey, and some are just unwise. I am a very straightforward individual and I ask lots of questions, but I also try to use wisdom and not breach anyone's privacy. I would not ask someone how much money he or she made, for example. I would never ask someone who was obviously over-weight how much he or she weighed. I would not ask someone how much he or she paid for an outfit of clothing unless it was someone to whom I was very close and whom I knew I would not offend. If someone is wearing what appears to be a large diamond, I would not normally ask if it was real or fake.

Because I am straightforward, I usually tell people, "If I ask you something you don't want to answer, just tell me, and I won't be offended." I am very open about my life and sometimes need to be reminded that not everyone is that way.

Be clear about what you want in relationships, and be ready to confront people lovingly when they do not honor your boundaries. The way you begin relationships is the way they continue, so if you don't approve of something, don't be afraid to speak up. When you let something go and don't deal with it, people view it as approval and usually get worse.

Very often people don't confront others, which is another way of saying they don't establish boundaries. Confrontation fre-quently offends people simply because unbridled human nature wants to do whatever it wants to do without concern for others. This is not healthy for any relationship or person. We all need to hear people say in various ways, "You can go this far and no farther."

We need to let people know what we are and are not willing to do. For example, grandparents should be able to say, "I will baby-sit once in a while, but not all the time." If they want to do it more, that is fine, but they should not be made to feel as if they are bad grandparents if they don't choose to. Once again, we should remember that we all have different lifestyles and tolerance levels, and no one should be shamed because he or she doesn't desire to do what someone else does.

My daughter's mother-in-law loves to watch the grandchildren. She does it all the time, many times for days at a time. I would not want to do that, not because I don't love my grandchildren—I do love them very much, and I minister to them in other ways—but my lifestyle would not permit me to spend most of my free time baby-sitting and at the same time remain happy. I would resent it.

Lots of people do many things they resent simply because they don't understand the importance of boundaries. Boundaries not only protect us, they protect other people and the longevity of relationships. Boundaries protect our peace!

Keep Wrong People Out of Your Life

Perhaps nothing affects us more than the people with whom we spend a lot of time. The Bible has a lot to say about what kinds of people we should not let into our lives.

For example, the Word tells us not to associate with someone who gets drunk or is a glutton or robber, who is guilty of immorality or greed, is an idolater, or is a person with a foul mouth (see Proverbs 23:20–21; 1 Corinthians 5:11). Why not? Simply because we are tempted to do what others do, and these behaviors lead to unhealthy ends. Have you ever decided you were not going to eat dessert and then changed your mind because others decided to eat it? Obviously I am not saying it is wrong to eat dessert; I am simply making the point that we are easily swayed by what others do.

If people have no measure of discipline in their lives, they may gossip and tell your secrets. Undisciplined people quite frequently live under the curse of a spirit of poverty, which literally affects every area of their lives. Prosperity or poverty is much more than merely a financial matter.

People who function under a poverty spirit will usually do everything poorly, or at best, mediocre; they never press into excellence. They are often late for appointments if they show up at all. They are in debt, and their possessions are in disarray. Things they own are dirty or in need of repair. They may have poor health and many broken relationships.

The people with whom we associate partially determine our reputations. I choose to associate with people of whom I am proud, not ashamed. Occasionally we spend time with people for the purpose of trying to help them, but we must have our boundaries so we make sure they don't eventually hurt us. Scripture warns us about associating with those who indulge in idle conversation: "He who goes about as a talebearer reveals secrets; therefore associate not with him who talks too freely" (Proverbs 20:19).

We can be sure if someone is talking to us unkindly about others, he will most likely talk the same way about us. I had many disappointments in relationships until I realized this truth and set boundaries on whom I choose for friends.

I once met someone I actually liked very much. We had a lot in common and could have been good friends, but I kept noticing that we never spent time together without this individual saying something derogatory about somebody. It actually made me afraid to go deeper in relationship because I felt sure this person would do the same thing to me. I might spend time with someone like that occasionally, but I would not let him or her get very close.

We should not be hesitant to establish boundaries to protect ourselves. If we want peace, we need to fellowship with people who work for and make peace too.

We should not develop relationships with people who have a spirit of rebellion. Paul said at the end of his message to believers in Thessalonica that they should not associate with anyone who refused to follow his instructions given in the letter (see 2 Thessalonians 3:14). In other words, avoid people who rebel against God's guidelines. In our society today, it seems that rebellion is rampant, and many think rebellion is cool, or a sign of freedom. However, this is the exact opposite of the attitude that God teaches us to have in His Word.

We are to submit to right authority in our lives, and those who refuse to do so have a serious problem. The Bible actually states that the spirit of rebellion at work in the world today is the spirit of antichrist (see 2 Thessalonians 2:7–8). We will never learn godliness from a rebellious person; instead, we will learn lawlessness. The following is a strong Scripture to which I have had to give much thought:

> But now I write to you not to associate with anyone who bears the name of [Christian] brother if he is known to be guilty of immorality or greed, or is an idolater [whose soul is devoted to any object that usurps the place of God], or is a person with a foul tongue [railing, abusing, reviling, slandering], or is a drunkard or a swindler or a robber. [No] you must not so much as eat with such a person. (1 Corinthians 5:11)

I believe the same guideline applies that I mentioned earlier: help people if you can, but don't let them hurt you. If we are spending time with people hoping to be able to help them, to be an example to them, or to minister to them, we certainly cannot do so by refusing ever to be near them. But we must influence them and not allow them to influence us. I often say we need to make sure we *affect* them, and they don't *infect* us.

Jesus ate with publicans and sinners, but He did so in order to help them see the light, and by His example, also see the life that was available to them. Jesus said we are the light of the world, and we should not put our light under a bushel. In other words, we cannot stay hidden all the time and do the world any good.

When I am with people I know have problems, and I don't want to have the same problems, I keep my heart guarded to a certain degree. Proverbs 4:23 says, "Keep and guard your heart with all vigilance and above all that you guard, for out of it flow the springs of life." In other words, I am especially careful not to adopt attitudes or opinions that are contrary to what Scripture tells me. I set a boundary, and I let people come close enough to try to help them, but not to hurt me.

BEWARE OF ENTANGLEMENTS

It is unwise to become entangled in other people's problems. Some individuals are what I call *drains*. They add nothing to my life, and Satan uses them to drain me of needed strength. Hebrews 12:1 states that we are to avoid every encumbrance and the sin that so readily entangles us. It is not only sin that does this, but also messy circumstances in other people's lives. They weigh us down and steal the energy we need in order to pursue the call of God on our own lives.

Second Timothy 2:4 encourages us as soldiers in God's army not to get entangled in things of civilian life. The word *entangle* is the key thing to consider. Of course, we will always be involved with people, and many of them will have problems; we will also try to help them in the love and mercy of Christ. The Scripture does not say, "Don't have *any* involvement with these types of people"; it says not to get entangled.

To *entangle* means to complicate or confuse, to get into a snarl or a tangle. These difficult relationships bring pain into our own lives, just as trying to comb a bad tangle out of our hair brings pain.

We comb our dog daily so her hair does not become tangled. On occasion, when we have let it get messy, it has been very painful and time-consuming to get the knots out. Likewise, we should watch over our lives and relationships regularly to make sure we are not out of balance, that we are not getting entangled in things that will drain us of energy and never really help anyone else.

I love people, and the call on my life is to help them in whatever way I can; however, I finally had to learn that not all the people I try to help will actually receive help. Even the ones who claim they want it won't always take what we offer. They may want to entangle us in their problems, they want to talk about them, go over and over them, and be bitter about them, but they don't really want to move on beyond them.

For some people, their problems have become their lives, and they wouldn't know how to spend their time without them. Their problems become who they are: persons with problems to whom everyone is supposed to cater. This may sound a bit too stern if you are tenderhearted or are blessed with the gift of mercy, but when enough people have stolen your time, people who will never change, you understand what I mean.

I spent three years ministering almost daily to a relative I loved and desperately wanted to help. The person claimed to want help and even made progress for periods of time, but the person always fell back into the same pit. It cost money, time, effort, and at the end, nothing was different from how it had been the day we began.

I am not sorry I did what I did; I don't regret any of the investment because I believe God often uses us to give people opportunity. All people are entitled to opportunity, but what they do with it is up to them. This individual had literally every opportunity to have an awesome life and still made a choice that brought more destruction.

I knew very definitely when the day came that I was finished. The desire to be further involved totally left me. I received phone calls from others telling me I needed to help, to do something, to provide an answer for the person, but I was finished. I could not let this person make me feel guilty because I knew that I had followed God not only in trying to help but also in letting go. I had to establish a boundary that in this case said "Keep Out."

If I could have been emotionally driven or accepted a false guilt, I would have become entangled in something that God would not have given me the grace to withstand. When we do things without God's grace, we are doing them in the energy of our own flesh, and it not only frustrates us, it also confuses and defeats us.

I wasted a lot of my life trying to do things myself, independent of God's help and approval. I flatly refuse to do so any longer. I will not be entangled with people who want me to use my time and energy trying to help them, when they really don't want to change. I will not permit them to frustrate me and therefore steal my peace.

Remember that Jesus said to stop allowing yourself to be "agitated and disturbed" (John 14:27). Some of the people and circumstances in life that upset us will never change until we establish boundaries and keep them out.

Of course, we have helped thousands of people over the years. People who had serious problems have received what we offered and completely changed for the better. We have also learned to recognize the signs of those who will never change. They have had eternal problems, they talk about them incessantly, their problems are always someone else's fault, they are hurt if you try to get them to face the truth or take any responsibility, and they won't follow a program that someone designs for their recovery. As before, they say they want aid, but they somehow never end up applying it.

You should never feel guilty about placing a boundary around your life that keeps out these types of people. You are actually not using wisdom if you don't establish such boundaries. God's Word calls us to peace, and boundaries are one thing that will help us keep it.

FAMILIARITY BREEDS CONTEMPT

Establishing and maintaining proper boundaries prevents familiarity. This is very important because familiarity breeds contempt or disrespect. Think of how a person treats a new car. He admires it, thinks it is beautiful, washes it all the time, and expects everyone to be very careful when inside it. He allows absolutely no dirty shoes or food in the car.

But what happens when the car has been around for a few years? It is now dirty all the time, dented, full of empty soda cans and hamburger wrappers. What happened? The owner became familiar with it, took it for granted, and no longer showed it the same respect he did when it was new. He could have kept it looking and running as if it was new had he given it the attention he had in the beginning.

When people first come to work for our ministry, they think it is the greatest thing that has ever happened to them, and they are amazed at and extremely thankful for the opportunity God has given them. However, if they are not very careful, after time goes by they find themselves complaining about the very things they previously thought were wonderful. Why does this happen? One reason and one only: familiarity.

We find a great example of the dangers of familiarity in the Bible concerning the ark of God. When David was attempting to bring it home, a man called Uzza put out his hand to steady the ark on the cart that was carrying it, and God struck him dead because no one was supposed to touch it (see 1 Chronicles 13).

Uzza knew the strict guidelines concerning the ark, so why did he touch it? I believe it was because it had been stored in his father's home for quite some time, and he had become familiar with it. Therefore, he felt he could take liberties. His respect level had lowered without his even knowing it, simply due to his being around the ark too much. In this case, familiarity cost him his life.

Perhaps familiarity costs us more than we realize in our own lives. Perhaps we let godly relationships with people slip away because we have lost sight of their value in our lives.

It is the same thing that happens in a marriage, or a friendship, or with any privilege we are afforded. New things seem wonderful, but when we become familiar with them, we begin to have less respect for them, or even contempt. A new bride may hang on her husband's every word and agree with him about each thing he says, admiring him openly for his wisdom. After ten years of marriage, she may be argumentative about all of his opinions, and yet someone she barely knows can have the same opinion as her husband and she will respect and receive whatever he says. Have you ever said to your spouse, "I told you the same thing they did, and you argued with me"? I have had it happen to me.

The Lord once spoke to my heart, saying, "If you would show your husband one half of the respect you show your pastor, your marriage would be a lot better." I am ashamed to admit that He was absolutely correct. Why did I behave that way? Not because I didn't love my husband, but I had let familiarity lessen my admiration and willingness to receive advice from him. The pastor was a newer addition in my life at that time, and I had not known him long enough for him to seem familiar.

How can we live with someone and not become familiar? Certainly we will know very well those with whom we spend a lot of time. But losing sight of *why* we first admired a person is what breeds familiarity and destroys the peace in God-ordained relationships.

For this reason, many people in authority feel they cannot spend a lot of time with those under their authority. Their experience has been that most people will lose respect through familiarity. It takes a wise person, who is very spiritually mature, to work under someone's authority and also be close friends with him or her.

People usually admire and look up to "the boss," which is a good thing; we are to give respect and honor to whom it is due. It helps us serve people properly if we really respect and admire those over us. Being around them a lot, however, can cause us to begin to look at them as "Good ole Joe" or "My buddy Charlie," and something happens in the heart that eventually kills the relationship. Respect is a key in good relationships, and I feel the lack of it is one of the main reasons that relationships are destroyed.

We should not allow ourselves to become too familiar with the things and people in our lives that are now special. Some things I own are very special to me; I treat them as valuable, taking precaution that they encounter no harm. How we view things determines how we will treat them. Even more, the people in our lives who are special to us we should treat with great respect, handle them carefully, be appreciative, thanking God for their friendship. Don't let what is special become mundane. To keep from taking each other for granted, we can practice remembering how precious people are and focus on thankfulness for their presence in our lives.

It may even be healthy to think about how it would affect our lives if we lost certain persons' presence or friendship. *What if So-and-so and So-and-so were no longer in my life? What if suddenly they were gone?* It could help us keep in the forefront of our thinking how vital they are and assist us in treating them as such. I have done this with my husband, Dave. I have thought about how it would change my life if he suddenly was not in it. He is very valuable to me, and I intend to treat him with respect and honor.

SET BOUNDARIES ON TEASING

I am aware of a relationship between two men who really enjoyed one another that was ruined through excessive joking. The relationship began with tremendous respect and admiration; they were both fun-loving guys who enjoyed teasing people. As they became more and more familiar with one another, the teasing took on a more tense nature. At first, their jesting was cute and funny, but it soon became a point of rivalry, and I noticed they used the pretense of "I'm joking" to make crude comments to each another when they were upset.

They should have shown respect for each other by practicing honest confrontation during a disagreement, but instead one would make a comment to the other that he intended to bring correction, but he did it under the guise of joking. Then the other one would respond with similar statements. This bantering would go back and forth, all, of course, under the mask of "I'm joking."

When someone's character, physical appearance, or family members are the brunt of "the joke," it ceases to be funny.

The comments became more and more rude and crude until these two men began to disrespect each other and lost the desire to have a relationship. I certainly did not enjoy being around them; their way of dealing with one another was uncomfortable. I could tell there was underlying strife. I could tell that the "joking" was not really as funny as they were pretending it was. The Bible says in Ephesians 5:4 that we are to rid ourselves of all "coarse jesting, which [is] not fitting or becoming," because it causes problems between people that in turn grieve the Holy Spirit of God.

They could have teased one another and enjoyed it, but only with boundaries. Even something like having fun must have boundaries, or it becomes an evil thing. In other words, we need to know how far to go and when to stop. We can set boundaries on ourselves and never put someone else in a position of having to enforce his own boundaries.

I know within myself when I am spending too much, talking too much, working too hard, and not getting enough rest. I also know that when teasing becomes rude, it has gone too far. At that point, I need to apologize and stay within God-ordained boundaries, or I may ruin an otherwise great relationship.

Familiarity is often the root cause of coarse jesting. When we don't know someone really well, we are more careful what we say, but it seems the better we know an individual, the more the "real us" pops out and the importance we place on good manners diminishes. It is better to remain respectful in all relationships and always to treat everyone with courtesy.

FOLLOW THE HOLY SPIRIT

Our goal is to let the Holy Spirit of God lead us into what will produce good fruit in our lives, such as discipline, which is another way of saying we have boundaries in our lives.

Without boundaries, everything is out of control. God wants to be in control, but He won't force us. We discipline ourselves to follow Him, which means we learn to live within boundaries.

We cannot follow the Holy Spirit and also follow people. We will either be God-pleasers or people-pleasers. If we establish boundaries for others as well as ourselves, we are on the pathway to being led by God's Spirit.

If you really think about it, life is filled with boundaries. A bedtime is a boundary. It says, "I will stay up until this time and no later." That boundary allows us to get good sleep and feel healthy the following day; it provides much needed energy. If we frequently ignore our boundaries in this area, it will adversely affect our health.

Stop signs and traffic lights are boundaries, as well as speed-limit signs and the yellow lines in the middle of the road. These boundaries are set in place for our safety.

Don't look at boundaries as something to be despised, but as something that provides safety and security for all of us. If *boundary* is a word you are not familiar with, I suggest you learn all you can in this area. I highly recommend Dr. Henry Cloud and Dr. John Townsend's book titled *Boundaries*. It was very helpful to me as well as several people I know. Without boundaries, we will never enjoy peace in our lives.

If you have made a decision to pursue peace, then establishing and maintaining boundaries must become a priority to you. Boundaries will protect you from being easily offended, which is the next way to keep your peace.

PEACEKEEPER #19

Let Go of Offenses

⌇⌇⌇

We must learn to pick our battles. There are simply too many conflicts in life to fight them all. We will have many major things to deal with, so the least we can do is practice letting go of all the little things that people do that irritate us. As we saw in the chapter on esteeming others, God may lead us to confront people for misconduct, or even for crossing our set boundaries, but there will be many little issues that we need to just ignore.

We are not alone in our dilemma; even the twelve disciples whom Jesus personally trained had relationship problems with each other. Peter asked Jesus how many times he must forgive his brother for the same offense (see Matthew 18:21–22). This indicates that someone, maybe one of the other disciples, continually irritated Peter in some way. It may have been as simple as a personality conflict or an irksome habit, but whatever it was, Satan used it to steal Peter's peace.

Jesus told him to forgive seventy times seven, which meant the perfect number of times. However many times it takes to remain in peace throughout our lives, that's how many times we are to overlook the offenses of others.

People should enter into close relationships with their eyes wide open, realizing there will be things about people that bother them. *After* we enter these relationships, we will have to *close our eyes* to many things. It will not do any good to concentrate on faults, because some of them may never go away. Some things change with people as the years go by, and others seem to remain forever.

"Love covers a multitude of sins [forgives and disregards the offenses of others]" (1 Peter 4:8). The Bible instructs us to make allowances for one another (see Ephesians 4:2). In other words, we are to allow people to be less than perfect.

I personally respond much better to people who allow me to be human than I do to those who expect me to be divine (perfect). I hate the pressure of trying to please someone in all things. It makes me uneasy and on edge, and I feel as if I must tiptoe around lest I offend in some minor thing. If I want to reap relationships that allow me to be myself, I must sow them.

I was recently speaking with my administrative assistant. We discussed the fact that it is impossible to spend as much time together as we do and never see each other's imperfect side. We must be generous with letting things go. That means we don't need to make a big deal out of every error and many times don't even need to mention them at all.

I have noticed in myself and others that even when we are willing to forgive, we want the person we are forgiving to *know* that we are forgiving him or her. We usually want to at least mention it.

You Will Be Tested Every Day

Why is it so hard to completely ignore offenses? We want to mention the fact that we overlooked their obnoxious behaviors so the people who offend us do not think they can treat us improperly and get away with it—it is a type of self-protection. But God wants us to trust Him to protect us as well as to heal us from *every* hurt and emotional wound, *every day.*

I wonder how weary we would be at the end of each day if God mentioned every tiny thing we do wrong. He does deal with us, but I am quite sure He also overlooks a lot of things. If people are corrected too much, it can discourage them and break their spirits.

We should form a habit of dealing only with what God Himself prompts us to address, not just everything we feel like confronting, or every little thing that bothers us. I am the type of person who would not be inclined to let anybody get away with anything.

I don't like feeling someone is taking advantage of me, partially because I was abused in my childhood and partially because I am human, and none of us embraces disrespect. In the past, I was quick to tell everyone his or her faults, but I have learned that is not pleasing to God.

Just as we want others to give us mercy, we must give it to them. We reap what we sow—nothing more or less. Even God may withhold His mercy from us if we are unwilling to give mercy to others.

We are to be Peacemakers, not Peace Breakers. Always remember that it takes two people to fight. If you respond with harsh words, you will stir up anger, but if you respond to an offensive statement with "a soft answer," you will "turn away wrath" (Proverbs 15:1). Someone has said that anger is one letter away from danger. Just add a *d*, which could well represent *devil*, in front of anger, and you see the trouble with rage.

I believe that our lives can be full of peace if we simply decide to do what is right in every situation that comes along. There is a right and a wrong way to handle the storms of life. But until I was filled with the Holy Spirit and began to learn about the power that is available to me as a believer to do the right thing, I never handled offenses right.

Jesus' economy is upside down from what the world teaches us. He says that we can have peace in the midst of the storm. Now just think about how awesome that would be, if *no matter what happened*, you could remain full of peace.

You can keep your peace in an unexpected traffic jam. You can keep your peace when you have to wait in the grocery store line, while the person in front of you doesn't have any prices on his products, the clerk runs out of cash-register tape, and she's new, and she doesn't know what she's doing anyway, and she is fumbling around trying to get the tape in the register, and you are in the biggest rush you have faced all week.

Even then, you can keep from losing your peace, from getting a headache or an ulcer, and from blowing your whole witness by acting like a fool. Even then, you can just stay steady because you have the power living in you to stay in peace.

Jesus said that He gives us power even to "trample upon serpents and scorpions, and [physical and mental strength and ability] over all the power that the enemy [possesses]" (Luke 10:19). He promised that nothing will harm us in any way. If we have the power over the enemy, surely we can overlook the offenses of others. He gives us the energy we need to treat people right.

Understand that every time you are tempted to be offended and upset, your faith is being tried. The Word says,

[You should] be exceedingly glad on this account, though now for a little while you may be distressed by trials and suffer temptations, so that [the genuineness] of your faith may be tested, [your faith] which is infinitely more precious than the perishable gold which is tested and purified by fire. [This proving of your faith is intended] to redound to [your] praise and glory and honor when Jesus Christ (the Messiah, the Anointed One) is revealed. (1 Peter 1:6–7)

Peter was saying, "Don't be amazed at the fiery trials that you go through, because they are taking place to test your quality." Every relationship test is an opportunity to glorify the work of God in you as a testimony to those watching you endure the offense.

Why do you think that in school you had to take final exams before passing to the next grade? You didn't graduate to the next level just because you showed up at school every day. You got a diploma only when you took the final exams and showed that you could answer the questions.

The Bible says that God will never allow more to come on us than what we can bear. But with every temptation, He also provides the way out. Remember, the only time we will not find the strength of God in our lives to do what is before us is if we're trying to do something that God never told us to do. He never told us to hold offenses against others. In fact, forgiveness is a very big issue with God.

Jesus said,

For if you forgive people their trespasses [their reckless and willful sins, leaving them, letting them go, and giving up resentment], your heavenly Father will also forgive you. But if you do not forgive others their trespasses [their reckless and willful sins, leaving them, letting them go, and giving up resentment], neither will your Father forgive you your trespasses. (Matthew 6:14–15)

DON'T ASK YOURSELF FOR ADVICE

Solomon said that he took counsel with his own mind, and in essence he concluded that it was like "searching after wind" (see Ecclesiastes 1:17). Our minds say to be upset if someone offends us, but God says to let it go.

I often share a teaching that I call "Shake It Off," which is based on the time Paul was on the island of Malta. He was helping some people build a fire when a poisonous serpent crawled out and attached itself to his hand. At first, when the people saw it they thought that he must be wicked to have such an evil thing happen to him. They watched, waiting for him to fall over dead.

But the Bible says that Paul simply "shook it off."

We can learn so much from that. When somebody offends or rejects us, we need to see it as a bite from Satan and just shake it off. If we hear that somebody has been talking about us, we need to shake it off. When we are sitting in a traffic jam and begin to feel upset, we need to let it go.

Frustration won't stop on its own. It keeps raising the pressure higher and higher, as if somebody is tightening the screws on our nerves. But when you feel that happening, you can literally shake it off and refuse to give in to it. Sometimes we make things bigger than they need to be; we blow them out of proportion. We can choose to let offenses go before they take root in us and cause serious problems.

Jesus told the disciples that if they entered towns that didn't receive them, they should just go to the next town. He told them to shake the dust off of their feet and move on. He didn't want the disciples to dwell on the rejection they had experienced; He wanted them to stay focused on sharing their testimony of His working in their lives.

Likewise, as we follow the Spirit, we can shake off offenses and hold on to our peace. When others see that we are able to remain calm even when "the serpent" bites us, they will want to know where that peace is coming from in our lives.

When we are in a state of upset, we cannot hear from God clearly. The Bible promises us that God will lead us and walk us out of our troubles, but we cannot be led by the Spirit if we are offended and in a dither.

We can't get away from the storms of life, or the temptation to be irritated at someone. But we can respond to offenses by saying, "God, You are merciful, and You are good. And I am going to put my confidence in You until this storm passes over" (see Psalm 57:1). We cannot prevent feeling negative emotions, but we can learn to manage them. We can trust God to give us grace to act godly even in an ungodly situation.

One day we were looking for a parking place, and a car was backing out, so Dave waited so he could get the spot. He had his blinker on, clearly showing that he was waiting to park. Well, a guy behind us on a bicycle was very put out because we had stopped. He was ranting and raving, and he pulled around Dave, but we held our peace and smiled at him. But while this guy was railing on us, somebody else took our parking place!

I can remember when that kind of thing might have really irritated us, but we've been through so many trials that we could shrug and say, "Bless you, hope you enjoy that parking place!" And we found another one. We've learned not to let offensive people steal our joy anymore. You might say that we have learned not to let offensive people offend us.

What good does it do to get upset at someone who takes your parking place? You can get all mad and bothered, but the other person will still have your spot. And you probably will never see that offensive person again as long as you live, so why let it steal your peace, even for a few minutes?

As soon as you lose your peace, the devil wins. If getting you offended works once, believe me, he will set you up with the same opportunity over and over.

Later, Dave said that person who took our place actually helped us. We didn't know that we were in the wrong block, and if we had parked there we would have been far from where we wanted to go. What Satan means for our harm, God intends for our good. Doing what is right leads to peace and joy.

Righteousness, peace, and joy in the Holy Ghost are a progression. If we don't know who we are in Christ, then we won't realize that we have His strength in us to do the right thing. Then we won't have peace, and if we don't have peace, we won't have joy. So if you have lost your joy, you need to back all the way up and find out where it was that you lost your peace, and then do what is right in that situation.

People without Christ, who don't live in the kingdom of God, don't have the power to keep from being offended. When they have a problem, they only have one choice, which is to get upset. But we have a choice. We can believe that Jesus is in our situation with us, and even though sometimes it feels as if He is sleeping through our storm, we can know that He is able to tell the storm to be still—and when He does, it will stop.

DON'T CRY OVER SPILLED MILK

If you are going to walk in peace, you have to be willing to be adaptable and adjustable to people and circumstances. When I lived in the "explode mode," it never failed that one of my children spilled something at the dinner table—every night. And every night I had a fit.

They would tip over their cups and start crying as soon as they saw their milk running under the bowls. I learned that when you spill something, you have to try to get to it before it gets to the crack in the table, because milk will sour quickly in there with all that other hidden dirt! And then eventually you will have to take the whole table apart and scrape dried milk and foodstuff out of its crevices with a table knife. (Now I have a table with a glass top, but everybody scratches it! You see, there is always something you will have to put up with and let go of in life.)

I used to shout at the kids, "Can't we ever have one meal in peace?" I didn't realize we could have had a meal in peace if I stopped shouting at everyone. I could have brought peace to our table every night if I had just cleaned up and shut up.

So, if you have wondered how to have peace, I can tell you that it will come if you will quit making a big deal about everything. You will have to be willing to let go of getting distraught over accidents or not getting your way.

One night I was under the table because whatever the kids had spilled had made it to the crack in the table before I got there, and the liquid was running down the center table legs. I was having a fit, and the kids were upset, and somebody kicked me in the head, and that made me even madder. I knew it was an accident, I knew he or she didn't do it on purpose. Poor Dave had to be weary from sitting down to dinner after working hard all day and having to endure my outburst. (And I couldn't figure out why he wanted to go to the driving range every night and hit golf balls, so I'd throw a fit about that too.)

So there I was, under the table, saying, "Every night somebody's got to spill something, and we just need some peace around here. . . . " And the Holy Ghost came unto me (right under that table), saying, "Joyce, once the milk is spilled, no matter how big of a fit you have, you are not going to get it to run back up the table legs, across the table, and into the glass." And He said, "Joyce, you need to learn how to go with the flow."

There are some things that we can do something about, but there are a whole lot of things that we can't do anything about. If it is something we can't do anything about, then we need to let it go and keep our joy. We need to hold our peace, do what is right, and let God work on our behalf.

When Jesus said, "Stop *allowing* yourselves to be agitated and disturbed; and do not *permit* yourselves to be . . . unsettled" (John 14:27, italics mine), He was saying that we must control ourselves.

For many years, I argued, "God, I don't want to act like that, but I just can't help it." The Bible says that self-control is a fruit of the Spirit, who dwells in us. We don't have to give way to unbridled emotions. God will give you power to do whatever you need to do, as often as you need to do it. God will help you manage your emotions. Be sure to read my book *Managing Your Emotions* if you frequently lose your peace through emotional responses to life's trials. Whether it is to help us not get upset over spilled milk or to forgive an offense, the Lord will give us grace as often as we need it.

The only way we will have peace is if we let little offenses and irritations go. Why not save some time and grief and just forgive people right away? When we are upset, we are much less likely to be led by the Spirit of God. We are not sensitive to His touch when we don't maintain a quiet inner life, which we will look at next.

PEACEKEEPER #20

Maintain a Quiet Inner Life

To enjoy more peace in our lives, we need to practice just being still and staying calm even when we feel like spilling out everything we think and feel. Many relationships break apart because everyone wants the last word. Sometimes, simply holding our peace is the right thing to do.

Although we have already talked about the importance of not speaking idle words, there is also great value in learning to entrust our battles to the Lord. Knowing He will fight for us fills us with deep peace that passes understanding, like the peace Daniel felt when he was thrown into the lions' den. David wrote some words that may express Daniel's feelings:

> He has redeemed my life in peace from the battle that was against me [so that none came near me], for they were many who strove with me. God will hear and humble them, even He Who abides of old—Selah [pause, and calmly think of that]!— because in them there has been no change [of heart], and they do not fear, revere, and worship God. (Psalm 55:18–19)

If we will spend time meditating on God's promises, considering the great things He has done in our lives, it will fill us with a deep peace that will cause us to be calm even when others seem full of fear, rage, or anxiety. Our peace will bring peace to others. The Word teaches that we will win the respect of other people by how we live our lives: "Make it your ambition and definitely endeavor to live quietly and peacefully, to mind your own affairs, and to work with your hands, as we charged you, so that you may bear yourselves becomingly and be correct and honorable and command the respect of the outside world" (1 Thessalonians 4:11–12).

God wants us to have a disposition that will bless others; we are ambassadors of Christ, Peacemakers who should demonstrate the calm, soothing presence of Jesus. God created us in His image, and our lives should be filled with the fruit of His indwelling presence.

Many people believe that if Jesus walked into a roomful of strife, it would take Him only a few minutes to bring peace to whatever the circumstances were. He had a soothing nature; He was clothed with meekness. He wasn't out to prove anything. He wasn't concerned about what people thought about Him. He already knew who He was, so He didn't feel the need to defend Himself.

In fact, even when Pilate brought charges against Him, Jesus made no answer (see Matthew 27:14). Other people got upset with Jesus and tried to start all kinds of arguments with Him, but His response was always peaceful and loving. His mellow disposition was the result of a quiet inner life, and a confident relationship with His Father. Inner peace produces outer peace.

Jesus was the fulfillment of Isaiah's prophecy:

Behold, My Servant Whom I have chosen, My Beloved in and with Whom My soul is well pleased and has found its delight. I will put My Spirit upon Him, and He shall proclaim and show forth justice to the nations. He will not strive or wrangle or cry out loudly; nor will anyone hear His voice in the streets; a bruised reed He will not break, and a smoldering (dimly burning) wick He will not quench, till He brings justice and a just cause to victory. And in and on His name will the Gentiles (the peoples outside of Israel) set their hopes. (Matthew 12:18–21)

God wants us to enjoy the same inner peace that was visible in the life of Jesus, and He expects us to bless others with the same grace. First Peter 2:15–16 confirms, "For it is God's will and intention that by doing right [your good and honest lives] should silence (muzzle, gag) the ignorant charges and ill-informed criticisms of foolish persons. [Live] as free people, [yet] without employing your freedom as a pretext for wickedness; but [live at all times] as servants of God."

The *Living Bible* (TLB) paraphrases this verse: "It is God's will that your good lives should silence those who foolishly condemn the Gospel without knowing what it can do for them, having never experienced its power."

MEDITATE ON GOD'S GOODNESS

Peter's letter called for believers to show respect for everyone and especially to love other Christians. We are to honor those in government and submit ourselves not only to those in authority over us who are kind, but also to those who are unjust (see 1 Peter 2:17–18). Keep in mind, the reason God asks us to do this is so that we are a testimony of His love to people who have never experienced His power. God does not delight in our suffering in these types of situations, but He does delight when we behave in a godly manner and glorify Him with our attitudes during them.

I know how difficult this sounds, but our peace must come from the confidence that the Lord will fight our battles for us. Hebrews 13:6 says, "So we take comfort and are encouraged and confidently and boldly say, The Lord is my Helper; I will not be seized with alarm [I will not fear or dread or be terrified]. What can man do to me?"

We are to keep our minds on God, who works "wonders in the earth" and makes wars cease. The Lord says, "Let be *and be still,* and know (recognize and understand) that I am God. I will be exalted among the nations! I will be exalted in the earth!" (Psalm 46:8–10, italics mine).

If we spend time meditating on the wonders that God is doing in the world and exalt Him above all of our differences with other people, we will enjoy a calm joy deep within our hearts. Then, when squeezed by the pressure of relationships and the trials of everyday life, we will emulate the soothing fruit of the Spirit.

We have outer lives and inner lives; there's more to us than what we see when we look in the mirror. There's another whole life going on inside each of us, and this inner life needs to learn to be still and know that God will work everything out for our good.

We know that people can pretend one thing on the outside and have something else totally different going on inside. And the Bible makes it very clear that our inner lives are more important than our outer lives to God, because He looks at our hearts. It was really life-transforming for me to realize that I might be fooling a lot of people, but I wasn't fooling God.

For me to act as if everything were okay while I had strife in my heart was not pleasing to the Lord. I decided I had to find a way to make things right inside of me. Real peace cannot be faked. Even though we may hide our real attitudes from people, we cannot hide them from God, because He lives *in* us.

KEEP GOD'S TEMPLE FULL OF PEACE

First Corinthians 3:16 says, "Do you not discern and understand that you [the whole church at Corinth] are God's temple (His sanctuary), and that God's Spirit has His permanent dwelling in you [to be at home in you, collectively as a church and also individually]?"

The Scripture teaches us that when we are born again, we become the home of God. Isn't that about the most awesome thing you can imagine? We are God's home, we are His dwelling place, and we should want Him to be comfortable living in us.

No one is comfortable living in a house of strife, and the Holy

Spirit is especially grieved when we are not in peace. All those years I spent in turmoil were wasted. The peace I enjoy now is so inspiring that I want to reach everyone in the world with the good news of its availability through Jesus.

Before I learned how to enjoy the inner life of peace, I was always angry; if not with somebody else, with myself. I found out that if I wanted to have peace, I had to choose peace.

When I read in First Peter 3:11 that we weren't to just "*desire* peaceful relations*" (italics mine), we are to pursue peace with everyone, I realized that this meant we aren't to just wait for peace to happen.

I believe a lot of people *desire* to have peaceful relations, but they are waiting for the other persons to act right so they can feel peaceful. I always remind people that they don't need a wishbone; they need backbone. We have to *make* peace happen.

Practice Being Still

I found out that in many instances, Dave and I could have peace if I adapted myself a little bit, or if I chose *not to say something that I really wanted to say*. I discovered that simply being still made peace happen.

See, in the beginning, I wanted peace, but I wanted Dave to give it to me. I wanted my children to give it to me. I wanted God to give me peace, and so I was always praying: "Oh, God, give me peace." But then I realized that Jesus had already left His peace with me, so begging God to give it to me was futile. I just needed to use the peace that was available deep within me.

I had enjoyed days when I was peaceful, I had plenty of money, nobody was bothering me, everybody was doing what I wanted, I was getting my way, I felt good, and the house was clean. But that was the kind of peace that the world gives us, and we don't need the power of the Holy Spirit to have peace on days when everything is going well.

The peace that Jesus said He left for us is a deep sense of knowing that even though everything isn't all right today, things will work out in the end. We believe *this too shall pass*. That peace is from the power of the Holy Spirit, and it equips us to have peace when it doesn't make any sense to have peace. As Spirit-filled believers, we have the strength of the Holy Spirit not to worry even when there are plenty of things to worry about.

Calming down is something you do on purpose. You can get upset without trying to, but if you're going to calm down, you will have to work at it. Keeping quiet is a powerful way to calm down. Often to have peace, as I just mentioned, I have to *not say* something that I really want to say. And I'm a talker, so usually it is *hard* for me not to make the point or have the last word. But I have learned that the fruit of peace is a greater reward than the temporary satisfaction of putting in my two cents. I'm learning that (as I said in chapter 16), being right is highly overrated. We usually strive to be right, but is it worth all we go through for the momentary, fleshly satisfaction we get from it?

Calming down is a decision. It has nothing to do with feelings. It is an act of obedience, and we do it to honor God because He lives in our house, and He's saying: "I want it—I want some peace in this house. I want it quiet in here. I want you to be full of peace."

What is normal for a Christian? Are we supposed to be all stirred up and anxious while trying to figure out something? Are we to be angry while wild thoughts and wicked imaginations go on inside of us? No. But it's amazing how many people live that way; they go to church on Sunday and think that's all it takes.

Having a right relationship with God is going to take a commitment of your time, and you're going to have to dedicate your inner life—not just church attendance, a few good works, and a little bit of your money—to the Lord. A quiet spirit is probably the greatest sacrifice we can offer up to God.

Watchman Nee, author of *The Spiritual Man,* was a gifted preacher of the gospel in China during the early 1900s. He wrote the following excerpt about how Christians are to have quiet spirits:

"To aspire to live quietly" (1 Thess.4.11). This is the duty of every Christian. Modern Christians talk far too much. Sometimes their unuttered words surpass in number those that are spoken. Confused thought and endless speech set our spirits to wandering away from the control of our wills. A "wild spirit" often leads people to walk according to the flesh. How hard it is for believers to restrain themselves from sinning when their spirit becomes unruly. An errant spirit invariably ends up with an error in conduct.

Before one can display a quiet mouth he must first possess a quiet spirit, for out of the abundance of the spirit does the mouth speak. We ought to carefully keep our spirits in stillness; even in time of intense confusion our inner being should nevertheless be able to sustain an independent quietude. A placid spirit is essential to anyone walking after the spirit: without it he shall quickly fall into sin. If our spirit is hushed we can hear the voice of the Holy Spirit there, obey the will of God, and understand what we cannot understand when confused. Such a quiet inner life constitutes the Christian's adornment which betokens something manifested outwardly.*

The thing we need to do when we are in trouble is hear from God. That's why it's so important that when we have some trial, some turmoil going on outwardly, we manage to keep our spirits quiet. If we get all stirred up inside, we are not going to hear from God. We cannot understand Him when we are confused and then cannot obey the will of God.

We will have peace when we learn to maintain an inner quiet. That's not a job we can give to God; we have the job of leaning on

*Watchman Nee, *The Spiritual Man,* Vol. 2 (New York: Christian Fellowship Publishers, Inc., 1968), 180–181.

the power of the Holy Spirit by faith to maintain a quiet spirit. Then we can hear from God and obey the leading of His Spirit. I share more about how to do this in my book titled *How to Hear from God*.

When we get disturbed in the flesh, we release idle words that cause damage. But being still isn't just refraining from speech; it is about living every day in a calm state of confidence in God that encourages the Holy Spirit to thrive in our house.

The serenity of God's presence makes us attractive to others and is a powerful testimony of God's work in our lives. I just love peace. I'm addicted to peace. Paul knew the value of peace, as we see when he was training Timothy, a young preacher. When he was giving Timothy instructions on how to handle his ministry, Paul told him, "Be calm and cool and steady, accept and suffer unflinchingly every hardship, do the work of an evangelist, fully perform all the duties of your ministry" (2 Timothy 4:5).

That is good advice for all of us. If we are calm and steady, people know they can depend on us. God can depend on us. No one has to wonder what we might be like one day from the next. When our unsaved friends see the calm and steady faith we have, they will be open to our testimony of the gospel. Stability is the fruit of living a peaceful life.

STABILITY RELEASES ABILITY

I believe that stability releases ability. I think a lot of people have ability because God has given them gifts, but they're not stable Christians, and so God cannot use their gifts publicly in ministry. They would end up hurting the cause of Christ because of their unpredictable behavior.

We can't be stable just when we're getting our way. We have to be stable when we're having trouble and trials, when people are coming against us, and when people are talking about us. Paul knew a lack of stability would hurt Timothy's witness and anointing; it would prevent him from hearing from God. We don't enjoy life unless we develop an ability to remain stable in the storm.

When we're upset, we are usually not listening. People don't hear because they don't get quiet enough to hear what God is saying. God isn't going to yell at you. He usually speaks in a still, small voice, and to hear Him, we must maintain an inner calmness. Actually, peace itself is a guideline for what God is approving and disapproving of in your life. We must all learn to follow peace if we intend to follow God.

You have to choose purposely to stay calm, to put your confidence and trust in God, and to be a ready listener for His voice. Then you have to be willing to make whatever adjustments are necessary to have peace in your life.

Some people might say, "Well, it's not fair for me to always be the one who's changing and adjusting to keep harmony with everyone else." It might not be fair, but God will bring justice in your life if you do what He's asking you to do. It might not be fair, but it will be worth it.

Just because somebody else is hard to get along with, we don't need to be hard to get along with too. We have to stop letting somebody else's bad behavior steal our joy.

I've mentioned that in the early years of our marriage, when I threw temper tantrums and didn't talk, Dave just stayed calm and happy. He went around the house singing and whistling; he went to play golf and watch football and play with the kids; he continued to enjoy life. When I was about to blow my cork in another room, he was steady and stable, and even though it made me so mad that I couldn't get him upset, he eventually won me over by the peace that he always maintained.

Unhappy people want to make other people unhappy; it irritates them to be around someone happy. But people who are full of peace can positively affect unhappy people. I saw Dave's example and became hungry for what he had. I know, without a doubt, if Dave had not had that stability in his life, I wouldn't be in ministry today.

I needed an example of peace because I grew up in a house of strife. I actually did not even know how to remain peaceful when I did not like my circumstances. Even someone preaching it to me would not have been enough; *I needed to see it.* His example was very important for what God had planned for me.

So, if you are in a relationship with somebody who is like I was— angry, upset, out of control, throwing temper tantrums, making bad choices—you can influence him or her to receive the grace of God to change if you will be stable in the power of the Holy Spirit.

It won't do any good to leave gospel tracts around the house or play my teaching tapes real loud. It won't help to leave books opened with underlined passages for that person to find. The Word says that we win people over, not by discussion, but by our godly lives (see 1 Peter 3:1). Of course, sometimes God uses our verbal witness to help others, but He uses our example even more.

Dave didn't preach to me: His life was a sermon. He lived his confidence in God in front of me. And his stability is one of the things that I still appreciate in him.

I grew up in a home where I never knew from one minute to the next what was going to happen. Somebody could be happy one day and ready to hit me the next day, and I didn't even know why. I lived through a lot of violence and anger, where ranting and raving was a daily event.

Perhaps you live in such a home now, but God can change it if you will abide in Him. Isaiah 32:17–18 promises this: "And the effect of righteousness will be peace [internal and external], and the result of righteousness will be quietness and confident trust forever. My people shall dwell in a peaceable habitation, in safe dwellings, and in quiet resting-places."

First Peter 3:2 gives us guidelines on how to live our lives to win over those who do not know about the grace of God. Though it is written in light of women with their husbands, the same principles apply to all relationships that we have with others. It says to conduct ourselves with reverence toward others, "to respect, defer to, revere, . . . esteem, appreciate, prize, and, in the human sense, to adore" and enjoy those whom God has given us to love. People's attraction to us will not be based on our outer lives, our hairstyles, or our pretty clothes.

Instead, we will draw people to us by "the inward adorning and beauty of the hidden person of the heart, with the incorruptible and unfading charm of a gentle and peaceful spirit, which [is not anxious or wrought up, but] is very precious in the sight of God" (1 Peter 3:4). We are true sons and daughters of God if we do right and let nothing terrify us, if we "don't give way to hysterical fears or [let] anxieties unnerve" us (v. 6).

Our circumstances won't change until we change. Remember, we are to keep our minds stayed on God, and He will keep us in perfect peace. And whoever heeds wisdom will "dwell securely and in confident trust and shall be quiet, without fear or dread of evil" (Proverbs 1:33).

Watchman Nee said that we should keep our spirits in a position of "being light and free all the time—keeping in mind that the outer man is different than inside." We can have raging storms taking place around us and still enjoy perfect peace on the inside.

I realize that I have already given you a lot of information on how to keep peace in your life, but in the next chapter I will share one more Peacekeeper that will keep you in God's will for the rest of your journey.

PEACEKEEPER #21

Aggressively Pursue Peace

❦

The main point I hope you remember from this study is to aggressively pursue peace. Through Jesus Christ, God has provided everything you need to enjoy a life of peace. The Word tells us, "*Strive* to live in peace with everybody and pursue that consecration and holiness without which no one will [ever] see the Lord" (Hebrews 12:14, italics mine).

The word *strive* has been translated in various Bible versions as "follow," "pursue," and "make every effort." It's important to understand that God expects us to interact with people. I know believers who withdraw from everyone, who don't think it is important to go to church or spend time with people. But that is not the heart of God. He wants us to find peace *with* people, not away from them. In fact, the Lord tells us to look after each other, helping each other to be built up in faith, as these next Scriptures command:

And let us consider and give attentive, continuous care to watching over one another, studying how we may stir up (stimulate and incite) to love and helpful deeds and noble activities, not forsaking or neglecting to assemble together [as believers], as is the habit of some people, but admonishing (warning, urging, and encouraging) one another, and all the more faithfully as you see the day approaching. (Hebrews 10:24–25)

God gives His blessings as a free gift, yet we receive or appropriate them through faith. If we don't release our faith in the promises of

God, they will not help us. We can encourage each other to remain faithful. We can pray for each other when our own faith weakens. Above all, we can encourage each other to aggressively pursue peace.

An aggressive peacemaker remains on watch to see that no one in the body falls away from God's grace. Hebrews 12:15 charges us to "exercise foresight and be on the watch to look [after one another], to see that no one falls back from and fails to secure God's grace (His unmerited favor and spiritual blessing), in order that no root of resentment (rancor, bitterness, or hatred) shoots forth and causes trouble and bitter torment, and the many become contaminated and defiled by it."

People could conceivably have money in the bank and yet live as those with none simply because they never went to the bank to get it. Jesus arranged for us to enjoy peace, but we must pursue it. Actually it is important to remember that God's Word says in Psalm 34:14 that we are to "*seek, inquire for, and crave peace and pursue (go after) it!*" (italics mine). When I saw this Scripture and then this similar one in 1 Peter 3:10–11, it was life-changing for me:

> For let him who wants to enjoy life and see good days [good—whether apparent or not] keep his tongue free from evil and his lips from guile (treachery, deceit). Let him turn away from wickedness and shun it, and let him do right. Let him search for peace (harmony; undisturbedness from fears, agitating passions, and moral conflicts) and seek it eagerly. [Do not merely desire peaceful relations with God, with your fellowmen, and with yourself, but pursue, go after them!]

When I first understood this Scripture, I realized that even though I prayed for peace regularly, there was something else I needed to *do*: I needed to pursue it, go after it in a strong way.

I began to study peace and examined what types of things caused me to lose my peace. I decided that I was absolutely unwilling to live my life frustrated and upset.

THINGS DON'T CHANGE OVERNIGHT

I would like to be able to tell you that things changed overnight; however, they didn't. I had to study the subject of peace for quite a long time and practice principles of peace until they became habit for me.

We form addictive habits throughout our lives. We learn to respond in certain ways and do so without even thinking about it. We must break these habits and form new ones, and this takes time. I want to *stress* that becoming a peacemaker and developing peaceful ways will take time, otherwise you may become discouraged in the beginning and just give up. I encourage you to stick with your pursuit until you experience victory, because it is well worth it.

One of the habits I had to break was getting upset whenever I did not get my way. I examined my pattern to understand why I always reacted like this. I realized that I had watched my father respond this way for years, while I was growing up. He was a very angry and controlling man and always got furious when things did not go his way.

As I have said before, my childhood home was filled with turmoil. It was our normal atmosphere. I doubt that I ever really enjoyed peace as a child. My alcoholic father was abusing me sexually, and he was violent toward almost everyone. My life was filled with fear: fear of being hurt, of someone's discovering what my father was doing to me, of no one's ever discovering it and helping me, of the fact that somehow it might be my fault, of making mistakes because I always got into trouble when I did. Fear! Fear! Fear! That was what life was to me.

I never learned peaceful ways as a child, but thank God we become new creatures when we enter a personal relationship with God through putting our faith in Jesus Christ (see 2 Corinthians 5:17). I share more about the story of God's redemptive work in my life and my father's in my newly revised book *Beauty for Ashes*. It bears our testimonies that we clearly receive a new beginning through faith in Jesus Christ; we can have our minds renewed and learn how to think and respond correctly to every situation in life.

God has blessed me with a strong personality. It helps me in many ways, but it can also be a great hindrance because I don't give up easily. In other words, if I have my mind set that something should be a certain way, it is not easy for me to let it go and trust God. Now, when I need to press through to the finish of something and refuse to give up, my personality is a benefit. But when I really cannot change a thing and need to let go and let God work, I have often found it difficult, to say the least. This is why I often say that it is so important to change what we can change, let go of what we cannot change, and have the wisdom to know the difference.

You might say, "Well, Joyce, I was not raised in a home filled with turmoil, and I don't even have the kind of personality you do. But I still don't have peace! So, what is my problem?" Satan works hard all of our lives to make sure we don't have righteousness, peace, and joy. He finds ways to steal from everyone.

We have examined many of the ways he will steal our peace in great detail, but the important thing is to be determined to have peace no matter how long it takes, or what it requires.

Crave peace, pursue and go after it! I love that statement. Each time I hear or read it, I feel a surge of determination within me to enjoy the life of peace that Jesus died to give me.

SATAN STEALS PEACE

Satan relentlessly attempts to steal everything God has provided for His children through Jesus Christ. Peace is one of the biggies; it is one of the things he works extra hard to prevent us from enjoying. Remember, *we have peace*—Jesus provided it—but *we must appropriate it.* Satan does everything he can to keep us from doing so, beginning with deception; he wants us to think that peace is not possible, that it is not even an option.

How can we remain peaceful while life seems to be falling apart around us? He screams into our ears when we have a challenging situation, "What are you going to do? What are you going to do?"

We frequently don't know what to do, nevertheless, Satan pressures us for answers that we don't have. He tries to make us believe it is our responsibility to solve our problems when the Word of God clearly states that our job as believers is to believe. We believe, and God works on our behalf to bring answers to meet our needs.

A good example appears in Exodus 14. The Egyptians were pursuing the Israelites; all the horses and chariots of Pharaoh, his horsemen and army were in pursuit of God's people. When the Israelites found themselves stuck between the Red Sea and the Egyptian army, it seemed hopeless. They could see no way out, so naturally, they became fearful and upset. They began to complain and make accusations against their leader, Moses. "Moses told the people, Fear not; stand still (firm, confident, undismayed) and see the salvation of the Lord which He will work for you today. For the Egyptians you have seen today you shall never see again. The Lord will fight for you, and you shall hold your peace and remain at rest" (Exodus 14:13–14).

It may have sounded foolish to the Israelites to stand still, hold their peace, and remain at rest, but that was God's instruction to them—it was their way of deliverance. When we remain peaceful in tumultuous circumstances, it clearly shows that we are trusting God. We often say, "God, I trust You," yet our actions show that we do not.

The lies of Satan steal our peace; however, the truth sets us free. Satan's lie is that we have to take care of ourselves: The truth is, God will take care of us as we place our trust in Him. When I began to practice this "peace principle" of simply trusting God, I actually felt guilty, as if I were not doing my part. I felt obligated to worry and try to figure out how to solve the current problem. This, of course, is exactly what Satan wants. He desires more than anything to bestir us to action that is useless. Then we end up exhausted and discouraged.

To enjoy a life of peace, you will need to examine your own life to learn what your "Peace Stealers" are. Satan uses some of the same things on everyone, but we also have things that are particular to each one of us. For example, one person may be very disturbed by having to do two things at one time, while another person may actually be challenged and energized by multitasking and doing several projects at once. We are all different, and we must learn to know ourselves.

My husband is not the least bit concerned about hearing that someone is talking unkindly about him, but he is easily disturbed when a driver does not stay in his lane of traffic or cuts in front of us. I am just the opposite. Although I would not appreciate unsafe driving, it does not disturb me as much as hearing I am being accused unjustly.

When our children are going through hard things, Dave says it is good for them and will help build their character; on the other hand, I want to rescue them. Since we are all different, Satan uses different things on each of us, and he usually has studied us long enough to know exactly what buttons to push at what time.

I can endure things better when I am not tired, and the devil knows this, so he waits to attack until I am worn-out. I learned by pursuing peace what Satan already knew about me, and now I try not to get overly tired because I know I am opening a door for Satan when I do.

It will be virtually impossible to enjoy a life of peace if you don't study to know what your Peace Stealers are. Keep a list of each time you get upset. Ask yourself what caused the problem, and write it down. Be honest with yourself, or you will never break free.

You may have things on your list like this:

- I didn't get my way.
- I had to hurry.
- I became impatient and got angry.
- Financial pressure upset me.

- I was too tired to deal with anything.
- I had to deal with a certain person who always frustrates me.
- A friend embarrassed me.
- I was in a traffic jam.
- A very slow clerk waited on me.
- A friend disappointed me.
- I got a stain on my dress.

You will have a lot of different things on your list, but it will help you to realize what bothers you. Remember, we cannot do anything about things we don't recognize. That the truth sets us free is a wonderful fact from God's Word that has truly been life-changing for me. Of course, truth must be faced in order for it to help anyone. This is often the painful part. Why does truth hurt? Simply because we don't like to see ourselves as we really are, and we have spent a lifetime developing systems of escape through making excuses and blaming others for our problems.

For many years, every time I became upset, in my mind it was always someone else's fault. I thought, *If Dave would just act differently, then I would not get upset. If life was not so challenging, then I could live peacefully. If my children would behave better, I could enjoy peace.* In my mind, my loss of peace was never my fault; it was always something and someone else's fault.

Only when I took responsibility for my reactions and decided to pursue peace did I begin to see change. Excuses and blaming others does us no good at all. If this has been your pattern, as it was mine, I strongly encourage you to ask the Holy Spirit to reveal the truth to you *about you,* and it will be the beginning of enjoying a life of peace.

PEACE EQUALS POWER

I have learned through my experience as well as God's Word that peace is power. That is one of the big reasons that Satan tries to steal our peace all the time. He wants all of God's children to be weak and powerless, not strong and powerful.

Maintaining your peace is your power over Satan. Consider this Scripture: "And do not [for a moment] be frightened or intimidated in anything by your opponents and adversaries, for such [constancy and fearlessness] will be a clear sign (proof and seal) to them of [their impending] destruction, but [a sure token and evidence] of your deliverance and salvation, and that from God" (Philippians 1:28).

We see that remaining peaceful is a clear sign to Satan of his upcoming defeat. *Peace is power!*

We studied in an earlier chapter that the Bible teaches us that staying calm and giving a "soft answer turns away wrath" (Proverbs 15:1). In other words, if someone is angry and yelling, answering him or her calmly and gently will change the situation and stop the possibility of an argument. How awesome! But in order for this to work, one of the people in the situation must be willing to humble him- or herself and respond the opposite of how he or she might feel like responding. Someone has to choose to be a peacemaker in every situation.

Even when a person is sick, staying peaceful and calm will help him or her recover more quickly. Just think of the instructions given to a woman in labor. I was told to "Breathe deeply," "Don't get tense," "Don't be fearful," "Stay calm," and that if I relaxed, the labor would be easier. In other words, when difficult situations face us, becoming upset only makes them worse—it does not help. Being upset steals our power; it does not release it.

The Word states that "the servant of the Lord must not be quarrelsome (fighting and contending). Instead, he must be kindly to everyone and mild-tempered [preserving the bond of peace]" (2 Timothy 2:24).

Why is a servant of the Lord required to be a peacemaker? I believe the Lord instructs us to avoid quarrels because they not only hurt our own witness to the world, but they also cause us to lose our power. We need to walk in this world with power—power against the forces of darkness. Satan seeks to stir up strife between people because we walk in power only when we walk in peace.

Second Timothy 2 continues to tell us clearly how a peacemaker is to train in the skill of keeping peace with others:

He must be a skilled and suitable teacher, patient and forbearing and willing to suffer wrong. He must correct his opponents with courtesy and gentleness, in the hope that God may grant that they will repent and come to know the Truth [that they will perceive and recognize and become accurately acquainted with and acknowledge it], and that they may come to their senses [and] escape out of the snare of the devil, having been held captive by him, [henceforth] to do His [God's] will. (2 Timothy 2:24–26)

I realized that often Dave and I got into arguments or experienced turmoil right before we went out to minister to people or conduct a seminar. It took a while for us to see Satan's plan, but finally we understood that the devil was "setting us up to be upset" so he could steal our power.

Proverbs 17:1 says that a house full of sacrifices with strife is not pleasing to the Lord. In other words, we could make all kinds of sacrifices of time and effort to try to help people, yet God is not pleased unless we stay in peace.

Pursuing peace means making an effort. We cannot maintain peace simply by our own fleshly effort; we need God's help, and we need grace, which is His power assisting us and enabling us to do what needs to be done. The effort we make must be *in Christ*. So often we just try to do what is right without asking for God's help, and that type of fleshly effort never produces good fruit. The Bible calls this a "work of the flesh." It is man's effort trying to do God's job.

What I am saying is, be sure you lean on God and ask for His help. When you succeed, give Him the credit, the honor, and the glory because success is impossible without Him. Jesus said, "Apart from Me [cut off from vital union with Me] you can do nothing" (John 15:5).

It takes most of us a long time to believe this Scripture enough to stop trying to do things without leaning on God. We try and fail, try and fail; it happens over and over until we finally wear ourselves out and realize that God Himself is our strength, our success, and our victory. He doesn't just give us strength—He is our Strength. He does not just give us the victory—He is our Victory. Yes, we make an effort to keep peace, but we dare not make an effort without depending on God's power to flow through us; failure is certain if we do.

The Lord blesses Peacemakers, those who work for and make peace. Peacemakers are committed to peace; they crave peace, pursue peace, and go after it. Jesus promised: "Blessed (enjoying enviable happiness, spiritually prosperous—with life-joy and satisfaction in God's favor and salvation, regardless of their outward conditions) are the makers and maintainers of peace, for they shall be called the sons of God!" (Matthew 5:9).

Peacemakers take the first step in working things out when disagreement, disharmony, or disunity exists. They work toward peace; they don't just hope or wish for it, they don't even just pray for it. They aggressively pursue it in the power of God.

Make a commitment to pursue peace from this day forward: to discover all you can about what your Peace Stealers are, to know yourself and face the truth that will set you free.

Call yourself a peacemaker, one who works for and makes peace with God, himself, and others.

About the Author

Joyce Meyer has been teaching the Word of God since 1976 and in full-time ministry since 1980. She is the bestselling author of more than fifty inspirational books, including *How to Hear from God, Knowing God Intimately,* and *Battlefield of the Mind.* She has also released thousands of teaching cassettes and a complete video library. Joyce's *Enjoying Everyday Life* radio and television programs are broadcast around the world, and she travels extensively conducting conferences. Joyce and her husband Dave are the parents of four grown children and make their home in St. Louis, Missouri.

To contact the author, please write:

Joyce Meyer Ministries
P.O. Box 655
Fenton, Missouri 63026
or call: (636)349-0303
Internet Address: www.joycemeyer.org

Please include your testimony or help received from this book when you write. Your prayer requests are welcome.

To contact the author
in Canada, please write:
Joyce Meyer Ministries Canada, Inc.
Lambeth Box 1300
London, ON N6P 1T5
CANADA
or call: (636)349-0303

In Australia, please write:
Joyce Meyer Ministries-Australia
Locked Bag 77
Mansfield Delivery Centre
Queensland 4122
AUSTRALIA
or call: 07 3349 1200

In England, please write:
Joyce Meyer Ministries
P.O. Box 1549
Windsor
SL4 1GT
UNITED KINGDOM
or call: (0)1753-831102

LIFE IN THE WORD DEVOTIONAL

BE ANXIOUS FOR NOTHING

BE ANXIOUS FOR NOTHING STUDY GUIDE

STRAIGHT TALK ON LONELINESS

STRAIGHT TALK ON FEAR

STRAIGHT TALK ON INSECURITY

STRAIGHT TALK ON DISCOURAGEMENT

STRAIGHT TALK ON WORRY

STRAIGHT TALK ON DEPRESSION

STRAIGHT TALK ON STRESS

DON'T DREAD

MANAGING YOUR EMOTIONS

HEALING THE BROKENHEARTED

"ME AND MY BIG MOUTH!"

"ME AND MY BIG MOUTH!" STUDY GUIDE

PREPARE TO PROSPER

DO IT AFRAID!

EXPECT A MOVE OF GOD IN YOUR LIFE . . . SUDDENLY!

ENJOYING WHERE YOU ARE ON THE WAY TO WHERE YOU
    ARE GOING

THE MOST IMPORTANT DECISION YOU WILL EVER MAKE

WHEN, GOD, WHEN?

WHY, GOD, WHY?

THE WORD, THE NAME, THE BLOOD

BATTLEFIELD OF THE MIND

BATTLEFIELD OF THE MIND STUDY GUIDE

TELL THEM I LOVE THEM

PEACE

THE ROOT OF REJECTION

IF NOT FOR THE GRACE OF GOD

IF NOT FOR THE GRACE OF GOD STUDY GUIDE

Don't miss Joyce Meyer's companion devotionals!

STARTING YOUR DAY RIGHT

Most of us agree that when we start the day off by seeking God, it gives us a positive outlook and a sense of peace that leads to a better day—and ultimately a better life. Now, Joyce Meyer provides us with a day-by-day guide for getting closer to God every morning of the year. Included in this 365-day devotional are such topics as:

- the keys to enjoying every single day
- balancing out extremes
- acting with discipline and self-control
- being happy
- living without fear

Through the inspirational thoughts in *Starting Your Day Right*, we're inspired each morning with a resurgence of hope and resilience in life, and never again want to leave home without first seeking the Lord.

ENDING YOUR DAY RIGHT

Many of us often start our day off with a devotion—a few minutes of prayer and Bible study. But how many of us take the time at night to spend a moment with God? Even when we do, it often amounts to nothing more than a hurried bedtime prayer. Now, Joyce Meyer offers *Ending Your Day Right*, a daily devotional aimed at helping us take time to acknowledge and give thanks for God's presence throughout our day, and to ask for his continued care throughout the night. Topics in this 365-day devotional include:

- the keys to letting go at the end of the day
- remembering to count our blessings
- living secure in God's love
- realizing our dreams and hopes
- giving thanks for the things we have

Ending Your Day Right is the perfect book to help us end the day on a positive note—and sleep easier, content in the love of God.

CHANGING EMPHASES
in American Preaching

CHANGING EMPHASES

in

American Preaching

The Stone Lectures for 1943

By

ERNEST TRICE THOMPSON

Professor of Church History and Church Polity,
Union Theological Seminary, Richmond, Virginia

Philadelphia
THE WESTMINSTER PRESS

TO MY FATHER

From whom came my earliest desire to be

a preacher of the Gospel

Preface

*I*N EXTENDING the invitation to deliver the Stone Lectures at Princeton Theological Seminary, President Mackay stated that it was the faculty's desire that I should choose some theme in the general field of American religious thought or history, and preferably in the history of American preaching. In response to this suggestion, I endeavored to speak — more briefly than I have written — on some of the changing emphases in American preaching which have particular significance for the present day; to consider the life and labors, and especially the theological or ecclesiastical significance, of five men who to an unusual degree reflect, or have helped to determine, important trends in the American pulpit.

It is the human story that I have tried to tell — the personal experience back of the Gospel which is proclaimed. As we follow the lives of these five men we see a little more clearly how preaching reflects its own age; how it stems from the preacher's experience of felt need; how it corrects the inadequacies of former generations, only itself to become distorted and partial; how it emphasizes neglected truth at the expense of old truth that will in the end inevitably rise to new life.

I wish to record my appreciation of the kindness of Dr. Mackay and of his colleagues on the faculty of the Seminary, and also of the interest and encouragement of the student body. I am indebted to the friends who read the manuscript and aided me with their advice, and especially to Rev. L. J. Trinterud, of The Westminster Press.

I wish to thank the Abingdon-Cokesbury Press for permission to quote from *Prophets of the Soul,* by Joseph M. M. Gray; the Association Press for permission to quote from

The Social Principles of Jesus, by Walter Rauschenbusch; Mrs. John C. Adams for permission to quote from *Horace Bushnell, Preacher and Theologian,* by Theodore T. Munger; The Bobbs-Merrill Company for permission to quote from *Saints, Sinners and Beechers,* by Lyman Beecher Stowe; John W. Buckham for permission to quote from his book, *Progressive Religious Thought in America;* the Trustees of the Columbus School for Girls, Columbus, Ohio, for permission to quote from the following books by Washington Gladden: *Recollections, The Church and Modern Life, Seven Puzzling Books, How Much Is Left of the Old Doctrines, Applied Christianity,* and *Social Salvation;* Doubleday, Doran & Company, Inc., for permission to quote from *D. L. Moody: A Worker in Souls,* by Gamaliel Bradford; Sheila Hibben for permission to quote from *Henry Ward Beecher, An American Portrait,* by Paxton Hibben; The Judson Press for permission to quote from *Bush Aglow — The Life Story of Dwight Lyman Moody,* by Richard Ellsworth Day; The Macmillan Company for permission to quote from: *Primitive Traits in Religious Revivals,* by Frederick Morgan Davenport; *D. L. Moody,* by William R. Moody; *The Forks of the Road,* by Washington Gladden; *Walter Rauschenbusch,* by Dores Robinson Sharpe; and the following books by Walter Rauschenbusch: *Christianity and the Social Crisis, Christianizing the Social Order,* and *A Theology for the Social Gospel;* The Pilgrim Press for permission to quote from *The Interpreter,* by Washington Gladden; the Fleming H. Revell Company for permission to quote from: *The Modern Movement in American Theology,* by Frank H. Foster; *D. L. Moody, His Message for Today,* by Charles R. Erdman; *The Life of Dwight L. Moody,* by W. R. Moody; and *Moody Still Lives,* by Arthur Percy Fitt; Charles Scribner's Sons for permission to quote from *Christian Nurture,* by Horace Bushnell, and *Faith and Nurture,* by H. Shelton Smith.

Contents

Chapter *I*

HORACE BUSHNELL
and the beginning of American Liberalism

*H*ORACE BUSHNELL was a theological pioneer, who,
a distinguished ecclesiastical historian has predicted, will go
down in history as " one of the greatest religious geniuses
which Christianity has hitherto produced." In a very real
sense he represents the later, the modern, development of
American religious thought, just as Jonathan Edwards represents the earlier. Edwards and Bushnell — these two men
are pivots on whom much of our intellectual history has
turned. The writings of Bushnell mark the close of one era
and the beginning of another. " In general and to the time
of the contemporaneous phase of American theological
thought which has followed the [First] World War, Bushnell's influence was felt and acknowledged," says Gaius
Glenn Atkins, " by all progressive religious thinkers, and reflected in the thinking of those who would not acknowledge
it." [1]

Yet Bushnell was not a professional theologian; he was
never a systematic thinker, and not always a consistent
thinker. Like Karl Barth, who found the message that has
shaken modern Christendom because he was required to deliver God's message to an expectant congregation amid the
uncertainties of a war-swept world, Horace Bushnell was a
preacher who wrote and spoke out of a compelling sense of
need. His first book, one of the most influential religious
publications ever to appear in America and still a classic in
its field, came as a protest against a revivalism that stifled

9

the proper religious development of American youth. His second volume was the outgrowth of a religious experience which he felt and declared to be a personal firsthand discovery of the Gospel. His last great work, some think his most significant work — on the vicarious sacrifice — marked a fourth and a final stage in his own religious development.

I

Horace Bushnell was born April 14, 1802, in Litchfield County, Connecticut, a rural county noted for its many distinguished sons.

His father, probably of Huguenot descent, and his mother, who had only a common-school education, were both plain farming people, whose ancestors had remained for eight generations in the same locality. When Horace was three, the family moved to New Preston, fourteen miles away, where the father, in addition to his farm, operated a small wool-carding and cloth-dressing establishment requiring the use of skilled handicraft and machinery.

The boy remained at home until he was twenty-one, attending the village schools, toiling between times on the farm and at his father's trade. In *The Age of Homespun,* one of our most enduring pictures of life on an early New England farm, he recalls "wrestling with the plough on the stony-sided hills; digging out the rocks . . . dressing the flax; threshing the rye; dragging home in the deep snows the great wood pile of the year's consumption; and then, when the day was ended, (taking his recreation with other members of the family) in reading or singing, or happy talk, or silent looking in the fire, and finally in sleep — to rise again with the sun and pray over the family Bible for just such another good day as the last."

From such a boyhood he carried through life a never failing love of nature, habits of close observation, and a keen, persistent interest in engineering and mechanics. As Munger says, " His deepest impressions did not come from books nor from contact with men, but from nature, and nothing was quite real to him until it had been submitted to its tests." [2]

Almost every biographer points out that the boy was not raised on the strict Calvinistic diet then prevalent in New England. This is only partially correct. His father, it is true, was a Methodist and his mother an Episcopalian, but both entered the Congregational Church in New Preston and became active workers in the Church. Horace was dutifully raised on the Westminster Shorter Catechism and listened respectfully with his parents to rigidly Calvinistic sermons on "freewill, fixed fate, foreknowledge absolute, Trinity, redemption, special grace, and eternity." He recalled, however, that his father, returning home, after second service, to a rather late dinner, would sometimes let the irritation of his hunger loose, in harsher words than were complimentary, on the tough predestinationism or the rather overtotal depravity of the sermon; whereupon, wrote Dr. Bushnell, " he encountered always a begging-off look from the other end of the table, which, as I understood it, said, ' Not, for the sake of the children.' "

The atmosphere of the home favored independent mental development. As Dr. Bushnell recalled it: " No hamper was ever put on our liberty of thought and choice. We were allowed to have our own questions and had no niggard scruples forced upon us. Only it was given us for a caution that truth is the best thing in the world, and that nobody can afford to part with it, even for an hour." [3]

The boy grew up good-natured, vigorous, and fond of outdoor sports, but serious, and overthoughtful. When he was seventeen, while tending a carding machine, he wrote out, a sentence or half a sentence at a time, a paper on the ninth chapter of Romans, in which he accepted the orthodox doctrines of the day on election, predestination, and the sovereignty of God, but argued that Paul was mistaken or inconsistent in wishing himself accursed from Christ for the sake of his brethren. Two years later he joined the Church and, for a while, shared enthusiastically in its religious activity.

In 1823, when he was twenty-one years of age, he entered Yale, older and more mature than the average student, but homespun still in manner and dress. His college life was marked by intellectual earnestness and a growing consciousness of power. Independence of thought, so characteristic of his later life, already was apparent. As one of his college chums expressed it, he thought for himself, and thought vigorously. But while moral earnestness remained, his religious convictions were fading. As his daughter described it: " A year to two before entering college, while still under the strong habitual influences of home, he had accepted, rather than wrought out, the faith of his youth. Now for the first time, the great untried world of thought opened before him, and his active mind launched out upon a sea of doubt " — a rising sea that in the end threatened to submerge him.

After graduation his plans for some time remained unsettled. He taught school, but after a few months abandoned the occupation as uncongenial.

His graduation essay led to employment on the editorial staff of the newly established *Journal of Commerce* in New York City. His editorials here attracted considerable attention, and a promising future was apparently opening before him. But he found the life a " terrible " one and before the year was out resigned his position to enter the law school at New Haven.

After six months he left the university, planning to practice law and enter politics in the new West. He returned to Yale, at the instigation of his mother, as a tutor. In this position he was more than ordinarily successful, gaining remarkable personal ascendancy over the students. Meanwhile he had resumed his study of law. He passed his examinations and was ready for admission to the bar, when unlooked for influences once more changed all his plans and purposes.

While he was groping for a career, his religious difficulties had steadily mounted. A year after graduation from college, he faced the fact that he could not possibly enter upon the preparation of theology as his mother had fondly hoped and planned from earliest childhood. "I was graduated," he wrote later, "and then, a year afterwards, when my bills were paid, and when the question was to be decided whether I should begin the preparation of theology, I was thrown upon a most painful struggle by the very evident, quite incontestable fact that my religious life was utterly gone down. And the pain it cost me was miserably enhanced by the disappointment I must bring on my noble Christian mother by withdrawing myself from the ministry. I had run to no dissipations; I had been a church-going, thoughtful man. My very difficulty was that I was too thoughtful, substituting thought for everything else, and expecting so intently to dig out a religion by my head that I was pushing it all the while practically away." [4]

Relief came from two sources. First, from prolonged meditation on one of the most influential religious books of the day, *Aids to Reflection*, recently published by the English poet-philosopher, Samuel Taylor Coleridge. As Williston Walker, professor of ecclesiastical history at Yale, has written: "New England, like the Anglo-Saxon world generally, had looked upon religious truth as capable of intellectual demonstration with all the logical sharpness of a problem in geometry. Its appeal was to the rational understanding, and with the assent of the intellect it stood or fell. Coleridge broke with this whole conception. To him Christianity is primarily graspable by intuition. Its appeal is not so much to the intellect as to the ethical and spiritual feeling." [5] Religion, he proclaimed in a characteristic passage, begins and ends with the heart. "Too soon did the Doctors of the Church forget that the *Heart,* the *Moral* Nature, was the beginning and the End; and that Truth, Knowledge and Insight were comprehended in its expansion. This was the first and true apostasy — when in Council and Synod the divine Humanities of the Gospel gave way to speculative systems and Religion became a Science of Shadows under the name of Theology, or at best a bare Skeleton of Truth, without life or interest, alike inaccessible and unintelligible to the majority of Christians." [6] Bushnell considered Coleridge the most fructifying writer he had ever read. In his own estimation, *Aids to Reflection* had greater influence on his life than any other book save the Bible. Study and reflection on this suggestive work, begun in college days and continued for years, with mental suspension and laborious self questioning, now began to bear fruit. Gradually he came "not merely to personal religious certainty, but to the conviction that the whole system of dependence on intellectual demonstration characteristic of the explanation of religion in that day was mistaken. Religion appeals, he became convinced, primarily to the heart and to the feeling for its compelling demonstration." [7]

The actual solution of his problem, the impetus needed for the precipitation of his doubts, came in connection with a revival in which he was called to act decisively in response to conscience. At the height of the revival, he and the students in his division, who were greatly influenced by his example, stood apparently unmoved, while other students with their tutors were in a spiritual glow.

Faced with a sense of unescapable responsibility, Bushnell found the God whose very existence he had begun to doubt by a moral decision to give himself unreservedly to the right and to the God, who, if he existed, was a God of right. He confessed later to his fellow tutors: " When the

preacher touches the Trinity and when logic shatters it all to
pieces, I am all at the four winds. But I am glad I have a
heart as well as a head. My heart wants the Father; my
heart wants the Son; my heart wants the Holy Ghost — and
one just as much as the other. My heart says the Bible has a
Trinity for me, and I mean to hold by my heart." [8]

Intellectual doubts continued for some time, but his ship
was launched; he was headed for the open sea. Henceforth
he was to be guided by heart as well as by head, to rely more
on feeling, on moral intuition, on observation and experience, than on cold, intellectual reasoning and logic that
draw relentless conclusions despite the warm, quivering protest of the moral sentiments, and spin lofty metaphysical
speculations with little meaning for life.

The question of a life calling now was fully settled. It
was to be, not the law for which his studies had prepared
him, but the ministry, to which he had been originally
pointed by his mother's hopes.

For his theological training, Bushnell chose Yale, then at
the height of its influence under Nathaniel W. Taylor, the
outstanding representative of the New England school which
since the days of Jonathan Edwards had sought to improve
and defend Calvinism against all its foes.

Bushnell was impressed and inwardly fortified by Taylor's sincerity, his courage, and his independence of thought,
but found little satisfaction in the main tenets of the " New
Haven theology," and grew increasingly distrustful of Dr.
Taylor's attempt to establish Christian theology as an intel-
lectually demonstrable system. Its logic, its metaphysics, its
systemization seemed artificial, too remote from life, and
too often abhorrent to the moral sense. Coleridge's great
work had convinced him " of a whole other world somewhere
overhead, a range of realities in higher tier," that he must
climb after, and if possible apprehend. Intuition, moral insight, experience, reason in its wider ranges, and nature as it

15

was open to the observing eye were the keys of this other world of realities.

2

Like most young ministers, Bushnell married shortly after the completion of his theological studies and soon thereafter entered upon his first and only pastorate at North Church in Hartford, Connecticut. The church was divided, as so often is the case, between conservatives and progressives, and the young pastor felt that he had been " daintily inserted between an acid and an alkali, having it for his task both to keep them apart, and to save himself from being bitten by one or devoured by the other." But the two factions rallied in quick loyalty to the young man whom they had called and stood unitedly and wholeheartedly behind their beloved pastor in all the stormy days that were to come.

A partial explanation for this early confidence, never forfeited, is found in a sermon which he preached during the first year of his ministry on " Duty Not Measured by Our Ability." It was a sermon which touched one of the most explosive theological questions of the day. But, as Theodore T. Munger has pointed out, " neither side heard what it expected. Old School and New School were ignored, or gently set aside to make room for a discussion that had nothing to do with their differences except to supersede or rather to absorb them in a more comprehensive view of the subject. Nothing was said of natural ability, or moral ability, or gracious ability, except that ' they raise a false issue which can never be settled.' To thus dismiss a controversy which had raged since Edwards, and was now embodied in the neighboring divinity schools, would have been regarded as a jest if his treatment of it had not been so serious. Instead of sinking himself and his hearers in ' the abysmal depths of theology,' he carried them into the world of human life and

Christian experience, where all was so much a matter of fact
that there was small room for question. Arminius and Edwards, Taylor and Tyler, would have listened without dis-
sent — bating a phrase or two — and for the time would have
forgotten their differences; or possibly, as often happens
with contestants when a greater truth is forced upon them,
they might have said, 'We always thought so.' For in truth,
Bushnell thus early was 'passing into the vein of compre-
hensiveness' of which he afterwards spoke — a phrase that
defines better than any other the method and spirit of the
man." [9]

As Bushnell explained in later years: " The effect of my
preaching [and we might add of his writing as well] never
was to overthrow one school and set up the other; neither
was it to find a position of neutrality midway between them;
but as far as theology is concerned, it was to comprehend,
if possible, the truth contended for in both." "The comprehensive principle," he was convinced, " is, in general, a possible, and, so far, the only Christian method of adjusting theologic differences." [10]

Bushnell's first published sermon was entitled " The Crisis
of the Church," a subject on which almost every minister
has spoken at one time or another, and was occasioned by
the mobbing of Garrison in the streets of Boston. Its chief
thought was that Protestantism and democracy were allied,
and that the principal dangers to the country were "slavery, infidelity, Romanism, and the current of our political
tendencies." As his biographer has declared, Bushnell held
to the Puritan conception of the state as moral and did not
hesitate to use his pulpit to enforce this conception and to
denounce any departure from it. He preached against slavery when the subject was still largely taboo in the pulpit,
though his position was moderate, not extreme. A fast-day
discourse, denouncing the Missouri Compromise, preached
in 1844, during the Presidential campaign, was widely cir-

culated as a campaign document, and was influential in defeating Henry Clay. In this sermon Bushnell laid down the proposition that "I cannot let politics alone until shown that politics are not under the government of God, beyond the sphere of moral obligation."

Printed, many of them, singly and then gathered into four widely circulated volumes, Bushnell's sermons spread his influence and his theology throughout the land and beyond the limits of his own lifetime. One of these sermons, entitled "Every Man's Life a Plan of God," has been termed one of the three most influential sermons ever preached in America. Another on "Unconscious Influence," according to some estimates, has been reproduced in more pulpits than any other sermon ever preached in England or America.

Principal George Adam Smith said once in conversation that Bushnell is the preacher's preacher as Spenser is the poet's poet, and that his sermons were on the shelf of every manse in Scotland. "Not an orator in the sense of dramatic effectiveness or emotional excitement," Dr. Williston Walker declared in 1902, "few men in the New England pulpit " — in the American pulpit he might have added — "have equalled Dr. Bushnell in his ability to present Christian truth in fresh and impressive guise, whether to the listener in the pew of a generation ago, or to the reader who follows his luminous page now that his voice has been silent for more than a quarter of a century." [11] Dr. W. W. Sweet, the eminent American historian, writing in 1937, adds: "I do not believe that it is an exaggeration to say that much of the best preaching in America during the last half century, at least, has been largely dependent upon Horace Bushnell." [12]

No less striking in their way and equally influential, are the long series of addresses which Bushnell began early in his ministry and continued to the end on a wide variety of subjects, some historical, some practical, but always with a definite and a natural religious message at their heart.

Theological suspicion was aroused against Bushnell in 1838, five years after the beginning of his ministry, by an article in the *Christian Spectator,* on " Revivals of Religion," an article which was to develop nine years later into his influential treatise on *Christian Nurture,* a landmark in the deliverance of childhood from the tyranny of theological dogmatism.

In 1839, Bushnell delivered an address at Andover which contained the germ afterward fully developed in his theory of language. In applying this theory regarding the nature and limitations of language to the central problem of the Trinity, Bushnell recognized quite clearly that he was risking not only his ministerial career but also, because of his precarious health, the financial security and protection of his home. In explaining the situation to his wife, he wrote, " I have withheld till my views are well matured; and to withhold longer, I fear, is a want of that moral courage which animated Luther and every other man who has been a true soldier of Christ."

This paper brought him into that world of suspicion and accusation from which he never thereafter wholly emerged.

Rising criticism; personal sorrow, including the death of his only son (from which he stated he " learned more of experimental religion than in all his life before "); together with laborious duties in his own parish and enlarging activities without, led to a physical breakdown when he was barely middle-aged. His sympathetic congregation increased his salary from twelve hundred dollars, the figure at which it had been fixed at the outset of his ministry, to fifteen hundred dollars, and granted him an extensive leave of absence.

3

Two years later, a year after his return to the pastorate, *Christian Nurture,* the first of Bushnell's major productions, and one of the most influential theological works ever published in America, was brought out under the imprint of the Massachusetts Sunday School Society.

The significance of this work can be understood only when we recall the background against which Bushnell wrote. Historically, Calvinism had included children in the household of faith and had regarded children, pledged in baptism to God by believing parents, as presumptively regenerated, and members, therefore, of the visible Church. Within the New England Churches, we find, from the beginning, two opposing ideas struggling for supremacy: one, the older Calvinistic view that children of believers were members of the Church by birth; the other, the independent or Congregational ideal of a regenerate Church membership, demanding evidences of conversion on the part of children as well as adults. This latter view was enormously strengthened by the Great Awakening, which was " the most far-reaching and transforming religious event " in the colonial period of our national history.

This revival not only powerfully stimulated the Christian life, but also changed the conception of entrance on that life in a way that has profoundly influenced the majority of American Churches almost to the present day. It emphasized the conception of a transforming regenerative change — conscious conversion after intense struggle, involving prolonged conviction of sin, and resulting eventually in the peace of God's forgiving love — as the normal method of entrance into the Kingdom of God. The child, even of Christian parentage, was commonly viewed as an alien from the divine promises — a ' child of wrath ' — until in years of approaching or actual maturity the divine Spirit could transmute him into a child of God.

Religious education, both in the home and in the Sunday School, was directed toward securing this " cataclysmic upheaval " in the lives of the children. The Churches gener-

ally felt that progress and development were impossible
without the emotional excitement and the spasmodic success of a revival. For more than a hundred years, up to the
eve of the Civil War, the evangelical Churches of America
made revivals their chief dependence for bringing children
as well as adults into the Christian life. The approved
method of becoming a Christian was to be converted in a
protracted meeting. Periods between revivals were considered periods of spiritual dearth, during which the Church
could only wait for the next outpouring of the divine
power.

As seen by Bushnell, this revival system had one great
merit and one great defect. "The merit is that it displaced
an era of dead formality, and brought in the demand of a
truly supernatural experience. The defect is, that it has cast
a type of religious individualism, intense beyond any former
example. It makes nothing of the family, and the church,
and the organic powers God has constituted as vehicles of
grace. It takes every man as if he had existed *alone;* pre-
sumes that he is unreconciled to God until he has undergone
some sudden and explosive experience in adult years, or
after the age of reason; demands that experience, and only
when it is reached, allows the subject to be an heir of life.
Then, on the other side, or that of the Spirit of God, the very
act or *ictus* by which the change is wrought is isolated or individualized, so as to stand in no connection with any other
of God's means or causes — an epiphany, in which God leaps
from the stars, or some place above, to do a work apart from
all system, or connection with his other works. Religion is
thus a kind of transcendental matter, which belongs on the
outside of life, and has no part in the laws by which life is
organized — a miraculous epidemic, a fire-ball shot from the
moon, something holy, because it is from God, but so extraordinary, so out of place, that it cannot suffer any vital connection with the ties, and causes, and forms, and habits,

which constitute the frame of our history. Hence the desultory, hard, violent, and often extravagant or erratic character it manifests. Hence, in part, the dreary years of decay and darkness, that interspace our months of excitement and victory." [13]

In opposition to this conception, which prevailed not only in New England but also throughout the nation, Bushnell developed as his fundamental thesis the then revolutionary proposition " that the child is to grow up a Christian, and never know himself as being otherwise."

In other words, " the aim, effort and expectation should be, not, as it is commonly assumed, that the child is to grow up in sin, to be converted after he comes to a mature age; but that he is to open on the world as one that is spiritually renewed, not remembering the time when he went through a technical experience, but seeming rather to have loved what is good from his earliest years." [14]

Bushnell did not neglect the doctrine of innate depravity, nor deny the necessity of regeneration and conversion. He did not overlook the value and the necessity of revivals. He insisted, however, that the means of grace ordinarily blessed of the Holy Spirit, and therefore the means on which the Church is primarily to rely for its preservation and also for its propagation, is the method of Christian nurture in the family and in the Church. According to Bushnell, regeneration of the child, baptized by believing parents, is not actual, but " presumptive, and every thing depends upon the organic law of character pertaining between the parent and the child, the church and the child, thus upon duty and holy living and gracious example." [15] " The very idea of Christian education," he said, is " that it begins with nurture or cultivation. And the intention is that the Christian life and spirit of the parents, which are in and by the Spirit of God, shall flow into the mind of the child, to blend with his incipient and half-formed exercises; that they shall thus beget their own good within him — their thoughts, opinions, faith and love, which are to become a little more, and yet a little more, his own separate exercise, but still the same in character." [16]

The second half of the book develops in detail, with a wealth of practical suggestion and a high degree of common sense, the means by which this result may be achieved.

When Dr. Bushnell's manuscript was first presented to the Massachusetts Sunday School Union, opposition was voiced on the ground that "it is new, it will make a stir, some persons will be startled by it." The publication attracted little attention, however, until an "Open Letter" appeared, having the sanction of the North Association of Hartford, Connecticut, and charging that the "Discourses" were full of "dangerous tendencies." Other critics then came forward, objecting to the book on the grounds that it was "naturalistic," that it seemed to imply that a man became a Christian by education rather than by the direct change of his heart by a sovereign act of God, or, as Dr. Charles Hodge of Princeton argued, "because it resolved the entire matter into organic laws, explaining away both depravity and grace." Bushnell soon discovered that he had "touched the quick of theologic odium," and was not greatly surprised when he learned that the Sunday School Union had decided to suppress the book. He saw that this would give him an opportunity to obtain a wider hearing and at once decided to republish it himself. In its final, revised form, this great work soon became a religious classic, widely accepted as a practical working method for the religious training of children. It remains to this day one of the most readable and one of the most helpful treatises we possess on the subject of Christian nurture. Its supreme value comes from the fact that it is based on observation and reality and is not a theory superimposed on life, and also, as Bushnell did not fail to point out, that it is in accord with the Scriptures and the ancient practice of the Church.

Its effect on American religious life is hard to overestimate. When Bushnell wrote, the effectiveness of the revival system had begun to wane, but there was nothing yet to take its place. *Christian Nurture* gave the Churches a better understanding of the laws of Christian growth and suggested a technique by which that growth might be realized. An even greater achievement was that it turned the current of Christian thought toward the young. Bushnell taught the American Churches that for their future growth they must depend, not entirely, nor even chiefly, upon revivals, but more and more upon the Christian nurture of the oncoming generation. He gave the primary and the most important stimulus to the development of modern religious education.

4

Bushnell's growing fame led in 1848 to invitations to deliver addresses before the Harvard Divinity School, Andover Theological Seminary, and the General Association of Connecticut.

In February of the same year he had had an unusual religious experience. Urged by a course of reading in the mystics to a search for a fuller Christian life, he enjoyed what seemed to him a vision of the Gospel in its reality, a " clearer knowledge of God " than any he had ever before known, an experience which he ever after regarded as marking a distinct stage in his spiritual development.

He accepted the three invitations which came to him a few months later as a providential opportunity to proclaim the truth that had been revealed to him. The three addresses, prefaced by a notable " Dissertation on Language " were published shortly thereafter under the title *God in*

Christ, his second major contribution to theological knowledge. A second bombshell also it proved to be in the closely formed theological ranks, one which plunged him into keener controversy than any he had hitherto known.

The "Dissertation on Language" which prefaced the new volume is not an unimportant work; in the words of his earliest and most intimate biographer, it is the "key to his thought," the necessary prelude to all his later theological contributions.

The great theologians of New England, as we have seen, thought that elaborate theological systems could be spun from Scripture by a rigid dialectical process. Definitions, formulas, and systems were accepted as final, exact statements of the truth. At least that was the goal toward which theology was ever striving. As a matter of fact each combatant in the theological arena "was sure to discover, through some unguarded loophole, truth lying outside of [his opponent's] definition that called for re-definition. Thus an endless process was established, consisting in efforts to bring the infinite within the finite." [17]

Seeking diligently for some way by which theology might be delivered from the morass into which it had floundered, Bushnell found it at length — so he thought — in the very nature of language. "In the misuse or abuse of this instrument," he affirmed, "a great part of our religious difficulties have their spring." All language, he proceeded to demonstrate, is divisible into two departments — a physical and an intellectual. In the lower department, words are names for objects designated; in the higher, they are more or less imperfect symbols of the intellectual or spiritual realities they typify. "Words of thought or spirit," he declared, "are not only inexact in their significance, never measuring the truth or giving its precise equivalent, but they always affirm something which is false, or contrary to the truth intended. They impute *form* to that which is really out of form. They are related to the truth, only as form to spirit — earthen vessels in which the truth is borne, yet always offering their mere pottery as being the truth itself." [18]

Not only is language inexact and inadequate in its representation of spiritual truth, but it also changes its meaning and reflects varying and shifting points of view, partial points of view, which need to be modified, corrected, or supplemented by divergent, often contrary symbols.

If this be true it follows that words can never adequately describe spiritual verities, and that Christian truth can never be brought within the molds of any dogmatic statement.

"Considering the infirmities of language," Bushnell concludes, " all formulas of doctrine should be held in a certain spirit of accommodation. They cannot be pressed to the letter for the very sufficient reason that the letter is never true. They can be regarded only as proximate representations, and should therefore be accepted not as laws over belief, or opinion, but more as badges of consent and good understanding. The moment we begin to speak of them as guards and tests of purity, we confess that we have lost the sense of purity." [19]

Bushnell believed that if his theory of language prevailed, the Scriptures would be studied more than they had ever been, but in a different manner — " not as a magazine of propositions and mere dialectic entities, but as inspirations and poetic forms of life; requiring, also, divine inbreathings and exaltations in us, that we may ascend into their meaning. . . . We shall seem to understand less, and shall actually receive more." [20]

" The two principal results which I suppose may follow, should these views of language be allowed to have their effect in our theology," he says, " are a more comprehensive, friendly and fraternal state than now exists between different families of Christians; and, as the confidence of dogma is mitigated, a more present, powerful and universal conviction entering into the Christian body, that truth, in its highest and freest forms, is not of the natural understanding, but is rather as Christ himself declared — spirit and life." [21]

The theological student will perceive that Bushnell developed here independently a point of view which has important affinities with the theology of Schleiermacher and Ritschl, later to bear their great influence in American thought. He opened in his day a new avenue of approach to spiritual truth, one which helped to free religion from the tyranny of words and from a dogmatic arrogance that not infrequently stifled spiritual life. At the same time he offered a cure so radical that, in the estimation of one sympathetic interpreter, "for those who accepted it too unreservedly it came near undermining not only rationalism itself, but the very foundations of theology as a science." [22]

It is not surprising that publication of this essay stirred the theological world of his day to the very core. As Munger says, "his entrance into the company of New England theologians with such a theory was like Copernicus appearing among the Ptolemaists." [23]

In the addresses that followed, Bushnell applied his theory to two of the major doctrines of Christendom. "I know no better method," he said, "than to accept these great truths of trinity and atonement as realities or verities addressed to faith; or what is not far different, to feeling and imaginative reason — not any more as logical and metaphysical entities for the natural understanding. . . . The essential matter seems to be that some trinity shall be held, such as will answer the practical uses of the life, and bring God into a lively, glowing, manifold power over the inner man — Father, Son, Holy Ghost, historically three, and also really one; — some scheme of atonement that upholds laws, as eternal verity and sanctity; delivering still from bondage under it, and writing it as a law of liberty in the heart." [24]

First, he considered the doctrine of the Trinity, which was

27

still a bone of contention between orthodox Congregationalists and the Unitarians.

Bushnell accepted the deity of Christ, wholeheartedly and
unreservedly, without attempting to solve the metaphysical
problem of the relation of the human nature to the divine.
In fact, considered from the orthodox point of view, his theory wavered on the human side rather than on the divine;
Christ's divine nature was definitely affirmed; his complete
human nature held in doubt. As Bushnell definitely declared, " he differs from us, not in degree, but in kind. . . .
He is in such a sense God, or God manifested, that the un-
known term of his nature, that which we are most in doubt
of, and about which we are least capable of any positive
affirmation is the human." [25]

But Bushnell was not concerned with metaphysical explanation. " As to any metaphysical or speculative difficulties
involved in the union of the divine and the human," he says,
" I dismiss them all by observing that Christ is not here for
the sake of something accomplished in his metaphysical or
psychological interior, but for that which appears and is outwardly signified in his life." [26]

Belief in the deity of Christ was imperiled, in his estimation, by false and inadequate views of the Trinity. The rise
of Unitarianism, which had split the New England Church
in two and still constituted a mighty peril for evangelical
Christianity, was, in part at least, a reaction against the popular tritheism which then prevailed in orthodox circles in
England and America. As stated by Bushnell: " It seems to
be agreed by the orthodox, that there are three persons, Father, Son, and Holy Ghost in the divine nature. These three
persons, too, are generally regarded as belonging not to the
machina Dei, by which God is revealed, but to the very *esse,*
the substantial being of God, or the interior contents of his
being. They are declared to be equal; all to be infinite; all
to be the same in substance; all to be one. . . . A very large

portion of the Christian teachers, together with the general mass of disciples, undoubtedly, hold three real living persons in the interior nature of God; that is, three consciousnesses, wills, hearts, understandings." [27]

Unitarians charged that evangelicals believed in three Gods — that Trinitarianism was a survival of polytheism and involved a logical contradiction. Three, they said, cannot be one, and one cannot be three.

Bushnell began in his own thought with the strict unity and the single personality of God — " one mind, will, consciousness." The Trinity became for him, accordingly, a trinity of manifestation, a trinity that results of necessity from the revelation of God to men. " I do not undertake to fathom the interior being of God, and tell how it is composed," he declared. " That is a matter too high for me, and I think for us all. I only insist that, assuming the strictest unity and even simplicity of God's nature, He could not be efficiently or sufficiently revealed to us, without evolving a trinity of persons, such as we meet in the Scriptures. These persons or personalities are the *dramatis personae* of revelation, and their reality is measured by what of the infinite they convey in these finite forms. As such, they bear, on the one hand, a relation to God, who is to be conveyed or imported into knowledge; on the other they are related to our human capacities and wants, being that presentation of God which is necessary to make Him a subject of thought, or bring Him within the discourse of reason; that also which is necessary to produce mutuality, or terms of conversableness between us and Him, and pour His love most effectually into our feeling." [28] To put it very simply, Bushnell presents God as a personal unity, working and revealing himself in different aspects as Father, Son, and Holy Ghost. The three persons of the Trinity are realized in experience, even if not fully understood by reason.

This was, of course, a modified Sabellianism, an interpretation regarded from ancient times as unorthodox, but an interpretation toward which modern Christian thought has increasingly gravitated. Many at the time were profoundly disturbed by Bushnell's presentation; many others, who believed in the deity of Father, Son, and Holy Ghost, were greatly helped. Bushnell had brought a theological stumbling block out of the realm of speculation into the more solid realm of Christian experience.

But Bushnell went farther in this weighty series of discourses. He passed from the person of Christ to his work, from his incarnation to his atonement, a doctrine expounded more fully in later years in his great work on *The Vicarious Sacrifice*. But already the germs of the later doctrine are apparent — Christ is a manifestation in humanity of the eternal life of the Father, entering into a prison world to set its soul captives free; by his incarnate charities and sufferings, he re-engages the world's love and reunites it to the Father; in one condensed, luminous utterance, every word of which is power, God was in Christ, reconciling the world unto himself.

Penal substitution in its traditional form was rejected as a "truly horrible doctrine"; the governmental theory of the atonement, then current in New England, was repudiated also on the ground that "no governmental reasons can justify even the admission of innocence into a participation of frowns and penal distributions."

At the same time the author argued that the life and the death of Christ do produce an impression in our minds of the essential sanctity of God's law and character, which it was needful to produce and without which any proclamation of pardon would be dangerous.

Thus Bushnell interprets the atonement as he had already interpreted the doctrine of the Trinity in terms of human experience. Any attempt to explain its influence on God, he claims, is beyond human power.

Bushnell concludes his triad of theological lectures with a discussion of "Dogma and Spirit," in which he points out the "mournful effect of dogma" throughout the history of the Church "as a limitation upon piety."

The first age of the Church he contends was "an age not of dogmas, or speculations, but of gifts, utterances and mighty works, and more than all, of inspiration, insight, freedom and power." Theology came with the triumph of Greek philosophy. "With it, of course, enters controversy, and controversy . . . whittles and splits the divine truth of the Gospel and shapes it into propositions dialectically nice and scientific, till at last the truth of Jesus vanishes, his triumphs are over, and his spirit even begins to die in the world." [29]

Luther, he argues, broke the incrustation of ages to rescue the true Gospel, but left the reign of dogma or speculative theology untouched. "Love, mercy, faith, a pure and holy life was still left a subordinate thing — important, of course, but not the chief thing. Christianity remained in the hands of schools and doctors. . . . Formulas still reigned over faith." [30]

It follows in the author's estimation that "nothing is wanted now, in order to realize a grand renovation of the religious spirit throughout Christendom . . . but simply to recover from this ancient lapse into dogma." [31]

He does not of course propose to make nothing of opinions and to abolish all confessions and creeds. He proposes no violent or abrupt change whatever. "Our platforms and church articles are generally too minute and theoretical . . . but we must feel our way in the preparing of changes. It will suffice to relax, in a gradual manner, the exact and literal interpretation of our standards; to lean more and more, as we have been doing for the fifty years past, towards the side of accommodation, or easy construction. This, too, in the hope which we may lawfully cherish, that it will, at last

31

be found amply sufficient as a term of fellowship, to unite in formulas far more simple and untheoretic than any which we have at present." [32] It was along this line that American Christendom was increasingly to move. Confessions and creeds do not possess the sanctity of former days. Systematic theology has fallen into disrepute. The laity are no longer instructed in a completely rounded Christian faith. Bushnell's writings gave a powerful impetus to this development.

With the publication of *God in Christ,* the storm of opposition broke. Representatives of Princeton, Yale, Boston, Bangor, and East Windsor, leaped into the fray. The theological seminaries of New Haven, Bangor, and Princeton, presented contradictory views of the atonement; Dr. Goodrich of Yale argued for a theory of the person of Christ which Dr. Hodge of Princeton declared had never been heard of; but all seemed determined to crush the man, " who, though he had denied none of the cardinal doctrines of Christianity, had ventured to express his faith in them under formulas and philosophic explanations somewhat different from those which were assumed to be canonically settled for all time." [33]

The Hartford Central Association, of which Bushnell was a member, declined to condemn the book, but the Fairfield West Association made repeated attempts to have Bushnell branded as a heretic by the General Association of Connecticut. For five years, from 1849 to 1854, the matter was in abeyance. The General Association steadfastly refused to act, not because it agreed with Bushnell theologically, but because heresy trials do not come easy in a congregational system of Church government and because it was difficult to proceed against one who was so evidently rooted in the essentials of religion. Bushnell's own Church withdrew from its local association to protect him against possible charges in that particular area, and for years none of his

Congregational brethren in the city would exchange pulpits or co-operate with him in any Christian effort. The college chapel and the Churches of New Haven, however, remained open to him, and he was in growing demand as a speaker on special and important occasions.

It was during this period that he gave his address at Cambridge on "Work and Play," and also that on "The Founders Great in Their Unconsciousness." Written at a time when his whole career was endangered, they reveal the essential spirit of the man. Work for a definite end may become a joy, Bushnell maintained, and this is what life is intended to be for a man. The founding fathers did not foresee the magnificent results of our political history. "I have even made it a part of their greatness that they did not. They stood for God and religion alone. They asked for nothing, planned for nothing, hoped for nothing, save what should come of their religion. . . . They did not begin at the point zero in themselves, or in their own human wisdom, but at duty; and they represent, at once, the infallible success and the majestic firmness of duty." [34] We could give no better monument than "for ourselves to receive the principle they have so nobly proved, that the way of greatness is the way of duty."

∫

Though he bore it for the most part with dignity and forbearance, this period of accusation broke down Bushnell's already enfeebled health. Granted a generous leave of absence, he spent part of the year 1855 in the South, and most of the following year in California, where he was instrumental in laying the foundation of what became its university.

Two years later he published his first volume of sermons — *Sermons for the New Life,* he called them — a volume which gathered up the fruitage of twenty-five years and which met with a popular response, in gratifying contrast to the reception of his book *God in Christ*.

In the same year appeared the work that cost Bushnell more than any other, *Nature and the Supernatural,* the most thorough and complete treatise ever to come from his pen, in his own estimation his best work, for the sake of which his life had been spared.

This volume, like the others, came as the result of a felt need, a practical religious need of his own day. Christians generally tended to regard the natural and the supernatural as two distinct orders, in antithesis one to the other. If the supernatural entered into the world of the natural, it was a miracle, and involved the breach, or at least a suspension, of natural law. But for increasing numbers breach or suspension of natural law had become inconceivable.

Christianity as a whole was affected. "Imprisoned by the terms and the method of nature, the tendency," Bushnell found, " is to find the whole system of God included under its laws, and then it is only a part of the same assumption that we are incredulous in regard to any modification, or seeming interruption of their activity from . . . the supernatural agency . . . [even] of God Himself." [35] The result is that for many " there is no incarnation . . . no miracle, no redemptive grace or experience, for God's system is nature, and it is incredible that the laws of nature should be interrupted." [36]

In Bushnell's estimation the defense of orthodoxy against this growing naturalism was lamentably weak. Four strategical mistakes he enumerates: (1) "We make up an issue for inspiration, so stringently close and verbal, that we take the short end of the lever ourselves, and give the long end to our adversaries; consenting that if we fail on syllables, they shall have their own way about chapters and books." (2) "We assert the supernatural in a way too fantastic and ghostly to admit a possible defence." . . . (3) "We define miracles to be suspensions of the laws of nature, and make it impossible, *gratis,* from that time forth, to offer an argument for them, which any bravely rational person, or mind well grounded in science can ever be expected to admit." And then, finally, we " surrender, in fact, the credibility of anything supernatural or miraculous by renouncing the credibility of any such thing occurring now." [37]

The thesis which Bushnell proceeds to develop is that nature and supernature are not antithetical, but complementary — coeternal factors in the universal system of God.

The system of nature constitutes " a chain of cause and effects, or a scheme of orderly succession, determined from within the scheme itself." [38]

The supernatural is anything "that is either not in the chain of natural cause and effect, or which acts on the chain of cause and effect, in nature, from without the chain." [39]

We do not need to look for marvels, or apparitions, or miracles in the ordinarily accepted sense, to find the supernatural. We find it " in what is least transcendent and most familiar, even in ourselves. In ourselves we discover a tier of existences that are above nature, and in all their most ordinary actions are doing their will upon it. The very idea of our personality is that of a being not under law of cause and effect, a being supernatural. . . . It is not said, be it observed, as is sometimes done, that the supernatural implies a suspension of the laws of nature, a causing them, for the time, not to be — that perhaps is never done — it is only said that we, as powers, not in the line of cause and effect, can set the causes in nature at work, in new combinations otherwise never occurring, and produce by our action upon nature results which she, as nature, could never produce by her own internal acting." [40]

" Finding now, that we ourselves are supernatural creatures . . . what shall we think of God's relation to nature? If it be nothing incredible that we should act on the chain of cause and effect in nature, is it more incredible that God should thus act? . . . Strange as it may seem this is the grand offense of supernaturalism, the supposing that God can act on nature from without, on the chain of cause and effect in nature from without the chain of connection, by which natural consequences are propagated — exactly that which we ourselves are doing as the most familiar things of our lives." [41]

Bushnell proceeds to argue that the world has been brought into a state of disorder by man's abuse of his freedom, that redemption for man and for society is possible only through the supernatural interposition of God in the Christian Gospel, and that, "taken in the whole comprehension of its import, our world is nothing but a vast, supernatural, reciprocal Providence in which our God is reigning as an ever present, ever mindful counselor and guide and friend, a Redeemer of our sin, a hearer of our prayers." [42]

But there is another point of real significance. According to Bushnell, the supernatural in God acts always according to law — not the law of nature, but the law of his own being; it is a result of his consistency, of his eternal righteousness, of his character. There is a sense then in which the Virgin birth, the resurrection, the regeneration of the individual, specific answer to prayer, all have happened, or do happen now, according to law — not natural law, but the law of Divine Being; i.e., if exactly the same events occurred in exactly the same way, God, as consistent being, would act again precisely as he had done before. Momentous consequences follow from this point of view, though not developed by Bushnell. It means for one thing that man need never fear what seems to be the discovery of law in the spiritual realm, only the philosophy that asserts that law leaves no place for the action of a supernatural personality.

Criticism came to this volume as to the other major works of Bushnell, and from opposite points of view. Unitarians opposed him on the ground that he was a "demolisher of nature"; Calvinists, on the ground that he had deferred "too much to nature." But many then, and many since, have found that it points to a way out of an intolerable impasse — making it possible for intelligent men, trained in the modern scientific point of view, to maintain their faith, not only in the natural, but also in the supernatural.

Dr. Bushnell had labored on the book in a time of great physical weakness; he had given himself unsparingly, without counting the cost; the reaction after its completion was followed by a physical collapse so serious that it seemed hopeless to him to attempt to continue a pastorate which had already been so seriously interrupted. In 1859, therefore, he finally and completely severed his relations with the Church that had been so patient with his infirmities.

6

The fifteen years of life that remained were years of increasing invalidism, years in which Bushnell continued to preach and write as he was able. A large part of his literary output, including some of the greatest and most enduring works of his life, came from these years of growing weakness, when as he felt he was pastor to the Church at large. As Williston Walker has said, they aroused less controversy than those that went before, but cost him even greater physical labor.

In addition to numerous articles and addresses, there were two books of sermons: *Christ and His Salvation* and *Sermons on Living Subjects;* two books of occasional articles: *Work and Play* and the *Moral Uses of Dark Things;* a book on woman suffrage, entitled *The Reform Against Nature;* and the final revision of *Christian Nurture.*

But the most important fruit of his declining years — in the estimation of some, his most significant and enduring work — was *The Vicarious Sacrifice Grounded in Principles of Universal Obligation,* issued in 1866. When the truth which he tried to present in this treatise began to dawn on his soul, five years earlier, it seemed as though he had reached the fourth distinct stage in his spiritual journey: first, his initial experience of God in early manhood; second, the resolution of his intellectual doubts, as he advanced into the clear moral light of Christ; third, the inward personal discovery of Christ that later found embodiment in *God in Christ;* and now the fourth state, in which he said: " I lay hold of and appropriate the general culminating fact of God's vicarious character in goodness, and of mine to be accomplished in Christ as a follower. My next stage of discovery will be when I drop the body and go home to be with Christ in the conscious, openly revealed friendship of a soul whose affinities are with him." [43]

The view of the atonement prevalent in America during the colonial period was that of penal substitution, the view that Christ had borne the exact quantitative penalty of man's sin, that he might satisfy divine justice and thus release God's forgiving grace for the salvation of men. Pressed by the difficulty of any scheme that supposes a literal satisfaction of God's justice, or the release of the guilty obtained by the penal suffering of the innocent, later New England theologians developed what is known as the governmental theory of the atonement, that Christ expressed by his death God's abhorrence of sin, the same amount as would have been shown by the punishment of the guilty. The righteousness of God therefore stands erect and fair, even though punishment is released. " Of all the theories of the atonement," says Williston Walker, " this is the most theatrical and least satisfactory, for the message of the Gospel is that in some true sense Christ died, not for general justice, but for *me*." [44] " It was a scholastic and not a human doctrine," agrees Theodore Munger. " It was far off and general. Simple souls wanted an atonement to sustain themselves rather than the government of God. It was not the maintenance of general justice that they felt the need of, but something that would help them to become personally just before God." [45]

In *The Vicarious Sacrifice,* Bushnell claims that all love that is worthy of the name in heaven or in earth is vicarious love, love that suffers with and for the sake of others, and that the mission of Christ is to be studied from this point of view.

Vicarious sacrifice, then, is no mysterious or incomprehensible transaction, no legal or governmental procedure by which Christ enables God to become gracious to men. " In what is called his vicarious sacrifice (Christ) simply engages, at the expense of great suffering and even of death itself, to bring us out of our sins themselves, and so out of their penalties; being himself profoundly identified with us in our fallen state, and burdened in feeling with our evils." [46]

This saving power comes from his life and death, as seen in the light of the resurrection; it is not omnipotent power that compels the will of men, but the moral power of God that renovates character, reconciles men to God, and induces them to love sacrificially, in turn, both God and man.

Other moral views had proved inadequate in Bushnell's estimation because they proposed Christ only as an example, or as a teacher, or as a revealer of the divine love. " The one fatal defect that vitiates all such conceptions and puts them under a doom of failure," he says, " is that they make up a gospel which has no law side of authority, penal enforcement, rectoral justice; nothing to take hold of an evil mind at the point of its indifference or averseness to good, nothing to impress conviction, or shake the confidence, or stop the boldness of transgression." [47] In Bushnell's own presentation, Christ is more than example, more than teacher, more even than the moral power of God. In addition — and for Bushnell this is fundamental — Christ, by his life and death, and by his teachings, "has set the law precept in a position of great honor and power, enduring it with such life and majesty, in men's convictions, as it otherwise never could have had." [48]

The second volume of *The Vicarious Sacrifice* was written ten years after the publication of the first, and was intended, not merely to supplement, but in a measure to substitute a belated idea for the latter part of the former volume. Though its effect on theological thinking has been small, its publication illustrates a fundamental trait in Bushnell's character — his readiness to change his opinion, to accept new light, and to modify old opinions, in an eager and never-ending search for the truth. As he explains in the introduction of this volume: "It seems to be required of me by the unexpected arrival of fresh light, that I should make a large revision of my former treatise entitled *The Vicarious Sacrifice.* . . . Having undertaken to find the truth on this great subject at whatever cost, I am not willing to be excused from further obligation because the truth appears to be outgrowing my published expositions. . . . There is no reason, personal to myself, why I should be fastened to my own small measures when larger measures are given me. Besides, how shall man ever get rid of his old sins, when he cannot let go his little outgrown opinions?" [49]

It is sometimes asserted that Bushnell in this volume found the moral view which he had previously advocated inadequate, and returned to the substitutionary view which he had formerly repudiated. But this is contrary to Bushnell's own explicit statement. He says: "I recant no one of my denials." "I still assert the 'moral view' of the atonement as before, and even more completely than before."

In his former work he had treated "the work of Christ as a reconciling power on man"; he now undertakes to treat it on the Godward side. Two things are necessary, Bushnell contends, for a man completely to forgive his fellow men —

first, a desire to win the wrongdoer; and, secondly, some sacrificial effort to accomplish this result. Only thus can he allay — or propitiate — the moral resentment which the transgression has properly aroused within his own breast. Assuming that this is true of all moral natures, why not of the Great Propitiation itself? God propitiates himself, Bushnell concludes, in the sufferings of Christ.

In presenting this theory, Bushnell sedulously avoids any thought of legal satisfaction. In direct contrast with the traditional method, he endeavors " to interpret all that is prepared and suffered in the propitiation of God and the justification of men by a reference to the moral pronouncements of human nature and society; assuming that nothing can be true of God, or of Christ, which is not true in some sense *more humano*, and is not made intelligible by human analogies. We cannot interpret God," he insists, " except by what we find in our own personal instincts and ideas." [50]

In spite of the inadequacies, the one-sidedness, the forced interpretation of Scripture texts to be found in *The Vicarious Sacrifice*, Bushnell had in fact rendered great service to our understanding of the work of Christ. For one thing he made it clear that the atonement is too large, too transcendent in its relation to the infinite and the eternal, to be illustrated by any one analogy, or to be comprehended and carried about in any single formula.

Then again he emphasized the fact, sometimes forgotten, that the end of the atonement, according to the usual Scripture text, is reconciliation of men to God rather than reconciliation of God to man (as in II Cor. 5:19), the renovation of character here on earth rather than a forensic transaction in heaven. As Peter puts it: Christ " bare our sins in his body upon the tree, *that* we, having died unto sins, might live unto righteousness " (I Peter 2:24).

In addition, Bushnell took the atonement out of the region of legalism, which had become dry scholasticism, and laid

41

it straight down upon life itself. "It is singular," one acute critic remarked at the time in a letter to a friend, "that men who, like Bushnell and Robertson, reject the full import of the death of Christ, should make Christ a far more living and effective power than the majority of those who receive it. It is singular, yet it must be confessed it is true." [51]

The criticism called out by the first volume of *The Vicarious Sacrifice* was severer than that visited on any previous book. Outside of New England, indeed, the condemnation on the part of the professional theologians was complete. But with the passage of the years the moral view set forth by Bushnell has met with increasing favor; it has become in its main outlines at least the characteristic view of the atonement held by American theologians. Unfortunately, as the manward aspects of the atonement have become predominant, the Godward aspects have tended to be forgotten.

Though his closing years were secluded years, Bushnell did not allow himself to be excluded from life. His mind continued to seek affiliation with the outside world. There was nothing in which he did not seem to take an interest, either in the world of affairs or in the world of thought. He had hoped to complete a new work on the Holy Spirit, but had strength to finish only a few pages. He had taken an active interest in the civic, as well as the religious, life of the city, and two days before his death the beautiful and spacious park which he had labored so long to secure for his native town was named in his honor. He was held in increasing veneration, not only in his own community, but throughout the state. When at last God took him, on February 17, 1876, he was at peace with all men.

7

Bushnell was a brilliant but not a balanced thinker. He wrote, read, and rewrote in the light of his enlarging experience and the practical needs of religious folk. He left behind him no complete system of thought and no school that could be called by his name.

And yet few American theologians have been so influential. His various writings are not read widely now, as once they were, but they have passed into the living structure of present-day religious thought. As Joseph M. M. Gray has said, they have "wrought themselves into the minds and lives of strong men who, through the alembic of their own thought and character, transmitted them to their contemporaries. Brooks, Gladden, Gordon, and a host of humbler and unnamed men whose works follow them, took their direction from his compass and found illumination at his insights. The body of reasoning into which he cast his discernments may lie moldering among the theological graves, but his spirit goes marching on." [52]

Theodore T. Munger, his most competent biographer, writing almost half a century ago, listed four specific contributions. Bushnell, he claims, brought relief, first, from a revivalism that ignored the law of Christian growth; secondly, from a conception of the Trinity bordering on tritheism; thirdly, from a view of miracles that implied a suspension of natural law; and fourthly, from a theory of the atonement that had grown almost shadowy under "improvements," yet still failed to declare the law of human life. In the estimation of John W. Buckham, a greater contribution was what he did toward the recovery of Christ as the central light and potency of Christianity. "It is true that the theological Christ essential to the 'plan of redemption' was made much of, but he was but a pale and unreal reflection of the Christ of the Gospels. Bushnell reillumined Christianity with the light of the true Christ. His was the 'Gospel of the Face' — a face which was 'as the sun shining in his strength' and lighting up all the heavy shadows and dark recesses of an otherwise dismal theological world." [53]

But more important than any specific contribution was the new approach to religious truth that he introduced into America. Over against dogmatic interpretations of Scripture taken as literal scientific fact, logical deductions from unexamined assumptions, metaphysical speculations remote from life, and finely spun webs of unimportant theory, Bushnell placed the emphasis on moral intuition, on religious feeling, on firsthand observation of nature, on the facts of religious experience, and on the Bible as read in their light. In a word he brought theology from the realm of mere logic to the realm of life. As his friend Amos S. Chesebrough remarked, "Christian doctrine was to him no longer a conclusion from a process of reasoning, but it was formulated Christian experience. It must be, not a speculation, not a piece of well-reasoned framework which nicely fits into a theological system, but something to live by — something firstly, secondly, always, vitally practical for the uses of the soul." [54] This is the key to all his writing, — the aim of all his preaching. *Christian Nurture, God in Christ, Nature and the Supernatural,* and *The Vicarious Sacrifice* — all yield rich treasure because developed by this method; they serve life because they arose out of life. As Dr. Leonard Bacon pointed out many years ago, his works have tended to make all the evangelical theology of our English tongue less rigidly scholastic, more Scriptural, broader in its views, more inspiring in its relations to the pulpit and to the Christian life.

At the same time it must be confessed that embedded in the writings of Bushnell there are seeds which, watered by the evolutionary philosophy that Bushnell himself repudiated, and fed by the theology of Schleiermacher and Ritschl, for whose reception Bushnell's writings prepared the way, have borne fruit in the present century that is not altogether good. H. Shelton Smith, in a recent book, *Faith and Nurture*, speaks of four tendencies in more liberal theology, all of them rooted in the writings of Bushnell, that have rendered modern liberalism bankrupt and have led modern religious education, in which he is specifically interested, to a decisive parting of the way.

The first of these is the philosophy of divine immanence. The God of the founding fathers was almost exclusively transcendent. The God of modern liberalism has become almost entirely immanent — a God in some cases actually identified with the forces of nature, or with the personality-producing and personality-responsive forces in the universe, or with the forces in the universe working for maximum mutuality. The transition from transcendence to immanence was powerfully stimulated by the writings of Horace Bushnell.

He himself believed in a God who was transcendent as well as immanent. He wrote his great work on *Nature and the Supernatural* to vindicate the rights of the latter. But his contention that the supernatural and the natural constitute a single order has been interpreted to mean that the supernatural is found only in the natural — that natural and supernatural are in fact identical, thus subjecting the supernatural to the very limitations from which Bushnell had sought to deliver it.

Theodore T. Munger, who did so much to extend Bushnell's influence, finds exaltation of nature to be the key to Bushnell. "Bushnell," he writes, "outrunning his day, conceived of God as immanent in his works — the soul and life of them. Their laws were his laws. Therefore if one would know how God feels and thinks and acts, one must go to nature, and to humanity as its culmination. God is the spiritual reality, of which nature is the manifestation." This is not Bushnell's own position, but it points to a direction in which the influence of Bushnell has been borne.

A second major concept in the development of liberal Protestantism is the idea of growth from within as over against change from without; the idea that regeneration is a natural process rather than the work of a supernatural agency, that religious education is dependent upon psychological processes and not upon the Holy Spirit. Bushnell himself recognized the need of divine regeneration. In *Christian Nurture* he rejects the view that growth in Christian character is a " vegetable process," a mere " onward development." " It involves," he says, " a struggle with evil, a fall and a rescue." This point of view is maintained even more strongly in his later writings.

Yet " the idea of progress in terms of gradual growth was cardinal with Bushnell. Revolutionary and catastrophic change was alien to his mode of life and thought." [55] And this aspect of Bushnell's thought was greatly stimulated by the general acceptance of the optimistic evolutionary philosophy so influential prior to the First World War.

A third idea widely influential in modern thought, whose falsity, we might think, has now been abundantly revealed, is the inherent goodness of the natural man. No idea in the orthodox theology was more repugnant to the rising liberalism of the nineteenth century than the doctrine of total depravity. Bushnell, as we have seen, did not deny the original " pravity " of man. Any analysis of Christianity in which sin and salvation from it by divine redemption figured lightly he would have repudiated. But his critics then, and his critics now, feel that he underestimated the prevalence of sin and its grip upon those whose habits are formed. There can be no doubt that his theory of Christian nurture had natural affinities with more optimistic theories of human nature. " Take any scheme of depravity you please," contends Bushnell, " there is yet nothing in it to forbid the

46

possibility that a child should be led, in his first moral act, to cleave unto what is good and right, any more than in the first of his twentieth year." [56] " Only unchristian education," he says, " brings up the child for future conversion." [57]

" When the twentieth-century movement of religious education emerged," Dr. Smith points out, " this phase of Bushnell's thought was revived and made basic. The lingering idea of Protestant evangelicalism that the child is alienated from the Kingdom of God was rejected. Children, it was held, are by nature already in possession of a life-principle which requires, not repentance, but spiritual development." [58] In the estimation of Dr. D. C. Mackintosh, Bushnell did more than any other preacher to discredit the old-fashioned teaching, " Ye must be born again." [59]

A fourth debilitating conception in modern theology is that of Jesus as an example, Jesus as a moral teacher, Jesus who is human as we are human, and divine in somewhat the same sense that all mankind is divine — a purely ethical comprehension of his person. Bushnell himself believed in the deity of Christ, including his Virgin birth and his resurrection from the dead. " He differs from us," he said, " not in degree but in kind." And yet Bushnell declared that the vicarious suffering of Jesus was " in no way peculiar to him, save in degree." Sacrifice in man is therefore not different from sacrifice in Christ, save that in man it " carries humbler effects."

In the estimation of Dr. Smith: " This element of Bushnell's thought is perhaps his most original contribution to the doctrine of Christian redemption. It has had a profound influence on the subsequent development of liberal views of the relation of Jesus Christ to men in the work of redemption." It contains " an element of truth that is essential to vital Christian discipleship. In an important sense the Christian is required to take up the cross and follow Christ. Yet in his tendency to equate the cross of Christ with that of

Christ's followers Bushnell set a trend toward an attenuated Christology." [60]

The same tendency has been powerfully stimulated by the readiness of some to assume that the essential contribution of *Nature and the Supernatural* is the asserted doctrine that man is of a nature kindred to God — that God and man enjoy the same essential life and personality. It is but a step from this point to the further view that Christ is divine only in the sense that man is divine.

More fundamental, perhaps, is the fact that Bushnell's emphasis on nature, experience, moral intuition, and the Christian sensibilities, though it freed the Gospel from many false dogmatisms and brought theology and the Bible to life, did tend to make man the measure of God, to lead him to seek the divine in the depths of his own being or in the world of nature around him rather than in the Scriptures of the Christian faith and in Christ in whom the Word has become flesh. Bushnell himself rooted, or attempted to root, his doctrines in the Scripture, and accepted the teachings of Christ as fully authoritative, but here as elsewhere many of those who felt his influence moved on to positions which he himself would not have taken.

To return to Horace Bushnell is impossible and, of course, not desirable. But Christians of every shade, liberals and conservatives, may learn from his spirit, share his passionate desire for the truth, be willing to revise their opinions in the light of new developments, keep their minds open to the divine Spirit, seek to bring religion into the realm of life, and realize that Christ himself is more important than beliefs about Christ.

Rev. Joseph H. Twichell, in his *Personal Reminiscences of Horace Bushnell,* says: " Never can I forget his witness concerning himself which it was once given me to hear. We were angling together on a mountain stream. I had happened to tell him what some one had recently told me of his obligation to him for aid in keeping the Christian faith, and he remarked that it must be a comfort to him to know that there were many to whom he had been the means of that sort of help. Whereupon he turned and faced me, and in a manner of utmost seriousness — almost solemnity — replied: ' The only thing that gives me the least comfort in myself is that I know and can testify that I have above all things else desired to know the truth.' " [61]

That was the secret of Bushnell's own life — his greatest legacy, it may be, to the Church.

Chapter II

HENRY WARD BEECHER
*and the popular revolt against
Calvinism*

*H*ENRY WARD BEECHER was the most popular preacher of his day; the most powerful preacher, many think, ever to appear in America; the greatest pulpit orator, some have even dared to claim, in the whole history of the Christian Church. For almost forty years he preached in a tabernacle lacking all architectural adornment, but so constructed as to carry his lightest whisper to every member of a congregation of almost three thousand, including, it seemed, every important visitor to our American metropolis. His words from the pulpit, on the platform, and in the religious and secular press, carried to the farthest confines of the English-speaking race. Lyman Abbott, a religious journalist, accustomed to assess the currents of American life, says that he has "probably done more to change directly the religious life, and indirectly the theological thought, in America than any preacher since Jonathan Edwards." [1] This no doubt is a partial judgment. "The significance of the man," writes Paxton Hibben, "is not that he lived as spectator or even incidental participant through so many years during which a tremendous transformation took place in the outlook and the lives of men, but that the life and conduct of Henry Ward Beecher were both barometer and record of these changes. More than any other man, he was their voice. . . . Beecher," he continues, "stood forth a prodigious figure, not by blazing a path in any wilderness, but by the fact that his inner experience was identical with that of millions of his fellow countrymen. His gift was merely that he was articulate while they were not. But he was articulate of the very intellectual processes and material growth by which the portentous America of today was evolving from the provincial, self-opinioned, ignorant and intolerant America of 1813." [2]

Though Hibben's picture of the Puritan prison house in which Beecher was born is woefully distorted, though his portrait of Beecher himself is a caricature, a ' psychological ' reconstruction of Beecher's inner life, weighted and determined by his own predilections, it must be admitted that the judgment just quoted is at least partially correct. Beecher was not a pioneer, an original thinker, like Bushnell; his influence, as some have claimed, may have been greater on the lay mind than on the American clergy and on the masses of the people than on the intellectual elite; nonetheless his life and career do reflect the fascinating sequences of American political, social, scientific, and theological history during a large part of the nineteenth century. Changing emphases in American preaching, including the popular revolt against Calvinism, which must be taken into account if we are to understand the present American scene, found in him both exemplar and voice.

I

Like Bushnell, Beecher had a long line of Connecticut forebears.

John Beecher, the first of the line; his wife, Hannah; and their son, Isaac, accompanied John Davenport to America in 1638, and were numbered with him among the first settlers of the colony.

Joseph Beecher, the fifth in order of descent; his son, Nathaniel; and his grandson, David, were blacksmiths, noted for their physical prowess. More important than physical prowess was intellectual alertness. David Beecher, grandfather of Henry Ward, was reputed to be one of the best-read men in New England, and his shop became a forum where all political ideas of the day were eagerly discussed.

Lyman Beecher, David's son, abandoned the family calling to become a minister. Early in his career he became recognized as one of the leaders of the New School theology, a follower of Timothy Dwight, the close friend and associate of Nathaniel W. Taylor, whose logical "abstrusions" and metaphysical subtleties proved so distasteful to Horace Bushnell. With Taylor, he opposed the idea of man's complete moral inability and helped to give the deathblow to the doctrine of infant damnation. He stressed instead man's freedom to respond to God's lawful requirements, the possibility therefor, and the duty of immediate repentance.

He labored under the firm conviction that he was freeing essential Calvinism from the philosophical encumbrances which had become attached to it from the time of the Reformation and from popular misunderstandings which facilitated the rise of Unitarianism. To this, his son, Charles Beecher, pointed out, he attributed all his success in revivals and the ability for so long to unite evangelical minds of opposite schools on common grounds.

His interests, as this reference indicates, were eminently practical. The labors of Timothy Dwight had helped to usher in the Second Great Awakening, as it is sometimes called, successive waves of revivals which constituted for many years the most powerful religious influence in America. Lyman Beecher had been "baptized into the revival spirit" at Yale. His all-absorbing aim throughout the whole of his career was to promote revivals, to lead men to submit themselves to the Lord Jesus Christ, in order that he might advance the coming of His millennial reign.

He advocated New School theology because, along with practical theologians, like Timothy Dwight and Nathaniel W. Taylor, and successful evangelists, like Charles G. Finney, he was firmly convinced that Old Calvinism, as he termed it, led to fatalism, obscured moral accountability, and made man unresponsive to the evangelistic appeal.

His career as a reformer was the outgrowth of the same all-absorbing interest. As he himself put it, " when I saw a rattlesnake in my path, I killed it." But unlike his more famous son he never went out of his way to hunt a rattlesnake and was only incidentally interested in social improvement.

As a young pastor in charge of the First Presbyterian Church at East Hampton, Long Island, he was horrified by the tragic death of Alexander Hamilton at the hands of Aaron Burr. He wrote a blistering sermon on the evils of dueling which helped to outlaw this pernicious custom and gave him something like a national reputation.

In his second pastorate at Litchfield, distressed by the ravages of drink on the lives of his people, he delivered six sermons on the evils of drinking, which were later published, translated into many languages, and widely circulated in this and other countries. More than any other man he was responsible for the launching of the great temperance campaign — whose end is not yet.

In 1826 he was called to the Hanover Street Church of Boston, that he might lead an aggressive fight against Unitarianism, which he regarded as " the deadly foe of human happiness, whose direct tendency was to prevent true conviction and conversion, stop revivals of religion, and leave men bound hand and foot under the power of the adversary." For six and a half years he labored in this lost Calvinistic bastion, and though Unitarianism was not put to rout, Trinitarian Congregationalism was immeasurably strengthened.

In his fifty-sixth year there came a new challenge to this doughty champion of the faith — this time from the West. Immigration was pouring rapidly into the Mississippi and Ohio valleys. Farseeing men in the Presbyterian Church had established Lane Seminary at Cincinnati. It was thought to be the strategic center for the training of ministers to take the western portion of the continent for Christ and to ward off the dangers of Catholicism that seemed to menace the future welfare of America. Lyman Beecher, the most prominent, popular, and powerful preacher in the nation, was invited to head the new institution.

"The exigencies of our country," said Beecher, "demand seminaries and exposition of doctrine and preachers of such zeal and activity as guarantee, by the grace of God, the increasing effusion of his Spirit. And the question whether the first and leading seminary of the West shall be one which inculcates orthodoxy with or without revivals, is a question, in my view, of as great importance as was ever permitted a single human mind to decide. If I accept I consider the question settled that a revival seminary takes the lead, and so much and so powerfully as inevitably to give a complexion probably forever to the doctrine and revivals of that great world." [3] Laboring under this point of view, Lyman Beecher came to Cincinnati as president of Lane Theological Seminary and pastor of the Second Presbyterian Church, the most aristocratic and influential Church in the city.

Unfortunately, Old School Presbyterians were on their guard. Their suspicions had been aroused against Dr. Beecher because, while he held to original sin, involving the certainty that infants will be "totally, actually depraved as soon as they are capable of accountable action," he also maintained that actual guilt results only from voluntary transgression of known law. Dr. Wilson, leading Old School divine in Cincinnati — according to Henry Ward Beecher, "as stiff a man, and as orthodox as Calvin himself, and as pugnacious as ten Calvins rolled into one" — greeted Dr. Beecher with a charge of heresy. He waited for presbytery, synod, and General Assembly to take action, and when this did not ensue, preferred charges himself, first before the presbytery and then before the synod.

Beecher was vindicated by both courts, but bitter contentions continued, and Lyman Beecher's acquittal was one of the major causes of the disastrous split of the powerful Presbyterian Church into Old and New School Assemblies in 1837. Lyman Beecher remained as president of Lane Seminary until 1850, by which time, in spite of many difficulties, it seemed established on secure foundations. In 1856, the aging warrior settled in Brooklyn that he might spend his closing days in the shadow of his illustrious son.

2

According to Theodore Parker, Lyman Beecher was the father of more brains than any man in America. There is basis for this distinction. Eleven of his thirteen children survived him. All seven sons entered the ministry, and most of them were distinguished. Catherine, his eldest daughter, was an outstanding pioneer in the education of women. Harriet, author of *Uncle Tom's Cabin* and a distinguished novelist, was the most famous American woman of her day.

Henry Ward, the seventh living child out of eight born to Lyman Beecher and his first wife, Roxana Foote, was born on June 24, 1813, during his father's second pastorate, at Litchfield. His mother, sensitive, gifted, gentle yet strong, with a love for the beautiful which her son was to inherit, died when Henry was only three, but as idealized by his father, remained a strong and potent influence in all his later life. His father, though he still loved to romp with his children and on rare occasions take all the family fishing on the neighboring pond, was by this time too absorbed in multifarious activities to devote much time to his little son. His second mother who came into the home within a year seemed cold. She inspired awe on account of her many excellencies, rather than love because of her sympathy and understanding. The boy grew up diffident and shy, unable to articulate clearly and longing vainly for affection.

His school days were unhappy. "I have not a single pleasant recollection in connection with them," he claimed in later years. This was due in part to the schools, but in great measure also to the fact that Henry Ward was painfully sensitive and showed little aptitude for learning.

At home he struggled with the catechism. "The other children memorized readily," Harriet recalled, "and were brilliant reciters, but Henry, blushing, stammering, confused and hopelessly miserable, stuck fast on some sandbank of what is required or forbidden by this or that commandment, his mouth choking up with the long words which he hopelessly miscalled, was sure to be accused of idleness or inattention, and to be solemnly talked to, which made him look more stolid and miserable than ever, but appeared to have no effect in quickening his dormant faculties." [4]

Hours in Church did not make religion any more attractive. He sat right under the pulpit in the minister's pew, which had sides so high that he could never see the speaker. Once to his great joy he was allowed to sit in the balcony, but a roguish boy pushed him off the hard bench so that he tore his coat, and his mother, not understanding, never allowed him the privilege again.

As he grew older, sermons on decrees, foreordination, election, and reprobation fascinated him, but raised disturbing questions about his own salvation. "My father's public teaching may be called alleviated Calvinism," he said in later life. "Even under that the iron entered my soul. There were days and weeks in which the pall of death over the universe could not have made it darker to my eyes than those in which I thought, 'If you are elected you will be saved, and if you are not elected you will be damned, and there is no hope for you.' I wanted to be a Christian. I went about longing for God as a lamb bleating longs for its mother's udder, and I stood imprisoned behind those iron bars: 'It is all decreed. It is all fixed. If you are elected you will be saved anyhow — if you are not elected, you will perish.'" [5]

His despair became deeper when his brother George, the next older, went to college and was converted. It seemed as though a gulf had come between them, and as though his brother was a saint on one side of it, while he was a little reprobate on the other side. "It was awful," he recalled. "If there had been a total eclipse of the sun I should not have been in more profound darkness outwardly than I was inwardly." [6]

Once on coming home he heard the bell toll and learned that it was for the funeral of one of his playmates. "I did not know that he had been sick," he said, "but he had dropped into eternity; and the ringing, swinging, booming of that bell, if it had been the sound of an angel trumpet of the last day, would not have seemed to me more awful. I went into an ecstasy of anguish. At intervals, for days and weeks, I cried and prayed. There was scarcely a re-tired place in the garden, in the woodhouse, in the carriage house, or in the barn that was not a scene of my crying and praying. It was piteous that I should be in such a state of mind, and that there should be nobody to help me, and lead me out into the light." [7]

The boy longed to open his soul to someone, but there was no one to whom he felt free to go. It would have been easier, he felt, to have had his head chopped off on the block than to reveal his thoughts to his mother. He did not dare to go to his father. As he explained in later years: "I do not recollect that to that day one word had been said to me, or one syllable had been uttered in the pulpit, that led me to think there was any mercy in the heart of God for a sinner like me. For a sinner that had repented it was thought there was pardon; but how to repent was the very thing I did not know. A converted sinner might be saved, but for a poor, miserable, faulty boy, that pouted, and got mad at his brothers and sisters, and did a great many naughty things, there was no salvation so far as I had learned." [8]

No one helped him in his hour of need except a scarcely literate Negro, Charles Smith, in whose room the boy was accustomed to sleep. Henry Ward Beecher lay on his cot at night and heard this poor Negro read his Bible and laugh and sing and pray, and thought how gladly he would change places with him, if only he could have his hope of heaven.

Unquestionably as a youth Henry Ward Beecher was lonely, self-centered, and repressed. Even so, he was not brought up in a Puritan prison house as sometimes charged. To be sure there was an unwholesome emphasis on theology, but the general atmosphere was one of intellectual virility. A spirit of cheerfulness pervaded the household. Henry Ward was grateful in later days for the freedom which he enjoyed, as well as for his participation in the family chores. During these days he laid the foundation for that magnificent physical vigor, that abounding health and good humor, that independence and self-reliance, which followed him all his life.

Yet, as Harriet Beecher Stowe has written, "he was not marked out by the prophecies of partial friends for any brilliant future." He was "a stocky, strong, well-grown boy, loyal in duty, trained in unquestioning obedience, inured to patient hard work, inured also to the hearing and discussing of all the great theological problems of Calvinism, which were always reverberating in his hearing; but as to any mechanical culture, in an extremely backward state — a poor writer, a miserable speller, with a thick utterance, and a bashful reticence which seemed like stolid stupidity." [9]

In Boston there was a changed atmosphere. Thomas K.

Beecher, a younger brother, remembers Henry Ward as a childhood hero, who owned a long sled and coasted down Copp's Hill, skated on the Mill Dam, ran to fires, played on the flute, jumped and whirled around the horizontal bar, and was not afraid of open stable doors and red cows with monstrous horns.

Harriet, who was about his own age, reports on the other hand that " the melancholy that brooded over his childhood waxed more turbulent and formidable. He grew gloomy and moody, restless and irritable." [10] At the Boston Latin School he absorbed only a minimum of learning and pondered the advisability of running off to sea.

His astute father, playing on his ambition to be a skilled mariner, packed him off to the Mount Pleasant Collegiate Institute at Amherst, saying, " I shall have that boy in the ministry yet." This school, newly opened on a pretentious scale by two Amherst graduates, had selected students from all parts of the world. The outlook of Henry Ward was broadened, while close friendships met the needs of his emotional nature. For the first time he began to make some progress in his studies. Meanwhile a gifted teacher of elocution helped to lay the foundation for his ultimate skill as an orator. When he came he still spoke as if he had pudding in his mouth, but now his slumbering ambition was aroused. He practiced long hours exploding vowels and making careful gestures, until at long last voice and body responded instinctively to every impulse of mind and heart.

While he was here there broke out one of those infectious religious revivals which Beecher came to feel " have no basis of judicious instruction but spring from inexperienced zeal. It resulted in many mushroom hopes, and I had one of them; but I do not know how or why I was converted. I only know I was in a sort of day-dream, in which I hoped I had given myself to Christ." [11] The religious feeling evaporated within a few weeks, but Henry, not daring to announce that there was some question about his conversion, was received into the Church.

In 1830, at the age of seventeen, he was enrolled at Amherst, then a struggling young college, ill-equipped and poorly endowed. Here, early in the course, he experienced his second " conversion." Once more it was a revival, a revival which produced a deep conviction of sin, for which despite earnest efforts he found little relief. " I remember with shame and mortification," he said, " the experiences through which I went, the pleadings for mercy, the longing for some token of acceptance, and the prayers that became ritualistic from their repetition, that I might have that that was hanging over my head, and waiting for me to take, and I did not know how, I did not know how." [12]

He made no reputation as a scholar at Amherst, in part because, while reading widely in the English classics and in subjects which really interested him, he studied hardly at all in those which he felt had no practical value. Contributions from his pen began to appear in the *Shrine,* one of the college papers, and he was making excellent progress as a debater. During the long winter vacation he taught school. When the opportunity offered he lectured and gave religious talks in neighboring schools and Churches.

On one occasion he walked to Brattleboro, Vermont, to deliver a lecture on temperance. The ten dollars he received for traveling expenses made him feel inexpressibly rich. Five dollars he took to buy an engagement ring. With the rest he bought books, particularly the works of Edmund Burke, which formed the foundation of his library and proved invaluable to him as a public speaker. By the time of his graduation he had fifty or more volumes. A year later there were one hundred and thirty-five (forty-two theological, seventy-one literary, ten scientific, and twelve miscellaneous). When he died, he had a library of ten thousand well and carefully selected volumes.

Already as a college student he was well versed in the fine points of theology. As he explained: " Growing constantly and warmly in sympathy with my father, in taking sides with orthodoxy, that was in battle in Boston with Unitarianism, I learned of him all the theology that was current at that time. In the quarrels also between Andover and East Windsor and New Haven and Princeton — I was at home in all these distinctions. I got the doctrines just like a row of pins on a paper of pins. I knew them as a soldier knows his weapons. I could get them in battle array." [13]

When he graduated from Amherst, he entered Lane Seminary, where his father was now the president. The only course which seems really to have aroused his interest was the Bible course offered by his prospective brother-in-law, Professor Calvin Ellis Stowe. " He led me," he said, " to an examination of the Bible and to an analysis of its several portions, not as parts of a machine, formal and dead, but as a body of truth instinct with God, warm with divine and human sympathies, clothed with language adapted to their fit expression and to be understood as similar language used for similar ends in every day life." [14]

Extracurricular activities absorbed much of his time. He sang in the choir and sometimes led it; taught a class of young ladies; gave a course of temperance lectures during the week; and preached whenever the occasion presented itself. For about six months he wrote editorials for the *Cincinnati Journal,* a religious weekly established by the Presbyterian Pastoral Association of Cincinnati to fight Roman Catholicism. After proslavery mobs had destroyed the printing press of James Birney, he had himself sworn in as a deputy marshall and patrolled the streets heavily armed and ready to shoot.

Theology was dished out to him, not only in the classroom, but also in the home. " Long, long discourses," recalled Thomas K. Beecher, " lasting till past midnight, and resumed at every meal, of 'free agency,' 'sovereignty,' 'natural and moral ability,' interpretations and such." Even more important in the education of Henry Ward Beecher was his father's heresy trial. He could never forget the anomaly — Lyman Beecher, the most eminent clergyman of his day, the champion of Trinitarianism against rampant Unitarianism, laboring sacrificially to build up a great theological institution in the expanding West, forced to leave the bedside of his dying wife to defend himself "for believing that a man could obey the commandments of God." After the trial was ended, there was the continued bitterness, a conspiracy so it seemed to crush the new seminary and its distinguished head. To champion his father, Henry Ward Beecher had become expert in theological technicalities, but he grew more and more impatient with theological partisanship and more and more convinced that theological controversies were futile and wicked. "By the time I got away from the theological Seminary," he confessed, "I was so sick — no tongue can tell how sick I was of the whole medley. How I despised and hated this abyss of whirling controversies that seemed to me to be filled with all manner of evil things, with everything indeed but Christ!"[15]

During his first two years in the seminary he seemed uncertain about his message, uncertain even about his call to preach. But one "blessed morning in May," shortly after he had read through one of the Gospels at a single sitting, there came the experience which he so lovingly recalled, "when it pleased God to reveal to my wandering soul the idea that it was His nature to love man in his sins for the sake of helping him out of them; that He did not do it out of compliment to Christ, or to a law, or a plan of salvation, but from the fullness of His great heart; that He was a Being not made by sin, but sorry; that he was not furious with wrath toward the sinner, but pitied him — in short, that He felt toward me as my mother felt toward me, to whose eyes my wrong doing brought tears, who never pressed me so close to her as when I had done wrong, and who would fain, with her yearning love, lift me out of trouble. And when I found that Jesus Christ had such a disposition . . . that it was Christ's nature to lift men out of weakness to strength, out of impurity to goodness, out of everything low and debasing to superiority, I felt that I had found a God. . . . Time went on, and next came the disclosure of a Christ ever present with me — a Christ that never was far from me, but was always near me, as a Companion and Friend, to uphold and sustain me. This was the last and the best revelation of God's Spirit to my soul." [16]

From the time when his soul was lifted up by these two great truths, God's nature as manifested by Jesus the Christ to love man in his sins for the sake of helping him out of them and the sustaining Christ ever present with individual men ('a real presence' of perennial spiritual influence), he sprang to his works, says John R. Howard, with an ardor that was unquenched to the end of his life. "God's love because of his fatherhood; man's worth and mutual brotherhood because of his sonship to God: these were the two halves of the one great theme which from that time to the day of his final silence, underlay his life, his words, his works." [17]

As Henry Ward Beecher himself described it: "I was like the man in the story to whom the fairy gave a purse with a single piece of money in it, which he found always came again as soon as he had spent it. I thought I knew at least one thing to preach. I found it included everything." [18]

3

Beecher's first charge was in Lawrenceburg, Indiana, a small town on the Ohio, in those days when the great rivers were pulsing arteries of trade.

His Church had twenty members, of whom nineteen were

women and the other — a cipher. With the help of the
Home Missionary Society, it promised to pay the new pastor
a salary of four hundred dollars a year. The only accommo-
dations available for his bride were two unattractive rooms,
heavily stained with tobacco juice, over a stable. Beecher
was not ashamed to wear the cast-off clothing of one of his
parishioners, but wished that the judge's figure was as robust as his own.

Oxford Presbytery, composed of stanch Old School Presbyterians, examined the son of Lyman Beecher with unusual
care and was amazed to find him orthodox. Henry Ward
was also surprised, but admitted that he had answered their
questions "some . . . directly, some intelligently, and others somewhat obscurely."

The next day presbytery affirmed its adherence to the Old
School Assembly and passed a resolution requiring its candidates and licentiates to do the same. Henry Ward could
not be thus disloyal to his father, and when the presbytery
refused to ordain him, he carried his Church into the New
School Assembly.

All through the West little Churches were dividing, one
faction into the Old School, the other into the New. "Going into my work in the midst of that state of affairs," wrote
Henry Ward Beecher, "I made up my mind distinctly that,
with the help of God, I would never engage in any religious
contention. I remember riding through the woods for long,
dreary days, and I recollect at one time coming out into an
open place where the sun shone down through to the bank
of the river, and where I had such a sense of the love of
Christ, of the nature of His work on earth, of its beauty and
its grandeur, and such a sense of the miserableness of Christian men quarrelling and seeking to build up antagonistic
churches — in other words, the Kingdom of Christ rose up
before my mind with such supreme loveliness and majesty —
that I sat in my saddle, I do not know how long . . . and

there, all alone, in a great forest of Indiana, probably twenty miles from any house, prayed for that Kingdom, saying audibly, 'I will never be a sectary.' I remember promising Christ that if He would strengthen me and teach me how to work I would all my life long preach for His Kingdom and endeavor to love everybody who was doing that work. Not that I would accept others' belief, not that I would embrace their theology, not that I would endorse their ecclesiastical organizations; but whatever their instruments might be, if they were sincerely working for the Kingdom of Christ I would never put a straw in their way and never strike a blow to their harm. By the grace of God I have kept that resolution to this day." [19]

In his own Church Beecher preached theology only when he had nothing else to preach. " I had one vivid point," he said, " the realization of the love of God in Christ Jesus."

He was popular in the village and drew people to the Church, but no one was converted under his preaching. " For three years," he said, " I did not make a sinner wink." Every Sunday he had a headache. And every Sunday night he went to bed vowing he would quit preaching and buy a farm.

After two years in Lawrenceburg, Beecher accepted a call to Indianapolis, the capital of the state. The town at that time had less than four thousand inhabitants. The roads had not yet been cleared of their stumps and at times became deep seas of mud.

The Second Presbyterian Church, to which Beecher came, was a New School Church, split off from the Old School, with a membership of about thirty. The Church was soon crowded as it had been at Lawrenceburg, but once more there was a discouraging lack of results.

In desperation Beecher went back to The Acts and studied the methods of the apostles. He found that they were accustomed, first, to feel for a ground on which the people and they could meet. Then general truth was presented on which all could agree. Then this mass of particular truth was brought to bear upon their hearers with an intense personal application and appeal — not in scholastic and scholarly language, but in the language of every day. He decided to follow this method, and " to present these truths in the language of the modern Hoosiers who sat before him instead of that of the ancient Hebrews."

The first time he tried this method, seventeen men were "awakened." "This," says Beecher, "was the most memorable day of our ministerial life. The idea was born. Preaching was a definite and practical thing. Our people needed certain moral changes. Preaching was only a method of enforcing truths, not for the sake of the truths themselves, but for the results to be sought in *men. Man* was the thing. Henceforth our business was to work upon *man;* to study him, to stimulate and educate him. A sermon was good that had power on the heart, and was good for nothing no matter how good that had no moral power on man." [20]

The results of this new type of preaching were soon apparent. A revival broke out, and nearly a hundred people were converted. A member of the congregation pictures Beecher in this revival, as " plunging through the wet streets, his trousers stuffed in his muddy boot-legs, earnest, untiring, swift, with a merry heart, a glowing face, and a helpful word for every one; the whole day preaching Christ to the people where he could find them, and at night preaching still where the people were sure to find him." [21] When the revival was ended he continued to preach twice on Sunday and five times during the week, in various parts of the town. During his long summer vacations he rode on horseback through the state of Indiana, from camp meeting to camp meeting, and from log hut to log hut, " preaching Christ for the hope of salvation." One spring in Indianapolis he preached seventy successive nights in revival effort.

When ministers said, as they sometimes did, "You are not orthodox," Beecher replied: "Very well, I am out on other business. I hear a call that has been sounding down the ages for two thousand years: 'Follow me, I will make you fishers of men.'" "Very soon," he recalled, "I came to the point in which I felt dissatisfied with the views of God that had been before given. I felt dissatisfied with that whole realm of theology, which I now call the machinery of religion. . . . I came [to feel] that it stood in the way of sinful men. I found men in distress, in peril of soul, on account of views which I did not believe were true, or if true, not in any such proportion. If you want to know why I have been so fierce against theology, that is it; because I thought with Mary, and I said time and again, 'They have taken away my Lord, and I know not where they have laid him.'" [22]

Beecher's supreme concern at this time was the salvation of men. He labored continuously and zealously for revivals. But, like his father, he killed rattlesnakes when he found them in his way. He sought to kill the most dangerous varieties to be found in the early frontier communities in a series of *Lectures to Young Men,* preached first to his own congregation, then published, and sold widely in successive editions over the nation.

The most divisive question in Indiana during Beecher's pastorates was the question of slavery. Abolition was unpopular in the state, and abolitionists were regarded as dangerous incendiaries. Beecher does not seem to have touched upon the subject in his first pastorate and not definitely in Indianapolis until his stay there was drawing to a close. Perhaps this was due to a sense of caution, to a feeling that his pastorate could accomplish more on other lines, or to a desire to let nothing interfere with his supreme concern of saving souls. In large part no doubt it was due to his profound distrust of the abolitionists, a distrust which he inherited from, and which he shared with, his father. In notes made for a debate in his seminary days he said of these extremists: "They have produced complete *reaction;* so far from aiding the cause and convincing the South, they have *driven* them through every middle ground onto the extreme of holding broadly and entirely that slavery is *right,* sanctioned by religion, ordained by nature, and essential to the successful progress of a republic — profitable, not immoral, desirable and positively needful." [23]

During the last year of Henry Ward Beecher's stay in Indianapolis, his presbytery requested all its ministers to preach on the subject of slavery at some time during the course of the year. In response to this request Beecher preached, not one sermon, but three. They aroused angry mutterings in the congregation, especially among the legislators who attended Beecher's Church in large numbers.

In Indianapolis as elsewhere Beecher made enemies, but they were far outnumbered by his friends. One thing that added to the young minister's popularity was his unconventionality. He was the first minister in Indianapolis to wear a felt hat in winter and a straw hat in summer; he spurned the immunity from service on the volunteer fire department which was offered to ministers of the Gospel; he painted his own house and dug in his own garden. "He chatted, joked and romped," wrote Jacob Piatt Dunn, in his *History of Greater Indianapolis,* "until he convinced the public that a man could be a Presbyterian preacher and still really enjoy himself." He read widely in horticulture as a diversion, and became editor of the *Western Farmer and Gardener,* published as a supplement of the *Indiana State Journal,* which, because of his sprightly writing, soon gained a national reputation. He was in growing demand as a lecturer, "incontestably," Hibben admits, "a person of consequence in the state of Indiana."

Eight years after coming to Indianapolis, Henry Ward Beecher received two calls, one to the famous and well-established Park Street Church in Boston, the other to a newly organized Congregational Church in Brooklyn. The first call he declined; the second, after considerable pressure, he accepted, leaving for Brooklyn, it may be noted, on the first passenger train to run out of Indianapolis. So began one of the most influential pastorates in the annals of the American pulpit.

4

Brooklyn, at the time, was a city of sixty thousand inhabitants; essentially, however, it was a part of New York City, and before Beecher had completed his ministry, its own population had increased to half a million. Plymouth Church, to which he came, had an initial membership of twenty-one members.

The new pastor's first step was to clear away the pulpit. He could never abide " swallow-nests " as he called them. He wanted to get nearer to his audience. He wished to stand clear, to be seen of his audience, to be free to move and gesticulate.

His primary purpose from the beginning was " to preach Christ for the awakening of men, for their conversion." He worked for revivals in Brooklyn as he had in Indianapolis, and up to the time of the Civil War revivals played a large part in the development of the Church. " My desire," he declared, "was that this should be a revival church — a church in which the Gospel should be preached, primarily and mainly for the recreation of man's moral nature, for the bringing of Christ as a living power upon the living souls of men." [24]

Theologically, the Church was orthodox. It adopted a creed which embodied the doctrines of the Fall, the depravity of the human race, the Trinity, the atonement, the inspiration and authority of the Bible, and the future judgment, with its final awards of everlasting punishment and eternal life. But, as Lyman Abbott indicates: " From the very initiation of the church its pastor's influence was steadily exerted in favor of substituting spiritual and ethical standards for intellectual standards of character. The questions asked in the examination of candidates for admission were practical rather than doctrinal. In the pulpit, in the prayer-meeting, and in the administration of the church the question, What do you believe? was rarely heard; the question, What is your life? was, in varying forms, constantly reiterated." [25]

At first the people came slowly, but after the first few months in ever increasing numbers. Fortunately the old church burned at the end of the second year and a new edifice was built after Beecher's own design. It was a bare auditorium, totally unadorned and making no appeal whatever to the aesthetic sensibilities. In place of the pulpit there was a long platform, with reading stand and chairs thrust out into the congregation, so that the speaker seemed surrounded by a sea of faces. There were seats for twenty-five hundred and room for five hundred more. The acoustical properties were perfect. Mr. Beecher could be seen, and his lightest whisper heard, by every member present.

From the beginning to the end of his long pastorate, even after the " Great Scandal " had besmirched his name, the great auditorium was crowded, morning and evening, predominantly by men, with hundreds turned away. Visitors, great and near great, came from all parts of the world. The membership, mostly middle class, increased until it reached a total of approximately twenty-five hundred.

The crowds were drawn by Beecher's personality, his " unconventionality, his audacity, wit and humor, his theological latitude, his dramatic ability, and picturesqueness of language, his friendly intimacy, and naturalness." [26]   But they were held by Beecher's messages, messages which for the most part, even through the bitterest antislavery days and in the midst of the Civil War, dealt with individual needs and with God's love which enabled a man to live up to his highest potentialities in Christ.

His influence was greatly extended by the press, which found his sermons good copy and broadcast his words through the length and breadth of the land.

Shortly after coming to Brooklyn, Beecher became a contributing editor of the *Independent*, a weekly religious journal whose circulation increased so rapidly (to more than one hundred thousand) that it soon became one of the major journalistic influences in the country.   Beecher's editorials, marked by a star and known therefore as his "star papers," were on a variety of subjects, but included vigorous and trenchant treatments of the questions of the day.   The *Cambridge History of American Literature* ranks them as among the "strongest editorials in the American press."

Through the pages of the *Independent* and increasingly in his pulpit, Henry Ward Beecher spoke his mind regarding the great moral issues of the time.   It was the prevalent opinion that a minister should preach nothing but the Gospel.   Political questions were to be carefully eschewed. Slavery, which Charles G. Finney and others had bitterly denounced, was still an unpopular topic in the pulpits.   The religious press was almost altogether proslavery or silent. The common feeling was that if men in sufficient numbers were converted, social problems would solve themselves.

Beecher held a different conception about the functions of the pulpit.   "I hold that it is a Christian minister's duty," he said, on the eve of the Civil War, "not only to preach the Gospel of the New Testament without reservation, but to apply its truths to every question which relates to the welfare of men." [27]

Justifying his course after the war had begun, he insisted: "I have a right to introduce into my sermons all secular topics as far as they are connected with man's moral character and his hopes of immortality. If I discuss them in a merely secular way, I desecrate the pulpit; but if I discuss them in the spirit of Christ, and for Christ's sake, that I may draw men out of their peculiar dangers, and lead them into a course of right living, then I give dignity and nobility to the pulpit." [28]

"A man," he agreed, "may preach politics too much. A man may do it foolishly. So a man may administer a bank foolishly, manufacture foolishly, or carry on any other business foolishly; but that is no reason why a bank should not be established, why a man should not engage in manufacturing, or why business of any sort should not be carried on. A minister may not be discreet in preaching upon secular topics, but that is no reason why they should not be preached upon. There have been indiscreet ministers from the days of the apostles, and it would be strange if in the future there should not be found here and there one that is not discreet. But the duty of introducing such topics is now generally acknowledged. I think that question is settled, for your life and mine, at least." [29]

Beecher's own example in dealing courageously with the public questions of the day had much to do with widening the range of the American pulpit — and incidentally with bringing on the Civil War. The effect of Beecher's ministry, says John Burroughs, "was to secularize the pulpit, yea, to secularize religion itself and make it as common and universal as the air we breathe."

In 1848, one year after his arrival in Brooklyn, Beecher, assuming the role of an auctioneer, raised two thousand dollars at a public meeting in the old Broadway Tabernacle for the purchase of a Negro woman who was about to be sent to the slave market in New Orleans. Later, on occasion, with the emotions of his congregation raised to the highest pitch, he auctioned off comely female slaves from his pulpit in Plymouth Church.

On February 21, 1850, he published a vigorous editorial in the *Independent* opposing the Clay compromises, entitled " Shall We Compromise," which made him overnight a national leader in the antislavery crusade.

From this time on until the outbreak of the Civil War, in the pulpit, on the platform, in lectures and addresses all over the North, especially through his editorials in the *Independent,* he labored to arouse the public conscience, to stir the public feeling, to shake off the public lethargy, to impress people with his own basic convictions: " The fundamental truth — that slavery is inherently and essentially wrong; the ultimate end to be constantly kept in view — the abolition of slavery; the means for the accomplishment of that end — the restriction of slavery within the then existing limits of slave territory; the underlying principle — no participation by the North in the sin of slavery, and therefore no return by the North of fugitive slaves; the spirit — one of good will alike to black and white, to slave and master; a chief instrument in the working out of this reform — the Church of Jesus Christ; the dominant, animating motive — love for Christ and loyalty to Him and His Kingdom." [30]

He bitterly opposed the repeal of the Missouri Compromise and the passage of the Kansas-Nebraska Bill. He urged Northern immigrants settling in Kansas to buy rifles and to use them if necessary to insure the entrance of Kansas into the Union as a free state. In this situation he declared that rifles were a greater moral agency than the Bible, and he pledged Plymouth Church to supply twenty-five of these for a colony being raised in New England. Without his knowledge some rifles were sent in boxes marked ' Bibles,' and from that time all rifles supplied to antislavery settlers were known as " Beecher's Bibles." When the new Republican

Party was organized, Beecher received a partial leave of absence from his pulpit and campaigned actively for the election of John W. Freemont. Four years later, he aided materially in the election of Abraham Lincoln.

He was, of course, frequently and violently denounced for bringing politics into the pulpit. In response to such criticism, Beecher replied: "It ought to be taught in the family, in the school and in the pulpit that it is a fault, a sin, for any man to be unconcerned in political duties. When the framing of the laws, the election of magistrates, the discussion of public civil interests, and the sacred function of the vote, are regarded as degrading to a religious man, the Republic is already on the broad road to destruction." [31]

It was not to be expected that this kind of preaching would make for universal popularity. Lyman Abbott described the situation exactly when he said that Henry Ward Beecher was "the most admired orator, and the most beloved preacher of his time," and also, with the exception of Theodore Parker, "the most bitterly hated."

∫

When news came that Fort Sumter had been attacked, Beecher preached a stirring sermon from Exodus 14:15 — "And the Lord said unto Moses, Wherefore criest thou unto me? speak unto the children of Israel, that they go forward." The war, he cried, " is not of our procuring." But now that it is brought to us "we must not stop to measure the cost . . . we must put our honor and our religion into this struggle . . . this matter must now be settled. . . . There are many reasons which make a good and thorough battle necessary." [32]

From this time on, in the newspapers, on the platform, in his pulpit, through the columns of the *Independent*, of which for a time he was editor, he sought to arouse the public conscience, the strength to will for war, and to press for the complete abolition of slavery. He wanted no business as usual, no shortsighted insistence on profits. "Taxation and national honesty are now synonymous," he wrote in the *Independent*, and concluded, "Every honest man in America ought to send to Washington one message in two words, *fight, tax*." The Churches, he argued, should lead men to regard their contributions to the Government as a religious offering. He instructed his wife to use all his own salary, now an ample one, over and above the necessary expenses, for the prosecution of the war. Three thousand dollars were raised in one service at Plymouth Church to equip a regiment. At another a fine outfit of Colt's revolvers were presented by the young men of Plymouth Church to a company. Mr. Beecher equipped one regiment at his own expense. He severely criticized Lincoln for his irresolution in regard to emancipation, and also for his unintelligent conduct of the war.

Beecher urged however that the war be waged without hatred and with no thought for vengeance. " I am for war," he exclaimed, " just so far as is necessary to vindicate a great moral truth. But one particle of violence beyond that is flagrant treason against the law of love." [33] Political sermons were still the exception rather than the rule. As he pointed out to his congregation on May 30, 1863, " By far the largest number of my sermons and the most of my preaching has been aimed at the conviction and the conversion of men." [34]

Later this same year Beecher visited England and in five remarkable addresses, delivered in the face of violent opposition, solidified British support in behalf of the Federal Government. One prophetic passage delivered in his Edinburgh address has particular interest in the light of subsequent events. "The day is coming," he predicted, "when the foundations of the earth will be lifted out of their places; and there are two nations that ought to be found shoulder to shoulder and hand in hand for the sake of Christianity and universal liberty, and these nations are Great Britain and America." [35]

When Beecher returned to the United States, he was given an ovation by his fellow countrymen. Popular opinion credited him with having turned the tide of British opinion toward the North. An article by Oliver Wendell Holmes in *The Atlantic Monthly* entitled "The Minister Plenipotentiary" described Beecher's British mission as "a more remarkable embassy than any envoy who has represented us in Europe since Franklin pleaded the cause of the young Republic at the Court of Versailles."

From this time on Beecher was regarded with high favor by the national Administration in Washington, and his influence in the nation was more powerful than ever before.

6

In April, 1865, an important delegation traveled to Charleston to raise over Fort Sumter the very flag which four years before had been dipped in surrender. Henry Ward Beecher was chosen by Secretary Stanton to be the orator of the occasion, the unofficial spokesman for the Administration. In the *Independent* he wrote: "If any man goes supposing that he accompanies me on an errand of triumph and exultation over a fallen foe, he does not know the first letter of my feelings." But in another column on the same page, the editor, Theodore Tilton, gloated over the fall of Richmond: "The City of Richmond . . . Babylon the Great, Mother of Harlots and Abominations of the earth. . . . Rejoice over her, thou Heaven, and ye holy apostles and prophets, — for God hath avenged you on her." [36] As Winifred E. Garrison has suggested, the actual spirit of the North lay somewhere between the kindly attitude of Beecher and the apocalyptic ravings of Tilton. But the reconstruction program which the Northern Churches generally supported had more in common with the latter.

True to his promise, Beecher raised his voice for conciliation — not yet, it is true, for the leaders of the Rebellion, "but for the people misled, for the multitudes drafted and driven into this civil war," he urged, "let not a trace of animosity remain." [37]

Before the party could return to the national capital, news came that Lincoln, who alone could have assured the triumph of this policy, had been assassinated. Almost immediately the country was divided. Andrew Johnson sought to continue the policy of his predecessor. The radical Republicans preferred to postpone the readmission of the Southern States until the rights of the Negro had been established, the people of the South duly chastened, and the continued dominance of the Republican Party fully assured.

Henry Ward Beecher, though he withdrew his personal endorsement of President Johnson, who had alienated many of his erstwhile supporters by intemperate language and unwise procedure, was more nearly in agreement with his program than any other conspicuous Churchman.

In the early stages of the debate over the restoration or reconstruction of the Southern States, he preached a sermon in Plymouth Church on the "Conditions of a Restored Union." "Now that war has ceased from out of our midst," he cried, "nothing can better crown its victories than a generous and trustful spirit on the part of the citizens of this nation toward those that have been in error. . . . There are many," he added, "who desire to see the South humbled. For my own part I think it to be the great need of this nation to save the self-respect of the South. . . . I think that he will be the wisest and most politic statesman who knows how to carry them through this terrible and painful transition with the least sacrifice of their pride, and with the greatest preservation of their self-respect; and if it can be done by the generosity of the North, a confidence will spring up at the South in the future that will repay us for the little self-sacrifice that we may make." [38] Many of the evils of reconstruction and much of its bitter legacy could have been avoided if the wise and Christian counsel of Beecher had been heeded.

He also gave good advice in regard to the Negroes. Certain of their rights, he agreed, had to be secured by legislation. He insisted however that ultimately the position of the Negroes in the South would depend on the good will of the Southern whites and the proved worth of the black man himself.

Two years after the close of the war, a convention of soldiers and sailors was held in Cleveland, under the auspices of conservative Republicans who opposed the continued exclusion of the Southern States from the Federal Union and approved in general the reconstruction policies of the chief executive. Henry Ward Beecher was asked to serve as chaplain. Unable to attend, he wrote a letter in which he advocated the immediate restoration of the Southern States to full participation in the national Government.

The position which he maintained was the same one which he had repeatedly advocated in the press and in the pulpit. Nonetheless lines had become more tense, and publication of this letter created a national sensation. Friends were alienated, personal bitterness aroused, and vituperative abuse evoked far surpassing anything he had heretofore experienced. Theodore Tilton, his erstwhile friend and protégé, now editor in chief of the *Independent,* and one of the most ardent of the radical Republicans who were clamoring for vengeance against the fallen South, caustically criticized Beecher in the columns of the paper, which at the same time discontinued the publication of his weekly sermons. Mr. Beecher thereupon broke off relations with the paper which he had so largely made, and three years later became the editor and part owner of a rival sheet, the *Christian Union,* whose popularity soon rivaled and threatened to surpass that of the *Independent.*

Only against this background can we understand the great accusation, the notorious scandal, which darkened his remaining days and is still used to besmirch his name.

The *Independent* lost ground, not only because of Beecher's withdrawal, but also because of Tilton's espousal of questionable views regarding "Love, Marriage and Divorce." Disquieting rumors were afloat regarding the latter's own moral conduct. When finally Tilton was relieved of his position as editor of the *Independent,* he held Beecher personally responsible. About the same time he began to accuse Beecher of making improper advances to his wife. For several years the charges were kept under cover. But finally, in 1874, after Beecher had refused demands which smacked of blackmail, Theodore Tilton brought suit against Henry Ward Beecher for alienation of affection, involving adultery.

It is doubtful if America has ever known a more delicious scandal, one that created a greater sensation or secured more publicity throughout the nation.

We cannot go into the tremendously complicated affair, or consider the rival accounts offered by Tilton and his supporters on the one hand and by Beecher and his friends on the other. There were many at the time who believed with Charles A. Dana, of the *New York Sun,* that " Henry Ward Beecher is an adulterer, a perjurer and a fraud, and his great genius and his Christian pretences only make him seem the more horrible and revolting." [39] Many others were convinced on the other hand that Beecher's enemies had engineered a gigantic conspiracy to destroy him.

A clear judgment is perhaps no longer possible. It should be noted, however, that a committee representing the Plymouth Church and composed of some of the leading citizens of Brooklyn, after an extensive investigation, exonerated Beecher from any wrongdoing with Mrs. Tilton or any other woman, although mildly censuring him for ' errors in judgment.'

The civil jury, after hearing exhaustive evidence on both sides, voted nine to three for acquittal.

A Congregational Church council, composed of two hundred and fifty of its most prominent representatives, drawn from all sections of the United States east of the Mississippi and including some who had come to the meeting convinced of Beecher's guilt, reviewed all the evidence for the third time and reported: "We hold the pastor of this church, as we and all others are bound to hold him, innocent of the charges reported against him until they have been substantiated by proof, and therefore we continue to extend to him our Christian fellowship and sympathy."

Judge Neilson, who presided over the civil trial, professed his belief in Beecher's innocence and became one of his warmest friends. William A. Beach, chief counsel for Beecher's accusers, stated that he had not been four days in the trial before he became convinced that Tilton's charges were unfounded. "I felt," he said, "as if we were a pack of hounds, endeavoring to pull down a noble lion."

The attack on Beecher would have blasted the reputation and destroyed the influence of any other man. Beecher's influence in the nation as a whole was seriously affected. But, with few exceptions, his own Church remained loyal and the congregations were undiminished to the end. His preaching was more inspiring than ever, and many who heard him felt that he walked with God. His productivity, both quantitatively and qualitatively, remained, in fact, unusually high during the whole period of tremendous tension.

After Beecher's trial was ended, he embarked on a series of annual lecture tours which continued up to the very year of his death. His manager, Major J. B. Pond, stated that he averaged one hundred and fifty lectures a year, and that during some seasons he lectured two hundred and fifty times, besides preaching every Sunday. The original purpose of these lectures was twofold: first, to reimburse Mr. Beecher for the expenses of his trial, which had left him heavily in debt; and, secondly, to disarm the criticism and allay the suspicion which the trial had occasioned. Both purposes were achieved, and although suspicion was never completely vanquished, hostility was greatly decreased.

After publication of the Cleveland letters and the storm of abuse which they had aroused, Beecher's activities in the political sphere were not quite so pronounced. He supported Grant, however, for both terms, in spite of the scandals which gathered about his regime, and wrote and spoke in behalf of both Garfield and Hayes. In 1884 he horrified his Republican friends and associates and stirred up a second storm of virulent opposition by espousing the cause and vigorously campaigning for the election of President Grover Cleveland.

He continued to manifest an interest in various social issues, although none were so significant as those of earlier years. Thus he advocated the rights of the Irish, rebuked anti-Semitism, opposed exclusion of Chinese immigrants, advocated woman suffrage, opposed prohibition as 'an absolute impossibility,' appealed for Civil Service reform, attacked judicial corruption, denounced Government repudiation of debts, and urged that public libraries, reading rooms, and picture galleries be opened on the Sabbath.

In 1878, speaking before the Society of the Army of the Potomac, he advocated universal military training. Wars are inevitable, he declared, until justice prevails and ignorance is enlightened. To prepare for war is often the way to prevent war. Though he had little to say about, and little understanding of, the problems of capital and labor, which were increasing rapidly in their gravity, he did foresee the growing danger of concentrated wealth in America. He viewed with equal alarm the growing movement for the organization of the American workingmen. "The movement," he prophesied, "is likely to draw to itself the indolent, the corrupt, the industrious poor, not enlightened, the laboring men by whom the great manufacturing interests of the world are conducted, and who are without real estate or capital. It will tend to organize labor as distinguished from capital in an antagonistic spirit. It will seek to resist the established methods of industry and commerce, by strikes, by unions, whose interior will embody the most absolute despotism known to mankind. . . . It will bring upon parties an influence which will corrupt political doctrines, breed demagogues like the frogs of Egypt, enfeeble the laws and emasculate the administration of government." [40]

7

At the outset Beecher's sermons had been chiefly evangelistic in their aim. As time went on they became more prevailingly ethical. After the Civil War there was another significant change. They became more intellectual, more philosophic. They were addressed less to the will and more to the reason. In the later years of his ministry he endeavored to relate the thinking of religious people to the advancing world of knowledge. It was here, in the estimation of many, that he rendered his most enduring service.

Perhaps the earliest reference to this fresh intent is found in a letter written to Theodore Tilton in 1867. "It seems to me that I discern, arising in studies in Natural Science, a surer foothold for these (evangelical) views than they have ever had," he wrote. "In so far as theology is concerned, if I have one purpose or aim, it is to secure for the truths now developing in the sphere of Natural Science a religious spirit and harmonization with all the cardinal truths of religion which have thus far characterized the Christian system." [41]

Five years later, speaking to the divinity students in Yale, he offered a timely word of warning: "There is another consideration," he said, "that we cannot blink, and that is, that we are in danger of having the intelligent part of society go past us. The study of human nature is not going to be left in the hands of the Church or the ministry. It is going to be a part of every system of liberal education, and will be pursued on a scientific basis. There is being now applied among scientists a greater amount of real, searching, discriminating thought . . . to the whole structure and functions of man . . . than ever has been expended upon it in the whole history of the world put together. More men are studying it, and they are coming to results, and these results are starting, directly or indirectly, a certain kind of public thought and feeling. In religion, mental philosophies of the psychological school are not going to run in the old grooves of Christian doctrine; they are not going to hold the same generic ideas respecting men. And if ministers do not make their theological systems conform to facts as they are; if they do not recognize what men are studying, the time will not be far distant when the pulpit will be like the voice crying in the wilderness. And it will not be 'Prepare the way of the Lord,' either. This work is going to be done. The providence of God is rolling forward a spirit of investigation that Christian ministers must meet and join. There is no class of people upon earth who can less afford to let the development of truth run ahead of them than they. You cannot wrap yourselves in professional mystery, for the glory of the Lord is such that it is preached with power throughout all the length and breadth of the world, by these investigators of his wondrous creation. You cannot go back and become apostles of the dead past, drivelling after ceremonies, and letting the world do the thinking and studying. There must be a new spirit infused into the ministry. Some men are so afraid that, in breaking away from the old systems and original forms and usages, Christianity will get the go-by! Christianity is too vital, too really divine in its innermost self to fear any such results. There is no trouble about Christianity. You take care of yourselves and of men, and learn the truth as God shows it to you all the time, and you need not be afraid of Christianity; that will take care of itself. You might as well be afraid that battles would rend the sky, or that something would stop the rising and setting of the sun." [42]

The new doctrine that theologians were required to assimilate at this particular time was the revolutionary and profoundly disturbing doctrine of organic evolution.

Darwin's *Origin of Species* had been published in 1859, and Herbert Spencer's *First Principles* in 1860–1862. Neither attracted much attention in America, probably because of our absorption in the conflict over slavery. But in 1869 John Fiske began to deliver his famous lectures on *Cosmic Philosophy*, and the next year Tyndall came to America on a lecture tour, followed by Spencer in 1872, and Huxley in 1876. Translated into common language for the common people through innumerable editorials and magazine articles, and rapidly finding its way into academic instruction in all the higher institutions of learning, evolution presented a challenge which the religious mind could no longer ignore.

Professor Asa Gray, the distinguished botanist at Harvard University, had dealt with the matter helpfully from the theistic point of view in 1860; John Fiske, also of Harvard, Dr. James McCosh, president of Princeton College, and others, took up the cudgels in its behalf shortly thereafter. But the theological mind was almost universally opposed. Professor Charles Hodge of Princeton, in 1874, concluded that " a more absolutely incredible theory (than evolution) was never propounded for acceptance among men." Mark Hopkins, ex-president of Williams, in a series of lectures at Princeton Seminary, agreed with Dr. Hodge that evolution was 'essentially atheistic.' And this seemed to be the prevailing point of view.

Henry Ward Beecher had retained a general interest in science since his college days. " I was convinced," he said, that " God had two revelations in this world, one of the Book, and one of the Rock, and I meant to read them both." [43] If there are any real discrepancies, he added, " it will be found that they lie in that human element which has been wrapped around the exposition of religion." [44] The theory of evolution seemed to fit in with the philosophy which slowly and obscurely he had been evolving through the whole of his ministry.

The influence of this new doctrine is found in the Old Testament Bible studies which were given during the autumn, winter, and spring of 1878. These studies were " designated to free the interpretation of the Word of God from superstition and to bring the Bible back into the atmosphere in which they were born." The Old Testament was accepted as a progressive revelation of God, but not as an infallible standard of belief.

About the same time Beecher began to question traditional views regarding everlasting punishment. On November 10, 1879, *The New York Times* quoted him as saying, " If I thought God stood at the door where men go out of life ready to send them down to eternal punishment, my soul would cry out: ' Let there be no God! ' My instincts would say: ' Annihilate him! ' " [45]

Three years later, Beecher summarized the recent progress of religious thought in America and gave a comprehensive statement of his own religious position. " There is a transition in theology," he pointed out, " and a gradual substitution of ' a theology of evolutionism ' for Calvinism." There is also " a strong and growing tendency to enlarge the

sphere of Divine Revelation by adding to the Bible the revelation of nature, and of man's reason and moral consciousness, which are a part of nature. In an important sense," he
affirmed, " the Sacred Scriptures are of God. . . . But they
claim no such mechanical perfection as has been claimed
for them. They have authority only concurrently with educated human reason and rational moral sense. . . . The alternative which every year will grow more and more vehe-
mently upon educated and thinking men," he predicted, " is
the enfranchisement of the Bible — or infidelity." [46]

The *Watchman and Reflector* complained that in this article Beecher " has emphatically stepped down and out from
any relation with Congregational Orthodoxy. He definitely
renounces the supreme authority of the Bible." [47] The growing volume of criticism from ministers in his own denomination, especially in his local association, provoked Beecher to
decisive action.

On October 11, 1882, he read before the Congregational
Association of New York and Brooklyn an assigned paper on
" Spiritual Barbarism." " The chapters of the Westminster
Confession of Faith concerning decrees, election, reprobation, as connected with the fall in Adam," he said, " I regard
as extraordinary specimens of *spiritual barbarism.* The
views therein given of the divine character and procedure
are wholly irreconcilable with the manifestations of God in
Christ Jesus. They stand over against the conception of
God as shining from the face of Christ as the Gorgon head
against an Apollo in the Grecian mythology. I hold it to be
a monster, and not a master of love that is there portrayed.
. . . Much of the violence sometimes manifested in my
preaching springs from indignation that I feel when the
loveliness, the beauty, the glory of God in Christ is trampled
under foot by such spiritual barbarism. It stands in the way
of thousands. It has turned more feet into the barren ways
of infidelity than any other single cause." Among other ex-

amples, he mentioned "the teaching that Adam stood for the whole human family, in such a sense that the race was revolutionized on account of his guilt, and that God has continued creating unaccountable millions of beings through thousands of years, whose inevitable destiny was eternal damnation! This," he cried, "is spiritual barbarism run mad!"[48]

Having given a negative statement of his views, Beecher asked permission to state affirmatively "what I do believe and teach, and what I have taught all through my ministry, lasting now more than forty-five years." In order that they might understand this, he described his religious experience along the lines previously sketched — his reaction against Calvinism, even the alleviated Calvinism of his father; his weariness of theological disputation; his dissatisfaction with the reigning orthodoxy, as mere straw without sustenance for the souls of men; the theology, centering about the love of God in Christ, which he had 'gradually' formed 'by practise.'

Fundamental doctrines he defined as those which are necessary for the conviction of sin, for conversion from sin, for development of faith, for dominant love of the Lord Jesus Christ, and for the building up of a Christlike character.

He proceeded to profess his faith in a God who is a personal Being, and accessible, as other persons are accessible, to the thoughts, the feelings, the wants, and the cares of men; in the Trinity — Father, Son, and Holy Spirit; in Providence, both general and special; in miracles; and in the efficacy of prayer. He believed in man's universal sinfulness (though not in total depravity) and in all men's need of regeneration. He accepted the inspiration of the Bible "with a few exceptions" as set forth in the Westminster Confession of Faith. He believed in the atonement, but not in any particular theory advanced in explanation thereof. "The Scriptures declare that the suffering of Christ secured the remission of sins," he declared. "They do not say how he secured it. . . . That part of Christ's mission, or that part of the Atonement . . . which flames through all the New Testament and which can be understood, is, that moral power which it exerts and those effects which through the Holy Spirit, are produced by it." And finally he expressed his faith in the future punishment. "The results of a man's conduct reach over into the other world on those that are persistently and inexcusably wicked, and man's punishment in the life to come is of such a nature and of such dimensions as ought to alarm any man and put him off from the dangerous ground and turn him toward safety. I do not think we are authorized by the Scriptures to say that it is endless in the sense in which we ordinarily employ that term." [49]

Having completed his statement on beliefs, Beecher presented his resignation from the New York and Brooklyn association of ministers, in order that no one might feel embarrassed by the supposition that they endorsed or were responsible for any of his views. Though urged to reconsider he declined to do so, and for the remaining five years of his life was the minister of a Congregational Church without personal denominational connection.

8

Early the following year, before a capacity audience in Cooper Union, he delivered the lecture, soon to be repeated through the length and breadth of the continent on *Evolution and Revolution.*

"A greater change," he said, "has taken place within the last thirty years, probably than ever took place in any former period of five hundred consecutive years. It has been a revolution; and yet the revolutionary tendencies of the doctrine of evolution are more in seeming than in fact, and, though extremely radical, are radical in the right direction, and are of the right kind. As contradistinguished from the old notion of creation by the instantaneous obedience of matter to the divine command, it is the teaching of the divine method of creation as gradual." [50]

The attempt to suppress the new doctrine, he prophesied, would fail. "The old folly of throwing the Bible at it," he warned, "ought not in our day to be repeated. They threw the Bible at the sun and the moon once, and it came back on their heads, and astronomy stands. They threw the Bible at geology, and geology stands. Let not the folly be repeated of throwing the Bible at the origin of man." [51]

The lecture was expanded into a series of eight sermons delivered shortly thereafter in Plymouth Church. During the whole period the Church was crowded, neither heat nor storm having any perceptible influence in diminishing the audience. The sermons were reported verbatim, telegraphed to Chicago, and published in full each Monday morning in the *Chicago Tribune*. In 1885 they appeared in book form under the title *Evolution and Religion*. It represents "the first avowed and complete adoption of evolution in its full extent among our theologians" and the first attempt to restate Christian theology upon the basis of that principle.

In the opening sermon Beecher expresses his sense of the pulpit's responsibility in accepting and interpreting this new truth: "I say to all those clergymen who are standing tremulous on the edge of fear in regard to the great advance that God is making today: 'Inside and outside of His Church you are bound to be the interpreters of God's providence to His people. And while you are not to be rash, nor to make haste unduly, nor to mix dross with the pure gold, yet, on the other hand, you must be sure to meet the Lord when He comes in the air, when He moves in the providences of the world, when He is at work in natural laws, when He is living in philosophical atmospheres, when He is shining in great scientific disclosures, when He is teaching the human consciousness all around; you are bound, because you are ministers of His Word, to meet the Lord, to welcome Him, to accept Him in all the new garments that He wears, and to see that the habiliments of Christ grow brighter and brighter, and nobler and nobler, from age to age, as He puts on righteousness and comes in all the glory of His Kingdom towards us.' " [52]

In developing his idea of evolution, " Beecher enunciates with great clearness, the first of the line of our liberal thinkers to do it completely and well," says Foster, " the fundamental idea of all genuine liberalism, that religious truth is discovered in the same way as all other truth, by the experience and study of man, not discovered, however, without the providence and illumination of God, whether in the natural or the religious sphere." [53]

He also drives home another fundamental tenet of liberalism, that certainty in religion does not depend upon the possession of an infallible Scripture. The Bible is " the book which has reached the highest conception of God, yet attained by human consciousness," a book which " gives the only grand ideal of manhood known to literature," a " living book " with " power of inspiring men with the noblest desires," a " book that creates life." But it is not inerrant: " The logical outcome of the theory of verbal and plenary inspiration," he insists, " is superstition on the one hand and infidelity on the other." [54]

Beecher also definitely repudiates the traditional idea of the Fall. In his usual extravagant style, he cried: " The old theory of sin — which will be exterminated, I think, by the new light thrown upon the origin of man and the conditions by which the race has been developed — is repulsive, unreasonable, immoral and demoralizing. I hate it. I hate it because I love the truth, because I love God, and because I love my fellow men. The idea that God created the race, and that two of them without experience were put under the temptation of the arch-fiend (or whatever the 'creature' was), and that they fell into disobedience for what they did not understand anything about, and that God not only thrust them out of the Garden of Eden, as no parent would ever treat a child in his own household, but that he then transmitted the corruption that was the result of disobedience through the countless ages, and spread it out and out and out, and kept on through the system of nature, mingling damnation on the right and on the left, before and behind — I hate it because I love God. I abhor it because I love justice and truth." [55]

Under the spell of the evolutionary philosophy, Beecher foresaw a steady progress upward. The human race would unfold, he predicted, "in the direction of reason and moral sense and affectionate sense." "Man," he cried, "is made to start and not to stop; to go on, and on, and up, and onward, steadily emerging from the controlling power of the physical and animal condition in which he was born and which enthrall him during his struggle upward, but ever touching higher elements of possibility, and ending in the glorious liberty of the sons of God." [56]

"Those who cannot be lifted, who prove themselves unsusceptible to all elevating influences," he concluded, "go down steadily lower and lower until they lose the susceptibility, the possibility of moral evolution, moral development; let them keep on and in the great abyss of nothingness there is no groan, no sorrow, no pain and no memory." [57] This doctrine of conditional immortality seems to have been Beecher's final view of the future life.

Through his lectures, his sermons, and his book, Beecher carried the evolutionary philosophy, a Christian philosophy of evolution, to multitudes of men and women throughout the nation who would never have read Darwin or Spencer or

Huxley, or understood a word if they had. "It was Beecher," says Gray, "who, more than any other preacher, made the first pathway for the average religious mind of his day from an unscientific to a scientific view of the world, and more than any other man at the time saved the religious situation in a day of misapprehended scientific change." [58] But while there were thousands who hung on his lips and were persuaded by his words, there were many others who once more heaped upon him vilification and abuse.

In 1886, Beecher revisited England. The trip, as Hibben acknowledges, was "a personal triumph — a round of public receptions and of lectures." The suspicions aroused by his trial seem to have been obliterated. He returned to America buoyant and seemingly in good health, and resumed work on his *Life of Jesus the Christ*. "No man could in a lifetime write all I now see," he said; "how can I put it into one book?"

On February 27, 1887, he preached his last sermon in Plymouth Church. Nine days later he was dead. Shortly before he had said to his friend, Rossiter W. Raymond, "When I am gone do not let it be forgotten that my one aim was the winning of the souls of men."

9

Whether Henry Ward Beecher determined the thought of his generation, or merely as a great preacher sensitive to the needs of people reflected changing currents of thought, we can see, clearly limned in his career, important tendencies which have continued unbroken until recent events have led men at last to question some of the things that they had long taken for granted.

In Beecher's ministry there is plainly apparent a movement away from Calvinism, a growing distaste for creeds, an increasing dislike for 'theology,' an evident weariness with theological disputes, a breaking down of denominational barriers, a hospitality to new currents of thought, in general greater breadth and catholicity. Old dogmas were being discarded, or if retained, retained only in form — among them belief in predestination, the Fall, total depravity, original guilt, substitutionary atonement, inerrant inspiration, and eternal punishment. There was growing reliance on experience and science as norms and sources of religious truth; a transition from belief to works as the test of one's faith; and a shift from justice to love as the most essential attribute of God. As Charles Howard Hopkins has well said: "Divine judgment was now tempered by a romantic optimism; the basic Christian concept of crisis was smoothed over by the softer idea of progress. The sympathizing Jesus gradually replaced the Christ of Calvary." [59] There was a concern for this life rather than for the life to come. A definite step was taken toward the modern conception that creation of a new social order founded on righteousness and love is the main concern of religion rather than salvation of souls and their training in this probationary period for a heaven beyond the grave.

There was, in brief, the beginning of a transition from Calvinism to a theology of evolutionism, from overemphasis on divine transcendence to overemphasis on divine immanence, from a theology interested too predominantly in God to a theology interested too predominantly in man, from an extreme view of total depravity to a delusive trust in man's inherent goodness.

With this change in the message came changes also in the methods of the preacher and in the spirit of the pulpit. It had grown less conventional and more natural, less scholastic and more popular, less theological and more human, less devoted to building up a system and more devoted to building up men.

Some of the reasons for this movement are revealed in the life of Henry Ward Beecher.

The old theology seemed more concerned with doctrines than with man — doctrines which ran contrary to human experience, which stood in the way of sinful men and hindered their approach to God, which emphasized nonessentials and caused needless strife and division among the followers of Christ, which offended the moral sensibilities and were turning multitudes away from God toward skepticism and unbelief. Increasing numbers of men were convinced that Calvinism obscured or falsified the character of God as revealed in Jesus Christ.

The old theology, which had dominated the outlook of America in the early days, had already lost its hold upon the affections of multitudes of people, when evolution, followed by historical criticism and the "new theology," appeared upon the scene. It found hearts that were swept and garnished, ready to welcome a new approach to religious truth.

"The children of Lyman Beecher," says Lyman Beecher Stowe, "helped to build the intellectual bridge between the theologians of the past, who placed the emphasis upon holding the correct doctrines and leaving everything else to God's divine intervention, and the spiritual leaders of the present, who care nothing for doctrines and do not believe in supernatural intervention. . . . Lyman Beecher mitigated the austerity of Calvin's God; Henry Ward Beecher and his brothers and sisters transformed Him into a God of love and service. . . . They paved the way for their successors of today to develop their God of love and service into the ideal, which shall spread the dominion of justice and brotherhood until there shall be developed a Heaven on earth." [60]

Mr. Stowe wrote when the clouds of the great Depression had begun to lift, and when Hitler was still only a tiny spot on the horizon.

The old theology, we begin to see now, had sounded

depths in its understanding of man's sin, and in its comprehension of the justice and mercy, the initiative and self-disclosure of God, that the new theology, with its evolutionary optimism, overlooked, but to which men in the end must return.

" The redeeming trait in Henry Ward Beecher's theology," commented Dr. Philip Schaff, " the crowning excellence of his character, the inspiration of his best words and deeds, was his simple childlike faith and burning love of Christ, whom he adored as the eternal Son of God, the friend of the poor, and the Savior of all men." [61]

Chapter III

DWIGHT L. MOODY
and the high tide of Revivalism

THE MOST far-reaching and transforming religious event in our colonial history was the Great Awakening, which flared up in New England under the preaching of Jonathan Edwards and was carried by George Whitefield through the length and breadth of the American colonies. It not only constituted a tremendous awakening of the religious life, but also, as we have seen, changed the conception of entrance upon that life in a way that has profoundly affected the majority of American Churches almost to the present day. The Great Awakening lost its force, however, with the approach of the Revolutionary War, and in the generation following the moral and spiritual life of America reached its lowest ebb. Less than seven individuals out of a hundred were members of the Church; atheism and skepticism were gaining ground; enemies of the Church predicted its early demise.

Then suddenly the Great Revival, which had continued to smolder especially in the South, burst once more into flame and ushered in one of the greatest periods of external growth and internal development that the Church has known in any age and in any land. This Second Great Awakening, as it is sometimes called, or the Great American Revival, as it is known to others, raged most intensely in the early part of the nineteenth century, but for several decades important revivals occurred every year in some part of the Church. They continued indeed, with less frequency and diminishing

101

intensity, until 1858 as the predominant feature of American religion. Since that last great unheralded awakening of the religious life which began in New York in the fall of 1857 and spread like wildfire during the following year over the major part of the continent, there has been no great nation-wide revival. But a continuous stream of great revivalists — Charles G. Finney, Dwight L. Moody, R. A. Torrey, Gypsy Smith, Sam Jones, B. Fay Mills, J. Wilbur Chapman, and William E. Sunday — have brought the tradition down almost to our own day. Largely through its revivals, protracted meetings at stated intervals in city and countryside, and steady evangelistic preaching by a host of faithful pastors, the Church in America has grown until, today, more than fifty individuals out of every hundred are numbered among its members, and the Church, with all its weakness, is immeasurably stronger than it was at the beginning of our national life.

Charles G. Finney, the most important evangelist in the opening half of the nineteenth century, marks a turning point in the history of American revivalism. In him new tendencies appeared, some of which were good and marks of a new age, but some of which were ultimately to bring professional evangelism into disrepute. Finney revolted against Old School Calvinism, in which he had been trained, because, like Lyman Beecher and many others, he felt that it cut the nerve of human effort — denying man's ability, and therefore his responsibility to turn unto the Lord. He aroused the opposition of Beecher, however, and of many of his contemporaries, by his ' new measures,' as they were called, his reliance on human ' means ' for bringing the sinner to the point of decisive action. He popularized, if he did not introduce, the ' protracted meeting ' and was responsible for the widespread use of the anxious seat. He prayed for the conversion of sinners by name and allowed women to pray as freely as men.

The new measures which were introduced so sparingly by Finney, and which brought down so much criticism by his contemporaries, were greatly multiplied by his successors. Dwight L. Moody, who followed in his footsteps, inaugurated evangelistic campaigns, in which the Churches of a city would unite in a series of meetings to win men to Christ. He also introduced the idea of the singing evangelist, taking with him, as his coworker, Ira D. Sankey, who did so much to popularize and make his work effective. It was the business genius of B. Fay Mills, however, which more than anything else is responsible for the revivalism which still lives in our memory. His careful preparation, thorough organization, and high pressure methods gave it business efficiency and promoted mass conversion, which sometimes resembled mass production. Mills's disciple was J. Wilbur Chapman, and he, in turn, passed the new system on to William A. Sunday, who brought it to its ultimate 'perfection.'

Unfortunately, the businesslike efficiency which these men introduced, the high pressure methods which they evolved, and the financial aspects which some of the later evangelists came to emphasize, brought in the end a reaction against evangelism as a whole from which we are not yet delivered.

Professor Davenport wrote his important book on *Primitive Traits in Religious Revivals* in 1905, before the movement had reached its climax, but already the handwriting was on the wall. "Along with the growing . . . ineffectiveness in the method," he pointed out, "has gone moral degeneration in its application. Revival crowds have become not gospel hardened so much as method hardened, and many and absurd are the devices employed to soften hard hearts. . . . Along with moral degeneration of method has frequently gone spiritual decay in revivalist personality. . . . We have had too many instances in the public view of formal, official, commercial, hypnotic manipulation of revival crowds." [1]

Washington Gladden, writing a few years later, agreed that the old type of evangelism was on its way out. "Strenuous efforts," he noted, "are put forth to revive it, but their success is meagre. It is easy by expending much money in advertising, by organizing a great choir, and employing the services of gifted and earnest men, to draw large congregations; but the great mass of those who attend these services are church members — the outside multitude is scarcely touched by them." [2]

Many factors must be taken into account if we are to understand the declining interest in revivals and their diminishing effectiveness in the life of the Church. The degeneration of revivalist personality, the taint of commercialism which became attached to the evangelistic enterprise, and reaction against the high pressure salesmanship of many latter-day evangelists undoubtedly played a part. The growing alienation of labor, a movement of vast importance, which we are to discuss in subsequent chapters, must also be considered. More important was the increasing secularization of modern life, accompanied by a marked decline in the sense of sin and a more critical attitude toward the Bible, resulting in popular ignorance and widespread rejection of evangelical truth. At the same time there was growing reliance — too great reliance, subsequent events have proved — upon 'religious education' as a substitute not only for revivalism but also for personal evangelism, with which it had been so long associated. Davenport himself thought that the declining efficacy of the revivalistic method could be explained by the mental evolution undergone by large areas of the American population. " The great growth in knowledge through public education, the enormously increased facilities for communication, the very struggle and competition of modern life, especially in the great centers," he wrote, "have developed in the average man an intelligence, a self-control, a power of rational inhibition, that makes him far less suggestible, less nervously unstable, less imitative, less liable to be swept away by great gusts of passion or emotion. He is in many respects less of a primitive and more of a highly civilized man, and over him the old revival method has correspondingly lost its power." [3] This explanation seemed more evident a generation ago than it does at the present time.

Whatever the cause, the fact itself cannot be overlooked. The definite collapse of the old-time revivalism came after the First World War. Since that time professional evangelism has come into disrepute. Men whose character is above reproach and whose methods are beyond criticism, able pastors with evangelistic gifts, find that revivals no longer attract the ' unsaved,' who are beyond the bounds of the Church. Some conclude that the day of mass evangelism is gone forever. For the future, they think, we must look to educational evangelism or to what is called clinical evangelism, an evangelism carried on through individual contacts. Whether or not this is the case, we must have methods different from the ones used by Finney, Moody, and Billy Sunday. New methods adapted to our own day are called for — methods that will bring the Gospel, in appealing guise and in a form that meets the needs of the modern day, to bear upon the consciences and the wills of men who have sought their own way rather than the way of God. As Finney put it: " New measures *we must have*. And may God prevent the church from settling down in any set of forms, and getting the present or any other edition of her measures stereotyped."

Whether we look backward, it may be with nostalgia, toward the revivalism which has had its day, or whether we look forward to the evangelism that is yet to be, it will help us to think for a few moments of Dwight L. Moody and the high tide of American revivalism. With only a district school education, "without a church or society behind him to support him, or a constituency except such as he himself created to afford him moral support, without any of the recognized graces of oratory," Dwight L. Moody spoke to more men (one hundred million it is estimated), converted more (a million perhaps), and established more permanent centers of religious activity than any preacher of his times. Few men in any age have worked "more passionately, more lovingly, and more successfully to bring God to man and man to God." And yet in Moody's own lifetime we can detect the slight, almost imperceptible turning of the tide. Before he reached the end of his remarkable and highly successful career the ebb of American revivalism had begun.

I

Dwight L. Moody was born in Northfield, Massachusetts, on February 5, 1837. His father was a mason, a competent workman who earned good wages, but one who was reckless and improvident, spending freely what he earned, and taking little or no thought for the morrow. He died when Dwight was four years old, leaving his widow and nine children nothing but a little house on the mountain side and an acre or two of land, heavily encumbered with debt. The creditors seized everything on which they could lay their hands, even the kindling wood stored up for the winter's fuel supply.

Mrs. Moody struggled desperately to keep her home together. She succeeded, but her hair turned quickly and completely white after her husband's death, and every night for a year the oldest daughter heard her sob herself to sleep.

Dwight grew up in an atmosphere of grinding poverty. His education was limited to a dozen terms in the little district school and profited him very little. This seems to

have been the boy's fault more than the school's. He loved
to play crude practical jokes but took no interest in his
books. He never overcame this early handicap and never
learned to speak without making grammatical mistakes.
He was not only educationally deficient but also spiritually
destitute. His mother was a Unitarian. She believed in
God and saw that her boy went to church, but took little
interest otherwise in his religious development. When he
left home he was almost totally ignorant of the Bible and
unacquainted with basic Christian truth.

There were also certain serious defects in his character.
For example, there was a native rudeness, which, uncurbed
in early life, fastened itself upon him and continued for
many years, leaving behind, to his own deep grief, a trail
of wounded feelings. George Pentecost was thinking of
this trait when he said, "Poor old Moody: we all love him,
but some of us don't like him." [4]

On his seventeenth birthday, Dwight left Northfield and
headed for Boston. He went to make his fortune, but as
one of his biographers suggests, it looked as though he were
headed for the city of destruction.

Instead, Boston marked a turning point in his career. He
secured a position in his uncle's shoe store, and won almost
instant success as a salesman. Two years later he went to
Chicago, then a lusty young city growing in the West,
where there was greater hope of financial reward. After
four years he had saved seven thousand dollars and was
making over five thousand dollars a year, which was worth
more then than it is now and was considered a very good income indeed for a young man not over twenty-four. A year
or two before his great ambition had been to save a hundred
thousand dollars and retire. He was well on the road to
success when suddenly he gave up his position to devote
himself entirely to religious work, with no assured compen-
sation whatsoever. To understand this unexpected decision

we must go back to his conversion, which had taken place in Boston a number of years before.

This was due largely to three individuals. First, to his Uncle Samuel, who made regular Church attendance one of the conditions for holding his position. Second, to Uncle Samuel's wife, Typhenia. She was the only one who seemed to understand this difficult and trying youth, and he went to her again and again to unburden his soul.

"I like the pastor," he said on one occasion, "and Mr. Kimball; but those rich and pious folks at Mt. Vernon make me sick and tired."

"Never mind, Dwight," she replied; "the Church is the bride of Christ."

"But the young folks are so lofty and proud. Is that Christianity?"

"Lad, we are to fight the fight of faith. Do you love the Church?"

"Well I guess I do," was the characteristic reply.

"Then forget the rest," she advised.[5]

Often when we think of the achievements of a man like Dwight L. Moody, we forget that back of him was an understanding woman like his Aunt Typhenia.

The third person responsible for his conversion was his Sunday School teacher, Mr. Kimball. We all know the story. Mr. Kimball had decided to speak to the youth about his soul. He walked toward the store where Dwight was employed, but as he drew near he began to reflect that the store would probably be crowded by customers, and the boy might be embarrassed. Before he realized it he had walked a block beyond his destination. He turned suddenly and dashed back, determined to have it over with. He found Dwight in the back of the store, wrapping up shoes. As Mr. Kimball told the story later: "I went up to him at once, and putting my hand on his shoulder, I made what I afterwards felt was a very weak plea for Christ. I don't know just what words I used, nor could Mr. Moody tell. I simply told him of Christ's love for him, and the love Christ wanted in return." And Moody gave his heart to Jesus.

Giving his heart to Jesus meant giving his life to Jesus. He wanted to tell others of the Saviour, but was disturbed over his limping speech. As usual, he went to Aunt Typhenia, with the burden on his heart.

"Do you love Christ?" she asked.

"Well I guess I do," was the enthusiastic response.

"Then don't worry, lad, over how you talk," she replied. "Just try to tell the people what He has done for your soul, and He'll do the rest." [6]

When he went to Chicago he joined a wealthy Church and rented a pew which he undertook to fill every Sunday with boys and young men from the boarding houses and off the streets. Before long he was filling four pews instead of one. But the Church seemed cold and unappreciative of Moody's talents. When he attempted to speak in prayer meeting, one of the deacons advised him that he could best serve God by keeping still.

Another critic commended his zeal in filling the pews he had hired but suggested that he should realize the limitations of his vocation and not attempt to speak in public.

"You make too many mistakes in grammar," he explained.

"I know I make mistakes," Moody replied, "but I am doing the best I can with that I've got." He looked at the man and added, "Look here, friend, you've got grammar enough — what are you doing with it for Jesus?"

Desiring a wider outlet for his energies, Moody found a mission Sunday School in the slums of Chicago and offered to teach a class. They told him he could have a room if he would secure the pupils. He brought in so many scholars that the building was soon crowded to its capacity. Two years after Moody came to Chicago, he had his own mission.

In a very short time it had an enrollment of more than a thousand pupils and was exerting a marked influence upon the community.

The success of this mission school compelled him to make a decision. "The greatest struggle I have ever had," he said years later, "was when I was faced with the problem of giving up business and devoting myself entirely to the work of the Lord." The crisis came in an unusual way.

There was a class of girls in the school. Moody said it was undoubtedly the most frivolous class of girls he had ever known. One day the regular teacher was absent, and Moody attempted to take his place. "They laughed in my face," he said, "and I felt like opening the door and telling them all to get out and never come back.

"That week the teacher of the class came into the store where I worked. He was pale and looked ill.

"'What is the trouble?' I asked.

"'I have had another hemorrhage of my lungs,' he replied. 'The doctor says I cannot live on Lake Michigan, so I am going to New York State. I suppose I am going home to die.'

"He seemed greatly troubled, and when I asked the reason he replied: 'Well I have never led any of my class to Christ. I really believe I have done the girls more harm than good.'

"I had never heard anyone talk like that before, and it set me thinking. After a while I said: 'Suppose you go and tell them how you feel. I will go with you in a carriage, if you want me to go.'

"He consented, and we started out together. It was one of the best journeys I ever had on earth. We went to the house of one of the girls, called for her, and the teacher talked to her about her soul. After he had explained the way of life he suggested that we have prayer. He asked me to pray. True, I had never done such a thing in my life

110

as to pray God to convert a young lady there and then. But we prayed, and God answered our prayer.

"We went to other houses. He would go upstairs and be all out of breath, and he would tell the girls what he had come for. It wasn't long before they broke down and sought salvation.

"When his strength gave out I took him back to his lodgings. The next day we went out again. At the end of ten days he came to the store with his face literally shining.

"'Mr. Moody,' he said, 'the last one of my class has yielded herself to Christ.'

"I tell you we had a time of rejoicing.

"He had to leave the next night, so I called his class together that night for a prayer meeting, and there God kindled a fire in my soul that has never gone out. The height of my ambition had been to be a successful merchant, and if I had known that meeting was going to take that ambition out of me I might not have gone. But how many times I have thanked God since for that meeting.

"The dying teacher sat in the midst of his class and talked with them and read the 14th chapter of John. We tried to sing ' Blest be the tie that binds,' after which we knelt down to pray. I was just rising from my knees when one of the class began to pray for her dying teacher. Another prayed, and another, and before we rose the whole class had prayed. As I went out I said to myself: ' O God, let me die rather than lose the blessing I have received tonight.'

"The next evening I went to the depot to say good-bye to that teacher. Just before the train started, one of the class came, and before long, without any prearrangement, they were all there. What a meeting that was. We tried to sing, but we broke down. The last we saw of that dying teacher he was standing on the platform of the rear car, his finger pointing upward, telling us to meet him in heaven."

That was the end of Moody's business career. What was

111

five thousand dollars a year, or even a hundred thousand, to the joy of leading souls to Jesus Christ? "I was disqualified for business," he said. "It had become distasteful to me. I had got a taste of another world, and cared no more for making money."

So Moody resigned his job, and without the assurance of any support gave himself entirely to religious work.

2

At first Moody's time was given mostly to his own mission. He had a Sunday School, we have seen, of more than a thousand members. It was the largest Sunday School in the West, and was second only to that of John Wanamaker in Philadelphia. Moody added Sunday evening services for the benefit of the parents, and before long evangelistic services were being held every night. Moody's own preaching started almost by accident. He had gone to a Sunday School convention with a friend. The expected speakers failed to arrive. The friend spoke, while Moody prayed for him; then Moody spoke, while his friend prayed. Sixty people were converted, and Moody was launched on his career as an evangelist.

The Chicago Mission soon became "the scene of some of the most remarkable reclamations of the vicious and depraved that any place on the globe has even witnessed." Moody "dragged men out of saloons, captured the children of drunkards, saved men from crime, brought relief to the poor and to the sick, and sunk his plummet down into the depth of human misery." [7] He learned to know men's needs, and the power of the Gospel to meet those needs, from actual experience.

At first his converts were urged to unite with the regular Churches in the neighborhood. But they liked Moody and his unconventional ways and did not feel at home in the established Churches. So the Mission was organized as a Church, and Moody became its pastor, though he remained unordained, a layman, all his life.

The remarkable success of Moody's Sunday School, together with his unique methods, attracted attention. He was invited to attend Sunday School conventions to explain his methods and to describe his work. He was elected a member of the Executive Committee of the State Sunday School Association and traveled widely through Illinois and other states arousing enthusiasm for the work. He advocated, along with other leaders, a uniform lesson and helped to set in motion the forces that issued ultimately in the International Sunday School lessons. The supreme service which Moody rendered the Sunday School movement, however, was through the emphasis he laid upon its evangelistic aim. He often turned state conventions into evangelistic campaigns, just as he frequently changed perfunctory teachers into earnest winners of souls. The constant burden of his heart is expressed in the message he delivered to the great International Convention in Boston only three years before his death: " If I had the trumpet of God and could speak to every Sunday School teacher in America, I would plead with each one to lead at least one soul to Christ this year."

Very early in his own life Moody formed the resolution never to let a day go by without speaking to someone about Christ.

" Are you a Christian? " he once asked a man just arriving in Chicago.

" It is none of your business," came the reply.

" But it is my business," was the answer.

" Then," said the stranger, " you must be D. L. Moody."

This incident is typical of the early Moody. His first attempts at winning souls were so crude and unconventional and at times even absurd, that he became known throughout Chicago as 'Crazy Moody.' Moody himself looked back upon these early years as exhibiting zeal without knowledge. But, as he often pointed out, "there is more hope for a man who has zeal without knowledge than for a man who has knowledge without zeal."

Moody persevered in his efforts and soon became known not only for his boldness but also for his skill in the fine art of personal evangelism. It is not true that Moody asked everyone he met if he were a Christian. In later life especially, he selected his subjects, was careful in his approaches, and cast his questions with care.

All this time Moody was going like a house afire. A contemporary said, "I never saw such high pressure; he made me think of those breathing steamboats on the Mississippi that must go fast or burst." [8]

But in the midst of this constant activity — he made two hundred calls once in a single day — there was little opportunity for spiritual replenishment or for intellectual growth. "I do not get 5 minutes a day to study," Moody wrote his brother, "so I have to talk just as it happens." [9] It is not surprising under the circumstances that his congregations began to fall off, and that Moody discovered ultimately that there was something lacking in himself. He felt that he was running dry; his sermons lacked power; he became oppressed with a sense of spiritual futility. "By the year 1867," says Day, "the consciousness of something wrong blackened his whole outlook. To meet the unidentified malady he plunged into the chasm Santayana described, 'redoubling one's efforts when he's losing his vision.'" [10]

His wife, realizing that something had gone amiss, persuaded him to go to England, hoping that contact with religious leaders there would lift him out of himself. In England, he met among others Henry Moorehouse, who was known as the 'boy preacher.' Moorehouse was attracted by Moody, and against Moody's wish, followed him to Chicago. He preached seven sermons in Moody's Mission, all on John 3:16: "God so loved the world, that he gave his only begotten Son, that whosoever believeth in him should not perish, but have everlasting life." Each sermon sent him ranging through the Bible from Genesis to Revelation " to prove that in all ages God loved the world, that He sent prophets and patriarchs and holy men to warn them and last of all sent His Son. After they murdered him, He sent the Holy Ghost."

"I never knew up to that time," said Moody, " that God loved us so much. This heart of mine began to thaw out, and I could not keep back the tears. It was like news from a far country. I just drank it in."

This incident made a lasting impression upon Moody. For one thing, it revealed to him the inexhaustible riches of the Bible. He began to study the Bible as he had never done before, to study it as Moorehouse taught him to do — topically, with the aid of a concordance, a method which greatly helped Moody, and which he subsequently popularized among large numbers of Christian people. He began not only to study the Bible but also to preach it. Hitherto his sermons had consisted of anecdotes drawn from his own experience and from those of his friends. Now the content was Biblical, though anecdotes were still used to illustrate and drive home his points.

This contact with Moorehouse also gave Moody a new comprehension of the love of God. "I used to preach," he said, " that God was behind the sinner with a double-edged sword, ready to hew him down. I have got done with that. I preach now that God is behind the sinner with love, and he is running away from the God of love." Umphrey Lee claims that John Wesley's great transforming experience was not an evangelical conversion, but a mystical conversion, in which he became overwhelmed with a sense of God's love. Like Wesley, Moody had been preaching for many

115

years, when that experience came which helped to transform his entire ministry.

Moody's spiritual depression continued however for a number of years. His prayer closet became a place of tears. "O God," he sobbed, "have mercy. There is something wrong with me. In His dear Name, correct me. I'd rather die than go on this way." [11]

Final deliverance from this crushing malady, which is apt to come upon a minister after he has been out in the work for a number of years, and which often leads to a crisis in his spiritual development, came in the year 1872, on the eve of his departure for England. For some time Moody had been praying that God would fill him with the Holy Spirit. On this occasion he was walking down Wall Street in lower New York. He was in a state of great spiritual exaltation. Every time he stepped, one foot said, ' Glory ' and the other responded, ' Hallelujah.' [12] Suddenly he prayed: "O God, why don't you compel me to walk close to Thee always? Deliver me from myself! Take absolute sway! Give me Thy Holy Spirit! "

I cannot describe what happened, Moody said later. "I seldom refer to it; it is almost too sacred an experience to name. Paul had an experience of which he never spoke for fourteen years. I can only say that God revealed Himself to me, and I had such an experience of His love that I had to ask Him to stay His hand." [13] From that time on Moody divided his life into three definite periods: a period of nature (before conversion), a period of grace (after conversion), and a period of power (after his filling, as he conceived it, with the Holy Spirit).

The sequel of that experience came just a little later. One day in Ireland he heard Henry Varley say very quietly to a group of Christian workers, " The world has yet to see what God can do with and for and through and in a man who is fully and wholly consecrated to Him."

Two days later Moody was in London, listening to Spurgeon, the great English preacher, for whom he had a great admiration. As he sat high in the balcony and looked over the vast audience and listened to the sermon, heaven came over his soul. Then suddenly he realized as he had never done before that it was not Spurgeon who produced the effect, but God speaking through the words of Spurgeon. And then he recalled the words of Henry Varley.

"He said a man," thought Moody. "He did not say a great man, nor a learned man, nor a rich man, nor a wise man, nor an eloquent man, nor a smart man, but simply a man. I am a man, and it lies with the man himself whether he will or will not make that entire and full consecration. I will try my utmost to be that man."

3

A few months later, under the most inauspicious circumstances conceivable, D. L. Moody began a series of evangelistic services that set first England and then America on fire with the Gospel of Jesus Christ.

At the first meeting in York there were less than fifty persons present, but the attendance grew until the Churches were taxed to seat the people. After five weeks there were two hundred and fifty converts. Moody, assisted by Sankey with his organ and his soul-stirring voice, went from one town to another in Scotland, Ireland, and England, the revival growing constantly in power until its great, smashing climax in London. The British Isles had never known such a revival, certainly not since the days of Whitefield and Wesley, and no religious movement since the Wesleyan revival has had such a permanent effect upon British life.

When Moody and Sankey returned to America they were two of the best-known individuals in all the world. Immediately they were besieged with invitations to conduct revival campaigns in the great American cities. They went in rapid succession to Brooklyn, Philadelphia, New York, Chicago, and Boston. And in the twenty years that remained of his life, Moody visited the great cities and larger towns in every part of America.

During his latter years Moody devoted relatively more time to the institutions which he had established: the Bible Institute and the Bible Institute Colportage Association in Chicago; in Northfield — the Seminary for Girls; Mt. Hermon School for Boys; the Bible conferences which have inspired summer Bible conferences all over the land; and the student conferences, forerunners of those numerous conferences for young people that hold so much promise for the Church. Out of these student conferences at Northfield came the World's Student Christian Federation and the Student Volunteers, which enlisted most of the great host of missionaries who during the last generation were determined to evangelize the world " in our generation." However, Moody continued his own evangelistic campaigns until the end.

Sometimes he was asked how many converts he had won. "I do not know," Moody replied; "thank God I don't have to keep the Lamb's Book of Life." His friends estimated, however, that he had "reduced the population of hell" by at least a million souls.

Among his converts were men who have come to play an outstanding part in the life of the Church — men like Sir Wilfred Grenfell, the apostle of the Labrador; D. E. Hoste, late director of the China Inland Mission; Dan Crawford, missionary to Africa; and J. Wilbur Chapman, outstanding Presbyterian evangelist. But over and above his converts were the large number of men who were profoundly influenced by his spirit. Richard E. Day suggests that they can be divided into a number of groups: (1) a group, who were already giants when Moody attracted attention, but who gave him their hearts and were profited by his spirit — men like John Kelman, Bishop Vincent, the two Bonars, Thomas Guthrie, and Alexander Duff; (2) a group of men about his own age who, though head and shoulders above him as scholars, received life's most significant impulse from his illumined personality — men like Henry Drummond, J. K. Studd, Theodore Cuyler, and F. B. Meyer; (3) hundreds of businessmen, so impressed with his merit and high purpose as to give him not only great sums of money but also their own active service — men like Richard C. Morse, John Wanamaker, Cyrus McCormick, R. K. Remington, W. E. Dodge, and George H. Stuart; (4) underprivileged boys in Moody's schools, for example, John McDowell and Sam Higginbottom; (5) powerful Christian leaders, his close friends, who felt somehow that D. L. Moody was a mystic center of power for his age — men like Henry Clay Trumbull, C. E. Scofield, Arthur T. Pierson, and G. Campbell Morgan; (6) last, but almost limitless, was the influence that Moody as an older man exerted on young collegians — men like John R. Mott, Robert E. Speer, Fletcher Sims Brockman, and Henry B. Wright of Yale.[14]

"Some day," said Moody, "you will read in the papers that D. L. Moody of East Northfield is dead. Don't you believe a word of it. At that moment I shall be more alive than I am now. I shall have gone up higher that is all — out of this old clay tenement into a house that is immortal; a body that death can not touch, that sin can not taint, a body fashioned like unto His glorious body. I was born of the flesh in 1837. I was born of the Spirit in 1856. That which is born of the flesh may die. That which is born of the Spirit will live forever."

And Moody will live forever, not only above where his spirit inhabits the heavenly mansions, but also in the institutions which he founded, in the men whose lives he transformed, and in countless others, who never heard his message, but who find their zeal rekindled by his own.

Yet, as Richard E. Day insists, he was not a great man; in fact, he was a very commonplace man, one who lacked any heavenly endowment and never recovered from the handicaps of his youth. What, then, was the secret of his power?

To answer this question, it will help us to look first at Moody's methods, then at his message, and last, and most important, at Moody the man.

4

Moody had many defects as a speaker. For example, he spoke too rapidly, used the wrong words — 'ain't' and 'tain't,' 'done' for 'did,' 'come' for 'came,' and mispronounced the right words — 'Daniel' became 'Dan'l,' 'Israel' was called 'Isr'l.' Dr. Pentecost once remarked in public, referring to Moody, "Anyone who can pronounce Jerusalem in two syllables can do almost anything." The English press gave considerable publicity to this remark, leading to Spurgeon's pointed reply, "I thank God there is one man in such hot haste to get the Gospel to the people that he does not stop to pronounce all the syllables of every word."

But Moody's defects were more than counterbalanced by his virtues. He was direct, sincere, and natural in his utterance. "If God has given you a message, go and give it to the people as God has given it to you," he advised. "It is a stupid thing to try to be eloquent." He was urgent. As Henry Moorehouse said, he preached "as if there never was to be another meeting, and as if sinners might never hear the Gospel again; these appeals to decide now are most impressive." His language was simple. Children gave him the same close attention as did the most highly educated. Sankey remarked: "Anyone, everyone understood what he said. His meaning was clear to every child." He was personal. Like Wesley and like Finney, he made everyone in the audience feel that he was speaking directly to him. If anyone showed signs of drowsiness, he would talk to that individual until he woke him up. His message came from the heart and reached the heart. Dr. Dale disliked evangelists, but he had a profound respect for Moody because he could never speak of a lost soul without tears in his eyes. "The heart," Moody cried, "always go for the heart. Speak to that, preach to that, if you want to carry men with you."

"That," says Dr. Erdman, "was the secret of his power, if there was any secret. He approached his audience with a tender heart, and no matter how severely he might denounce sin or how faithfully he might warn against punishment, he was obviously and always seeking the good of his hearers and sympathizing with them in their weakness and need." [15]

Last, but not least, Moody believed absolutely and implicitly in his message. "Why do you go to hear Moody?" a scoffer asked his friend. "You don't believe what he preaches." "No," his friend replied, "but he believes it, with all his heart, and it is refreshing to meet such a man in these days of doubt and uncertainty." [16] And many who came to scoff remained to pray.

Like Wesley, but unlike Finney, Moody made large use of music in his revival services. There was one interesting difference, however, between Moody and Wesley. Wesley was himself musical while Moody was barely able to distinguish one tune from another. He utilized trained musical leaders — men like P. P. Bliss, George C. Stebbins, and especially Ira D. Sankey — not because he himself enjoyed the music, but because he realized its value.

As we have seen, Moody inaugurated the idea of a united evangelistic campaign. Another unique feature of his revivals was the "inquiry room." Whenever a tabernacle was constructed for him, he always had an inquiry room at the front. He invited those who were interested to come forward into this room during the singing of the last hymn. This involved no commitment on their part but prevented their being swept out by the crowds. Moody's labors in the inquiry room were spent largely in personal conversation with those who had become concerned as to their spiritual welfare. "This exhausting toil," as Dr. Erdman points out, "was an expression of the deepest conviction of his soul: namely, that public proclamation of the truth does not fulfill all the responsibility of the Christian worker, but that he must deal face to face with anyone who can be persuaded to talk about Christ; and, further, that if a spirit of inquiry or a new interest has been aroused in any auditor by an evangelistic appeal then that very hour, avoiding the danger of delay, a definite commitment to Christ should be made." [17]

Moody believed in advertising his evangelistic meetings, though not in the sensational fashion which later became common. He was careful to avoid any charge of commercialism. He was concerned with the smallest details in regard to the physical arrangements. The room must not be too hot or too cold; there must be plenty of fresh air, but no drafts. Moody was convinced that he was an instrument in God's hands, that *God* was working through him, but *through him* for the salvation of men. No detail was too insignificant, no expenditure of effort too great, to win a single soul to Jesus Christ.

5

Moody's message came from the Bible. He spoke of Biblical characters, utilized Biblical parables and Biblical incidents, and drove home Biblical truths. He had wonderful power to make the Bible vivid and real.

Gamaliel Bradford claims that in Moody's estimation to question the Bible was infidelity and led to hell. There are passages in his sermons which give strong support to this contention. He himself accepted the Bible implicitly as the absolutely inerrant Word of God. And he insisted that it was to be taken as an unbroken whole. "The moment you can break down that word in one place," he said, "and make out that it is not true, then, of course, the whole word goes." [18] This was an unfortunate statement, a dangerous 'mistruth,' which on the lips of Moody and others like him was to cause unnecessary difficulties for individuals and the Church in the days that lay ahead. But Moody was not at all troubled about questions which had begun to trouble many of his contemporaries. According to his own confession, he was quite ready to believe that Jonah had swallowed the whale, if the Holy Scripture so declared. "Take the Bible," he urged his contemporaries, "study it . . . pass on the message; be obedient to commands; waste no time in discussion; let speculation and theorizing pass into the hands of those who like that kind of study." [19]

The doctrine of evolution, which Henry Ward Beecher had espoused, and which was so greatly to influence the Christian message and the atmosphere in which all preachers were henceforth to labor, was scarcely noticed by the great evangelist. Once, and only once (so far as known), he spoke of it publicly: "It is a great deal easier to believe that man was made after the image of God than to believe, as some young men and women are being taught now, that he is the offspring of a monkey." [20]

Moody read little besides the Bible, the older commentaries that clarified the text, and the sermons of Spurgeon. History, philosophy, science, and poetry did not appeal to him. Novels he abhorred. His theology came from men he had known and admired, especially those who had influenced him in his formative years.

We might sum it up by saying that he was a conservative, evangelical Christian, who preached salvation by faith in a crucified and risen Saviour. "The utter depravity of human nature, free salvation by Christ, the imminence of death, the necessity to salvation of a complete supernatural change of character and emotions" were the subjects which he emphasized according to contemporary accounts. Lyman Abbott, writing only a little before Moody's death, concluded that the evangelist's power was due first to his emphasis on God's love, which rarely fails to meet a response "when it comes to men who are hopeless of ever becoming worthy of doing anything worthy," and, secondly, to his insistence on the facts of a present loss and a present salvation. "It was his thought," said Abbott, and Moody's sermons sustain the point, "not that the world will be lost, but that it is lost; not that the Christian will be saved, but that he is saved. And he made this message of a present salvation effective because the message grew out of his own personal experience. He did not promise a future hope, which may be realized and may not; he promised a present experience, which he was sure can be realized because he had realized it himself." [21]

Moody's message was based on the cross. When British Christians questioned him about his creed he referred them to the fifty-third chapter of Isaiah. "If you wish to know the secret of our success," he said, speaking of the revival in Great Britain, "it is this: we have stood fair and square on the Bible doctrine of substitution. Oh! that is what is needed by a dying world, Substitution! If you take that out of the Bible, you can take the Bible along with you. The scarlet thread is unbroken from Genesis to Revelation." And yet, as Dr. Erdman has pointed out, "he did not fall into the error of preaching a dead Christ, nor into the more subtle error of urging men to seek salvation by putting their trust in a dogma relative to the death of Christ. He taught

men to have faith in a Person, and not in a doctrine. . . .
His message began at the cross, but never ended there.
. . . His definite aim was to persuade men to yield themselves in obedience to this living Lord and in all things to
do his holy will. He pled with men to forsake sin, and he
promised victory to all who looked to Christ for help." [22]

Moody believed in hell. He said once: "If I believed
there was no hell, you would not find me going from town
to town, spending day and night preaching and proclaim-
ing the Gospel, and urging men to escape the damnation of
hell. I would take things easy." [23] But he did not dwell
upon this aspect of the Gospel. It was not the chief motive to which he appealed. He laid a great deal more emphasis, as we have seen, upon the love of God, God's infinite
love as revealed in the gift of His Son. "There was a time,"
he admitted, "when I thought a good deal more of Christ
than the Father. I thought Christ came in to act as media-
tor between me and an angry judge, and Christ seemed far
nearer to me than the Father, but since I became a father
that feeling is all gone. It must have taken more love for
God to give up His Son than it did for Christ to come and
suffer." [24]

"Salvation," he insisted, "is instantaneous. I admit that
a man may be converted so that he cannot tell when he
crossed the line between life and death, but I also believe a
man may be a thief one moment and a saint the next. I believe a man may be as vile as hell itself one moment, and
be saved the next," [25] or, as he put it on another occasion,
"saved like Zacchaeus between the branches and the
ground."

Only as men were thus converted — supernaturally regenerated — was there any hope of human brotherhood.
"I have no sympathy," he emphatically proclaimed, "with
the doctrine of universal brotherhood and universal Fatherhood. A man must be born into the household of faith by

the Spirit, through Christ, before he becomes my brother, or a son of God." [26]

Moody was an old-fashioned premillennialist (not a modern dispensationalist). He believed that the return of Christ might occur at any moment but had no program for the last days and did not allow his beliefs to separate him from Christians who held the contrary view. His doctrine prevented him, however, from working directly for the betterment of social conditions. He believed, of course, that the Gospel must manifest itself in life. "Christianity isn't worth a snap of your fingers if it doesn't straighten out your characters," he cried, and he never failed to assist in local charities which sought to alleviate misery and suffering. Nonetheless, Moody remained blind to the great social issues that were rapidly growing in importance — issues which, as we shall see later, were to affect profoundly the message of the American pulpit and determine the attitude of multitudes of people toward the Church. He believed that things were going to the bad and would continue to do so until the "final crash," which was to precede Christ's return.

As Henry Ward Beecher said, "He is a believer in the second advent of Christ, and in our own time. He thinks it is no use to attempt to work for this world. In his opinion it is blasted — a wreck bound to sink, and the only thing that is worth doing is to get as many of the crew off as you can, and let her go."

Some, of course, were not attracted by this and other aspects of Moody's Gospel. As George Adam Smith, a great friend and admirer, said, "much of Moody's teaching repels a whole side of the Church and diminishes his authority with thinking men and women." His later missions to Great Britain did not achieve the same success as the Great Revival of 1873–1875. Paul D. Moody, the great evangelist's younger son, suggests that this may not be due to the change which came over the religious atmosphere in Great Britain after the heresy trial of Robertson Smith in 1876. In America, the crowds remained undiminished to the end, but there were not so many converts. After one series of meetings in New York City, for example, there were only thirty-three new members received into the Churches. Moody complained that the Church people, his numerous friends, crowded out the unconverted. Since he could not preach to non-Christians as once he had done, he sought to lay the obligation upon the Christians who so largely made up his audiences.

More likely Moody's failure to reach the unconverted in the same measure as formerly was due to the great changes that took place in America's mental and religious outlook during the closing years of his life. "New ideas and new conditions had arisen," explained Charles F. Goss, just after the great evangelist's death. "With these Mr. Moody was not perfectly in touch. He did not fully understand them. This was not strange. In fact, it was inevitable. No man ever lived perhaps (unless it was Gladstone) who was able to keep pace with the rapid changes from one period to another during a long life. Men grow up into a certain set of conditions, adjust themselves to them, become hardened in them, and stay there, while a new generation arises with new needs and new notions, passes on, and leaves them behind.

"Mr. Moody helped to make an epoch. His influence upon the religious life of the generation playing its part in human affairs between 1860 and 1890 was that of a formative force. He moulded thought, action, worship. It would be too much to expect that his mind thus hardened in its habits of thought and feeling should be able to adjust itself to the enormously altered conditions of the last decade. In order to have done this he would have had to alter himself, and this was impossible to a nature like his. I said to him once, in 1897: 'You are at odds with much of modern life. Why do you not conform to the new epoch? You were a leader of a great movement a generation ago, and you are still young enough to head the religious life of the new age if you will only comprehend it and accept it.'

"He fixed those great deep eyes upon me," says Goss, "with one of those long stares which seemed to penetrate into my very soul, and shook his head. What I said did not appeal to him. He knew no other methods. He could grasp no other ideas." [27]

Moody himself realized, however, that the times were changing. "Thirty years ago," he said, "pretty much everybody believed that the Bible was true. They did not attack it or question it. They believed that the Lord Jesus Christ by dying on the cross had done something for them, and that if they received Him they would be saved. And my work was to bring them to a decision to do what they already knew they ought to do. But all is different now. The question mark is raised everywhere, and there is need for teachers who shall teach and show the people what the gospel is." [28]

But changing times did not mean for Moody a changing gospel. "Ministers are abreast of the time," he cried, "if they preach the old gospel faithfully. . . . The gospel has stood the test of nineteen centuries, and it has never failed once. I know what the gospel will do for sin-sick souls, for I have seen its power for forty years. Why should I try a new remedy of whose value I know nothing? Why should I spend years in studying up a possible cure for sin when I have a sure remedy . . . ? I have only one message, for men of every class." [29] "What we want today," he added, "is men who believe in [the Bible] from the crown of their heads to the soles of their feet; who believe the whole of it, the things they understand, and the things they do not understand." [30]

So Moody, great soul that he was, helped to identify evangelism with a theology that was losing its hold upon large sections of the American people.

6

To understand Moody we have to take into account, not only his methods and his message, but also his personality. It is of course impossible to analyze a man's character without somehow losing the man. It will help us, however, to note some of the qualities which most impressed his contemporaries.

First, there was his tremendous energy. He seemed tireless. No difficulty or opposition could daunt him, and no fatigue could wear him out. He could not only set a dozen men to work but could outwork them and a team of horses. In his early days he sometimes neglected the laws of health. "I didn't know much at this time," he wrote later. "After going from early morning until late at night with only a few crackers and cheese, I was faint and fatigued. Sometimes after such a day I imagined that I sinned in going to sleep over my prayers, when actually I was a fool for neglecting the dictates of common sense. God is not a hard taskmaster, and in later years I have learned that to do your best work, you cannot afford to neglect the common laws of health." But he continued to abhor laziness. Unbelief was the sin against which he preached, but his family entertained a secret suspicion that in his innermost soul he detested laziness fully as much. "If a man's lazy, what can you do for him?" he would inquire. "Other faults a man may overcome, but I almost despair if a man is lazy."

He loved practical jokes, and could take as well as give them. He was habitually cheery and sunny, in the home and out of it. He did not believe in being worried or anxious about the Lord's affairs or about his own. "It's worry that kills," he would say, and after the most exacting work he would be able to relieve his mind of all anxiety and rest as quietly as a child. He believed, and lived as he believed, that one should do his best and then cast his burden on the Lord.

Moody was a thorough conservative. But he invited all kinds of Christians to his Northfield platform, if he knew they had a positive evangelical message. One of the men greatly drawn to Moody was Henry Drummond, whose own influence was so great among university men in the English-speaking world. When Drummond published his *Natural Law in the Spiritual World* and publicly espoused the theory of evolution, many of Moody's friends urged him strongly to drop him from his program. But Moody refused to budge and stuck by him to the end. When finally news came of Drummond's death he burst into tears and declared he was the most Christlike man he had ever known. Later he wrote a tribute for the *Record of Christian Work* in which he said: "My own feelings are akin to those of David on the death of Jonathan. When at last we meet again before our Lord and Master Jesus Christ, whom we both loved and served together in years gone, things which we could not see alike here below we shall fully know in the light of his countenance who brought our lives together and blessed them with a mutual love."

Paul D. Moody, ghosting for his father, once represented him as saying that higher criticism was less dangerous than unchristian attacks on it. The article was submitted for the evangelist's approval. "I queried," says the son, "what I had written myself, for while it was my own immature conviction I was not certain he would subscribe to it. He pondered it for a little time thoughtfully and then replied that he would let it stand." [31]

In the last year of his life Moody wrote to friends in England: "Destructive theology on the one side and the no less evil spirit of extreme intolerance on the other side have wrought wide dissensions in many communities in America. Instead of fighting error by the emphasis of truth, there has been too much 'splitting of hairs' and too often an unchristian spirit of bitterness. This has frequently resulted in depleted churches and has opened the way for the entrance of still greater errors." [32]

But if Moody was unwilling to criticize others, there were many who were ready to criticize him. As A. P. Fitt, who served as his secretary and later became his son-in-law, points out: "There were criticisms and hostilities and prejudices in England and in America: ministerial criticisms, false rumors and insinuations, ridicule, misjudgments, oppositions of atheism and other 'isms.' But he outlived them all. He turned criticism into a means of grace and learned from it. He was ever ready to rectify mistakes in judgment or conduct, to ask forgiveness for even unintentional hurts and wrongs, and he tried never to repeat his mistakes. He could not work until he was at peace with everyone." [33]

Through Moody's introduction, Rev. Charles F. Goss was elected pastor of Moody's old Church in Chicago. After a few years and a very unhappy experience, he was compelled to resign. He came to Northfield to talk it over with Moody. The evangelist heard him patiently and then advised him: "Goss, whatever you do, keep sweet! I have been misunderstood, maligned, abused, but I made up my mind to keep sweet. . . . You cannot do any good unless you keep sweet. . . . My advice to you is to keep sweet." [34]

As we have seen, Moody avoided all taint of commercialism in his evangelistic campaigns. Along with Sankey, he could have become wealthy from the sale of their Gospel hymns alone — the royalties totaling more than a million dollars. Both men refused, however, to make material gain out of this or any other aspect of their work. Large sums of money passed through Moody's hands, but he passed it on to his institutions, and when he died left practically nothing to his children.

Moody was not spoiled by his success or by the tremendous flattery which everywhere attended him. Gamaliel Bradford speaks of the enormous laudation, just plain glory, that followed him wherever he went. "Great men bowed down to him, learned men deferred to him, rich men opened their purses freely. If he would, he might have had a train of adoring women; but it is one of the fine things about him that the adulation of women did not appeal. As Mr. Duffus puts it: 'He never let gushing women make a fool of him.'" [35]

He remained sincerely humble, feeling that God could not use him if he became in the least bit conceited. Dr. Torrey, who knew him well, said: "He loved to put himself in the background and put other men in the foreground. . . . He made no pretense to a humility he did not possess. In his heart of hearts he constantly underestimated himself and overestimated others." [36]

Henry Drummond was accustomed to say that Moody was the greatest human he had ever known. He was interested in nature, in animals, but especially in people — he loved them, and they naturally loved him in return. This love knew no difference between rich and poor, between the powerful and the weak. Men and women of every class had souls that needed to be saved and that were worth saving. To Moody nothing else mattered.

Everyone was attracted by the evangelist's sincerity, naturalness, and common sense.

The characteristic which impressed his contemporaries the most, however, was his thorough consecration to what he considered the will of God. Gamaliel Bradford, with all his skill as a delineator of character, could not fully understand Moody because he did not share his faith. Yet he wrote: "No one can dwell with Moody long without being convinced that he would have thrown over all his glory and success in a moment, if he had been convinced that God willed it. It is said that in later years he deliberately changed his methods, dividing his audiences in a way to yield less personal triumph for himself, but greater results." Gamaliel Bradford must have known how difficult such procedure would be — even for a preacher. But he adds, " I have no doubt it is true." [37]

His son says, " He lived solely for the glory of God and for the spread of the Gospel of Jesus Christ." And his son's wife, who saw him intimately in the little affairs of the home, as well as in the great things of the Kingdom, and who watched him narrowly for at least some transient inconsistency, added: " Here I suppose is the ultimate secret of Moody's success. Of course he had gifts, gifts which some of the rest of us do not possess, but God could use him mightily because he put what gifts he had absolutely at God's disposal."

One of his contemporaries remarked: " After I'm with him a while, it's Christ I think of, not Moody. He's such a plain person; but I soon forget that too." His biographer comments, " Somehow one couldn't be with him half an hour, without becoming conscious of — Another." [38]

" The rapture of flight in writing of Moody," he adds, " has never arisen from admiration of his genius. It is said respectfully, and in so saying Infinite Grace is magnified, Moody was essentially commonplace. For this I thank God. . . . It has come as a song in the night to find in Dwight L. Moody sure proof that the loftiest achievement is merely ' my human best filled with the Holy Spirit.' " [39]

Or, as Moody himself said, " Today's broken world needs nothing more than men and women on fire with the Fire of heaven — not great men, but true, honest persons whom God can use."

Chapter *IV*

WASHINGTON GLADDEN
and the development of the "New Theology"

WASHINGTON GLADDEN was born February 11, 1836, in Potts Grove, Pennsylvania. He died eighty-two years later, in the midst of the first World War, active, alert, forward-looking until the end. There is no minister whose life reveals more clearly the vital changes that were taking place in the religious thought of America during these important years when America was growing to maturity. The development of American liberalism, whose germs we have discovered in Horace Bushnell; the popular reaction against Calvinism, reflected so clearly in the experience of Henry Ward Beecher; the passing of the old time revivalism, seen at its best in the career of Dwight L. Moody; the beginning of the social gospel, whose mature development we are to study in the life and writings of Walter Rauschenbusch — all are mirrored in the life and labors of Washington Gladden.

I

His father — Solomon Gladden — was a schoolteacher, born in Southampton, Massachusetts; his grandfather, a shoemaker, laboring in the summer on the neighboring farms; his great-grandfather, a veteran of the Revolutionary War, who had wintered with Washington in Valley Forge. The boy's mother was also a schoolteacher, the daughter of a shoemaker, living in Owego, New York, so that Washington Gladden was descended on both sides from humble but industrious parentage.

Solomon Gladden died when his son was only six. Washington spent a year on his grandfather's farm in Massachusetts and then came to live with his mother's brother, who managed to wring a living from a stony little farm three miles from Owego.

The schooling of this uncle, who became a second father to the boy, had been limited to three or four brief winter terms. It was enough, however, to develop an intense love of reading, which became his one and only recreation. In the long winter evenings, after the chores were done, he gathered his family together and, by the flickering light of pine knot or tallow dip, read aloud the books he was able to secure from the school library. As he grew older, Washington was allowed at times to share in this sacred privilege. Says Gaius Glenn Atkins: "He could never, I think, have repaid his uncle for this. No one who heard him in after years could ever forget the timbre of his voice, its characteristic modulations, its restrained passion when the banked fires of indignation or noble affirmation broke through. I can hear the music of it now across the years." [1]

Washington Gladden began his own education in the district school, where each child used whatever textbook the family could provide. After his eighth summer, his labors were needed on the farm, and he was able to attend only the brief winter's term — four months out of the year.

From earliest childhood he had been bathed in an atmosphere of contagious piety. His father and mother, as well as the uncle and aunt with whom he was now living, were all deeply religious. Over and over again the great family Bible was read through in family prayers. The Westminster Catechism was learned by heart and accepted without questions of any sort. "It would be difficult," Washington Gladden wrote in his *Recollections*, "to convey to most of those who will read these pages any adequate sense of the positiveness with which these doctrines were held in the circles in which my life was spent. We did not admit to ourselves the possibility of any error in their statement, and we guarded ourselves carefully against any influence which would tend to weaken our hold upon them." [2]

Every Sunday the boy went with the rest of the family to Sunday School and two preaching services in the Presbyterian Church at Owego. There were frequent revivals. Washington heard, among others, the well-known Baptist evangelist, Elder Knapp, who was accustomed to give lurid descriptions of the burning pit, with the sinners trying to crawl up its sides out of the flames, while devils stood by with pitchforks to fling them back again. It was in the days of the Millerite hysteria, when thousands of Christians believed that the day of the Lord was at hand. When Washington was seven years old, he heard a lecture in the Baptist Church in which the lecturer, with figures drawn from the prophecy of Daniel, proved with chalk upon a blackboard that the world was going to be burned up in 1843. There was a blazing comet in the sky that winter — "wonders in the heavens above and signs on the earth beneath," the preacher said. Every night the boy saw that comet through his bedroom window and hid his head under the covers to escape the terrible portent.

As Washington grew older, he came to desire above all other things that spiritual experience of which he had heard others testify, and which he believed to be the supreme good. Yet he was unable to find his way into the peace of God. He understood that he, with all the rest of mankind, had by the fall "lost communion with God" and was "under his wrath and curse, and so made liable to all the miseries of this life, to death itself, and to the pains of hell forever." "Of the exact truth of this statement I had not the shadow of a doubt," he says. "But I understood that there

was a way by which I could escape from this curse and re-
gain this lost communion. That was the one thing, above
all others, that I wanted. I would gladly have exchanged
for it not only every sinful pleasure, but all the pleasures
that were not sinful. It will hardly be credited today, but I
felt that being a Christian would mean, for me, giving up
all my boyish sports — ball-playing, coasting, fishing; and I
was more than ready to make that sacrifice. So I kept trying
for years, to gain that assurance of the favor of God of which
I heard people talking, and which, I felt sure, some of them
must possess. I listened, in prayer meeting and revival
meeting, to what they said about it; I noted with the greatest care the steps that must be taken, and I tried to do just
what I was told to do. I was to ' give myself away,' in a serious and complete self-dedication. I suppose that I shall be
far within the truth if I say that I tried to do that, a thousand
times. But I understood that when I had done it, properly,
I should have an immediate knowledge of the fact that it had
been properly done; some evidence in my consciousness that
could not be mistaken; that a light would break in, or a burden roll off, or that some other emotional or ecstatic experience would supervene; and when nothing of the kind occurred, the inevitable conclusion was that my effort had
been fruitless; that I had failed to commend myself to the favor of God, and was still under his wrath and curse." [3]

Years later, when Washington Gladden was a pastor in
Springfield, Massachusetts, he wrote his first distinctive religious book, *Being a Christian and How to Begin.* It was
written to make plain the way of Christian discipleship to
young people who were attracted by the Christian life but
did not know how to start. Very simply he explained that
to be a Christian means something more than to submit to
certain rites (as the ritualist says), or to believe certain doctrines (as the dogmatist says), or to experience certain emotions (as the sentimentalist says). To be a Christian means

to believe on Christ, to learn of Christ, and to follow Christ
— and the way to begin is just to begin. The widespread
popularity of this little book makes it plain that its message
was still needed as late as 1876, and that many young people
were troubled, as Washington Gladden had been troubled
a generation earlier, because their conversion did not follow the conventional pattern set by certain popular evangelists.

When young Washington Gladden was sixteen years old
he left his uncle's farm to become a printer's apprentice in
Owego. He broke for a while his strict religious habits but
was led before long into the Congregational Church by a
sane and sensible evangelist who showed him a way out of
his religious difficulties.

This Church was formed by a group seceding from the
Presbyterian Church which he had attended in earlier years.
Its pastor ventured one day to pray for the slaves. The el-
ders, fearing that he might be an abolitionist, forced him out
of the pulpit. A small group thereupon left the Church and
called the ousted minister back from New England. This
new Church, as might be expected, shared to the full in the
new humanitarian sentiments that were beginning to rise in
the American Churches, especially among the Congregationalists. The *Independent,* carrying the sermons and the flam-
ing editorials of Henry Ward Beecher, warmed the hearts
and stirred the consciences of its members. It was this new
ethical concern that captured the interest of Washington
Gladden, rather than the theological pabulum, the controversies over predestination and the proper mode of baptism,
or the revivalism that still furnished the staples of religion
for the Churches as a whole. Throwing himself wholeheartedly into the work of this Church, it was not long before he
formed the purpose of entering the ministry. "It was not an
individualistic pietism that appealed to me," he said; " it was
a religion that laid hold upon life with both hands, and pro-

posed, first and foremost, to realize the Kingdom of God in this world. I do not think that any other outlook upon the work would have attracted me. . . . I wanted to be — if I could make myself fit — the minister of a church like that. I could not think of any life better worth living." [4]

To prepare himself for his new life's calling, he toiled for a year and a half at Owego Academy, following with four years at Williams College, whose president, the famous Mark Hopkins, was then at his prime. The course which Dr. Hopkins taught his seniors on the Westminster Shorter Catechism was regarded as a good equivalent for a seminary course in systematic theology.

2

After Gladden had graduated from Williams College, he taught for a while in the public school at Owego. Meanwhile he read theology with the young Congregational pastor, who had but recently graduated from Andover. It was hoped that Gladden might prepare himself to preach in the neighboring schoolhouses and in the small Churches near by which were without a regular pastor. He ministered temporarily to a small Church across the Pennsylvania line and then, in 1860, accepted a call to a newly organized Methodist Congregational group in Brooklyn. Here, on November 15, 1860, he was ordained to the Congregational ministry.

The Churches in Brooklyn, Gladden found, were little moved by the intense political excitement which then filled the air. Even "right-minded people," it seemed, were determined to keep the Church out of politics. Henry Ward Beecher, it is true, thundered mightily at times against slavery, but he was an exception. On the other hand, one of the most honored and influential of the Presbyterian pastors, Henry J. Van Dyke, preached a sermon that summer which was a closely reasoned and forcible argument to prove that abolitionism and infidelity are synonymous terms, and that no man could be an abolitionist without being an infidel.

After the election of Lincoln, when it became clear that the mind of the South was set on secession, Northern sentiment, for a time uncertain, shifted definitely to the policy of compulsion, and the Civil War was the inevitable result. "As I recall those anxious days of November and December, 1860," Washington Gladden wrote in 1909, "I cannot help wishing that the ethical passion of the North for liberty had been matched with a faith, equally compelling, in the cogency of good will. One or two sermons, yellow with age, bearing those dates, testify of a strong desire to find a better way out of the trouble than the horrible way of war, and I am not ashamed of the youthful faith that a better way was possible." [5]

The strain and anxiety of this difficult period brought Gladden to the verge of nervous collapse, and shortly after the outbreak of the war he accepted what seemed to be a less exacting work in Morrisania, New York, a small town two miles north of the Harlem River, now a part of New York City.

Having a little more time now for study, he sought to compensate for his lack of theological training. He spent much time in the Astor Library and attended lectures in Union Theological Seminary in New York. Of far greater consequence, however, was his discovery of the sermons of F. W. Robertson and Horace Bushnell, which revealed a new world to his delighted gaze. "Here were men," he says, "to whom spiritual things were not traditions but living verities; men who knew how to bring religion into vital touch with reality. What I found upon these throbbing pages was what Dr. Munger afterward described as 'The Appeal to Life.' I can never tell how much I owe to these two men — to Robertson, first, for opening my eyes; to Bushnell, chiefly, for teaching me how to use them." [6]

Someone to whom Gladden expressed his indebtedness called his attention to Bushnell's earlier work, *God in Christ*, a book which he procured, and with which he lived for some months. " The introductory essay, on Language," he says, "was, for me, a ' *Novum Organon*,' giving me a new sense of the nature of the instrument which I was trying to use, and making entirely clear the futility of the ordinary dogmatic method. And in the three great discourses which followed . . . I found an emancipation proclamation which delivered me at once and forever from the bondage of an immoral theology. That there was a gospel to preach I had no longer any doubt, for I had been made to see that the Judge of all the earth would do right. That was the foundation of Bushnell's faith; his heresy was the unfaltering belief that God is just." [7]

So it seemed to Gladden. The popular revolt against Calvinism, encouraged by Henry Ward Beecher and carried a step farther by Washington Gladden, was, in large part, a revolt of the popular moral sentiment against what appeared to be the immoral trends of the orthodox theology. Reliance upon the moral sentiment, insistence upon ethical religion, a strong conviction that God's character and providential government of the universe cannot be contrary to man's own highest moral insights are keys which enable us to understand the further development not only of Gladden's religion, but also of that of his age.

On the first Sunday after Lee's surrender, Gladden declared that the people of the North had, in the midst of their joy, a sincere pity for the vanquished. " I most firmly believe," he said, " that by a hearty and considerate kindness to the Southern people we can restore the old relations of amity; nay, that we can establish new relations of friendship, which shall be far closer and more enduring than the old ones were." [8]

Any chance that these sentiments might prevail in the

nation as a whole were promptly destroyed by the assassination of President Lincoln. There was a general feeling that the South as a whole was responsible and popular support swung quickly to the more rigorous, the more vindictive, policy of the radical Republicans. The pulpit which might have been expected to exert a modifying influence added additional fuel to the flames. Funeral services were held widely over the country on April 19 as Lincoln's body was carried to its final resting place. Most of the preachers, as Gladden recalled, seized the occasion to demand a vigorous policy in dealing with treason. There were exceptions — Henry Ward Beecher, breaking with lifetime associates, and, among others, Washington Gladden, an inconspicuous pastor in an unimportant town. "Of the few hundreds who listened," he wrote, "a score may have been convinced; but a voice like this affected the raging of the populace about as much as the chirping of the swallows on a telegraph pole." [9] An emotional cyclone, he continues, swept a whole nation out of the ways of sanity and practically destroyed the finer growths of tolerance and magnanimity. As a result, seeds of distrust and ill will were widely and deeply sown, and through the entire period of reconstruction the nation was gathering the harvest.

"For myself," says Gladden, "I must confess that if I had ever cherished any fond belief in the infallibility of the populace, that illusion was forever dispelled by the spectacle of those days. It became only too apparent that a whole people, swept by a flood of excitement, may go hopelessly wrong. Burke says that it is difficult to draw up an indictment against a whole nation. Difficult it may be, but it is sometimes necessary. That entire populations are subject to epidemics of unreason is historically true. And the only hope for this democracy is in the rise of a class of leaders who have the courage to resist the mob, and to speak the truth in the days when the truth is the last thing the people want to hear. . . . Our business," he adds, "is 'to make reason and the will of God prevail.'"[10]

3

In 1866, Gladden accepted a call to a Congregational Church in North Adams, Massachusetts, a small factory village of something more than eight thousand inhabitants, where he remained for the next five years. A series of Sunday evening lectures, delivered to his young people, were condensed into a series of weekly articles for the *Springfield Republican* and published later in book form. It was the first of a long series of books, thirty-eight in all, that were to flow from his pen, all virile productions, concerned with vital problems, and all widely read.

One of his first magazine contributions raised the question, "Are Dr. Bushnell's views heretical?" A Congregational council in Illinois had refused to ordain a candidate for the ministry because he sympathized with Bushnell's view of the atonement. Gladden had been persuaded by Bushnell " that there could be no such thing as judicial transfer of blame or penalty from a guilty to an innocent person; that the entire transaction was within the ethical rather than the forensic realm." He wrote now to set forth the substance of Bushnell's teaching and to acknowledge it publicly as his own. If this was heresy, he declared that he also must be counted among the heretics. And he extended the right hand of fellowship to the young man who had been rejected for teaching it. This article brought a grateful response from the venerable Dr. Bushnell and was the beginning of a close fellowship that further influenced Washington Gladden's views on religion.

In 1871, Gladden accepted the position of religious editor of the *New York Independent,* which was still widely read and greatly influential, despite the defection of Henry Ward

Beecher and the recent dismissal of Theodore Tilton. It was Gladden's responsibility to survey and comment on the entire field of religious thought and action.

When he began his task the theological world was still placid and serene. "But signs of disturbance began to appear after a year or two," Gladden recalled. "I can hardly tell how it began; some indications of restiveness under the restraints of the traditional orthodoxy were audible in certain quarters. The *Independent* was interested in such phenomena and began to take an active part in discussing them. Nothing very radical was contended for; the point mainly insisted on was that theology must be moral." [11]

Typical of this attitude is an editorial in the issue for July 3, 1873, entitled "Immoral Theology." "To teach that God is a being who has a perfect right to bring into the world a creature with faculties impaired, with no power to resist temptation, utterly unable to do right, powerless even to repent of the wrong which he is fated to do, and then send to everlasting misery this helpless creature for the sin which he could not help committing — to teach such a doctrine as this about God," wrote the editor, "is to inflict upon religion a terrible injury and to subvert the very foundations of morality. To say that God may justly punish a man for the sins of his ancestors, that God does blame us for what happened long before we were born, is to blaspheme God, if there be such a thing as blasphemy. To say that any such thing is clearly taught in the Bible is to say that the Bible clearly teaches a monstrous lie. Yet such theology as this is taught in several of our theological seminaries and preached from many of our pulpits. It is idle to say that it is nothing but a philosophical refinement, that the men who come out of our theological seminaries with these notions in their heads never make any use of them in their pulpits. They do make use of them. They are scattering this atrocious stuff all over the land. They are making infidels faster than they are converting sinners. Men say, 'If this is your God, worship him, if you want to, but do not ask us to bow down to your Moloch!' Who can blame them? For our own part we say, with all emphasis, that between such a theology as this and atheism we should promptly choose the latter."[12]

These two quotations reveal clearly the underlying assumptions of the new theology — and one of its most impelling motives. To increasing numbers of men Calvinism had become unreal; it seemed remote from life, a legal fiction. To increasing numbers it had become morally offensive. It was assumed that man's moral sense reflected the divine attributes, that between God and man there was a common measure of morality, and that both God's character and God's actions could be judged by man's own moral sensibilities. The new theology endeavored to heal the breach between men's consciences, their increasing ethical sensitiveness, and their religion. It was becoming more and more plain that men generally would not accept a religion that offended their fundamental moral convictions. The new theology sought to check a growing defection from the Church. Unfortunately it tended to make man's conscience the measure of divine truth. It threatened ultimately to lose the idea of special revelation, on which historic Christianity depends, in the shifting sands of a general revelation, so shifting and so uncertain as to become almost meaningless.

Gladden resigned his position on the *Independent* in 1875 because he could not approve the advertising policy of the paper. For the next seven years he was pastor of the North Congregational Church in Springfield, Massachusetts.

The theological question continued to attract him. A Congregational council meeting near Springfield had refused to install a young minister, Rev. James F. Merriam, who was unwilling to assert that all who die impenitent suffer everlasting torment. A few weeks later a different council installed without question Rev. Theodore T. Munger, who rejected orthodox views on future punishment even more emphatically than had Mr. Merriam. As a result there was widespread discussion among Congregationalists regarding the conditions of fellowship. Some maintained that consensus of doctrine determined the matter. But there was no such consensus. Others argued that self-discipline should be relied upon — that those who found themselves out of harmony with their brethren should withdraw voluntarily from the Church.

This proposal did not commend itself to Washington Gladden or to any of the steadily increasing number of liberals in the Congregational Churches. "It may be absurd," Gladden wrote, but the liberal "cannot help thinking that in some, at least, of the things concerning which he disagrees with his brethren, he is right and his brethren are wrong. He believes that the truth which God has given to him is truth which his brethren need. Fidelity to his Master and love for his brethren constrain him to continue in the fellowship. He will differ with them as kindly as he can; he will not emphasize his difference in divisive and unseemly ways, but he will be faithful to the truth as he sees it, in order that those with whom he walks may be led to see it also." [13]

4

In 1882, Washington Gladden began his long and influential pastorate in the first Congregational Church of Columbus, Ohio. He came to this city of fifty-three thousand inhabitants, the political and intellectual capital of the state, in his physical prime. He died thirty-six years later, vigorous in mind and body until the end.

Throughout this entire period he was held in increasing honor in the city of Columbus, in the state of Ohio, and throughout the nation. He was much in demand in the leading colleges and universities, and a number of his books were delivered first as lectures in one or more of these institutions. His influence was especially strong among the younger generation of ministers. It is doubtful, says Gaius Glenn Atkins, " if the ministry of any preacher of his times reached further, or was of more pregnant quality." [14]

Most of his energies during this long period were given to his own Church and to the ordinary parish problems faced by every successful pastor. In the morning he was accustomed to preach on some theme of personal religion, and several volumes of sermons attest to the high inspirational value of his ordinary preaching. In the evening his thought took a wider range, religious, theological, and social. And many of these Sunday evening lectures, as in his other pastorates, were later printed in more permanent form.

Though he was not a profound scholar, he was a tireless and discerning reader in many different fields. He kept himself in touch with advancing theological thought, and he also sought to keep his congregation informed, not only as a matter of interest but also as a measure of safety; not only that theological reconstruction might keep pace with truth as he saw it, but also that members of his congregation, particularly the large number of college and university students who attended on his ministrations, might not have their faith undermined by advancing thought, by problems which intelligent and inquiring minds could no longer avoid.

In 1886 he was invited to deliver a series of lectures to the students of Ohio State University. These lectures, reported in the *Christian Union* and then in the *Christian World* of London, were published, first in England and then in this country, under the title, *Burning Questions of the Life That Now Is and of That Which Is to Come*. The supreme question facing young college men at the time in the field of religion was the question of evolution and its bearing upon religion. " It is thought by some and feared by many," Gladden stated in his opening lecture, " that the religious beliefs which have been regarded throughout Christendom as most fundamental, have been undermined by recent discoveries in physical science; it is loudly said that Christianity is doomed, and that the Churches must give place to other forms of social organization. . . . It is of the utmost consequence that we know the truth about this matter. . . . The discourses that follow will be devoted to a discussion of some of the fundamental doctrines of Christianity under the light of modern science." [15]

Gladden agreed with Beecher, who the year before had thrown his great influence decisively in favor of the new theory, that evolution was an aid rather than a hindrance to faith. " In the splendid array of organized facts which constitute modern science," he said, " there are proofs of creative Mind far more impressive than any that were visible to the men of a former generation." [16]

In the remaining lectures the speaker defended man's ability to know the Infinite and Eternal Power behind all phenomena (in opposition to Herbert Spencer); man's moral freedom (against materialists in the scientific field and predestinarians in the theological realm); the value of prayer (without breach of natural law); the deity of Jesus Christ; the historical trustworthiness of the Gospels; and the hope of immortality. " The fact that theology is becoming more and more ethical, that it is dropping those dogmas such as original sin and unconditional election, which confound our moral sense," was given as one of the marks of the advancing Kingdom of God.

" The central truths of the Christian religion," the lecturer concluded, " stand as firmly today as ever they stood. Criticism has demolished some of the cumbrous and obstructive outworks of our theology; it was a good service and ought to be frankly acknowledged; but the assaults of destructive criticism upon the citadel of our faith have been impotent.

The things that can be shaken are disappearing . . . the things that cannot be shaken will remain. Science can neither confute nor demonstrate the first truths of religion, but science has made these truths more probable than once they were." [17]

The second great question which Gladden felt compelled to face was the question of inspiration. When he began his ministry in Springfield, in 1875, higher criticism had not forced man to face the issue; when he came to Columbus, less than a decade later, the issue could no longer be avoided. The work of the English revisers on the King James Version of the Scriptures had emphasized the uncertainties of the text. But the majority of ministers seemed reluctant to acquaint laymen with the simplest facts which they themselves accepted as a matter of course. On one occasion Washington Gladden discovered that he was the only minister in a group of twenty who felt that it was safe to inform laymen that all scholars recognized I John 5:7 as an interpolation.

Gradually, however, the results of the new critical studies carried out in Germany began to come to the popular attention. They were reported, not only in the new Biblical commentaries and in an occasional ' heretical ' book, but also in newspapers and magazines. Gladden's work brought him into intimate contact with young men in the university and in the medical schools. Many of them, he found, had been convinced by the lectures of Robert Ingersoll that the Bible contained discrepancies and contradictions, as well as various moral blemishes. " When, therefore, they were told by their pastors and teachers that the admission of a single error in the Bible rendered it worthless, they saw no other way than to cast it aside, and this they were doing by scores and hundreds." [18]

Gladden was deeply pained by this growing contempt for the Bible on the part of young men who ought to become the leaders of the Church. He was convinced that it came from an unfortunate attempt to force upon men a theory of the origin of the Bible to which its own pages gave overwhelming contradiction. He proceeded therefore to deliver a series of Sunday evening lectures to his congregation on the origin of the Bible. The lectures were attended by the largest congregations he had yet known, and though some were apprehensive at first, they became more sympathetic as the course of lectures unfolded. Gladden was more convinced that ministers were too apprehensive about the risks they ran in telling the truth. "If we speak kindly and considerately with due regard for the convictions of those who differ from us," he said, "truth speaking is not ordinarily a dangerous venture." These lectures were subsequently published under the title of *Who Wrote the Bible* and were more widely circulated than any other of his books, being used for many years as a manual of instruction in Bible classes and in the Y. M. C. A.

In the earlier chapters the author gives the literary history of the Bible as understood by the best scholars of the day. In the final chapter he concludes that the Bible is "a book of righteousness" and a "record of the development of the Kingdom of righteousness in the world." It is not, however, an infallible book, scientifically, or historically, or morally. It was plain that Washington Gladden and a host of others no longer accepted the unconditioned authority of the Scriptures.

A supplement to this book, entitled *Seven Puzzling Bible Books,* published half a dozen years later, insists that it is safe to inform the laity of the results of Biblical criticism, and that it is the duty of the minister so to do even where it is not desired, because concealment of the truth is likely to result in serious practical error. "It is not safe," Gladden asserts, "to put the Bible into any man's hands until you have told him distinctly that it is not the kind of book which many people suppose it to be. . . . A long dark catalogue of crimes and wrongs can be traced directly to a misunderstanding of the true character of the Bible by men who believed themselves to be doing God's will." " The fundamental error of many of those who have found warrant in the Bible for cruelty and oppression," he adds, " was not merely their failure to get the true meaning of the writers but their failure to understand the true nature of the book — their erroneous belief that the Bible in all its parts is equally inspired and equally authoritative. That is a dangerous belief as history abundantly proves. It is not only safe, therefore, to tell the people the truth about the Bible, it is very unsafe to conceal from them the truth and to leave them under the bondage of an erroneous tradition." [19]

The deepest reason why some are unwilling to abandon the dogma of Biblical infallibility, he found, is the notion that some kind of infallible guide is necessary in religion. " It is now about time," he believes, " to see that [this] fundamental assumption is all wrong; that no infallible rule in religion is either desirable or possible." [20] " The revelation which we need from God is not an infallible rule, applicable to all conditions of life and grades of intelligence; it is rather a path of light through the ages, giving us direction, but leaving us free, in the light of great principles, to settle for ourselves the problems of every hour and of every generation. Such a guide the Bible is." [21]

5

The widespread abandonment of inerrant inspiration and the general acceptance of the theory of evolution, along with growing reliance on moral intuition and experience as tests of Christian truth, led to increasing modification of the traditional doctrines on the part of leading Christian thinkers. As the century drew to a close (1899), Washington Gladden issued a new volume, *How Much Is Left of the Old Doc-*

trines — A Book for the People, based as before on a series of Sunday evening lectures to his own congregation. "I am going to maintain," he asserted at the outset, "that the intelligent Christian may stand in the presence of modern thought and accept everything that has been proved by science or history or criticism, and not be frightened at all by any of it; firmly believing that the great verities of the Christian faith will still remain untouched." [22]

Frank H. Foster complains that this volume reveals an element of inconsistency in Gladden's thinking. Doctrines are accepted, and others discussed, simply because they are found in the Bible or in the creeds of the Church. "To drop the idea of the authority of the Bible has not yet come to mean to drop also all those doctrines which depend solely upon the Bible, and are the efforts of men to explain matters which are either better explained in some other way, or else need no explanation, such as the Trinity, Incarnation, and Atonement." [23] At least his words suggest the lines along which some modern thought would soon begin to move.

Fourteen years after the publication of *How Much Is Left,* Washington Gladden, now seventy-seven years of age, attempted once more to bring his congregation up to date on the most recent theological developments. In these lectures, published under the title of *Present Day Theology,* Gladden sought to present the ideas "which thoughtful and intelligent men of all denominations are accepting." He was moved to treat this subject once again because he had discovered that doctrines presented in their traditional form failed to produce conviction. Young men and women attending college and university, who were unable to reconcile their inherited religious notions with demonstrated truth in other fields, fell naturally and inevitably into agnosticism. Many painful cases had come to Gladden's attention.

"What right," he indignantly explodes, "has any minister of the Gospel to send out young men and women from his church into the world in such a benighted condition, liable to be wrecked in their religious thinking, as soon as they come in contact with the living and constructive thought of their generation? If he is so stupid or so ignorant or so indolent or so cowardly that he cannot find out and deliver the truth that God is revealing to the world today, let him get out of the pulpit. A coal mine would furnish him a more fitting environment and a far more useful occupation." [24]

In developing the fundamental tenets of *Present Day Theology*, Gladden does not advance for the most part beyond the positions which he had set forth in his previous volume.

The central truth of the Reformed theology on which America had builded was the sovereignty of God; the ruling concept of the new theology, as explained by Gladden, was belief in the divine immanence, the fact that God is in nature, especially human nature, working out his great designs; that nature exhibits the method of his working; that history reveals him; that what we call progress is only the carrying forward of his eternal purpose; that all the good deeds and the loving services of men are the signs of his presence; that therefore there is more of God in the world today than ever before.

This doctrine of divine immanence affects greatly one's idea of ultimate religious authority. In one of his most important books, *The Church and Modern Life*, written five years earlier, Gladden had recognized three sources of religious truth — nature, humanity (attaining its perfection in Jesus Christ), and "that divine Spirit who is always in the world, and always waiting upon the threshold of every man's thought." [25] Almost inevitably the last tended to become the more important. In present-day theology that trend is made implicit.

"I do not see," Gladden says, "how any man who believes

156

in a living and present God, a God who is dwelling among his people and educating them by His Spirit, can help seeing that theology, which is simply man's explanation of God's relation to them and to the world, *must continually change as their education progresses,* and as they get clear and more adequate ideas about him. The notion that theology can be tied up to one set of formulas . . . seems to me a flat . . . and even contemptuous denial of the one sublime and vital truth of religion — the fact of God's constant presence in the world and of the leadership of his Spirit in our study of the truth." [26] Some may object that theology is given once for all in the Bible. Gladden replies: " I do not admit the truth of this, but if it were true, the case would not be altered in the least, because man's interpretation of the Bible must change as man's spiritual vision is enlarged and purified." [27] And the same argument applies if Christ be taken as the revelation of the truth, " for our interpretation of Christ changes equally with enlarging vision." Gladden puts it very succinctly: Present-day theology is " the explanation given by the Christian consciousness of this time of the truths of Christianity." [28] Present-day theology, he says again, even more simply, " finds the revelation of essential truth in the social consciousness." [29]

" So far as the relations of God and man are concerned," writes Gladden, " what has happened to the old theology, what has transformed it into the new theology, is simply this, that the ruling conception of God as Sovereign, Ruler, Moral Governor, has been exchanged for the ruling conception of God as Father." [30]

No changes are more important than those which this new theology brought concerning nature and the supernatural. In the old theology, says Gladden, the relation was one of contrast; in the new theology the distinction between the two ceases, or becomes thoroughly unreal. Natural and supernatural have in fact become identified.

157

The new theology is willing to admit that we inherited from our first ancestors weakened or impaired moral natures, tendencies to evil, but rejects original sin in its traditional form, particularly the "horribly unethical" notion of original guilt. The old theology thought of the penalty of sin as the suffering inflicted upon the sinner by a judicial process in the future life. The new theology thinks more of the natural consequences of sin in the present life, a mode of thought which does away "at once and forever with all theories of legal substitution." Its prime concern is to save men, not from the consequences of sin in this world or in the next, but from sin itself.

Heaven and hell are not primarily places; they are states of character. They are not figures of speech; they are present realities of human experience. Death works no miraculous change in the human heart. Probably, says Gladden, we shall go as the Scripture says, each to his own place; that is, we shall find the associations and occupations that are congenial. As so many of his contemporaries, Gladden could not accept the idea of the persistence of evil in the universe. "Evil," he said, "may come to an end through the final restoration to virtue of all wandering and sinning souls, or it may cease through the sinking into non-existence of the disobedient and the incorrigible." [31]

The old doctrine of Christ's person, based on two contrasted natures, is no longer tenable, in the opinion of Dr. Gladden. Modern theologians, he explains, begin with the human Christ. And the view most commonly held is that of Albrecht Ritschl, who goes no farther than to say that to the Church, Christ has the value of God. According to this view, Christ is more than other men, "so much more that we have no terms in which to express the difference; more, but not *other;* his nature is the same as ours; and towards that glorious perfection we are called to rise. . . . 'This is not to say that we shall never reach that standard, too, quite the contrary. We must reach it in order to fulfill our destiny and crown and complete his work.'" [32] This would seem to mean that Washington Gladden had rejected the essential deity of Christ which once he affirmed. Christ is simply the first-born among many brethren; ultimately we shall become divine, in the same sense in which he is divine.

To an increasing number of men and women in Gladden's day the old doctrines had ceased to carry conviction; they seemed remote from experience; they collided with the rising moral sentiments. As a result, traditional theology, based on metaphors that had lost their vitality, actually appeared to be an immoral theology. The theory of evolution, now generally accepted; the philosophy of divine immanence, to which it naturally gave birth; the new views of natural law, which seemed to rule out the supernatural as it was popularly understood; the accepted results of historical criticism which could no longer be ignored — all seemed to necessitate a modification, a restatement of theological beliefs in terms which were intelligible and could be accepted by modern minds. Ministers like Washington Gladden who developed the "New Theology," as it was called, and sought to transmit it to their congregations were motivated not only by a zeal for the truth, but also by love for God who had manifested himself supremely in Jesus Christ, and by love for men who were sons of a common Father.

There can be no doubt that they rendered the Church valuable service in pruning off excrescencies, which had become liabilities instead of assets; in making it possible for thoughtful, well-informed men, imbued with the new scientific outlook, to maintain their connection with the Church; in relating religion to men's actual experience, and in making it more vital and real.

At the same time it becomes increasingly apparent that in their readiness to accept the philosophy and scientific outlook of their own day they surrendered or at least jeopardized essential Christian truth. In the conviction that between God and men there is a common measure of morality, they tended to make man — man's moral sentiment, man's modern sentimentality — the measure of divine action and the touchstone for divine truth. In their emphasis on the divine immanence, they increasingly ignored the divine transcendence, and tended to confine God within the bounds of the natural. In their insistence on God's present-day revelation in nature and in the moral consciousness of mankind, they tended to lose sight of God's historic revelation in the Bible. Their view that Christ is the culmination of an evolutionary process made him in the last analysis merely a man, and thus cut the roots of Christianity as a continuing force in the life of mankind.

On the other hand, it must be remembered that Gladden's theology, like the New Theology as a whole, was definitely Christocentric. "The manifestation of the life of God in Jesus Christ we call The Incarnation," Gladden wrote; "and it was a manifestation so much more perfect than any other that the world has seen that we do well to put the definite article before the word." [33] Gladden's own supreme loyalty to Christ cannot be doubted. His peculiarity among the ministers and the theologians of his day was not his theology, which he held in common with many of his contemporaries. Neither was it his energy and his success in popularizing this theology throughout the Church.

It was, rather, his conviction, and his readiness to act upon the conviction, that Jesus had revealed God's law for all human life, and that his principles, faithfully applied, would solve the problems of industry, the problems of government, all the deep-rooted, dangerous, running sores of civilization. "It is open to any man," he said to the theological students of Drew Seminary, "to say that Jesus Christ knew nothing about the proper ordering of social relations, that while he may be a safe guide for those who wish to find the way to heaven, he is not to be trusted as a social philosopher. And this is practically what is said by a good many persons in the Church as well as out of it. Those who are most eager to affirm his divinity are often most bold to deny his authority when he speaks of human relationships and obligations. For my own part, I must confess that I cannot so divide his words; and that his teaching respecting the divine Fatherhood, with its corollary (the brotherhood of man), appears to me to be the very substance of his mission." [34]

It was in his varied application of these twin truths to the problems of his own day that Gladden made his most significant contribution to the onward march of the Gospel. His theology reflects the thought of other men, but in this field, the field of applied Christianity, the movement that came to be known as the Social Gospel, he was a pioneer.

6

Washington Gladden's concern for the social application of the Gospel grew out of his practical experience as a pastor.

He came into contact with the nascent labor problem in North Adams. When he took up his position, the relation between employer and employee was still personal and essentially democratic. Before he left the situation had begun to change. Strikebreakers had been imported and the old relations had altered, never to return.

When Gladden arrived in Springfield, the industrial issue was becoming acute. Two years before there had been a financial collapse. In 1875, when he assumed this new pastorate, large numbers of steady and industrious workingmen were still unable to secure employment. Meetings were being held in the city hall, agitators were at work, and the situation was growing dangerous. The new pastor was asked to address the group. Gladden did not at this time recognize the obligation of the community to provide employment for men thrown out of work through no fault of their own as he did at a later time. He pointed out some of the difficulties in the way and then urged the men to accept any work that offered itself, regardless of pay. It was better, he said, to work under any conditions than to beg or to resort to violence. The next Sunday he explained the plight of the unemployed in Springfield to his own congregation, and urged that those who were able provide work, and, if necessary, make work. There was a remarkable response to this plea, and the situation in the city was relieved.

It was apparent to Mr. Gladden, however, that a new problem had appeared — a problem which would become increasingly acute not only in America, but throughout the world; a problem in which the Church must be concerned, in which indeed its very life was at stake. It was essentially, he felt, a problem of conduct, of human relations — a problem which could be solved, but could be solved only by an application of the law of Christ. The Church, it seemed to him, ought to know how to apply this law to industry as to the rest of life.

Strangely enough, this was a novel idea. Men generally believed that application of the law of Christ to industrial life was not the Church's business. The Church's single concern, they declared, was to save souls; if that were done, the industrial problem would solve itself. It was easy to point out that this was not true to life; that it was an unreal judgment, with no basis in fact. Men whom the Church regarded as converted, and who must be accepted as regenerate men, were not always characterized by social understanding or even by social sympathy. " Many of them," Gladden found, " were practising injustice and cruelty, without any sense of the evil of their conduct. They were nearly all assuming that the Christian rule of life had no application to business; that the law of supply and demand was the

162

only law which, in the world of exchanges, they were bound to respect. If a man was converted and joined the church, it did not occur to him that that fact had any relation to the management of his mill or his factory. Business was business and religion was religion; the two areas were not coterminous; they might be mutually exclusive. Nothing was more needed in the church," he concluded, "than the enforcement upon the consciences of men of the truth that the Christian law covers every relation of life, and the distinct and thoroughgoing application of that law to the common affairs of men." [35]

But there was another objection to the discussion of such topics in the pulpit, Washington Gladden discovered, that was even more prevalent than the former — the common feeling that ministers were not competent to deal with such matters. Since they had no knowledge of business or of economics, they were advised to let them alone.

Gladden recognized that for many ministers this was the easiest way to dispose of the matter. It would exempt them from a good many knotty problems and a good many painful experiences, if only they could get a dispensation from their consciences to evade the subject. And considerable pressure would be brought to bear upon them to follow this course. But Gladden felt that it was a question which ministers could not afford to ignore. Their business is to save souls. Souls are men. "How to save men, their manhood, their character" — that is the minister's chief problem. There is no realm where character, manhood, is more rapidly and more inevitably made or lost than that of industry. "Is the man saved," he asked, "who, in his dealings with his employee or his employer, can habitually seek his own aggrandizement at the cost of the other? Is not the selfishness which is expected to rule in all this department of life the exact antithesis of Christian morality? Is there anything else from which men need more to be saved than from the habits of thought and action which prevail in the places where 'business is business'? " [36]

In time another consideration came to weigh even more heavily upon Gladden's mind, and that was the growing alienation of labor from the Church. Careful investigation and long experience convinced him that this significant phenomenon was due to the steadily increasing hostility between employer and employee and to the steadily widening breach between the rich and the poor. The working people were convinced that the Churches were mainly under the control of the capitalists and those sympathetic with their point of view. " It is sadly true," Gladden wrote in 1908, " that there are many among these toiling millions who are embittered against the Church, who have no faith in it, and no expectation that any good will come out of it; but the great majority are not hostile to the Church; at worst they are indifferent, and this indifference is due to their belief that the Church no longer represents Jesus Christ." [37] The only way in which the Church could reverse this movement of the working class away from the Church, he felt, was by manifesting an intelligent and sympathetic concern in their aspirations and in their difficult struggle for economic justice.

In this question regarding capital and labor, Gladden believed that the Christian Church was facing its crucial test. If it met this question squarely and solved it successfully, its future was secure. It would have won its right to the moral leadership of society. If it failed to meet the challenge, if this important problem was worked out without its aid, the world would have very little use for it in the generations to come. " The Church is in the world to save the world; if it lacks the power to do this, and industrial society plunges into chaos, are there any ecclesiastics infatuated enough to believe that the Church can save itself out of that wreck?

No," Gladden replies; " it must save society or go to ruin with it." [38]

It seemed to Gladden that a teacher of religion who confessed that he was unfit for effective service in the area of life where character was mainly won or lost, where the life of the Church was at stake, and where the destiny of the nation was trembling in the balance, was failing at the most crucial point. It was as if a physician should declare that he would prescribe for nettle rash and chicken pox, but must decline to deal with tuberculosis or typhoid fever or any of the great maladies that take such a terrible toll of human life.

Moved by such considerations, Washington Gladden delivered a series of Sunday evening lectures to his Springfield congregation on "Workingmen and Their Employers." In these lectures, later printed in book form, Gladden defended the right of workingmen to organize, so long as they abstained from violence and relied upon reason and moral influence, though he was not so sympathetic toward the unions as he became in later years. His principal contention, and one from which he never departed, was that a solution for industrial problems could be found only in co-operation, based on Christian motives of love for one's neighbor as well as love for one's self. In later years it did not seem to him that this was an important book, but it was a serious attempt to deal with an important question, and it was the first of a series of volumes dealing more vitally with the same issue.

Gladden believed that co-operation should prevail, not only in industry, but also among the Churches. The days when "keen contempt and bitter abuse were common currency among the sects" were in process of passing; some persons were even beginning to look forward to organic unity of some, or all, of the great branches of Christendom.

But little or nothing had been done to promote effective co-operation among the Churches, and to Gladden's practical mind this seemed the more promising line of procedure. In 1883 he wrote a series of four articles for *The Century* telling how the Christians of a little New England town came together and united their forces in practical Christian work, and how the movement grew until it culminated in "The Christian League of Connecticut," whose influence was being felt in this and other lands. These articles, later printed in book form, proved to be the most popular of all the many magazine articles that he wrote and stimulated co-operation and consolidation in many overchurched communities.

7

Shortly after Gladden came to Columbus, the Hocking Valley strike once more brought the industrial issue before him and made him realize as never before "the critical character of the relations between the men who are doing the work of the world and the men who are organizing and directing it." Company officials, who were members of Gladden's own congregation, informed their pastor that they intended to crush the union at any cost. They succeeded for the moment — at terrific cost to themselves and to the men. But within a year the union was again organized, collective bargaining was the practice, and the manager of the company admitted that it was better to have an organized and disciplined force to deal with than a mob. Gladden felt that this mounting tension between capital and labor brought questions which he, as Christian teacher, moral counselor and guide, could not avoid.

About the same time a fierce strike broke out in the city of Cleveland. Washington Gladden was invited as one reasonably impartial to address a mass meeting of employers and laborers. "Is it peace or war?" was the question he put to his audience. The great combinations effected by capital, he held, necessitated combinations of labor as measures of defense. Such combinations under the present competitive system meant war. And war is a great evil — but not, said Gladden, the greatest evil. "The permanent degradation of men who do the world's work would be a greater evil." But industrial warfare, he proceeded to point out, threatened to become disastrous to both parties. "It is a sorry comment on our civilization that here, at the end of the nineteenth Christian century, sane and full-grown men, whose welfare depends wholly on the recognition of their mutual interests and on the co-operation of their efforts, should be ready to spend a good share of their time in trying to cripple or destroy one another. It is not only wicked, it is stupid; it is not simply monstrous, it is ridiculous." [39] After addressing words of practical counsel to both employers and employed, he closed with the questions: "Is it well, brother men, is it well to fight? Is it not better to be friends? Are you not all children of one Father . . . members one of another? . . . Promise that you will do what you can, every one of you, to bring the day when between Labor and Capital there shall be no longer war but peace for evermore." [40]

The laboring group, who dominated the meeting and had evidently come in a critical mood, were won by Gladden's recognition of the right of labor to organize. They cheered him so heartily at the close that he was convinced that the "hearts of fifteen hundred workingmen were in the right place." The following week the same address was delivered to a notable assemblage in Boston, composed mostly of the employing class, and the following week, at their suggestion, to a group of workingmen in Boston, including a number of outstanding labor leaders. The hearty reception of this speech by both groups persuaded Gladden that at this time "the chasm between the contending classes was not so wide but that it could be spanned by reason and good will." And this impression was deepened by several conferences carried on at the instigation of Gladden between employers and labor leaders at Columbus and Toledo.

The address delivered at Cleveland, along with other addresses on this and allied subjects delivered to his own congregation on Sunday evenings and later published in *The Century*, were brought together in an important volume entitled *Applied Christianity*. The publishers hesitated at first over the adjective, but were led to see that it carried the whole significance of the book; that " the thing which the world needed most was a direct application of the Christian law to the business of life." The book was tremendously popular and made common a phrase which carried the heart of Gladden's message. To the end of his life he was convinced that the disorders of the industrial world and all the disorders of society could be solved, and could be solved only by the application to them of the Christian law of life, particularly as embodied in the Second Great Commandment: " Thou shalt love thy neighbor as thyself."

The industrial problem was during this period the most pressing problem, and it continued to engage much of his interest. It was treated again at length in a course of lectures delivered on the Lyman Beecher Foundation at Yale in 1889, and published under the title of *Tools and the Man;* touched upon in a series of lectures delivered in Chicago and to the students of Iowa College and published under the title of *Social Facts and Forces;* and in a series of lectures given to the students of Drew Seminary in 1905 and published under the title of *Christianity and Socialism*. It was treated again in his important book on *The Church and Modern Life,* and in *The Labor Question* in 1911.

Over and over again Gladden insisted that labor had a

right to organize — that it must organize, indeed, in spite of inevitable abuses, to defend itself against the powerful combinations of capital. The organization of capital and labor under our present competitive system, however, means war, which is disastrous to the interests of both capital and labor, and to the nation as well. For many years Gladden argued that the solution for this impasse was some sort of industrial partnership, some type of profit-sharing, which would give capital and labor a mutual interest in the success of industry. In his later years he was forced to recognize that labor and capital had drawn steadily apart, and that the good will of former times had largely evaporated. This was due in part, he felt, to the unreasonable attitude of labor and in part to the almost vindictive opposition of some employers.

This growing cleavage between workingmen and their employers, between capital and labor, troubled Gladden more than anything else. He felt the evil of men out of work, of families living in want in the presence of unexampled abundance, but more serious still, and more ominous for the future, was the growing alienation and enmity by which social classes were set against one another — " the cold, haughty temper of the House of Have and the envy and hatred of the House of Want."

Industrial warfare, Gladden was convinced, could not endure forever. Socialism, which increasing numbers looked to as the only alternative, he rejected as impracticable — better than the prevalent individualism, but carrying new dangers of its own. The remedy, he pointed out, must be evolutionary and not revolutionary, and this meant increasing Government ownership and control.

Though Gladden, along with other early advocates of the Social Gospel, regarded the labor problem as the most pressing question before the American public, his interests

ranged out over the whole of life. In his second series of
lectures on the Lyman Beecher Foundation, published under the title of *Social Salvation,* he gave his attention "to
other problems with which the Christian pulpit needs to
concern itself" — the poor, the unemployed, prisoners, social vices, public education, and the redemption of the city.
This latter problem, indeed, was one which was much on
his mind. As religious editor of the *Independent* he had
taken an active part in arousing popular indignation against
the Tweed Ring in 1871. From the start he had taken a
keen interest in the civic life of Columbus. In the early
nineties the looseness and inefficiency of municipal governments in America began to arouse public concern. Washington Gladden wrote three articles for *The Century* on
"The Cosmopolis City Club," an imaginary story telling
how a group of men in an American city organized a club
for the study of municipal conditions, how they investi-
gated and exposed abuses, and how they effected a more
satisfactory municipal organization. Publication of these
articles in book form in 1893 was followed by a rapid increase in the number of municipal clubs, many of them pat-
terned after the Cosmopolis Club of Washington Gladden.
In 1900, Gladden was elected a member of the city council
of Columbus and played a modest part in solving some of
the city's most pressing problems. As he drew toward the
close of his career, he was forced to admit that not much
progress had been made in the matter of civic reform. No
plan can be devised, he said, which will give us good city
government, so long as the great majority of our citizens are
unwilling to pay the price. He remained convinced, however, that if the Kingdom of God was to come to any city, it
must come in and through the city hall.

Out of such practical interests, Washington Gladden, with other pioneers, developed what came to be known as the Social Gospel.

The end of Christianity, as he saw it, was twofold, a perfect man in a perfect society. "These purposes," he reiterated again and again, "are never separated; they cannot be separated. No man can be redeemed and saved alone; no community can be reformed and elevated save as the individuals of which it is composed are regenerated." [41]

To accomplish this twofold aim, the Church must begin where Christ began — with the individual. It must seek, as he sought, first of all to bring men into filial relations with God. If, however, a man comes into right relations with his Father in heaven, he cannot remain in wrong relations with his brother on the earth.

The Church is not an end in itself — it is an instrument — a means employed by God for promoting the Kingdom of Heaven. "The Kingdom of Heaven," says Gladden, "is not an ecclesiastical establishment; it includes the whole of life — business, politics, art, education, philanthropy, society in the narrow sense, the family: when all these shall be pervaded and controlled by the law of love, then the Kingdom of Heaven will have fully come. And the business of the Church in the world is to bring all these departments of life under Christ's law of love. If it seeks to convert men, it is that they may be filled with the spirit of Christ and may govern their conduct among men by Christ's law. If it gathers them together for instruction or for inspiration, it is that they may be taught Christ's way of life and sent out into the world to live as he lived among their fellow men. Its function is to fill the world with the knowledge of Christ, the love of Christ, the life of Christ." [42]

In seeking to carry out this obligation the Church is to

rely entirely on moral and spiritual instruments. It cannot use force in any way, nor enter into any coalition with Governments that rest on force. It should not attempt to dictate or prescribe the form of industrial society or even to take sides in the present controversy between collectivism and private enterprise. "Its business is to fill men's minds with the truth as it is in Jesus, and to make them see that that truth applies to every human relation; and it ought to believe that when this truth is thus received and thus applied, it will solve all social problems." [43]

Ministers cannot fulfill their own responsibility, or create in the Church an eager desire to lessen the sorrow, the suffering, and the injustice, as well as the sin, of the world, by purely abstract teaching. They must be ready in wise proportion to " set forth the law of love, as it applies to the institutions and the customs of society, and show what evils result from its violation, and what blessings flow from obeying it." [44] "For although it is not the business of the Church to furnish to the world an economic programme, it is her business to see that no economic programme is permitted to exist under which injustice and oppression find shelter. The right to reprove and denounce all social arrangements by which the few prosper at the expense of the many is one of her chartered rights as the institute of prophecy. A church which fails to exercise this function is faithless to her primary obligation." [45]

But though it is the duty of the Church " to bring home to men the obligations of the law, and to show them wherein they are failing to obey it," its primary task is to preach the Gospel, to revitalize social morality by the spirit of religion. No social morality can endure unless it have a religious foundation. Nothing, therefore, is ultimately so important as the deepening of men's faith in the great religious verities. No social reform will be adequate unless it springs from a genuine revival of religion. The religion, however, " which needs to be revived is not that which puts the sole emphasis on the safety and welfare of the individual, but that which equally exalts the social welfare; which identifies the interest of each with the interests of all; which makes men see and feel that no salvation is worth anything to any man that does not put that man into Christian relations with his neighbors. Nothing but religion will do this for any man, and the religion which fails to do this is a spurious Christianity." [46]

Gladden felt that the Church of his own day was weakened by its lack of faith — not in the person of Christ, but in the teachings of Christ. "It believes the Nicene Creed," he lamented, "but it does not believe the Sermon on the Mount." [47] It was weakened, likewise, by its subjection to orthodoxism, the assumption that essential truth had been sought out, registered, and certified once for all and finally. Its sectarianism also weakened it. To this Gladden returned again and again. The Church's first duty in the light of the world's pressing need is to recognize and realize its own unity. The need is not that of organic unity, but of effective co-operation, and the most important place to begin is in the local community, the city, or the village. Still another cause of the Church's enfeeblement, which Gladden sought to emphasize, was its too close reliance upon the principles and forces of the material realm. He was disturbed because the Church had forfeited the confidence and lost the sympathy and support of the working people, who were bound increasingly to dominate the society of the future; it had been too ready, he felt, to sacrifice truth for the revenues of the rich or the friendship of the strong.

It was this conviction that led Dr. Gladden, when he was Moderator of the Congregational Church, to protest vigorously against a large gift made to the Mission Board of his Church by Mr. John D. Rockefeller. He made his protest under the impression that the gift had been unsolicited.

It was revealed thereafter that the Mission Board had sought the gift over a period of several years, but in Dr. Gladden's estimation this only made the situation worse. It was just after Ida Tarbell's strongly documented *History of the Standard Oil Company* had called public attention to the sources of Mr. Rockefeller's wealth and aroused heated indignation against Mr. Rockefeller and the business methods which he embodied. In Dr. Gladden's estimation the money was "tainted money" which the Church had no right to receive. He did not suggest that the Church must examine scrupulously every cent of its income and refuse to receive all that had not been earned in accordance with the Christian ideal. He did argue that reception of money by Churches or by Church institutions from sources that were notoriously corrupt tended to shut the Church's mouth against those particular evils, to set up false standards of value in the eyes of those dependent on the Church's teaching, and to impair its prestige among the poor.

The widespread agitation to which Dr. Gladden's attack gave rise seemed to settle nothing. The Mission Board did not return the money, nor did it ever acknowledge its mistake. But in Dr. Gladden's own estimation it cleared the air. "Even the man in the street," he wrote in his *Recollections,* "is able to see that the alliance of churches and colleges with public enemies is not a good thing; that one man's money is decidedly not as good as another man's — when the acceptance of the money involves partnership with evil-doers or condonation of nefarious conduct." Even politicians, he claimed, were tending to become sensitive about such matters, and added, "I have no doubt the churches and the colleges will be more so, one of these days." [48]

Gladden was convinced that in time Christ's law would become supreme in all of human society. This optimistic attitude, which he shared with other early advocates of the Social Gospel, was stimulated no doubt by the theory of evolution, along with the new theology's fundamental conviction that man is essentially good. In Gladden's estimation it resulted from faith in Christ's teaching as the only workable rule of life. "All the signs indicate," he wrote early in the present century, "that modern society is being forced by the disastrous failure of the methods of strife to entertain the possibility of co-operation as the fundamental social law. The multiplication of armaments has become not only an enormity, but a howling farce; it is impossible that the nations should go on making fools of themselves after this fashion. The industrial conflict is no whit less irrational. And the terrible collapses in big business during the last decade have reduced to absurdity the scheme of the graspers. Who wants to climb to their bad eminence? If there are still many who do, there is certainly an increasing of those who feel that such success is a dismal failure. And the conviction grows that the Golden Rule is, after all, the only workable rule of life; that we must learn how to live by it. This is the sign of promise. Is He really coming to his Kingdom? One would like to live fifty years longer just to see." [49]

Gladden's optimism was grounded also in his faith in God. He believed with H. G. Wells that something goes on "that is constantly working to make order out of casualty, beauty out of confusion, justice, kindliness, mercy out of cruelty and inconsiderate pressure." "My own confidence," he affirmed, "goes down to the bedrock of all my beliefs that what ought to be is going to be. If I believe in God at all, I must believe that." [50]

To men of the present day it is easy to see that Gladden was overly optimistic; too imbued with the idea of progress; too ready to believe that the problems of society could be solved by the development of good will, motivated by Christ and guided by an enlightened social intelligence; too prone to rely on moral suasion and on rational appeals to the intellect. He did not see how deeply rooted sin is in the human heart, how it distorts and blinds the vision of all men — even the best of them — how difficult it is for any social group voluntarily to surrender power or prestige, and how violently such a group will react when its prerogatives are seriously threatened. He was not sufficiently aware of the powerful social forces that were even then hurrying mankind toward destruction. As he failed to understand man's nature realistically, so also he failed to grasp fully the sterner aspects of God's character, to realize that in the divine Providence there is judgment as well as mercy and crisis as well as progress. And yet Washington Gladden was among the first to catch the significance of the labor movement for society and also for the Church; one of the first to recognize the danger that threatened civilization when a large and dynamic section of the general population had no real stake in the maintenance of that civilization. He was one of the first to attempt to turn Christian thought from its preoccupation with the individual to the steadily mounting problems of the social order, and one of the first to recognize that Jesus who is alone able to save the individual is also alone able to save society.

9

With others of his generation, Washington Gladden held high hopes of a warless world. "We are going to make an end of international wars very soon," he wrote in 1909; "the absurdity of that way of settling the disputes of nations is becoming apparent to all civilized peoples." [51]

The outbreak of the World War in August, 1914, was a shock to him as it was to others, but it did not shake his fundamental convictions. He set forth his idea of the genesis of the war and his cure for war in a little book, published in 1916, entitled *The Forks of the Road,* a book which was awarded the prize offered by the Church Peace Union for the best essay on war and peace.

Co-operation, Gladden repeated, is not only the law of Christ; it is also the law of life. Disregard of this law brings inevitable suffering to mankind. Three realms — industry, politics, and international relations — have remained outside the pale of Christian ethics. Most powerful of these kingdoms of Antichrist is the last, where it has been the rule for each nation to seek its own interests at the expense of its neighbors. The militaristic policy, based on the assumption that all nations are enemies and developed most fully in Germany, has led the world through centuries of steadily accumulating disaster to this culminating catastrophe, in which civilization itself is now imperiled.

The crucial question for mankind is whether or not this lesson is being learned, whether militarism will be repudiated at the peace table, whether the nations will build on the old system of hatred and war, or on the new system of brotherhood and peace. Gladden did not attempt to suggest details of the plan that must be formulated to achieve this end. He did suggest, however, the advisability of a League of Peace, with an international police force to insure that its policies should be enforced.

The Church, he argued, is also standing at the forks of the road. Its fundamental convictions regarding the Fatherhood of God and the brotherhood of man wipe out all distinctions of caste, annul all repugnances of race, and break down the barriers of nationality. " If anything is central in Christianity, it is this obliteration of the lines of division between races and nationalities and the inclusion of the world in one brotherhood. Whatever other truths might be made subordinate or secondary, this truth of the divine Fatherhood and the human Brotherhood were to be lifted into the light and held before the thought of the world." [52] But the Church in the past has diluted her mes-

sage. She has incorporated in her teaching " large elements
of the tribalism and the egoistic imperialism whose bread
she has been eating, which is the flat contradiction of the
doctrine of Christ, and which is the efficient cause of war." [53]
She has failed to grasp and enforce the central truth of the
Kingdom which Jesus lived and died to reveal.

The present debacle of civilization, Gladden prophesied,
"will be but a ghastly horror, an eclipse of faith, if it does
not usher in a new day, with new international relationships, new bonds of unity, new guarantees of friendship,
new hopes of permanent peace. If such a day as that is
coming, the Christian Church ought to have the vision to
see it and the heart to meet it. She will have done far less
to bring it in than she ought to have done; it will come,
if it comes, rather as the result of a fearful retribution than
as the willing acceptance of the law of life.

"But when the nations, taught by whatever fiery tuition,
conclude that the way of Christ is the right way to live together, the Church ought to be ready to confirm their decision and to strengthen their purpose. But she ought also
to be able to see that if she would be of any service in this
new day some radical reconstructions will have to take place
in her doctrine and in her life. She will have to eliminate
the tribalism and the heathenism and the particularism of
her theology. She will have to tell the truth about the
Bible and put the life-giving spirit above the brain-befog-
ging and conscience-clogging letter. She will have to get
rid of her intolerant and divisive sectarianism and quit un-
churching and cursing men for differences of theological
opinion. She will have to cast into the abyss a good share
of her *Aberglaube* and her ecclesiastical flummery and come
back to the simplicity that is in Christ. And above all she
will have to take the great central truth of the divine Fatherhood with all its corollaries and make it the heart of
her teaching, and the inspiration of her life." [54]

When the United States itself finally entered the war, Gladden continued to hold out the same ideals for both Church and State. As always, he kept his eye on the future — the task that still needed to be done. " If after the war the Church keeps on with the same old religion," he warned in his New Year message for 1918, " there will be the same old hell on earth that religious leaders have been preparing for centuries, the full fruit of which we are gathering now. The Church must cease to sanction those principles of militaristic and atheistic nationalism by which the rulers of the earth have so long kept the world at war. We must not wait till after the war. That may be too late. Is not now the accepted time? " [55]

His last book, a series of sermons entitled *The Interpreter*, came from the press before the issues of the war had been decided and only a few months before his death.

God " is doing all that infinite love can do to fill the world with righteousness and peace," he said in a sermon on *Worlds in the Making*. " The one thing that infinite love cannot do is to take away from men the chance to be men. . . . This world will be Paradise as soon as men want Paradise enough to pay the price of it in labor and patience. God is always doing his part, but he will never do ours. . . . Worlds in the making! Races in the making! Nations, states, communties in the making! Men in the making! Our Father who has been working hitherto is as busy as ever today upon this work. Some of us know now how far it is from being finished. But it is a great joy and a great honor and a great inspiration that we may have some knowledge of what he is doing and some part with him in the work." [56]

These words might well be taken as Gladden's final message to the Church. But there are other words by which he is better known and by which he will be longest remembered. They were written when he was a young pastor in

Springfield, at a time when he was feeling keenly his position of theological isolation. More than any others they give us the secret of his life:

" O Master, let me walk with Thee
In lowly paths of service free;
Tell me Thy secret; help me bear
The strain of toil, the fret of care.

" Help me the slow of heart to move
By some clear, winning word of love;
Teach me the wayward feet to stay,
And guide them in the homeward way.

" Teach me Thy patience; still with Thee
In closer, dearer company,
In work that keeps faith sweet and strong,
In trust that triumphs over wrong;

" In hope that sends a shining ray
Far down the future's broadening way;
In peace that only Thou canst give,
With Thee, O Master, let me live."

Chapter V

WALTER RAUSCHENBUSCH
and the challenge of the
Social Gospel

$\mathcal{A}$ RECENT student has claimed that the "Social Gospel" is America's most unique contribution to the great ongoing stream of Christianity.[1] This characteristic expression of American religion began to develop shortly after the close of the Civil War. It was the Church's response to the rapidly expanding industrialism of the postwar period, the increasing tension of capital and labor, the widening breach between irresponsible wealth on the one hand and insufferable poverty on the other, leading to growing indifference and mounting hostility to the Church on the part of great masses of the people.

Among the myriad voices raised in advocacy and exposition of the Social Gospel, the clearest and most compelling was undoubtedly that of Walter Rauschenbusch. No man did more than he to arouse the social consciousness of American Christians; no one did so much to reveal the social implications of the Gospel. In the estimation of Reinhold Niebuhr, Rauschenbusch was "not only the real founder of social Christianity in this country, but also its most brilliant and generally satisfying exponent to the present day."[2] Ambrose White Vernon, in the *Cambridge History of American Literature*, describes him as "perhaps the most creative spirit in the American theological world." Henry Pitney Van Dusen thinks that in the last fifty years he has influenced the life and the thought of the Church more than any other single individual. "Probably the three most influential men in American Church history upon the thought of the Church," he continues, "have been Jonathan Edwards, Horace Bushnell, and Walter Rauschenbusch." [3]

I

The last of this trio was the seventh in a line of ministers, some of whom achieved considerable distinction, in a family whose heritage was deeply rooted in Pietism. His father and grandfather had been Lutheran pastors in the ancient town of Altena, in Westphalia, Germany. The former came to America in the disturbed decade of the 1840's as a missionary to his fellow countrymen who had emigrated to the land of promise. Shortly after his arrival here he became a Baptist and, in 1858, began to teach Church history and other subjects in the German department of Rochester Theological Seminary, a post which he retained for more than thirty years. He was an able teacher, strongly evangelical, and aggressively conservative.

Walter was born in Rochester on October 4, 1861. His mother, as Sharpe has said, had "quality," and from her Walter derived his urbanity, his strongly pronounced sense of humor, and his intense love of nature, coupled with habits of keen observation. The home atmosphere was strongly religious, centering about the Church, the Sunday School, and the family altar. It nurtured old-fashioned piety, but lacked social vision.

When the boy was three and a half years old, his mother returned to Germany, where she remained for the next four years. Walter began his schooling in the land of his fathers and continued it in Rochester, first in a private school and then in the Free Academy. Four more years were spent in travel and study in Germany. Young Rauschenbusch graduated with first honors from the Evangelical Gymnasium of Gütersloh in Westphalia and spent part of a year in the University of Berlin. Returning to Rochester, he took simultaneously his senior year at the university and his first year at Rochester Theological Seminary. He graduated from the former in 1884, from the German department of the latter in 1885, and from the English division in 1886.

He wished to go as a missionary to India, but one of his professors in the theological seminary objected to his 'liberal' views on the Old Testament, and the Baptist Board refused to appoint him.

Shut off from foreign mission fields, Rauschenbusch accepted the pastorate of a small Baptist Church in New York City, located in the tough West End, adjoining a region popularly known as Hell's Kitchen. His congregation was composed entirely of working people, a part of that vast flood of cheap labor drawn from the reservoirs of Europe and crowded now into the tenements of New York.

Rauschenbusch came to his first pastorate expecting to save souls "in the ordinary religious sense," but soon discovered that the old-fashioned gospel, taken by itself alone, could not adequately solve the problems of the New York slums.

America was prosperous; the wealth of the nation was mounting rapidly; but the people of Hell's Kitchen did not share in the good times. When work was plentiful they got along; when it was scarce they suffered; when hard times came, as they frequently did, they "sank into destitution, demoralization, prostitution and crime." Rauschenbusch lived among these people, saw their needs, and shared their sorrows. He counted the times a mother had to lift her carriage before she could find a square yard of grass for her baby. Many of these children died, he knew, of malnutrition and the indescribable living conditions of the New York tenements. The endless procession of men "out of work, out of clothes, out of shoes, and out of hopes" that wore down his threshold also wore away his strength. He

185

fell an easy victim to the influenza epidemic raging in New York during the winter of 1888. Venturing out too early in the great blizzard of that year to minister to sick and needy parishioners, he was again stricken, and as a result largely lost his hearing. Rauschenbusch was a sensitive man, unusually dependent on his friends, and this deafness, which in large measure shut him off from his fellows and doomed him to physical loneliness, was a tragedy, bravely borne, but keenly felt to the day of his death.

The burden of his people bore more heavily still upon his heart. He sought to apply his inherited religious ideas to the conditions he found, and discovered that they did not fit. Acceptance of Jesus Christ could give inner strength to the individual but had no effect on the system that continued to destroy the bodies and souls of men, to crush and destroy the spirits and the lives of little children. Armed with the simple Gospel of his fathers, following the traditional pattern of Church ministration, he and all the other ministers about him could not save souls as fast as they were destroyed in Hell's Kitchen.

"My social view," he said later, "did not come from the Church. It came from outside. It came through personal contact with poverty, and when I saw how men toiled all their life long, hard, toilsome lives, and at the end had almost nothing to show for it; how strong men begged for work and could not get it in hard times; how little children died — oh, the children's funerals! they gripped my heart — that was one of the things I always went away thinking about — why did the children have to die?" [4]

Henry George, passionate crusader for social justice, was campaigning vigorously at the time for election as mayor of New York. Rauschenbusch was deeply stirred. He felt that the Single Tax, using the unearned increment in land values for the common good, offered a way out. To this agitation, he confessed later, he owed his first awakening to the world of social problems. He began to read widely on economic and social matters — to absorb the ideas and the ideals of men who felt keenly the problems of the masses of the people. Before 1886 he had read the sermons of D. L. Moody, Alexander MacLaren, J. Hudson Taylor, and Henry Drummond. Now he read the words of the leading economists and found help and inspiration in men like Bellamy, Mazzini, Tolstoi, and Ruskin, the last of whom he described as the most Christlike thinker in all literature.

Meanwhile, he did not neglect the practical measures that lay at hand. With Jacob Riis he labored successfully for the establishment of playgrounds for the children of the slums and for fresh-air centers for the babies.

Looking back upon this period, Rauschenbusch said: " In the early dawn of the Social Awakening, we young men were groping in the dark. All our Christian intuitions assured us that this new call for social justice was of God, and that the very spirit of our Master was urging us on. But the older brethren told us that the true function of the ministry was not to ' serve tables,' but to save the immortal souls of men. One told me that these were ' mere questions of mine and thine ' and had nothing to do with the Gospel. A young missionary going to Africa to an early death implored me almost with tears to dismiss these social questions and give myself to ' Christian work.' Such appeals were painfully upsetting. All our inherited ideas, all theological literature, all the practices of church life seemed to be against us." [5]

This criticism of his fellow ministers, including some of his closest friends, the feeling generally prevalent that all this " social stuff " had nothing to do with religion, forced Rauschenbusch back to his Bible to see whether he or they were right. As he discovered the burning social interests of the prophets and the Master's similar passion for social justice, his own convictions were deepened.

187

He began to write on social questions for the religious papers and also for the secular press. In 1889 he and a number of friends united to publish *For the Right,* a monthly paper in which the " interests of the working class " were discussed "from the standpoint of Christian socialism." In the columns of this paper, for the next three years, Rauschenbusch gave his best thought on religious and social issues.

"One of the peculiarities which distinguished *For the Right* from many other papers akin to it," he wrote, " is that it stands for a combination of personal regeneration and social reform. Most of the social reformers claim that if only poverty and the fear of poverty could be abolished, men would cease to be grasping, selfish, overbearing and sensual. We do not see it so. . . .

" On the other hand we differ from many Christian men and women in our insistence on good institutions. They believe that if only men are personally converted wrong and injustice will gradually disappear from the construction of society. It does not appear so to us. Revivals in the South were not directly followed by a general freeing of slaves. Revivals in the North do not ease the pressure of competition in a community or stop speculations in land. Special work and hard work has to be done in pointing out a social wrong and thinking out its remedy, before the righteous purposes of a community can be brought to bear on it. This is essentially a function of those who profess to know and love God's will, and we raise the charge of negligence and sloth against the church of God in suffering injustice to be incorporated in the very construction of society." [6]

From these fundamental convictions — the necessity of individual regeneration, and its complement, the necessity of social reconstruction — Rauschenbusch never departed till the end of his days.

As he labored and wrote, his mind became more clear. He was convinced that his interest in the welfare of humanity was a religious interest and that his work on behalf of the poor was in accordance with the mind of the Master; but his religious life was not yet unified, and so he could not rest. He longed for a faith that would cover his whole life, and the traditional religious conceptions seemed to cover only a part of it. They explained how the individual could be saved, but said nothing about the salvation of society. That was his difficulty — " how to find a place under the old religious conceptions for this great task of changing the world and making it righteous; making it habitable, making it brotherly."

With this question still unresolved, Rauschenbusch sailed in 1891 for a year of study in Europe.

He spent much time with the great British economists, Sydney and Beatrice Webb, and became interested in the Rochdale Co-operatives and in Fabian Socialism. He followed closely the work of the Salvation Army in the slums of London, but recognized that " it would be necessary to go deeper than Booth and his Army, that instead of touching up bad conditions by relief work — mopping up the floor — and then allowing people to go on with all the concentration of wealth that produced poverty and the slums, that it would be necessary to turn off the spigot." [7]

It was in Germany, seemingly, that he found the answer to his quest. He spent a year of study there, partly on the teachings of Jesus and partly on sociology. " That is a good combination," he said, " and likely to produce results. In the Alps I have seen the summit of some great mountain come out of the clouds in the early morn and stand revealed in blazing purity. Its foot was still swathed in drifting mist, but I knew the mountain was there, and my soul rejoiced in it. So Christ's conception of the Kingdom of God came to me as a new revelation. Here was the idea and purpose that had dominated the mind of the Master himself. All his teachings center about it. His life was given to it. His death was suffered for it. When a man has once seen that in the Gospels, he can never unsee it again.

"When the Kingdom of God dominated our landscape," he continued, "the perspective of life shifted into a new alignment. I felt a new security in my social impulses. The spiritual authority of Jesus Christ would have been sufficient to offset the weight of all the doctors; and I now knew that I had history on my side. But in addition I found that this new conception of the purpose of Christianity was strangely satisfying. It responded to all the old and all the new elements of my religious life. The saving of the lost, the teaching of the young, the pastoral care of the poor and frail, the quickening of starved intellects, the study of the Bible, church union, political reform, the reorganization of the industrial system, international peace — it was all covered by the one aim of the Reign of God on earth. That idea is necessarily as big as humanity, for it means the divine transformation of all human life." [8]

From this time on the theology — the very life — of Walter Rauschenbusch centered about the idea of the Kingdom.

Back in New York, he joined with a few intimate friends to found the Brotherhood of the Kingdom — perhaps the most influential of all the many organizations formed during this period to promote the interests of social Christianity. The purpose of the organization was to make central in Christianity the idea of the Kingdom of God, "to re-establish this idea in the thought of the church and to assist in its practical realization in the world." Each year from 1892 until after the outbreak of the Great World War, interdenominational leaders met annually at the summer home of Leighton Williams at Marlborough-on-Hudson for conference and study concerning the various aspects of the Kingdom.

In 1907, Rauschenbusch gave his own estimate of the movement's accomplishments. "I am impressed," he said, "with the amazing changes in public thought since the Brotherhood was founded. All these things for which we then stood, according to our light, have come to the front and fill more and more of the horizon, like a hill toward which an express train is running. We stood for Christian Union, and today that sentiment has spread so that kindred groups of churches are coalescing by formal vote. . . . We stood for an historical study of the Bible, and today that method is triumphant among all Biblical scholars. . . . We stood for purer politics, for the abolition of privilege, for the rights of the people against the corporations, and today the United States are moving with almost revolutionary speed toward a new political era. We stood — though not unanimously — for Christian Socialism, and today that is capturing the heart of the intellectual and moral aristocracy of our people. We stood for the pre-eminence of the Kingdom of God in Christian thought and thereby . . . tended to substitute a power, more ethical, more synoptic, of a more Christian type of doctrine for the old 'scheme' of salvation, and all theology is drifting that way. It would be folly for us to claim that we created these changes, but I think that we can in proud humility claim that by a divine vision we foresaw God's future and offered ourselves *by our organization* for the realization of His great ends. We did *help* to create the change. And where we supposed we were losing our lives, we found them." [9]

In the same year in which this letter was written, Rauschenbusch published the first of his revolutionary volumes, the most dynamic and compelling book yet written on the Social Gospel, a book which so nearly expressed the ideals of the Brotherhood that it was seriously suggested that the organization might disband with its work accomplished.

For ten years, now, Rauschenbusch had been a professor in Rochester Theological Seminary. He had resigned his pulpit in Hell's Kitchen for a chair in a theological seminary because he saw an opportunity to impress his thoughts and experiences on young men who were giving their lives to Christian service. Articles on some phase of the social question flowed from his pen in ever increasing volume, but he was not widely known outside his own denomination until he wrote his first great work — *Christianity and the Social Crisis* — in 1907. He wrote the book, as he himself disclosed, to discharge a debt to his former parishioners. He gave the manuscript to his publishers and sailed for Europe, uncertain as to its reception. He returned to find himself famous, catapulted into the leadership of the movement for social Christianity almost overnight.

2

Rauschenbusch wrote his great book in the opening decade of the present century, seven full years before the outbreak of the First World War. According to present-day critics, it was a time when advocates of the Social Gospel were misled by the scientific theory of evolution and blinded by the myth of inevitable progress. Certainly this was not true of Walter Rauschenbusch. With clear understanding, he pointed out that Western civilization was passing through a social revolution "unparalleled in history for scope and power." Not only the older European countries, but also the United States of America, he held, were approaching a crisis. In this momentous hour the Church could not remain neutral. It must throw its immense weight on one side or the other. "If it tries not to act, it thereby acts; and in any case, its choice will be decisive for its own future." [10]

According to Rauschenbusch, the Church is committed to the task of social reconstruction by its historic origins. The Old Testament religion reached its highest development under the prophets, all of whom "interpreted past history, shaped present history, and foretold future history on the basis of the conviction that God rules with righteousness in the affairs of nations, and that only what is just and not what is expedient or profitable shall endure." [11]

Jesus, though greater than the Old Testament prophets, was still one of the prophets. Like them, he put conduct above ritual; like them, he was concerned with public and not merely with individual morality; and, like them, his sympathies went out predominantly to the poor. His message was centered on the Kingdom of God. To the ordinary reader of the Bible, inheriting the Kingdom of Heaven simply means being saved and going to heaven. For others it means the millennium. For some, the organized Church. For others, the invisible Church. For the mystic it means the hidden life with God. What, then, did the Kingdom mean to Jesus? There is only one way in which we can answer this question, replies Rauschenbusch. We must discover what Jesus' contemporaries understood by the Kingdom, the ideas which Jesus knew he would arouse when he proclaimed, "The kingdom of heaven is at hand"; and second, what modifications Jesus introduced into the current ideas. When we follow this course of investigation, there are several ideas that stand out very prominently.

1. The Kingdom of God was a social hope for Jesus as well as for his contemporaries. In other words, it involved not only a redemption of individuals, but also a redemption of society.

2. Jesus repudiated the idea of bloodshed and violence as a means of ushering in the Kingdom.

3. He taught that it would come by organic growth rather than by divine catastrophe.

4. He made it, not a Jewish, but a universal Kingdom.

5. He taught that it was a present reality and not merely a future hope.

Rauschenbusch recognized, of course, that this was a point on which New Testament scholars were at odds.

Many believed then, as they do now, that Jesus shared the eschatological hopes of his day — that he looked for the imminent coming of a supernatural kingdom through some divine catastrophe. Rauschenbusch admitted that the New Testament affords material for this point of view. But the eschatological interpretation cannot be harmonized, he held, with the central teaching of Christ; more likely the verses that bear this meaning reflect the viewpoint of Jesus' disciples, who had been infected by the popular hope. Rauschenbusch recognized, however, that Jesus looked forward to a final, apparently a supernatural consummation.

The ethics of Jesus, the author continued, were ethics of the Kingdom — ethics that would usher in the perfect society. They centered about love, because love is par excellence the society-building quality. They were revolutionary in their implications and, if applied, would remold every human institution.

At the same time, Rauschenbusch recognized clearly that Jesus was not primarily a reformer, or even a teacher of ethics. "Beyond the question of economic distribution," he said, "lies the question of moral relations; and beyond the moral relations to men lies the question of the religious communion with that spiritual reality in which we live and move and have our deepest being — with God, the Father of our spirits. Jesus had realized the life of God in the soul of man and the life of man in the love of God. That was the real secret of his life, the well-spring of his purity, his compassion, his unwearied courage, his unquenchable idealism: he knew the Father. . . .

"No man is a follower of Jesus in the full sense who has not through him entered into the same life with God. But on the other hand no man shares his life with God whose religion does not flow out, naturally and without effort, into all relations of his life and reconstructs everything that it touches. Whoever uncouples the religious and the social

194

life has not understood Jesus. Whoever sets any bounds for the reconstructive powers of the religious life over the social relations and institutions of men, to that extent denies the faith of the Master." [12]

In spite of the fact that our records are scanty and partial, in spite of the fact that there was an inevitable decline from the position of Jesus, primitive Christianity retained a strong social impetus which we do not sufficiently take into account.

This social interest, Rauschenbusch points out, took two divergent forms, being connected, first, with the return of the Lord and, second, with the formation of the new society.

Jesus declared he would come again. His disciples confidently expected his early return. They believed he would set up the Kingdom at this time. Bound up with the Kingdom and the millennium there was — for many at least — the continued hope of a redeemed society. As time went on and Jesus did not come, the hope of his immediate return faded and with it to a certain extent the hope of the Kingdom. Its place was taken by the expectation of personal immortality. Christianity stresses both — salvation for the little personality of man and for the great collective personality of mankind. But in so far as Christianity retained the first impact coming from Jesus and the Baptist and the prophets of Israel, its hope was predominantly the latter.

The social hope of the early Christians took a more wholesome direction in the " New Society." The Early Church confidently believed that they were the coming people who would absorb all others. Inspired by this ideal, a new society was actually formed which — not perfectly, of course, but to a large degree — did measure up to the apostles' ideal. It was a society which raised the moral standards of its members, tore down old barriers which divided man from his fellow man, and cared for the poor and needy. It carried with it also a new leaven of democracy and protest, manifested in dissatisfaction with harsh conditions of life, the position of women, the organization of the family life, the position of slaves, and man's relation to the state.

All the theories of primitive Christianity involved a bold condemnation of existing society. "Whether that society was to be overthrown by a divine catastrophe of judgment or displaced and absorbed in the higher life of the Christian community, in any case it was to go. The future of society belonged to that new life originated by Christ." [13]

But if the social hope was so powerful in the prophets of Israel and in Jesus and in the early Christian communities, why has Christianity never undertaken the work of social reconstruction? In the early centuries, Rauschenbusch replies, social propaganda was impossible; many postponed all idea of social redemption to the time of the Lord's return; Christians generally seemed to despair of both empire and civilization.

When at last the Church became the Church of the empire other factors were operative. There was the blighting effect of custom and precedent; the increasing otherworldliness of Christianity; the tendency toward asceticism, developing ultimately into monasticism; the absorption of religion in sacramentalism, dogma, and ecclesiasticism. As Rauschenbusch puts it, "the Church substituted itself for the Kingdom of God, and thereby put the advancement of a tangible and very human organization in the place of the moral uplifting of humanity." [14] Important, too, was the subservience of the Church to the State. And, as Rauschenbusch points out, "the limits set by a despotic age have continued into our democratic age. They have become theological tradition." [15] Thus many have actually come to believe that religion has nothing to do with politics and with society. This conception was furthered by the disappearance of Church democracy; the development of an autocratic Church, which is inevitably a conservative Church; and last, but not least, the lack of any scientific comprehension of social development.

"If any considerable portion of the argument has been correct," argues Dr. Rauschenbusch, "it follows that the failure of the Church to undertake the work of a Christian reconstruction of social life has not been caused by its close adherence to the spirit of Christ and to the essence of its religious task, but to the deflecting influence of alien forces penetrating Christianity from without and clogging the revolutionary moral power inherent in it." [16]

Encouragement, however, is to be found in the fact that all these limitations have at last been removed.

"For the first time in religious history," Rauschenbusch declares, "we have the possibility of so directing religious energy by scientific knowledge that a comprehensive and continuous reconstruction of social life in the name of God is within the bounds of human possibility." [17]

With the foundation thus laid, Dr. Rauschenbusch proceeds to consider the present crisis. Underlying causes, he held, were the industrial revolution, the rise of capitalism, and the private ownership of land. Manifestations of the crisis were found in the exploitation of labor, unequal and unjust distribution of wealth, and destruction of the workers' morale. "The constant insecurity and fear pervading the entire condition of the working people is like a corrosive chemical," he warned, "that disintegrates their self-respect." [18] A similar corrosive influence is the hatred generated by our economic system among both employers and employed. Rauschenbusch could see the danger, but neither he nor anyone else could see the movements to which this hate and this insecurity would give rise in other lands where it was more pronounced than in our own. Other manifestations of the crisis in America were the physical decline of the people (the results of overcrowding and of unhealthy environment); the wedge of inequality constantly widening; hardening class distinctions after the European pattern; the crumbling of political democracy, as capitalism extends its power over the machinery of government; the tainting of the moral atmosphere — inevitable because a competitive system puts a premium on unsocial conduct and exalts selfishness to the dignity of a moral principle; and the undermining of the family.

It has become the fashion today to state that prewar liberals believed that progress was automatic and inevitable for the entire human race. Certainly Walter Rauschenbusch harbored no such romantic illusion. In a period when the average American took little thought for the morrow, when evangelicals generally thought that the Church had no responsibility for social problems and no stake in their solution, this vigorous prophet warned that " the continents are strewn with the ruins of dead nations and civilizations. History laughs at the optimistic illusion that ' nothing can stand in the way of human progress.' It would be safer to assert that progress is always for a time only, and then succumbs to the inevitable decay." [19] " The cry of ' Crisis! crisis! ' " he admits, " has become a weariness. Every age and every year are critical and fraught with destiny. Yet in the widest survey of history Western civilization is now at a decisive point in its development." [20] It is quite possible, he thinks, that some Gibbon of Mongol race will sit by the shore of the Pacific in the year A.D. 3000 and write on the " Decline and Fall of the Christian Empire." Rauschenbusch was not mistaken about the crisis of civilization. But the hour was later than he, or even the most pessimistic observer could suppose.

Does the Church have any stake in the social movement? Of course, replied Rauschenbusch, and warned among other things that there is danger that the working people will pass from indifference to hostility, and from religious enthusiasm to antireligious bitterness. " The crisis of society," he concluded, " is also the crisis of the Church. . . . If society continues to disintegrate . . . the Church will be carried down with it." [21] Communism then was hardly a cloud upon the sky, Fascism was not yet in the cradle; but their coming makes it clear that Walter Rauschenbusch is also to be counted among the prophets.

What, then, is to be done? " The fundamental contribution of every man," Rauschenbusch asserts, " is the change of his own personality. We must repent of the sins of existing society, cast off the spell of the lies protecting our social wrongs, have faith in a higher social order, and realize in ourselves a new type of Christian manhood which seeks to overcome the evil in the present world, not by withdrawing from the world, but by revolutionizing it." [22]

" The ministry, in particular," he adds, " must apply the teaching function of the pulpit to the pressing questions of public morality. It must collectively learn not to speak without adequate information; not to charge individuals with guilt in which all society shares; not to be partial, and yet to be on the side of the lost; not to yield to political partisanship, but to deal with moral questions before they become political issues and with those questions of public welfare which never do become political issues. They must lift the social questions to a religious level by faith and spiritual insight. The larger the number of ministers who attempt these untrodden ways, the safer and saner will those be who follow. By interpreting one social class to the other, they can create a disposition to make concessions and help in securing a peaceful settlement of social issues." [23]

Christianity and the Social Crisis appeared at an opportune moment. The current financial panic, the excitement aroused by various muckraking articles and books, the increase of public concern, the restlessness of labor, the growing interest in social religion — all these and other currents of the time predisposed the public mind to welcome this crackling volume, written, as some one has said, "with the learning of the scholar, the vision of the poet, and the passion of the prophet."

Of course there was criticism, but the book was more widely acclaimed than Rauschenbusch had dared to hope. It was read and discussed by all ministers, it seemed, and by a large number of laymen. It was translated, as were his later books, into many foreign languages. The Kingdom of God movement sponsored by Kagawa before the outbreak of the present war was the result, in part, of the impact of the thought of Walter Rauschenbusch upon the mind and soul of a sensitive young Japanese.

Rauschenbusch could never, after this, answer the demands made upon his time. He spoke constantly to religious groups, to social workers, to laboring men, and to students, before conferences and open forums, all over the country. He was widely quoted in the secular press. Magazine articles, which continued to flow from his pen, reached an ever widening circle of readers.

No one would affirm that Rauschenbusch launched the Social Gospel movement in America. Washington Gladden was older by a quarter of a century; many others preceded him, or were his contemporaries in the movement. But no one did so much to arouse the social conscience of the American Churches as Walter Rauschenbusch, and no one contributed so much to what he termed the "Social Awakening."

3

Rauschenbusch believed that ultimately the Church would have to recast its systematic and practical theology, its ritual, its prayers, its hymns, and its evangelism to make room, not simply for the terminology, but for the aims, the motives, the passions, and the philosophy which are summed up in the newly recovered concept of the Kingdom of God.[24] His second significant book — *For God and the People: Prayers of the Social Awakening* — was offered as a pioneer effort in this direction. It is a slender volume of only one hundred and fifty-four pages, and yet, in the estimation of many, it will prove to be his most enduring work.

The volume opens with a discussion of the social meaning of the Lord's Prayer, a theme familiar now, but novel at the time. Then follow beautiful and moving prayers for different occasions and causes and for various social classes. No other writing so reveals the quality of the man's spirit; nothing else bares so completely the religious atmosphere in which the Social Gospel of Walter Rauschenbusch had its birth.

Many of the prayers were written on railway trains, as he meditated on the life problems of the people he had seen. He put out of his mind everything else but the needs of these people. And the prayers seemed to come as the fruitage of a real mystical withdrawal into communion with God. So, reports Sharpe, "he described it in a dinner table conversation, but he did not then add the detail, known to his intimates, that on some of these occasions he was moved to such deep feeling that the tears welled out of his eyes and blotted the paper on which he was writing." [25]

Nothing like these prayers had ever been published before; no prayers combining so successfully social passion with profound religious insight and soul-stirring expression have been published since. All recent Protestant liturgies reflect their influence. For many ministers and laymen prayer breathes a new spirit; it has taken on a new dimension.

4

Five years after the appearance of *Christianity and the Social Crisis* came a sequel, *Christianizing the Social Order,* prompted by the unexpected popularity of the former book and the new questions which were insistently asked of its author.

He begins by noting the heartening signs of social awakening in the nation and especially within the Church, rising like " an equinoctial gale in March." Before 1900 those who were interested in social thought were few, and it seemed as though they were voices shouting in the wilderness. But now social religion has been admitted within the organization of the Church. Since the publication of his first great book, most of the larger denominations have discussed social problems at their national conventions, and have created permanent organizations to educate the rank and file of their members. The development of the social point of view is discernible also in the institutional agencies of the Churches; for example, in the newly organized Federal Council of Churches (described recently as "the lengthened shadow of Walter Rauschenbusch"); in the Religious Education Association; in the Y. M. C. A., which used to stand for religious individualism; and in the Y. W. C. A., which was more conservative, but has now "definitely committed itself to the business of securing a living wage and a maximum working day for the women workers, for whose welfare it exists."

These movements, says Rauschenbusch, represent the more progressive forces in the Church. But even those citadels of conservatism which make a speciality of what is safe — the denominational publishing houses and the theological seminaries — have been affected. The former are issuing literature which "really sets forth the forward thought of the Church on social questions." And practically all first-class seminaries have introduced chairs devoted to "Social Ethics" or "Christian Society."

In the opinion of Dr. Rauschenbusch, the social awakening constituted the beginning of a new epoch in the history of the American Churches. The social mission of the Church was not universally accepted by all denominations or by all members of the more progressive denominations, but "the Church is moving and the Master of the Church is behind it."

But though Rauschenbusch was plainly encouraged by the remarkable progress made in appreciation of the Social Gospel in recent years, he was by no means blind to the difficulties in the way. He proceeded to set forth some of the obstacles to progress: (1) the innate conservatism of human nature; (2) the active opposition of the dominant social classes to any change that would affect adversely the interest of their own class (including the possibility of what we today would term a Fascist coup); (3) the psychological conservatism of age — including the most influential section of the population; (4) the power of institutionalized tradition; (5) and too often the influence and weight of the Church. "The power of religion is almost illimitable," he declares, "but it is not necessarily beneficent." In the past the Church has been the most conservative of all institutions. And it can not be denied that in Europe "all the great national churches . . . have opposed the conquering role of political democracy.

"It is, therefore, a vital question for the social progress of our country what fundamental attitude the churches of America are likely to take to the forces that are striving to renovate our social order." [26] If they espouse the *status quo*, change becomes difficult. If they espouse the cause of the people, the whole situation is changed. "Once more the fate of a nation is rocking in the balance. Let the Church of Christ fling in, not the sword, but the cross, not against the weak, but for them! " [27]

To encourage it to a right decision, Rauschenbusch argues once more along historical lines for the revolutionary destiny of the Church.

"The chief purpose of the Christian Church in the past," he declares, "has been the salvation of individuals. But the most pressing task of the present is not individualistic. Our business is to make over an antiquated and immoral economic system; to get rid of laws, customs, maxims, and philosophies inherited from an evil and despotic past; to create just and brotherly relations between great groups and classes of society; and thus to lay a social foundation on which modern men individually can live and work in a fashion that will not outrage all the better elements in them. Our inherited Christian faith dealt with individuals, our present task deals with society." [28] Acceptance of this mission he regarded as a return to Jesus' faith in the Kingdom of God, which had been lost for many centuries but now had been recovered in our own.

According to Rauschenbusch, the largest and hardest part of the task has been accomplished. The family, the school, and the Church have been reclaimed, and are now essentially Christian. The decisive victory has been won, also, in the political realm. True, its character leaves much to be desired. It is newly saved and not yet sanctified; but the power of special privilege has been broken, and democracy has the means of redemption within its grasp. Only the economic order remains. If business can be made thoroughly Christian, if capitalism, a competitive order which stimulates selfishness and makes good will more difficult, can be replaced by a co-operative system, like Socialism, which calls out the instincts of good will and solidarity, the task will be done.

To the development of this theme, a frankly socialistic critique of capitalism and the presentation of a religious foundation for social reformation, Rauschenbusch devotes the major part of his work.

While Socialism, as such, has made little headway in the Church, as among the masses of the American people, many if not most of the specific reforms, the immediate steps advocated by Rauschenbusch, have since been incorporated into American life. And economic development continues to be along the lines which he foresaw.

Rauschenbusch fears that some readers will conclude that his book has fallen away from high religious ground and has sagged down to the level of mere economic discussion. He insisted, however, that his book was religious from beginning to end: "Its sole concern is for the Kingdom of God and the salvation of men. But the Kingdom of God includes the economic life; for it means the progressive transformation of all human affairs by the thought and spirit of Christ." [29]

"On the other hand, no outward economic readjustment will answer our needs. It is not this thing or that thing our nations needs, but a new mind and heart, a new conception of the way we ought all to live together, a new conviction about the worth of a human life and the use God wants us to make of our own lives. We want a revolution both inside and outside. We want a moral renovation of public opinion and a revival of religion." [30]

"We must begin at both ends simultaneously. We must change our economic system in order to preserve our conscience and our religious faith; we must renew and strengthen our religion in order to be able to change our economic system." [31]

If the social order is to be Christianized, we must have converted men. "Create a ganglion of redeemed personalities in a commonwealth and all things become possible," says Rauschenbusch. "Here is one of the permanent functions of the Christian Church. It must enlist the will and the love of men and women for God, mark them with the cross of Christ, and send them out to finish up the work which Christ began." [32]

To accomplish this end the Church "must come out of its spiritual isolation. In theory and practice the Church has long constituted a world by itself. It has been governed by ecclesiastical motives and interests which are often remote from the real interests of humanity, and has almost uniformly set church questions ahead of social questions. It has often built a sound-proof habitation in which people could live for years without becoming definitely conscious of the existence of prostitution, child labor or tenement crowding. It has offered peace and spiritual tranquility to men and women who need thunderclaps and lightnings. . . .

"We do not want to substitute social activities for religion," Rauschenbusch declares. "If the Church comes to lean on social preachings and doings as a crutch because its religion has become paralytic, may the Lord have mercy on us all! We do not want less religion; we want more, but it must be a religion that gets its orientation from the Kingdom of God. . . .

"This, then, is one of the most practical means for the Christianizing of the social order, to multiply the number of minds who have turned in conscious repentance from the old maxim, the old admirations, and the old desires, and have accepted for good and all the Christian law with all that it implies for modern conditions. When we have a sufficient body of such, the old order will collapse like the walls of Jericho." [33]

Christianizing the Social Order gives us Rauschenbusch's most careful thought on the application of Christian principles to the problems of society. Though it did not achieve the popularity of his earlier books, its influence, some think, has been even greater. For example, this book was made required reading for every young minister entering the Methodist Episcopal Church. According to Roy L. Smith, this served to shift the homiletical emphasis in this powerful body over to an entirely new basis. "Pulpits which had echoed to debate on baptism and prevenient grace now resounded with discussions of wages, working conditions, housing, sanitation, collective bargaining, and trade unionism. Young theologues who had considered writing their graduate theses on 'Messianic Ideas in the Old Testament' suddenly shifted to economics and wrote on 'The Theory of the Minimum Wage.'" [34]

ſ

When Rauschenbusch wrote his third great book, Christianizing the social order did not seem to be beyond the realm of practical possibility. Though he shared the common evolutionary philosophy of his age, and in his book actually equated the Kingdom of God with the theory of evolution interpreted in terms of religious faith, he never made the mistake of thinking that the evolutionary advance of the Kingdom for which he hoped was automatic or certain. Nonetheless he was reasonably hopeful. The larger part of the task had been accomplished. And the widespread evidence of the social awakening was distinctly encouraging.

The war which broke out in August, 1914, was a rude shock which brought Rauschenbusch "emotional anguish, deep uncertainties, especially for the future of social Christianity, and chilling fear for the whole future not only of countries which he loved but for civilization itself." [35] But despite his growing concern for the war and the burden of sorrow which it pressed upon his heart, his devotion to, and his faith in, the coming Kingdom was not diminished.

In 1916 he wrote a brief study book for the International Y. M. C. A. on *The Social Principles of Jesus*. It is not generally included among his major productions, but it was one of the most widely distributed. Moreover, the fact that it circulated so extensively among college men and women suggests that its influence may have been fully as great as that of some of his more pretentious volumes.

Rauschenbusch confesses in this book that the task has been rendered more difficult and its final achievement more uncertain by the war. "The common people," he writes,

"have secured some participation in political power and
have been able to use it somewhat for their economic betterment. . . . Before the outbreak of the Great War it seemed
safe to anticipate that the working people would secure an
increasing share of the social wealth, the security, the opportunities for health, for artistic enjoyment, and of all that
makes life worth living. Today the future is heavily clouded
and uncertain, but our faith still holds that even the great
disaster will help ultimately to weaken the despotic and ex-
ploiting forces, and make the condition of the common people more than ever the chief concern of science and states-
manship." [36]

But if this goal is to be realized new problems must be
faced. " Here are the enormous tasks of international relations, which the Great War has forced us to realize — the
prevention of armed conflicts, the elimination of the irritant
causes of war, the protection of the small nations which possess what the big nations covet, the freedom of the seas as
the common highway of God, fair and free interchange in
commerce without any effort to set up monopoly rights and
the privilege of extortionate gain, the creation of an institutional basis for a great family of nations in days to come.
These are some of the tasks," he emphasizes, " which the
men and women who are now young must take on their
minds and consciences for life, and leave to their children
to finish." [37]

As American sympathies for the Allies became more pronounced, and the United States moved slowly but steadily
toward participation in the spreading conflict, Walter Rauschenbusch found himself increasingly out of touch with
popular sentiment. Shortly after the outbreak of the war
he wrote an article entitled " Be Fair to Germany, a Plea for
Open-mindedness." Later, in collaboration with Dr. Aked,
he prepared a widely circulated manifesto — entitled *Private
Profit and the Nation's Honor* — in which he objected stren-

uously to the manufacture and sale by America of munitions of war for the Allies. It was, he argued, a step leading us into war as a part of the economic and military machine of Great Britain. He also took an active part in opposing the preparedness campaign which seemed to him to be preparedness for war against Germany. Most dangerous of all, when the Lusitania was sunk, Rauschenbusch refused to join in the chorus of denunciation. To the public his silence seemed to give consent. Popular antagonism grew. Invitations were withdrawn. Ugly editorial references began to appear in the press.

As Sharpe says, "Rauschenbusch was not entirely unused to public reproach and misrepresentation, but when close friends and collaborators turned against him, he was cut to the quick." [38] And yet, throughout this difficult period, "when friend and foe alike flung hot words at him and heaped bitter invective and scorn upon him, there is not to be found a mean, harsh, bitter retort in any of his correspondence or utterances. Cogent argument and brave defense of his position there are, but no malice. Perhaps at no time in his life did he more perfectly manifest the spirit of Jesus Christ, of whom it was said, 'Who when he was reviled, reviled not again; when he suffered, threatened not.'" [39]

As the war dragged on, Rauschenbusch's moral distaste grew more pronounced. He had never been an absolute pacifist; it is not certain that he became one. But he joined the Fellowship of Reconciliation, a newly organized pacifist organization, and made an address which leaned strongly in that direction.

To understand Rauschenbusch's attitude during these trying days we must remember that "war represented to him the negation of Christianity and of social progress, the two things he had given his life to promote." [40] He disliked British imperialism, and, as Sharpe says, "probably never

entirely understood England and the English." Though
wholly loyal to America, he could not join what seemed to
be partisan denunciation of a land to which he was bound
by so many ties. Also, he did not share the popular hope
that the victory of the Allies would insure a better world.
He saw some of the dangers ahead, and some of the weaknesses manifested later in the League of Nations. To a former friend, who had attempted to place him " on the grill "
he wrote: " I can see only a step ahead, and that little step
consists in keeping our nation within the area of peace. I
am afraid of those who want to drag our country in to satisfy
partisan hate, or because they think universal peace will result from the victory of the allies." [41] His position in brief
was similar to that of some of our isolationist ministers before Pearl Harbor. But in that day among the prominent
clergymen of America, Rauschenbusch stood almost alone.

6

In the spring of 1917, at the very time when America was
finally compelled to enter the conflict, Rauschenbusch delivered the Nathaniel W. Taylor lectures at Yale University. For many years he had felt the need for a theology
" large enough to match the social gospel and vital enough
to back it." These lectures, which were expected to deal
with some aspect of doctrinal theology, gave him the desired
opportunity. Gathered up later in a book entitled *A Theology for the Social Gospel,* they present his mature thought,
his final reflection, against the background of the world's
mounting tragedy, on the subject to which he had so largely
devoted his life. Lacking the literary charm of his earlier
books, it was perhaps his most creative work. Like his
Prayers of the Social Awakening, it cultivated a new field —
a field which he felt must be tilled and developed if the social movement was not to become irreligious and, therefore,

ineffective, and if theology itself was to remain a vital force in the life of the world.

Rauschenbusch was acquainted with the development of modern theology, though he was not a professional theologian. He acknowledged his indebtedness to Schleiermacher, Ritschl, Troeltsch, and a host of others. His assumptions regarding inspiration and the development and modification of Jesus' thought were definitely liberal. But his main departure from the traditional formulation was in its center of gravity, its organizing principle. Not justification by faith as in the Lutheran theology, and not the sovereignty of God as in the Reformed theology, but the Kingdom of God was the center to which all else must be related. Thus the negations of Liberalism were for the most part avoided; many orthodox conceptions were unaffected; some were gently laid aside as meaningless, while others were enriched.

In Rauschenbusch's own estimation the Social Gospel was only the old message of salvation enlarged and intensified. The changes required to make room for it were not destructive, but constructive. They involved addition, rather than subtraction.

The doctrines most affected are those of sin and redemption, and it is to the modification of these two doctrines viewed in relation to the Kingdom of God that Rauschenbusch devotes the major portion of his book.

The author points out in the beginning that every religious movement must be tested by its bearing on the religious consciousness of sin. The Social Gospel does not lessen man's sense of sin, but, emphasizing classes of sin largely overlooked by traditional theology, it plunges him into a new baptism of repentance.

Traditional theology is inclined to emphasize the "Fall" of our first parents and to neglect the contribution which our more recent forefathers have made to the sin and misery of mankind. The Social Gospel concentrates its energies on

211

the present and active sources of evil and leaves the question of its origin to God. Traditional theology, taking its start from the sin of Adam in the Garden of Eden, stresses the individualistic aspects of sin. The new theology, based on positive ideals of social righteousness embodied in the Kingdom of God, sees sin as the treasonable force which frustrates and wrecks these ideals and despoils the earth of their enjoyment. Traditional theology is right in emphasizing the fact of original sin, but has slighted or overlooked the fact that sin is also transmitted along the lines of social tradition. This channel is at least as important and far more susceptible to religious influence and control.

To deal with sin realistically in the modern world, we have to recognize the authority of the social group in justifying, urging, and idealizing wrong, together with the decisive influence of economic profit in the defense and propagation of evil. Individualistic theology has not trained the spiritual intelligence of Christian men and women to recognize and observe these superpersonal forces of evil. It does not, therefore, adequately conceive what Rauschenbusch describes as the Kingdom of Evil, in which the factors enumerated above converge and find their complete and final meaning. "The social gospel," he claims, "is the only influence which can renew the idea of the Kingdom of Evil in modern minds because it alone has an adequate sense of solidarity and a sufficient grasp of the historical and social realities of sin." [42]

It is evident, even from this brief analysis, that Walter Rauschenbusch did not share the optimistic view of human nature so often attributed to advocates of the Social Gospel. His recognition that sin is transmitted, not only through biological inheritance, but also through social tradition; his exposure of the vast network of organized sin which he called the "Kingdom of Evil"; his presentation of sin in its social context, as sin which is found not only in individuals, but also in all human relationships, were definite contributions to theological thought and enable us to understand more clearly the "world-rulers of this darkness" against which Christians must continually war. Unfortunately, many of Rauschenbusch's successors became so absorbed in the evil to be found in man's environment and in society as a whole that they ignored or forgot the more fundamental sources of evil which are found in man himself. A realistic reading of human nature agrees with Christian revelation that "the ultimate source of sin and evil" is found not "in superpersonal groups and social systems," but "rather in the private order of the human self." [43]

The Social Gospel enlarges not only the doctrine of sin, but also the doctrine of salvation.

Whatever others may have taught, Rauschenbusch never made the mistake of thinking that society could be saved apart from redeemed personalities. But the experience of salvation, including both regeneration and sanctification, receives new orientation, correction, and enrichment when brought into proper relation with the idea of the Kingdom. Thus salvation is not complete unless it commits a man to the ideals of the Kingdom, unless in some germinal and rudimentary form he has turned from a life centered on self toward a life going out toward God and his purposes for mankind. "Conversion," as Rauschenbusch indicates, "has usually been conceived as a break with our own sinful past. But in many cases it is also a break with the sinful past of a social group." [44]

The new thing in the Social Gospel however is "the clearness and insistence with which it sets forth the necessity and the possibility of redeeming the historical life of humanity from the social wrongs which now pervade it. . . . Its chief interest is concentrated on those manifestations of sin and redemption which lie beyond the individual soul." [45]

Rauschenbusch has already emphasized the importance

213

of the social group as a superpersonal entity "dominating the individual, assimilating him to its moral standards and enforcing them by the social sanctions of approval or disapproval." "In our age," he continues, "these superpersonal forces present more difficult problems than ever before. The scope and diversity of combination is becoming constantly greater. The strategy of the Kingdom of God is shortsighted indeed, if it does not devote itself to their salvation and conversion." [46] The salvation of these superpersonal beings, like the salvation of the individual, consists in their being brought under the law of Christ. In the case of professions and various economic groups, it means willingness "to give up monopoly power and the incomes derived from legalized extortion, and to come under the law of service, content with a fair income for honest work. The corresponding step in the case of governments and political oligarchies, both in monarchies and in capitalistic semidemocracies, is to submit to real democracy. Therewith they step out of the Kingdom of Evil into the Kingdom of God." [47]

What is the function of the Church in this process of salvation? The Church, as Rauschenbusch sees it, is the social factor in salvation. Such a superpersonal being, organized around Jesus Christ as its indwelling power, is indispensable if the individual is to be saved and if society itself is to be redeemed. "The saving power of the Church does not rest [however] on its institutional character, on its continuity, its ordination, its ministry, or its doctrine. It rests on the presence of the Kingdom of God within her." [48]

This Kingdom may be defined as humanity organized according to the will of God as revealed by Jesus Christ. It is always coming, always pressing in on the present, always big with possibility, and always inviting immediate action. Its realization in the life of humanity is the supreme purpose for which the Church exists. The doctrine of the Kingdom is one which theology neglects at its own peril. For unless the Church has a vision of redeemed society more compelling than any other, it will not for long maintain the spiritual leadership of mankind.

What place does Jesus have in this doctrine of the Kingdom? Rauschenbusch admits that the Social Gospel is not greatly interested in metaphysical questions as to the nature of Jesus' person. It is more interested in Jesus, who actually inaugurated the Kingdom of God, and who set in motion the historical forces of redemption which are ultimately to overthrow the Kingdom of Evil. The Social Gospel wants to see a Personality able to win hearts and dominate situations, able to bind men in loyalty and make them think like himself, and able to set revolutionary social forces in motion. It interprets all the events of his life, including his death, by the dominating purpose which he consistently followed, the establishment of the Kingdom of God.

The main purpose of Rauschenbusch in this important volume is to show how the Social Gospel affects the doctrines of sin and salvation. He recognizes, however, that every essential change or enlargement of these fundamental conceptions is bound to affect all related doctrines. In the closing chapters he endeavors to suggest how the Social Gospel would affect some of the more important of these.

The doctrine of God, he believes, will be democratized. In other words, God will be regarded as Father, rather than as Sovereign, an immanent God, who invites man's co-operation and aid.

Inerrant inspiration, he contends, was a conception not held by the Apostolic Church. Its historical result has been to discourage prophecy in the Church, for no one wishes to claim inerrancy. "The social gospel . . . feels the need of present inspiration and of living prophetic spirits in order to lead humanity toward the Kingdom of God. . . . Wherever the Kingdom of God is set to the front, inspiration will spontaneously spring into life at points where the conflict is hot and active in the present. A theology adapted to the social gospel, therefore, will recognize inspiration as an indispensable force of our religion and an essential equipment of redemption. The social order can not be saved without regenerate men; neither can it be saved without inspired men." [49]

The sacraments commit us to the realization of Jesus' ideal — the Fatherhood of God and the brotherhood of man.

The future development of the race should have a larger place in practical Christian teaching. God is in history. He has the initiative. Where others see blind forces working dumb agony, we must see moral will working toward redemption and education. Sin ruins, righteousness establishes, and love consolidates. In the last resort the issues of future history lie in the moral qualities and religious faith of nations. This is the substance of all Hebrew and Christian eschatology. The millennial hope of the Early Church was crude in form but right in its substance. The ideal of a social life in which the law of Christ shall prevail and in which its prevalence shall result in peace, justice, and a glorious blossoming of human life is a Christian ideal. An outlook toward the future in which the spiritual life is saved and the economic life is left unsaved is both unchristian and stupid.

We must shift our hopes, however, for the coming of the Christian ideal of society from catastrophe to development. In this connection, Rauschenbusch presents his final views regarding the eschatological views of Jesus. He recognizes that the school which emphasizes Jesus' apocalyptic expectations has done valuable work, but believes that the future will probably show that it has overworked its hypothesis. Critical analysis eliminates a good deal of eschatological material as later accretions. We see the situation incorrectly, he thinks, when we assume that the ideas of Jesus were uniform through his ministry. It is vital to this problem to know in what direction Jesus was working. He was shaking off catastrophic ideas and substituting developmental ideas. In short, apocalypticism was part of the environment in which he began his thinking; it was not his personal product; he was emancipating himself from it.

Insistence on continuous development, however, does not eliminate the possibility and value of catastrophe. Political and social revolutions may shake down the fortifications of the Kingdom of Evil in a day. The Great War is a catastrophic stage in the coming of the Kingdom of God. Its direct effects will operate for generations.

"An eschatology which is expressed in terms of historic development has no final consummation. . . . Its consummations are always the basis for further development. The Kingdom of God is always coming, but we can never say, ' Lo here.' . . . A progressive Kingdom of righteousness happens all the time in installments, like our own sanctification. . . . Meanwhile we are on the march toward the Kingdom of God, and getting our reward by every fractional realization of it which makes us hungry for more." [50]

Belief in a future life, Rauschenbusch says, is not essential to religious faith. Plainly, however, a man has a larger and completer hope if he looks forward to eternal life for himself as well as to a better destiny for the race. The most unattractive element in the orthodox view is the eternal fixity of the two states. No one, Rauschenbusch contends, deserves an eternity in hell. On the other hand, it jars the sense of justice to see some totally exonerated. Rauschenbusch himself inclines to believe in the just effects of sin and in the operation of saving mercy for all.

Last of all, Rauschenbusch considers the atonement — a doctrine which he thought the Church was better prepared to understand than ever before. Three questions he endeavors to answer:

First, how did Jesus bear sins which he did not commit? According to Rauschenbusch, he bore the weight and suffered the consequences of public sins — social sins in which all men share, and for which all men therefore are partly responsible. "In so far as the personal sins of men have contributed to the existence of these public sins, he came into collision with the totality of evil in mankind. It requires no legal fiction of imputation to explain that 'he was wounded for our transgressions, he was bruised for our iniquities.'" [51] It is explained by the fact of human solidarity.

Secondly, how did Christ's death affect God? Christ, replies Rauschenbusch, has begun to lift men to a new basis of spiritual existence. He has altered the relation between God and humanity "from antagonism to co-operative unity of will; not by a legal transaction, but by the presence of a new and decisive factor embodied in the racial life which affected its spiritual value and potency." [52] When men learn to understand and love God, and when God by anticipation sees his own life appropriated by men, God and men enter into a state of spiritual solidarity which is the only effective reconciliation.

The third important question is, How does Christ's death affect man? Rauschenbusch mentions three ways out of many: (1) It is the conclusive demonstration of the power of sin in humanity; (2) it is the supreme revelation of love (a monumental fact telling of grace and inviting repentance and humility); and then finally (3) it displays the power of prophetic suffering for the redemption of mankind and inspires Christ's followers to carry on the work which he has begun.

A year after the delivery of these lectures, Rauschenbusch was forced to retire on account of ill health. Shortly thereafter he wrote a letter to his old friend Dr. Cornelius Woelfkin, in which he effectively answered many of the false charges which had been leveled against him in regard to the

Great War. " A victory for the central powers," he recognized, would fasten the philosophy of imperialism and militarism on the world. " I should regard this as a terrible calamity to the world and have always feared a German triumph." But he added, " I am not as sure as others that a victory for the allies would, of itself, free the world from imperialism. . . . The controlling influence of America in the final and decisive phases of the struggle," he continued, " opens a great historic opportunity for our nation. . . . We [alone] can lift the whole contest above a fight for territory and trade privileges and make it a battle for the freedom of the nations and the achievement of international order and peace." He foresaw, however, that President Wilson would have a tremendous task " to translate his idealistic utterances into realities against the pressure of selfish interests at home and abroad. Again and again in the past, the peoples have been led to slaughter by noble hopes only to be cheated at the peace table. Therefore, the President deserves our earnest support in standing for the nobler ends to which he has given such remarkable expression." [53]

This letter was accepted by most of his friends as an evidence of his changed attitude toward the war, but for Rauschenbusch it was a matter of small concern — the days of his earthly pilgrimage were drawing to a close. In a revealing letter describing the development of his personal religion, he confessed: " My life has been physically very lonely and often beset by the consciousness of conservative antagonism. I have been upheld by the comforts of God. Jesus has been to me the inexhaustible source of fresh impulses, life and courage. . . . It has been my deepest satisfaction to get evidence now and then that I have been able to help men to a new spiritual birth. I have always regarded my public work as a form of evangelism, which called for a deeper repentance and a new experience of God's salvation." [54]

Two months later, when he was only fifty-seven years of age, Walter Rauschenbusch died. At the time many believed, and some since have continued to believe, that he died with a broken heart. D. R. Sharpe, his confidential friend and official biographer, denies that this was the case. He insists that Rauschenbusch never lost his gallant faith in the eternal purpose of God and in its certain realization within human society, and that he passed out into that larger life with a stout heart and with a resolute and unfaltering step.

7

Rauschenbusch predicted that after the war the Social Gospel would " come back " with pent-up energy and clearer knowledge. Instead, it appeared to some that the social movement was about to collapse. "The mood of hope, good will and optimism disappeared." Idealism was replaced by cynicism, the desire for reform by a longing for normalcy.

Lack of concern for the historic doctrines of Christianity on the part of early advocates of the Social Gospel tended, on the one hand, to alienate conservative Christians from social religion and, on the other hand, to make it easier for later proponents of the movement to ignore its distinctive religious aspects. Among many of the successors of Rauschenbusch the Social Gospel became less a gospel and more of a movement for social and ethical reform.

Some, who lacked Rauschenbusch's own realistic insight into the forces of evil against the Kingdom and had believed that the new age of humanity was about to dawn, were disillusioned. Others, who had tended to substitute the message of social redemption for the historic message of individual salvation through Christ, discovered the inadequacy of their new gospel and drew sensibly nearer to the faith of their fathers, or found dwindling response on the part of religious people who were more concerned with their own individual needs than they were with the ideals of the Kingdom.

Opposition to the Social Gospel came for many years from economic conservatives who desired the maintenance of the *status quo,* and from theological conservatives who linked the movement with " Modernism " or feared that enthusiasm for Christian social ethics was doing violence to the historic concern of Christianity for the redemption of individuals. Today, as F. Ernest Johnson has pointed out, a new group has been added, the neo-orthodox, who criticize the movement " on the ground that it is theologically shallow — that it has missed the real meaning of the Kingdom of God in relation to history, that it is ' humanistic ' and lacking in recognition of the supernatural factors in redemption, that it has glorified the immanence of God at the expense of his ' otherness '; that it is hopelessly romantic in its conception of human nature, that it has substituted for divine architecture the work of men's hands." [55]

As the world crisis has developed, some have tended to despair entirely of man's effort and to trust only in divine catastrophe as the final act of human history. The Kingdom, they say, is not a goal to be attained by human effort; it is something given in God's own time apart from the processes of history. Everywhere there is a growing recognition of the continuing evil in man's nature and of the basic and never-ending conflicts in human society. John Bennett states that the present state of Christian thinkers in America — as a whole — is one of profound puzzlement and social fear. " Hope," he says, " is not dead but eager expectation is dead. Our sense of what is possible in history is being revised. Many of us are seeking for a basis for loyalty to the purposes of God in history, which does not depend upon expectation of results in our time." [56]

But though corrections will be made, and the inadequacies and one-sidedness of the so-called Social Gospel must and

will be corrected, its permanent contribution to an understanding of the religion of Jesus Christ, its recovery of forgotten or neglected elements in the Church's mission, can
never again be lost.

Walter Rauschenbusch held before his generation the
hopes of a redeemed society — a goal which he saw, and
which we recognize more clearly now, can never be wholly
realized in history, but toward which we must constantly
struggle. The course of world events has left us no alternative. We must engage in ceaseless effort to advance God's
reign on earth — the Kingdom of God which forever eludes
us, and which only he can finally bestow, or else civilization
itself, and along with it the Church as an effective agency
for the redemption of mankind, will vanish from the earth.

NOTES

Chapter I
HORACE BUSHNELL
and the beginning of
American Liberalism

1 *Master Sermons of the Nineteenth Century*, p. 133. Willett, Clark & Company.
2 Munger, Theodore T., *Horace Bushnell, Preacher and Theologian*, p. 6. Houghton Mifflin Company. Used by permission of Elizabeth Munger Adams.
3 Cheney, Mary Bushnell, *Life and Letters of Horace Bushnell*, p. 30.
4 *Ibid.*, p. 32.
5 Bushnell, Horace, *Christian Nurture*, 1923 Edition, pp. xxiii, xxiv. Used by permission of Charles Scribner's Sons, publishers.
6 Coleridge, Samuel Taylor, *Aids to Reflection*, p. 123.
7 Bushnell, *op. cit.*, p. xxiv.
8 Cheney, *op. cit.*, p. 56.
9 *Op. cit.*, p. 53.
10 Quoted by Munger, *ibid.*, p. 54.
11 *Bushnell Centenary*, p. 20.
12 *Makers of Christianity from John Cotton to Lyman Abbott*, p. 299. Henry Holt and Company, Inc.
13 Bushnell, *op. cit.*, pp. 158, 159.
14 *Ibid.*, p. 4.
15 *Ibid.*, p. 35.
16 *Ibid.*, p. 21.
17 Munger, *op. cit.*, p. 102.
18 *God in Christ*, Centenary Edition, p. 48. Charles Scribner's Sons.
19 *Ibid.*, p. 81.
20 *Ibid.*, p. 93.
21 *Ibid.*, p. 96.
22 Buckham, John Wright, *Progressive Religious Thought in America*, p. 13. Houghton Mifflin Company. Used by permission of the author.
23 *Op. cit.*, p. 109.
24 *God in Christ*, p. 111.
25 *Ibid.*, p. 123.

26 *Ibid.*, p. 163.
27 *Ibid.*, p. 130.
28 *Ibid.*, p. 137.
29 *Ibid.*, p. 287.
30 *Ibid.*, p. 290.
31 *Ibid.*, p. 352.
32 *Ibid.*, pp. 341, 342.
33 Munger, *op. cit.*, p. 143.
34 *Work and Play*, pp. 160, 161.
35 *Nature and the Supernatural*, Second Edition, p. 20.
36 *Ibid.*, p. 21.
37 *Ibid.*, pp. v, vi.
38 *Ibid.*, p. 37.
39 *Ibid.*, p. 37.
40 *Ibid.*, p. 43.
41 *Ibid.*, pp. 58, 59.
42 *Ibid.*, p. 408.
43 Cheney, *op. cit.*, pp. 445, 446.
44 *A History of the Christian Church*, p. 457.   Charles Scribner's Sons.
45 *Op. cit.*, p. 399.
46 *The Vicarious Sacrifice*, p. 41.
47 *Ibid.*, p. 399.
48 *Ibid.*, p. 321.
49 *Ibid.*, Vol. II, p. 11.
50 *Ibid.*, pp. 14, 15.
51 Munger, *op. cit.*, p. 271.
52 *Prophets of the Soul*, p. 160.   Used by permission of the Abingdon-Cokesbury Press, publisher.
53 Buckham, *op. cit.*, p. 26.
54 *Bushnell Centenary*, p. 47.
55 Smith, H. Shelton, *Faith and Nurture*, p. 11.   Used by permission of Charles Scribner's Sons, publishers.
56 *Christian Nurture*, p. 9.
57 *Ibid.*, p. 10.
58 Smith, *op. cit.*, p. 120.
59 *Personal Religion*, p. 284.   Charles Scribner's Sons.
60 Smith, *op. cit.*, pp. 23, 24.
61 *Bushnell Centenary*, p. 79.

Chapter II
HENRY WARD BEECHER
and the popular revolt against
Calvinism

1 *Henry Ward Beecher,* p. xii.   Houghton Mifflin Company.
2 *Henry Ward Beecher, An American Portrait,* p. vii.   Double-day, Doran & Company, Inc.   Used by permission of Sheila Hibben.
3 Beecher, Charles, *Autobiography and Correspondence by Ly-man Beecher,* Vol. II, p. 273.
4 Stowe, Harriet Beecher, *Men of Our Times,* p. 512.
5 Abbott and Halliday, *Henry Ward Beecher,* p. 490.
6 Beecher, William C., and Scoville, Samuel, *A Biography of Rev. Henry Ward Beecher,* p. 79.
7 *Ibid.,* pp. 79, 80.
8 *Ibid.,* p. 80.
9 Stowe, *op. cit.,* p. 512.
10 *Ibid.,* p. 517.
11 Beecher and Scoville, *op. cit.,* p. 98.
12 Abbott and Halliday, *op. cit.,* p. 606.
13 *Ibid.,* p. 490.
14 From *Saints, Sinners and Beechers,* p. 251, by Lyman Beecher Stowe.   Copyright, 1934.   Used by special permission of the Publishers, The Bobbs-Merrill Company.
15 Abbott and Halliday, *op. cit.,* p. 490.
16 *Ibid.,* pp. 36, 37.
17 Howard, John R., *Patriotic Address,* p. 43.
18 Stowe, Harriet Beecher, *op. cit.,* p. 541.
19 Beecher and Scoville, *op. cit.,* pp. 167, 168.
20 *Ibid.,* p. 188.
21 Stowe, Harriet Beecher, *op. cit.,* p. 544.
22 Abbott and Halliday, *op. cit.,* p. 603.
23 Quoted by Stowe, Lyman Beecher, *op. cit.,* p. 268.
24 Quoted by Abbott, *op. cit.,* p. 243.
25 *Ibid.,* pp. 83, 84.
26 *American Dictionary of National Biography,* Vol. II, p. 132. Charles Scribner's Sons.
27 *Sermons,* Vol. I, p. 29.
28 *Ibid.,* Vol. II, p. 199.

29 *Ibid.*, p. 186.

30 Abbott, *op. cit.*, p. 195.

31 Quoted by Stowe, Lyman Beecher, *op. cit.*, p. 284.

32 Howard, *op. cit.*, pp. 284, 285.

33 *Lecture Room Talks*, p. 117.

34 Quoted by Abbott, *op. cit.*, p. 243.

35 Howard, *op. cit.*, p. 513.

36 *Independent,* April 6, 1865, quoted by Garrison, W. E., *The March of Faith,* p. 17. Harper & Brothers.

37 Howard, *op. cit.*, p. 689.

38 *Ibid.*, pp. 714, 718.

39 *New York Sun,* April 16, 1876, quoted by Hibben, *op. cit.*, p. 251.

40 Howard, *op. cit.*, p. 820.

41 *Theodore Tilton vs. Henry Ward Beecher,* Vol. I, p. 485, quoted by Hibben, *op. cit.*, p. 338.

42 *Yale Lectures on Preaching,* 1st Series, pp. 87–89.

43 Stowe, Lyman Beecher, *op. cit.*, p. 262.

44 Beecher, *Sermons,* Vol. I, p. 392.

45 Quoted by Hibben, *op. cit.*, p. 332.

46 *North American Review,* August, 1882, pp. 106, 107.

47 Quoted by Garrison, *op. cit.*, p. 95.

48 Abbott and Halliday, *op. cit.*, pp. 482, 483.

49 *Ibid.*, pp. 504, 505.

50 *Ibid.*, p. 566.

51 *Ibid.*, p. 567.

52 *Evolution and Religion*, p. 24.

53 Foster, Frank H., *The Modern Movement in American Theology*, p. 89. Used by permission of Fleming H. Revell Company, publishers.

54 *Evolution and Religion*, p. 61.

55 *Ibid.*, p. 90.

56 *Ibid.*, p. 91.

57 Abbott and Halliday, *op. cit.*, p. 602.

58 Gray, *op. cit.*, p. 169.

59 *The Rise of the Social Gospel in American Protestantism*, p. 19. Yale University Press.

60 *Op. cit.*, pp. 392, 393.

61 Bok, Edward W., *Beecher Memorial*, p. 88.

Chapter III
DWIGHT L. MOODY
and the high tide of
Revivalism

1 Davenport, Frederick Morgan, *Primitive Traits in Religious Revivals*, pp. 208, 209. Used by permission of The Macmillan Company, publishers.

2 *The Church and Modern Life*, p. 179. Houghton Mifflin Company. Used by permission of the Trustees of the Columbus School for Girls, Columbus, Ohio.

3 *Op. cit.*, p. 213.

4 Quoted by Day, Richard Ellsworth, in *Bush Aglow — The Life Story of Dwight Lyman Moody*, p. 56. Copyright, The Judson Press. Used by permission.

5 *Ibid.*, p. 63.

6 *Ibid.*, p. 64.

7 Goss, Charles F., *Echoes from the Pulpit and Platform*, p. 40.

8 Quoted by Day, *op. cit.*, p. 107.

9 *Ibid.*, p. 116.

10 *Ibid.*, p. 121.

11 *Ibid.*, p. 126.

12 *Ibid.*, p. 136.

13 Quoted by Fitt, Arthur Percy, *Moody Still Lives*, p. 29. Used by permission of Fleming H. Revell Company, publishers.

14 *Op. cit.*, pp. 291–294.

15 Erdman, Charles R., *D. L. Moody, His Message for Today*, p. 100. Used by permission of Fleming H. Revell Company, publishers.

16 Moody, W. R., *D. L. Moody*, p. 489. Used by permission of The Macmillan Company, publishers.

17 *Op. cit.*, p. 101.

18 *The Great Redemption*, p. 140.

19 Moody, W. R., *The Life of Dwight L. Moody*, p. 497. Used by permission of Fleming H. Revell Company, publishers.

20 *Heaven*, p. 9. Fleming H. Revell Company.

21 Goss, *op. cit.*, p. 29.

22 *Op. cit.*, pp. 90, 91.

23 *The Way Home*, p. 81.

24 *The Great Redemption*, p. 260.

25 *Pleasure and Profit in Bible Study,* p. 91.
26 Quoted by Day, *op. cit.,* p. 217.
27 *Op. cit.,* pp. 103, 104.
28 Quoted by Fitt, *op. cit.,* pp. 144, 145.
29 *Ibid.,* p. 145.
30 Moody, *Pleasure and Profit in Bible Study,* p. 33.
31 *My Father,* p. 44. Little, Brown & Company.
32 Moody, W. R., *The Life of Dwight L. Moody,* p. 496.
33 *Op. cit.,* p. 59.
34 *Ibid.,* pp. 59, 60.
35 From *D. L. Moody: A Worker in Souls,* by Gamaliel Bradford. Copyright, 1927, by Doubleday, Doran & Company, Inc.
36 Torrey, R. A., *Why God Used D. L. Moody,* p. 28. Bible Institute Colportage Association.
37 *Op. cit.,* p. 135.
38 Day, *op. cit.,* p. 287.
39 *Ibid.,* p. 279.

Chapter IV
WASHINGTON GLADDEN
and the development of the "*New Theology*"

1 *Religion in Our Times,* p. 49. Round Table Press, Inc.
2 P. 37. Houghton Mifflin Company. Used by permission of the Trustees of the Columbus School for Girls, Columbus, Ohio.
3 *Ibid.,* pp. 35, 36.
4 *Ibid.,* pp. 63, 64.
5 *Ibid.,* p. 106.
6 *Ibid.,* p. 119.
7 *Ibid.,* pp. 119, 120.
8 *Ibid.,* p. 147.
9 *Ibid.,* p. 153.
10 *Ibid.,* pp. 156, 157.
11 *Ibid.,* p. 223.
12 Quoted, *ibid.,* pp. 224, 225.
13 *Ibid.,* pp. 270, 271.
14 *Op. cit.,* p. 53.
15 *Burning Questions,* pp. 4, 5.
16 *Ibid.,* p. 37.
17 *Ibid.,* p. 247.

18 Gladden, *Recollections,* p. 319.
19 Pp. 3, 5, 6. Houghton Mifflin Company. Used by permission of the Trustees of the Columbus School for Girls, Columbus, Ohio.
20 *Ibid.,* p. 36.
21 *Ibid.,* p. 40.
22 Pp. 15, 16. Houghton Mifflin Company. Used by permission of the Trustees of the Columbus School for Girls, Columbus, Ohio.
23 *Op. cit.,* p. 147.
24 P. 5.
25 P. 26.
26 *Present Day Theology,* pp. 15, 16.
27 *Ibid.,* p. 19.
28 *Ibid.,* p. 19.
29 *Ibid.,* p. 67.
30 *Ibid.,* p. 29.
31 *Ibid.,* p. 113.
32 *Ibid.,* p. 141.
33 *The Church and Modern Life,* pp. 24, 25.
34 *Christianity and Socialism,* pp. 29, 30.
35 *Recollections,* pp. 251, 252.
36 *Ibid.,* p. 253.
37 *The Church and Modern Life,* p. 145.
38 *Recollections,* p. 254.
39 *Applied Christianity,* p. 131. Houghton Mifflin Company. Used by permission of the Trustees of the Columbus School for Girls, Columbus, Ohio.
40 *Ibid.,* p. 145.
41 *Tools and the Man,* p. 1. Houghton Mifflin Company.
42 *The Church and Modern Life,* pp. 85, 86.
43 *Ibid.,* p. 150.
44 Gladden, *Social Salvation,* p. 18. Houghton Mifflin Company. Used by permission of the Trustees of the Columbus School for Girls, Columbus, Ohio.
45 Gladden, *The Church and Modern Life,* p. 156.
46 *Ibid.,* p. 167.
47 *Ibid.,* p. 106.
48 *Recollections,* pp. 408, 409.
49 *Ibid.,* pp. 419, 420.
50 *Social Salvation,* p. 230.
51 *Recollections,* p. 306.

52   *The Forks of the Road,* pp. 123, 124.   Used by permission of The Macmillan Company, publishers.
53   *Ibid.,* pp. 130, 131.
54   *Ibid.,* pp. 134–136.
55   *The Pacific,* January 17, 1918, quoted by Buckman, J. W., *op. cit.,* p. 247.
56   Gladden, *The Interpreter,* p. 39.   Used by permission of The Pilgrim Press, publisher.

Chapter V
WALTER RAUSCHENBUSCH
and the challenge of the Social Gospel

1   Hopkins, Charles Howard, *The Rise of the Social Gospel in American Protestantism, 1865–1915,* p. 3.   Yale University Press.
2   *An Interpretation of Christian Ethics,* Preface.   Harper & Brothers.
3   Quoted by Sharpe, Dores Robinson, *Walter Rauschenbusch,* p. 410, from Van Dusen in a letter from Beaven to Mrs. Rauschenbusch.
4   Address, Central Y. M. C. A., Cleveland.   Printed in *Association Monthly,* January, 1913.   Quoted by Sharpe, *op. cit.,* pp. 428, 429.
5   *Christianizing the Social Order,* p. 92.   Used by permission of The Macmillan Company, publishers.
6   *For the Right,* August, 1890.   Quoted by Sharpe, *op. cit.,* pp. 92, 93.
7   Sharpe, *op. cit.,* pp. 427, 428.   Used by permission of 'The Macmillan Company, publishers.
8   *Christianizing the Social Order,* pp. 93, 94.
9   *The Kingdom,* Vol. I, No. 2, September, 1907.   Quoted by Sharpe, *op. cit.,* pp. 137, 138.
10   *Christianity and the Social Crisis,* p. xii.   Used by permission of The Macmillan Company, publishers.
11   *Ibid.,* p. 9.
12   *Ibid.,* pp. 48, 49.
13   *Ibid.,* p. 140.
14   *Ibid.,* p. 181.
15   *Ibid.,* p. 189.
16   *Ibid.,* p. 198.

17 *Ibid.*, p. 209.
18 *Ibid.*, p. 237.
19 *Ibid.*, p. 279.
20 *Ibid.*, p. 285.
21 *Ibid.*, pp. 332, 341.
22 *Ibid.*, p. 412.
23 *Ibid.*, pp. 412, 413.
24 *Christianizing the Social Order*, p. 95.
25 *Op. cit.*, p. 274.
26 *Christianizing the Social Order*, p. 36.
27 *Ibid.*, p. 39.
28 *Ibid.*, p. 41.
29 *Ibid.*, p. 458.
30 *Ibid.*, pp. 458, 459.
31 *Ibid.*, p. 459.
32 *Ibid.*, p. 462.
33 *Ibid.*, pp. 464, 465.
34 *The Revolution in Christian Missions*, pp. 35, 36. Abingdon-Cokesbury Press.
35 Sharpe, *op. cit.*, p. 356.
36 P. 42. Used by permission of the Association Press, publisher.
37 *Ibid.*, p. 144.
38 *Op. cit.*, p. 378.
39 *Ibid.*, p. 391.
40 *Ibid.*, p. 379.
41 *Rochester Herald*, August 23, 1915. Quoted by Sharpe, *op. cit.*, p. 379.
42 *A Theology for the Social Gospel*, p. 87. Used by permission of The Macmillan Company, publishers.
43 Smith, Shelton, *op. cit.*, p. 97.
44 Rauschenbusch, *A Theology for the Social Gospel*, p. 99.
45 *Ibid.*, p. 95.
46 *Ibid.*, pp. 110, 111.
47 *Ibid.*, p. 117.
48 *Ibid.*, p. 129.
49 *Ibid.*, p. 194.
50 *Ibid.*, p. 227.
51 *Ibid.*, p. 248.
52 *Ibid.*, p. 265.
53 Quoted by Sharpe, *op. cit.*, pp. 387, 388. From a letter by Rauschenbusch to Dr. Woelfkin.

54   Quoted, *ibid.*, pp. 434, 435.
55   *The Social Gospel Re-examined*, pp. 2, 3.   Harper &
Brothers.
56   *The Church Through Half a Century*, p. 119.   Charles
Scribner's Sons.